Recovery from Schizophrenia

Recovery from Schizophrenia, from its first publication, was acclaimed as a work of major importance. It demonstrated convincingly, but controversially, how political, economic and labor market forces shape social responses to the mentally ill, mold psychiatric treatment philosophy, and influence the onset and course of one of the most common forms of mental illness.

In this revised and updated third edition, Dr Warner analyzes the latest research to extend the conclusions of the original work, and tells us whether conditions and outcome for people with schizophrenia are getting better or worse for people in Britain and America. In addition, he:

- Critiques recent approaches to preventing the occurrence of schizophrenia.
- Suggests innovative strategies for advancing the economic situation of people with mental illness.
- Describes the latest advances in the rehabilitation of people with schizophrenia.
- Provides a guide on how to combat the stigma of mental illness at the local and national level.

Recovery from Schizophrenia's radical analysis of the factors affecting the outcome of schizophrenia is essential reading for all psychiatrists, mental health professionals, mental health advocates, social workers, rehabilitation personnel, and psychologists.

Richard Warner is the Medical Director of the Mental Health Center of Boulder County, Colorado and Clinical Professor of Psychiatry and Adjunct Professor of Anthropology at the University of Colorado.

Recovery from Schizophrenia

Psychiatry and Political Economy

Third Edition

Richard Warner

Brunner-Routledge
Taylor & Francis Group
HOVE AND NEW YORK

First edition published 1985
by Routledge
11 New Fetter Lane, London EC4P 4EE

Second edition published 1994 by Routledge

Reprinted 1997 by Routledge

Third edition published
by Brunner-Routledge
27 Church Road, Hove, East Sussex BN3 2FA

Simultaneously published in the USA and Canada
by Brunner-Routledge
29 West 35th Street, New York NY 10001

Brunner-Routledge is an imprint of the Taylor & Francis Group

Copyright © 2004 Richard Warner

Typeset in Times by RefineCatch Limited, Bungay, Suffolk
Printed and bound in Great Britain by
MPG Books Ltd, Bodmin, Cornwall
Paperback cover illustration by Gary Sims
Paperback cover design by Anú Design

British Library Cataloguing in Publication Data
A catalogue record for this book is available from the British Library

Library of Congress Cataloging-in-Publication Data
Warner, Richard, 1943–
   Recovery from schizophr   ia / Richard Warner.—3rd ed.
      p.   cm.
Includes bibliographical references and index.
   ISBN 0-415-21266-9
   1. Schizophrenia—Treatment—Political aspects.
2. Schizophrenia—Treatment—Economic aspects.
3. Schizophrenia—Treatment. I. Title.
   RC514.W24 2003
   362.2′6—dc21   2003008633

ISBN 0-415-21266-9 (hbk)
ISBN 0-415-21267-7 (pbk)

To those who suffer from schizophrenia

Contents

Acknowledgments

Several people were kind enough to give me criticism and encouragement when some of the ideas in this book were first drafted in the form of a long article. Among these reviewers were John Strauss, John Wing, Loren Mosher, Solomon Goldberg, Lewis Wolberg, Bernard Bloom and Maxwell Jones. I am most grateful for their advice.

I am also indebted to those who have discussed this research with me and reviewed sections of the book. I have received valuable critiques from the following colleagues in various departments of the University of Colorado: Robert Freedman, Thomas Mayer, Edward Greenberg, and Paul Shankman. Jani Little and Charles Judd have been invaluable statistical advisors and Gary McClelland provided advice and instruction about probability theory and the prevention of schizophrenia. At the Mental Health Center of Boulder County, my associates Phoebe Norton and Ruth Arnold have made useful comments on sections of the manuscript. Julian Leff and Andrew Scull carefully reviewed large sections of the work and made many helpful suggestions.

I gained a great deal from discussions with Loren Mosher, Julian Leff, Paul Polak, Robert Freedman, James Mandiberg and Ezra Susser. Robert Freedman contributed to the development of the theory about the occurrence of schizophrenia in Chapter 9. Much of the discussion in Chapter 10 about the economic advancement of the mentally ill in the community is a result of my collaboration with Paul Polak. Ezra Susser has helped me with epidemiological advice on many of the themes in the book. Sue Estroff and Joe Morrisey have often helped with ideas, information and insights. My research collaboration with Dawn Taylor, Giovanni de Girolamo, Peter Huxley and Sherrill Evans, among others, has allowed many of the ideas in the book to be tested. Many colleagues associated with the World Psychiatric Association global anti-stigma program have increased my understanding of how to tackle stigma; they include Hugh Schulze, Everett Rogers, Corinne Shefner-Rogers, Otto Wahl, Heather Stuart and Norman Sartorius. Gyles Glover, of the University of Durham, gathered the data on National Health Service expenditure on mental illness, which are referred to in Chapter 6.

I have been fortunate to work with many creative and talented colleagues at the Mental Health Center of Boulder County in the past quarter-century. Their devotion to excellence in creating innovative services for people with mental illness has been an inspiration. The leadership and human values of Phoebe Norton has made possible the formation of a system of care that embodies many of the principles set out in this book.

A great deal of credit is due to Marilyn Rothman, the librarian who, with great energy and skill, helped me assemble the many sources cited here. Jennifer Johnson cheerfully and efficiently located recent articles on outcome from schizophrenia for this edition. I am especially grateful to my wife, Lucy Warner, for her unflagging support, astute criticism and editorial advice.

Gary Sims, who created the cover art used for each edition of this book, died in 1993, loved and missed by many. I thank his parents for their permission to use the design for the paperback cover of this edition.

The following figures are reprinted from other sources by permission of the publisher or author. Figure 1.3 is taken from Gottesman, I.I., *Schizophrenia Genesis: The Origins of Madness*, New York, W.H. Freeman, 1991, p. 96, ©1991 Irving I. Gottesman. Figure 2.1 is taken from Brenner, M.H., "Fetal, infant and maternal mortality during periods of economic instability," *International Journal of Health Services*, 3: 145–59, 1973, p. 153, ©1973 Baywood Publishing, Farmingdale, New York. Figure 5.1 is taken from Bockoven, J.S., *Moral Treatment in Community Mental Health*, New York, Springer, 1972, p. 56, ©1972 J. Sanbourne Bockoven.

Material in Chapters 3 and 6 has previously been published in Warner, R., "The influence of economic factors on outcome in schizophrenia," *Psychiatry and Social Science*, 1: 79–106, 1981, ©1981 Universitetsforlaget, Oslo. The research at the end of Chapter 4 has previously been published in Warner, R., "The effect of the labor market on mental hospital and prison use: an international comparison," *Administration in Mental Health*, 10: 239–58, 1983, ©1983 Human Sciences Press, New York. Chapter 7 has previously appeared in essentially similar form as Warner, R., "Recovery from schizophrenia in the Third World," *Psychiatry*, 46: 197–212, 1983, ©1983 William Alanson White Psychiatric Foundation, Washington, DC. Some of the material on combating stigma has been seen before in Warner, R., *The Environment of Schizophrenia*, ©2000 Brunner-Routledge, London.

Introduction

Does the way we make our living or the level of economic development of our country affect whether or not we become mentally ill? Does social class or the state of the economy influence whether people with schizophrenia recover from their illness? Has industrial development affected the number of people with schizophrenia who become permanently and severely disabled – lost to their families, costly to the community and leading lives of emptiness and degradation? These questions are at the heart of this book.

My original intent was to uncover what the natural course of schizophrenia had been before the antipsychotic drugs were introduced, but this simple goal led to the realization that some current beliefs about the illness, widely accepted in psychiatry, are not accurate. We may well have been too pessimistic about the course of untreated schizophrenia and overconfident about the benefits of modern treatment. The antipsychotic drugs, it emerges, have not appreciably improved the long-term outcome from the illness; these drugs alone did not unlock the doors of our mental institutions and make possible the community treatment of people with psychosis. Despite a massive annual investment in the treatment of schizophrenia, the outcome from the illness in modern industrial society is no better than in the Third World.

Each change in our treatment approach to schizophrenia, moreover, is not necessarily an advance. A treatment method of demonstrated effectiveness – moral management – was laid to rest in the mid-nineteenth century only to be resurrected in a similar form nearly a hundred years later. Much of what today is called community treatment is, in fact, the antithesis of treatment; people suffering from psychosis are consigned to a sordid, impoverished existence in which even basic needs, such as food and shelter, are not met. To understand how such aberrations and misconceptions have come about, to appreciate what has shaped the course and occurrence of schizophrenia, and to see what has molded psychiatric ideology and the social response to the person with schizophrenia, we need to step outside psychiatry. We have to venture into the territory of the sociologist, the anthropologist and the historian; we must enter the province of epidemiologists, social psychologists, economists and political scientists.

A NOTE ON THEORY

The materialist theoretical approach I have used throughout this book is not commonly applied to questions in psychiatry. The central premise of the approach is that in order to understand human thought and behavior it is essential to begin with the material conditions of mankind's existence and productive processes. The origins of philosophical and social change, the materialist argues, are likely to be found in changes in technology. Values, attitudes and ideology are likely to be shaped by political and domestic economy (for example, family patterns, social stratification and political organization); and these aspects of society, in turn, tend to be molded by the forces of production and reproduction, by the technology of subsistence and population control and by labor requirements.[1]

A materialist research strategy, for example, allows us to generate the hypothesis that social attitudes towards the mentally ill partly reflect the usefulness of the person with psychosis in the productive process; that psychiatric ideology is influenced by economic conditions; that the course of schizophrenia is influenced by class status, sex roles and labor dynamics; or that variations in the occurrence of the illness may reflect differences in the circumstances of different classes and castes under different modes of subsistence and production. Such hypotheses, of course, must be tested against alternative explanations, and that is what this book sets out to do.

I do not wish to suggest that material conditions *create* schizophrenia in any simple, deterministic way, but rather that they *mold* the course and outcome of the illness and *influence*, along with other factors, its incidence. Psychiatric ideology is obviously not wholly determined by the economy, but it could be significantly affected by such factors. The materialist perspective allows for the operation of any number of causes besides technological, environmental and production-related forces. People in similar environmental settings will not all develop schizophrenia; biology must be crucial in determining who develops a psychosis. Inbreeding could produce isolated populations with an increased genetic predisposition to schizophrenia. Individual psychology is also relevant; the psychotic or pre-psychotic person's behavior or response to circumstances may sometimes create the stresses that precipitate or worsen his or her illness. The materialist researcher would expect, however, that if we look at a large number of instances we will often find material forces to be important. It is not only biological, genetic or psychological factors that determine the distribution and course of schizophrenia. We should be prepared to expand our concern with social factors beyond family dynamics and socio-economic status. It is in the relationship between all of these potential causes and the economic, technological and environmental facts of our existence that we may gain the broadest understanding of why some people become schizophrenic and why some of them never recover.

CHAPTER TOPICS

The opening chapters of the book establish the background for the subsequent analysis. The first chapter outlines what is known about the factors that promote the appearance of schizophrenia and that shape the course of the illness. The material is presented in such a way that readers who are not already familiar with the facts and features of the illness will learn enough to understand the rest of the book. The next chapter provides details of the ways in which mental and physical health are influenced by the economy, by social class and by the conditions of labor.

The middle section of the book looks at the impact of political economy on schizophrenia. Chapter 3 is an analysis of outcome studies of schizophrenia since the beginning of the twentieth century and tries to establish whether changes in the long-term course of the illness are linked to large-scale fluctuations in the economy. The extent to which political, economic and labor market forces shaped the postwar policy of deinstitutionalization is examined in Chapter 4; and the role of similar forces in the development of institutions for the mentally ill in the eighteenth and nineteenth centuries and in molding the treatment philosophy of the period is discussed in the following chapter.

Chapter 6 looks at possible reasons for the link between the economy and outcome from schizophrenia, and Chapter 7 attempts to explain why schizophrenia is a less malignant condition in the Third World. The plight of the person with schizophrenia in Western society and the way in which the social role and alienation of the psychotic person shape the course of the illness is examined in Chapter 8. Moving from the course of schizophrenia to its prevalence, Chapter 9 analyzes how economic development, social stratification and birth complications influence the appearance of the illness. The issue of the prevention of schizophrenia is also addressed in this chapter.

The final section deals with issues of treatment and social integration. Chapter 10 evaluates the limitations of the antipsychotic drugs and their proper role in treatment. The importance of work, and strategies for employing people with mental illness are covered in Chapter 11. Consumer involvement and community support in the management of psychosis are covered in the final chapter, along with methods for fighting the stigma of schizophrenia.

Part I

Background

Chapter 1

What is schizophrenia?

Schizophrenia is an illness that is shaped, to a large extent, by political economy. The thrust of the following chapters will be to document this claim. First, though, we must be clear what it means. What is political economy? What is schizophrenia, and how can it be "shaped"?

WHAT IS POLITICAL ECONOMY?

All social groups survive by exploiting their environment and by limiting their population size to whatever their technology and the environment can sustain. The !Kung Bushmen subsist in the arid Kalahari Desert by camping in small bands near the few waterholes that exist and foraging over wide areas for nuts, berries, roots and melons.[1] Industrial societies sustain dense populations through increasingly intensive exploitation of land and sea for food, fuel and raw materials by means of elaborate forms of technology. Whatever the level of complexity of a society, however, it must possess a social structure that regulates the basic mechanisms of production and reproduction – a structure that governs the relationships among the productive and non-productive members of the society; that controls population size; and that regulates the distribution of labor power and energy in the society. All these functions may be subsumed under the term *economy*. Where the social structure is primarily seen as influencing domestic roles and relationships we speak of *domestic economy*. When we are considering larger political groupings (clans, bands, classes, castes and nations) we refer to *political economy*.[2]

We shall be looking, then, for influences on the occurrence and course of schizophrenia that lie in differences in the modes of production of various societies – hunting and gathering, subsistence farming and industrial capitalism, for example. What was the impact of the Industrial Revolution upon insanity and the insane? How is schizophrenia affected by styles of labor use, by Third World migrant labor patterns, by unemployment, by land-tenure arrangements, by the social stratification of class and caste, by the fluctuations of the business cycle, by poverty, by welfare support and by variations in family organization that are consequences of political-economic forces?

WHAT IS SCHIZOPHRENIA?

Schizophrenia is an illness (or, equally, a group of illnesses). Psychiatrist Thomas Szasz would disagree, arguing that the whole concept of mental illness is a fabrication – scientifically worthless and socially harmful.[3] Indeed there are many conditions treated as illnesses by psychiatrists that might more logically be considered as non-medical forms of deviance – for instance, nicotine dependence, transvestism and conduct disorder of childhood (to name just a few), all mental disorders listed in the fourth edition of the American Psychiatric Association *Diagnostic and Statistical Manual* (DSM-IV).[4] Schizophrenia, nevertheless, fulfills any criteria we might wish to establish to define an illness. It is a non-volitional and generally maladaptive condition that decreases the person's functional capacity and that may be identified by a reasonably circumscribed set of characteristic features. Within rather broad limits, the age of onset and the expected course of the condition may be specified. Researchers have identified anatomical, physiological and biochemical abnormalities in the brains of people exhibiting features of schizophrenia. The predisposition to develop the condition appears to be inherited, and in essentially similar forms the disorder is universally identifiable in all societies around the globe with (as we shall see, in Chapter 9) a surprisingly similar incidence rate. We may regard schizophrenia as an illness, but it will be apparent that it is an illness that is strongly affected by the sufferer's environment.

Schizophrenia is a *psychosis*. That is to say, it is a severe mental disorder in which the person's ability to recognize reality and his or her emotional responses, thinking processes, judgment and ability to communicate are so affected that his or her functioning is seriously impaired. Hallucinations and delusions are common features of psychosis.

Schizophrenia is one of the *functional* psychoses. These are the disorders in which the changes in functioning cannot definitely be attributed to any specific organic abnormality in the brain. As more is learned of brain pathology in mental illness this distinction has become less relevant. It allows us, however, to distinguish certain mental illnesses from such organic mental disorders as the pre-senile dementias (like Huntington's chorea), drug-induced psychoses (such as those that amphetamine may cause) or delirium tremens (secondary to alcohol withdrawal).

The two most common functional psychoses are schizophrenia and bipolar affective disorder (also known as manic-depressive illness). The distinction between the two is often not easy to make and, as we shall see, psychiatrists in different parts of the world at different times have not drawn the boundaries in the same way. In essence, however, bipolar disorder is an episodic and recurrent disorder in which the psychotic symptoms are associated with severe alterations in mood – at times elated, agitated episodes of *mania*, at other times *depression*, with physical and mental slowing, despair, guilt feelings and low self-esteem.

Schizophrenia, on the other hand, while it may be episodic, will tend to relapse at irregular intervals, unlike the more regular, cyclical pattern of bipolar disorder; or it will demonstrate a continuous but fluctuating course. Furthermore, although schizophrenia may be associated with depression, elation or agitation at times, it is often free of these features and the mood is likely, instead, to be blunted, lacking in spontaneity or incongruous. Markedly illogical thinking is common in schizophrenia. Auditory hallucinations may occur in either bipolar disorder or schizophrenia, but in the latter they are more likely to be commenting on the patient's thoughts and actions or to be conversing one with another. Delusions, also, can occur in both conditions; in schizophrenia they may give the individual the sense that he or she is being controlled by outside forces or that his or her thoughts are being broadcast or interfered with. Both bipolar disorder and schizophrenia are most likely to begin in late adolescence or in early adult life.

Despite common features, different forms of schizophrenia can appear quite dissimilar. One person, for example, may be paranoid and hostile in certain circumstances but show good judgment and high functioning in many areas of life. Another may be bizarre in manner and appearance, preoccupied with delusions of bodily disorder, passive and withdrawn. So marked are these differences, in fact, that many psychiatrists believe that, when the underlying neurophysiological and biochemical mechanisms of schizophrenia are worked out, the illness will prove to be a set of different but related conditions that lead, *via* a final common pathway of biochemical interactions, to a similar series of consequences. This view of schizophrenia as a federation of states has been present from the time of its earliest conception. To understand why these conditions were united in the first instance we must look at the history of the development of the idea.

EMIL KRAEPELIN

The concept of schizophrenia was formulated by the German psychiatrist Emil Kraepelin. Studying, over the course of years, patients admitted to the insane asylums of the late nineteenth century, he observed that certain types of insanity with an onset in early adult life and initially rather varied features seemed to progress ultimately to a similar deteriorated condition. To accentuate the progressive destruction of mental abilities, emotional responses and the integrity of the personality that he saw as central to this condition, Professor Kraepelin termed it dementia praecox – dementia of early life. Against considerable professional opposition, he took the position in 1887 that three conditions, previously considered separate, were in fact subtypes of this single disease entity. These conditions were hebephrenia, marked by aimless, disorganized and incongruous behavior; catatonia, in which the individual might be negativistic, motionless or even stuporose or, at other times, extremely agitated and incoherent; and finally, dementia paranoides, in which delusions of persecution and grandeur were predominant.

In defining dementia praecox, Kraepelin was particularly concerned to show how it differed from other forms of insanity and from idiocy. Unlike cerebral syphilis, no specific cause of the condition could be identified; in contrast to the psychogenic psychoses, dementia praecox did not appear to be an acute response to stress; and it was to be distinguished from manic-depressive insanity by its progressive deteriorating course and by the absence of clear-cut mood swings from elation to melancholia.

Emil Kraepelin's description of dementia praecox continues to serve us well, with some exceptions, as a picture of modern-day schizophrenia. Some of the characteristic features that he identified are listed in Table 1.1. Where his observations no longer appear relevant is in his description of the symptoms associated with catatonic schizophrenia – automatic obedience, stereotypic movements, waxy flexibility, echolalia and echopraxia (see Table 1.1). Kraepelin's treatise on dementia praecox is illustrated with photographs of catatonic patients sitting and standing rigidly in bizarre and contorted postures, preserving poses into which they were set by the photographer. It was not unusual for Kraepelin's patients to repeat involuntarily the words and movements of those around them or to stand or kneel for days or longer in the same spot.[5] Patients with such features could still be seen on the wards of old-style institutions after the Second World War, but they are now very rarely seen in the industrial world. Catatonic schizophrenia, however, is still one of the commonest forms of the disorder in the Third World.

It is possible, as social psychiatrist Julian Leff argues, that these catatonic symptoms are a somatic expression of delusions of influence, symbolic thinking and pathological fear, much as the bodily symptoms of hysteria are a somatic conversion of anxiety. Both hysteria and catatonic symptoms have receded in the West, Dr Leff suggests, as the population has developed a capacity for expressing emotions in verbal and psychological terms rather than as somatic symptoms.[6] It may also be true that the harsh and regressive conditions of asylums around the beginning of the twentieth century tended to provoke and worsen catatonic symptoms, which persisted as a physical expression of the patient's dependent status and barren existence.

Even more probable, these same asylum conditions may have brought about the deteriorating course that Kraepelin saw as central to his concept of the illness. Therapeutic nihilism, extended hospital stays and coercive management within the asylum walls, and poverty and unemployment beyond them, during these years of the late nineteenth-century Great Depression

Table 1.1 Features of dementia praecox identified by Emil Kraepelin

Feature	Description
Hallucinations:	
Auditory	At the beginning these are usually simple noises, rustling, buzzing, ringing in the ears (p. 7). Then there develops . . . the *hearing of voices*. Sometimes it is only whispering (p. 7). What the voices say is, as a rule, *unpleasant* and *disturbing* (p. 9). Many of the voices make remarks about the thoughts and doings of the patient (p. 10). It is quite specially peculiar to dementia praecox that the patients' own *thoughts appear to them to be spoken aloud* (p. 12).
Visual	Everything looks awry and wrong (p. 14). People appear who are not there (p. 14).
Delusions:	
Paranoia	The patient notices that he is looked at in a peculiar way, laughed at, scoffed at . . . People spy on him . . . persecute him, poison the atmosphere (p. 27).
Guilt	The patient has by a sinful life he believes destroyed his health of body and mind (p. 27).
Grandiosity	The patient is 'something better,' born to a higher place, . . . an inventor, a great singer, can do what he will (p. 29).
Ideas of influence	Characteristic of the disease . . . is the feeling of one's thoughts being influenced (p. 12).
Thought transference	The patient sometimes *knows the thoughts of other people* (p. 13).
Ideas of reference	Indifferent remarks and chance looks, the whispering of other people, appear suspicious to the patient (p. 31).
Thought disorder:	
Poverty of thought	There is invariably at first a *loss of mental activity* and therewith a certain poverty of thought (p. 19).
Loose associations	The patients lose in a most striking way the faculty of *logical ordering* of their trains of thought. . . . The most self-evident and familiar associations with the given ideas are absent (p. 19).
Incoherence	By these disorders, which . . . remind one of thinking in a dream, the patients' mental associations often have that peculiarly bewildering incomprehensibility. . . . It constitutes the essential foundation of *incoherence of thought* (p. 20).
Thought block	There can be a sudden 'blocking' of their thought, producing a painful interruption in a series of ideas (p. 22).
Affect (emotional expression):	
Blunting	Singular indifference . . . towards their former emotional relations, the extinction of affection for relatives and friends. . . . 'No grief and no joy' (p. 33).
Inappropriateness	One of the most characteristic features of the disease is a frequent, causeless, sudden outburst of laughter (p. 33).
Lability	*Sudden oscillations of emotional equilibrium* of extraordinary violence may be developed (p. 35).

Table 1.1 – continued

Feature	Description
Speech:	
Abnormal flow	The patients become monosyllabic, sparing of their words, speak hesitatingly, suddenly become mute . . . let all answers be laboriously pressed out of them (p. 56). In states of excitement . . . a prodigious *flow of talk* may appear (p. 56).
Neologisms	There may be produced . . . quite senseless collections of syllables, here and there still having a sound reminiscent of real words (p. 68).
Autism:	Patients with dementia praecox are more or less inaccessible, . . . they shut themselves off from the outside world (p. 49).
Stupor:	The rigid, impenetrable shutting up of themselves from all outer influences (p. 50).
Negativism:	Stubborn opposition to interference of all sorts (p. 47).
Lack of drive:	The patients have lost every independent inclination for work or action (p. 37).
Automatic obedience:	
Waxy flexibility	The preservation of whatever positions the patient may be put in, even although they may be very uncomfortable (p. 38).
Echolalia	The involuntary repetition of words said to them (p. 39).
Echopraxia	The imitation of movements made in front of them (p. 39).
Mannerisms:	They add flourishes by which the movements become unnatural, affected and manneristic (p. 45).
Stereotypy:	Continuance in the *same positions* as well as . . . the reception of the *same movements* or *actions* (p. 43).
Intellectual deterioration:	The patients are distracted, inattentive, tired, dull, . . . their mind wanders, they have no perseverance (p. 23).
Deterioration of judgment:	The faculty of judgment in the patient suffers without exception severe injury (p. 25).
Personality deterioration:	Their thinking, feeling, and acting have lost the unity . . . of the psychic personality, which provides the healthy human being with the feeling of inner freedom (p. 53).

Source: Kraepelin, E., Dementia Praecox and Paraphrenia, Edinburgh: Livingstone, 1919.

combined to limit the chances of recovery from dementia praecox. Few psychiatrists since Kraepelin, as we shall see in Chapter 3, have found the course of schizophrenia to be as malignant as originally portrayed. As Kraepelin's classification was adopted around the world, nevertheless, so was the impression that the illness was inevitably progressive and incurable. To varying degrees the same view holds sway today – that without treatment the outlook is hopeless – despite considerable evidence to the contrary.

EUGEN BLEULER

Twelve per cent of Emil Kraepelin's patients with dementia praecox recovered more or less completely – few enough, but a sufficient number to cause concern about the central diagnostic criterion being poor outcome. In the more prosperous years of the early twentieth century in Switzerland and in the therapeutically progressive atmosphere of the renowned Burghölzli Hospital, psychiatrist Eugen Bleuler presented a more optimistic view of the outcome from the illness. Stimulated by the psychoanalytic theories of his assistant, Carl Jung, Dr Bleuler formulated a new unifying concept for the condition and gave it a new name. To Dr Bleuler the identifying characteristic of the illness was not poor outcome but a specific psychological picture – a lack of continuity in the associations between the patient's thoughts and a restricted or incongruous expression of emotion. Other symptoms that he regarded as fundamental were ambivalence and autism (a preoccupation with the inner world leading to detachment from reality). From the fragmentation of thinking and feeling, Eugen Bleuler derived the term *schizophrenia* – split mind. The hallucinations and delusions that were commonly part of the psychotic picture, Dr Bleuler considered to be merely secondary to the more fundamental defects.[7]

Dr Bleuler's 1911 monograph, *Dementia Praecox or the Group of Schizophrenias*, contains many examples of patients who fail to show Kraepelin's progressive deterioration and who often recover a high level of functioning.

> A young farm girl, age seventeen, has been catatonic for a period of two years. Then she became a nursing attendant. Two years later she was released. She then became a midwife. She married, her husband had a difficult time with her. For example, she would not permit him to sing while he worked. She formed strong unfounded sympathies and antipathies. At the age of thirty-eight, she was again mildly catatonic for some six months. Since then she has been working for eight years outside the hospital, but not as a midwife.[8]

Another of Bleuler's examples:

Physician: Neurasthenia at twenty-nine. Then at thirty-one after typhoid fever, catatonic. At forty-seven, apparently "cured". He then resumes his practice, marries. Has been well for the past two years.[9]

Bleuler's impression was that few, if any, of his patients with schizophrenia completely recovered without some vestige of their illness remaining. Far-reaching improvement, however, was common. Fully 60 per cent of his patients recovered sufficiently from their first schizophrenic episode to return to work and support themselves.[10] Such "social recoveries" cannot be directly compared with Kraepelin's 12 per cent of patients, who may well have shown signs of more complete symptomatic recovery. There can be no doubt, though, that the course of the illness in Bleuler's patients was much more benign than in Kraepelin's hospital in Munich. So much so, that Bleuler was able to assert that

the therapy of schizophrenia is one of the most rewarding for the physician who does not ascribe the results of the natural healing processes of psychosis to his own intervention.[11]

It would be hard to find in modern psychiatry such an optimistic view of the natural course of schizophrenia.

Bleuler's treatment methods

Why should the outcome for Bleuler's patients have been so superior? He may well have broadened the diagnosis of schizophrenia to include some less severely disturbed patients. But it is also likely that Bleuler was too modest about the value of treatment, and that his methods of management maximized the chances of his patients' recovery. The description of his treatment methods from the first decade of the twentieth century reads like a model of the approaches introduced a half-century later in the social psychiatry revolution of postwar northern Europe (to be described in Chapter 4) or like the principles of humane care abandoned half a century earlier at the end of the moral-treatment era (described in Chapter 5).

Institutional care, for instance, was to be minimized. "It is preferable to treat these patients under their usual conditions and within their habitual surroundings," Dr Bleuler insisted. "The patient should not be admitted to hospital just because he suffers from schizophrenia, but only when there is a definite indication for hospitalization." Furthermore, "one can consider it an established rule that earlier release produces better results."[12] If the patient cannot return to his own family, "the care he may receive from a strange family often serves as an adequate substitute."[13] In pursuing this policy of active community rehabilitation Bleuler may have been aided by the low levels of poverty and unemployment in Switzerland at that time. It is certain, at any rate, that his discharge policies were much more liberal than those of Kraepelin.

The return to an appropriate occupation, Bleuler believed, was vital to the patient's health. "Idleness facilitates the predomination by the complexes over the personality," he argued, "whereas regulated work maintains the activity of normal thinking."[14] But he emphasized that "faultless perform-ance can hardly be expected and the unavoidable rebukes can greatly endanger the entire pleasure that the patients take in their work."[15] Dr Bleuler recognized that a number of other stresses might threaten the patient's recovery – too much responsibility at work, for example, family troubles or a sense of failure.

Within the institution close attention was to be given to the quality of the patient's environment. "Good surroundings have a very different influence on the patient than unpleasant and noisy ones."[16] The use of mechanical restraints was limited. Patient self-reliance was encouraged and occupational therapy was considered essential. "Every mental institution should have the kind of set-up that will make it possible to offer every patient some kind of work at all times."[17] On Sundays, "generally a bad day" for the patients as there was no work, "special care should be taken to provide sufficient opportunity for entertainment."[18]

Although Bleuler demonstrated that the outcome of schizophrenia was often benign, Kraepelin's more pessimistic view has proven more popular. Why should this have been so? Partly, perhaps, because patient management, economic conditions and community acceptance of the mentally ill in most places through many of the subsequent years have been sufficiently poor that outcome from the illness has seemed closer to Kraepelin's experience than to Bleuler's. (This possibility will be examined in some detail in subsequent chapters.) In part, the modern pessimistic view of the untreated course of schizophrenia may have developed because the introduction of the anti-psychotic drugs in the mid-1950s and their subsequent, virtually universal, employment in the treatment of psychosis has masked what was previously known of the natural history of the illness. Finally, some diagnostic reforms have tended to follow Kraepelin's lead in attempting to limit the use of the term schizophrenia to only those cases that do not recover.

DIAGNOSIS

It is by no means universally clear what is schizophrenia and what is not, and before we can study the course of the illness in more detail it will be necessary to examine the different approaches to defining its boundaries.

Scandinavian psychiatrists have tended to use a rather narrow definition of schizophrenia in an attempt to adhere to Kraepelin's emphasis on poor out-come. In this they have followed the course set by psychiatrist G. Langfeldt in

1937. He distinguished between a core group of people with *process* or *nuclear* schizophrenia, on the one hand, who demonstrated an insidious onset of illness and a deteriorating course and, on the other, a *reactive* group, who tended to show signs of better social functioning before becoming psychotic, to have a more acute onset and to display a better prognosis. Those with reactive psychosis, for whom the outlook is brighter, have been separated from "true" schizophrenia in Scandinavian psychiatric terminology and labeled as suffering from *schizophreniform psychoses*.[19] In Britain this approach has not been generally adopted, nor was it much used in the United States until recent years.

Soviet psychiatrists, particularly in Moscow, also emphasized the course of the illness in developing their classification of schizophrenia. In this instance, however, the result was a broad definition. The Moscow-school psychiatrists spoke of *periodic* schizophrenia, consisting of acute episodes with normal remission; *stepwise* schizophrenia, in which each acute episode led to a period of lowered social functioning; and *sluggish* schizophrenia, with a course of progressive deterioration. Among those with periodic schizophrenia were to be found patients who would probably have been diagnosed in Western Europe as suffering from manic-depressive psychosis. The Soviet emphasis on social adjustment in diagnosing schizophrenia, in a society where dissidence and non-conformity were seen as pathological, led to the use of the label schizophrenia for individuals who might elsewhere have been considered merely eccentric or iconoclastic.[20]

In the United States, until the mid-1970s, the diagnostic approach to schizophrenia was also extremely broad, leading to the labeling of many patients as schizophrenic who in Europe would have been considered manic-depressive or non-psychotic. This diagnostic practice came about not through an emphasis on the course of the illness but as a result of giving weight to certain intrapsychic mechanisms (under the influence of psycho-analytic theory) that were thought to be basic to schizophrenia. Thus, American psychiatry, like the Soviet system, expanded the concept of schizo-phrenia to include patients with no clear psychotic features. In the United States these patents were labeled *latent* and *pseudoneurotic* schizophrenics.

In the 1960s a research project used a standardized method of diagnosis (built around British criteria) to compare the diagnostic approaches of psy-chiatrists in New York and London. Comparing the hospital diagnoses given to hundreds of patients admitted in these two cities on opposite sides of the Atlantic, it was found that American psychiatrists were roughly twice as likely to diagnose schizophrenia, compared with the research team's standardized approach, four times as likely to diagnose psychotic depression and ten times less likely to label a psychotic patient as suffering from mania. The diagnoses given by the psychiatrists working in London hospitals, as might be expected, were very close to those of the project psychiatrists (who were using a British diagnostic approach).[21] Plainly, at this time, American psychiatrists were labeling patients as having schizophrenia who would have been considered to have manic-depressive illness in Britain.

The underlying problem was that schizophrenia and bipolar disorder (manic-depressive illness) share many common symptoms. During an acute episode it may not be possible to tell them apart. The distinguishing feature is often likely to be the prior history of the illness. The records of patients with bipolar disorder (unless they are too early in the course of the illness) should reveal prior episodes of depression and mania with interludes of normal functioning. From 1950 until the mid-1970s, however, American psychiatrists paid little attention to the course of the psychosis in diagnosing schizophrenia and emphasized instead the presence of supposedly "schizophrenic" symptoms and defects. The result was an over-inclusive pattern of diagnosis in comparison with European approaches.

We may view the problem of the diagnosis of schizophrenia in even broader cross-cultural perspective through the findings of the International Pilot Study of Schizophrenia. This large-scale project of the World Health Organization looked at two issues – the diagnosis of schizophrenia around the world (which is what concerns us here) and the course and outcome of the illness. Their findings on the latter question will be discussed later in the book. Using a standardized, British diagnostic approach (incorporated in a computer program), the project evaluated the symptoms of psychotic patients admitted to treatment in 1968–69 in nine centers in the developed and developing world – in cities in Colombia, Czechoslovakia, Denmark, India, Nigeria, Taiwan, UK, USA and the USSR.

Comparing the diagnoses made by the local hospital psychiatrists and the uniform research method, the project revealed that the diagnosis of psychosis, in general, and schizophrenia, in particular, was reasonably similar in the European and Third World centers. The serious discrepancies lay in the Soviet and American diagnostic approaches. A large proportion of the patients who were labeled as having schizophrenia by psychiatrists in Moscow and Washington, DC did not meet the research definition and would have been diagnosed as suffering from manic-depressive psychosis or a neurosis elsewhere in the world.[22]

The diagnostic approaches of American psychiatrists changed suddenly and radically in the late 1970s. Much greater attention was paid to discriminating manic-depressive illness from schizophrenia. The stimulus to this movement was clearly the introduction of lithium carbonate to US psychiatry. This drug, a simple salt, is highly effective in the control of manic-depressive illness in many patients and it is more pleasant and probably less potentially harmful to use than the most common alternative category of drugs at that time, the antipsychotic medications. Lithium carbonate, however, is generally not beneficial for people with schizophrenia.

Research published as early as 1949 in Australia[23] and in 1954 by researchers in Scandinavia[24] demonstrated the effectiveness of lithium salts in manic-depressive illness, and the use of the drug was widespread in Europe and other countries throughout the 1960s. Despite these facts, lithium carbonate was not commonly used in the United States until the mid-1970s. This delay of ten years or more is usually attributed to the concern over accidental poisonings resulting from the use of lithium chloride as a salt substitute for cardiac patients in the United States during the 1940s. Lithium was taken off the market until the US Food and Drug Administration gave permission for its use in the treatment of mania in 1970.[25]

Some observers, however, have suggested that the delay in the marketing of lithium in the United States was due to a lack of enthusiasm on the part of the major pharmaceutical companies. Lithium carbonate is such a simple substance that it could not be patented. Consequently, since its introduction, it has sold for only slightly more than the cost of aspirin. The profit margin for manufacturers is therefore a good deal lower than with other products. (As an illustration of this point, US psychiatrists who receive several visits a month from representatives of pharmaceutical companies marketing patented drugs, did not see a salesman for lithium carbonate from one year to the next.)

Whatever the reasons for the delay in the introduction of lithium to the United States, the advent of the drug was followed within a few years by a major revision of the US classification system for mental disorders. These changes meant more for the diagnosis of schizophrenia, however, than a tightening of the criteria to exclude manic-depressive illness. The concept of schizophrenia was narrowed down to include only those patients with the worst prognostic outlook. With the publication in 1980 of the third edition of the American Psychiatric Association *Diagnostic and Statistical Manual* (DSM-III), American psychiatry switched from one of the broadest concepts of schizophrenia in the world to one of the narrowest – a diagnostic approach similar to the Scandinavian system. No psychotic patient, for example, could any longer be labeled as suffering from schizophrenia if he or she had been continuously disturbed for less than six months. Thus, a patient who had experienced several schizophrenia-like episodes, each briefer than six months, was not to be considered as having schizophrenia. Nor was a patient who did not show a clear deterioration in functioning. Patients who failed to meet these criteria but appeared schizophrenic in other ways were to be diagnosed as suffering from brief reactive psychosis, schizophreniform disorder or atypical psychosis. Those patients who could not be definitely diagnosed as suffering from either manic-depressive illness or schizophrenia, having features of both conditions, were previously labeled as "schizoaffective" and included within the schizophrenia category; now they were to be excluded.[26] This narrow diagnostic scheme was essentially unchanged by the publication in 1994 of fourth edition of the American Psychiatric Association *Diagnostic and Statistical Manual* (DSM-IV).

A number of practical implications flow from these geographic and temporal variations in the diagnosis of schizophrenia. In particular, whatever we have to say about the prevalence and course of the illness has meaning only if we define which diagnostic approach is being used. For every narrowly defined case of schizophrenia in the population there can be as many as four more people who meet broadly defined criteria for the illness.[27] Where the diagnostic concept is deliberately shaped to exclude patients who recover, we must expect the outcome to be worse. In this book, the term schizophrenia, unless otherwise qualified, refers to a middle-of-the-road definition – not as exclusive as the Scandinavian or modern American approach, nor as broad as the Soviet or earlier American systems. The definition used here will essentially be the one in use in British psychiatry and the one which, as the WHO Pilot Study shows, is most commonly used around the world. This definition, while clearly differentiating cases of bipolar disorder, does not exclude psychoses of short duration or those with features of good prognosis. It does, however, exclude patients who fail to show clear-cut psychotic symptoms.

COURSE AND OUTCOME OF SCHIZOPHRENIA

A thorough analysis of the outcome of schizophrenic illness will be attempted in Chapter 3. At this point it is necessary to give an idea of the wide variation that occurs in the course of the condition. A Swiss psychiatrist, Professor Luc Ciompi, provides a useful analysis of the course of schizophrenia followed into old age. In the late 1960s Dr Ciompi traced 289 patients, all more than 65 years of age, who had been admitted for treatment of schizophrenia to the University Psychiatric Clinic of Lausanne at various times throughout the century. For most of these patients the history of the illness extended back for more than thirty-five years, in many cases for more than fifty years. This is one of the longest follow-up studies in the literature. Dr Ciompi describes in detail his diagnostic criteria, which are those of Emil Kraepelin and Eugen Bleuler – neither particularly narrow nor broad.

Figure 1.1 is a diagrammatic representation (adapted from Dr Ciompi's paper) of the onset, course and outcome of the illness in the 228 patients for whom the information could be determined with certainty. Dr Ciompi found that the onset of the illness had been either acute (with less than six months from first symptoms to full-blown psychosis) or, conversely, insidious, in roughly equal numbers of cases. Similarly, the course of the condition was episodic or continuous in approximately equal numbers of patients; and the outcome was moderate to severe disability in half the cases and mild disability or full recovery in the other half. Full recovery was noted in more than a quarter of the patients.[28] The outcome from schizophrenia varies from one period to another and from place to place. These results, like Eugen Bleuler's, are somewhat better than average and, as we shall see (in Chapter 6), this may be a consequence of the superior economic conditions in Switzerland

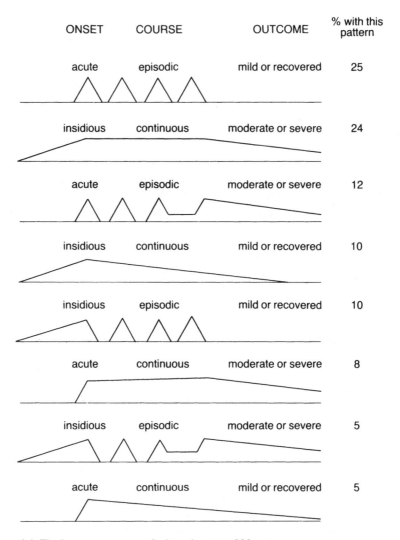

ONSET	COURSE	OUTCOME	% with this pattern
acute	episodic	mild or recovered	25
insidious	continuous	moderate or severe	24
acute	episodic	moderate or severe	12
insidious	continuous	mild or recovered	10
insidious	episodic	mild or recovered	10
acute	continuous	moderate or severe	8
insidious	episodic	moderate or severe	5
acute	continuous	mild or recovered	5

Figure 1.1 The long-term course of schizophrenia in 228 patients

Source: Ciompi, L., "Catamnestic long-term study on the course of life and aging of schizophrenics," *Schizophrenia Bulletin*, 6: 606–18, 1980.

throughout most of the twentieth century. We can see from these results, nevertheless, that the course of schizophrenia varies a good deal between patients and that the outcome is often favorable – regardless of treatment.

Many attempts have been made to predict which patients will have a benign course and a good outcome – good-prognosis schizophrenia – and to identify the features that will distinguish them from patients with poor-prognosis schizophrenia. (This distinction is similar to Dr Langfeldt's differentiation of process and reactive schizophrenia mentioned earlier.) The results of this work will be discussed in some detail in Chapter 10. Here we may briefly state that it is the patient with higher levels of functioning (social, sexual and vocational) before developing a psychosis who tends to do better. A sudden onset to the illness and an onset late in life are also good prognostic features.

HOW WIDESPREAD IS SCHIZOPHRENIA?

Results of prevalence studies range from as few as one person with schizophrenia for every 1,000 adults in one community to one for each 60 adults in others. This wide variation is in part due, as we have seen, to differences in diagnostic practices and, in part, to differences in recovery and death rates for people with schizophrenia in different parts of the world. It is possible that there are also variations in the true frequency of occurrence of the illness, but a World Health Organization multi-national study makes this seem less likely. The WHO research demonstrates that the rate of occurrence of *new* cases (the incidence) of narrowly defined schizophrenia is surprisingly similar in ten widely dispersed countries.[29] Chapter 9 will examine differences in the prevalence of schizophrenia in detail and the possibility of environmental effects on the frequency of the illness. The studies analyzed in that chapter indicate that in many industrial world settings the prevalence of schizophrenia is close to one in every 200 adults.

Schizophrenia is found in every culture. The content of the patient's hallucinations and delusions varies from one social group to another – the delusions of villagers living in the north of Ghana are associated with the local fetish system, for example, but among the city dwellers of Accra in the south of that country ideas of influence and control by electricity and radio are more common.[30] The form and basic features of schizophrenia, nevertheless, are similar around the world, as the WHO Pilot Study shows.

WHAT CAUSES SCHIZOPHRENIA?

Tuberculosis is the result of an infection by a bacillus. In the early decades of the twentieth century, however, when the disease was widespread, although a huge proportion of the population became infected with the organism, only a relatively small number went on to develop clinically recognizable evidence of the disease. What caused the manifest symptoms of the illness to appear in those few, in some cases years after the initial infection? Poor social conditions were known to increase the susceptibility to the illness, and improvements in diet and housing were linked to a decline in the death rate from tuberculosis long before effective drug treatment was introduced. The irritant effects of coal dust on miners, pregnancy in women and the debilitating influence of secondary illnesses, all could reduce an individual's resistance to the disease. What, then, is the cause of tuberculosis? The tubercle bacillus? Overcrowding? Poor diet? The stresses of lower-class living? Or any of the other environmental, occupational or constitutional factors that increase the individual's susceptibility? Clearly any and all of these factors may be considered contributory, and the reduction in the prevalence of the illness had as much to do with elimination of some of the social causes and with the increase in the resistance of the population by vaccination as with the direct attack on the infective organism by chemotherapy.

The same principles apply to schizophrenia. We do not know with certainty of a specific organic defect or infective agent that is critical in the development of schizophrenia (although there are a number of theories and there has been an expansion of knowledge in this area). We do know, however, of several factors that increase the susceptibility to this illness and that may provoke its appearance. To grasp how these factors may influence the development and the course of schizophrenia we need to use an interactive conceptual model such as the one proposed by American psychiatrists John Strauss and William Carpenter.

An adaptation of the conceptual scheme offered by these authors[31] is given in Figure 1.2. An interactional model allows for various types of explanation to assume importance at different stages in the individual's development. The genetic contribution, damaging intrauterine effects and birth trauma might each play a part in forming the newborn infant's predisposition to developing schizophrenia. The vulnerability to the illness might theoretically be heightened during childhood development by brain damage, for example, or by unusual family communication patterns.

Whether or not the illness becomes manifest in later life is likely to depend upon the extent of the vulnerability and the subsequent exposure to a variety of stresses. Precipitating stresses may be biological in nature (such as hallucinogenic drug abuse), or psychosocial. In the latter category are life events (such as starting work, leaving home or bereavement), environmental influences (criticism or intrusiveness at home, for example) or existential concerns (loss of a sense of purpose or belonging).

Once an episode of psychosis has begun, these same stressors and new ones, together with the degree of vulnerability, will determine the subsequent course and outcome of the illness. Labeling and social stigma may affect the individual's sense of self-worth, as may his or her success in reintegrating with the social group and in returning to a valued social role. Criticism, rejection, restriction, confinement or idleness might well limit the individual's capacity for recovery from schizophrenia.

The strength of some of these potential causes of vulnerability and precipitants of psychosis has been better demonstrated than others. On the following pages a few of the more important will be briefly outlined.

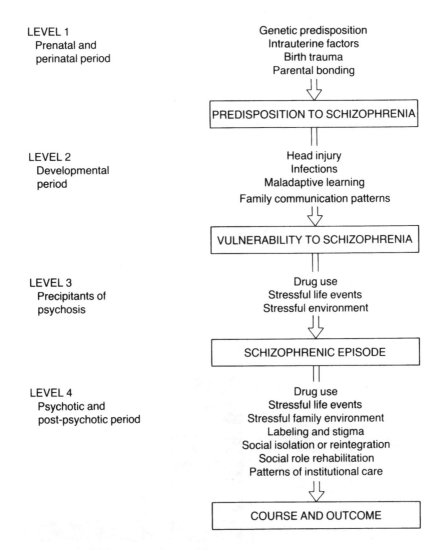

LEVEL 1
Prenatal and
perinatal period

Genetic predisposition
Intrauterine factors
Birth trauma
Parental bonding

PREDISPOSITION TO SCHIZOPHRENIA

LEVEL 2
Developmental
period

Head injury
Infections
Maladaptive learning
Family communication patterns

VULNERABILITY TO SCHIZOPHRENIA

LEVEL 3
Precipitants of
psychosis

Drug use
Stressful life events
Stressful environment

SCHIZOPHRENIC EPISODE

LEVEL 4
Psychotic and
post-psychotic period

Drug use
Stressful life events
Stressful family environment
Labeling and stigma
Social isolation or reintegration
Social role rehabilitation
Patterns of institutional care

COURSE AND OUTCOME

Figure 1.2 Interactional model for factors possibly affecting the onset, course and outcome
of schizophrenia

Inheritance

If inheritance is important in the development of schizophrenia, relatives of
people with schizophrenia will have a greater risk of developing the illness
than others – and they do. One would also expect the risk to be progressively
greater in relatives who are more genetically similar to the schizophrenic
person. Epidemiologist Irving Gottesman, drawing data from about 40

European studies conducted between 1920 and 1987, compiled a comparison of the average lifetime risk of developing schizophrenia for people with different degrees of relationship to someone with schizophrenia. His findings, shown in Figure 1.3, indicate that the closer the similarity in genetic make-up, the greater the risk. The identical twins of people with schizophrenia, who have precisely the same genetic constitution, run the greatest risk of developing the illness – nearly 50 per cent. The offspring of parents both of whom have schizophrenia have a similar risk. The rate is less for first-degree relatives

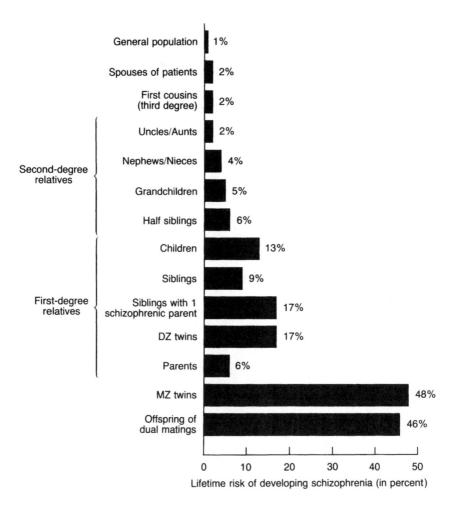

Figure 1.3 The average risk of developing schizophrenia for relatives of a person with the illness; compiled from family and twin studies conducted in Europe between 1920 and 1987

Source: Reprinted by permission of the author. From Gottesman, I. I., *Schizophrenia Genesis: The Origins of Madness*, New York: W. H. Freeman, 1991, p. 96, © 1991 Irving I. Gottesman.

such as non-identical siblings and progressively declines through second-degree and third-degree relatives to the general population risk of around one per cent.[32]

Studies of people adopted in infancy suggest that the increased risk of schizophrenia in the relatives of identified cases is related to inheritance rather than environment. The children of people with schizophrenia have a similar increased prevalence of the illness whether they are raised by their biological parents or by adoptive parents. Likewise, the family history of people with schizophrenia brought up by adoptive parents reveals an increased prevalence of the illness among their biological relatives but not among their relatives by adoption.[33]

Genetic factors appear to be important in the development of schizophrenia but are not sufficient to explain the entire pattern of occurrence. As we have seen, although identical twins have exactly the same genetic make-up, the risk of the second twin developing schizophrenia is only 50 per cent. One may conclude that genetic factors play a major part in establishing the vulnerability to the illness but that environmental factors (including the intrauterine experience) must also play important roles before schizophrenia becomes manifest. Nearly two-thirds of people with schizophrenia, moreover, have no relative at all with the illness.[34] If a genetic vulnerability is always present in schizophrenia it must skip generations; the interaction of more than one gene and environmental factors may be necessary for the illness to become apparent.

Studies of twins reveal additional information about the inheritance of vulnerability to schizophrenia.[35] When one of a pair of identical twins has a severe and deteriorating form of schizophrenia, it is virtually certain that the other twin will show signs of the illness; but if one identical twin has a mild form of the psychosis, the chances of the other twin developing schizophrenia are very much lower – around 25 per cent.[36] This observation suggests that the genetic vulnerability influences both the onset and the course of the illness. The identical twins of people with schizophrenia, furthermore, if they do not develop schizophrenia, run an increased risk of developing other psychiatric disorders – alcoholism, neurosis or personality problems.[37] What is inherited is, perhaps, not specifically a vulnerability to schizophrenia but, instead, an underlying biochemical and functional disturbance that may express itself in somewhat different ways under the influence of environmental stresses.

Recent genetic linkage studies have led to the identification of several suspected gene locations each associated with a proportion of the risk of developing schizophrenia; a single major gene locus has not emerged. Genetic susceptibility regions have been detected on chromosomes 5, 6, 8, 15 and 22, and each region could harbor one or more relevant genes. Genetic researchers suspect that susceptibility genes are present in a large proportion, perhaps seven to ten per cent, of the general population, and that the interaction of multiple genes and additional environmental factors are necessary to produce the illness.[38]

Just what is the deficit that might be inherited?

Brain chemistry

Emotions and thought processes are regulated by the complex interaction of systems of nerve cells throughout the brain. Each nerve cell (or neuron) exerts its effect by the release of a chemical mediator at the synapse – the point of contact with another neuron. Biochemical theories attempting to explain the appearance of symptoms of schizophrenia have focused on abnormalities in the action of some of these chemical neurotransmitters.

A prominent biochemical theory of schizophrenia – the dopamine hypothesis – suggests that the underlying abnormality may be a relative overactivity of tracts of neurons in which dopamine is the chemical mediator. Acute stress, leading to sudden increases in dopamine turnover, could thus precipitate an episode of psychosis in a vulnerable individual.[39] It is likely, however, that the disturbance of dopamine function is a consequence other abnormalities elsewhere in the brain which have not yet been clearly identified. Attention has been focused, for example, on whether an abnormality in the functioning of the inhibitory interneurons, which release gamma-amino butyric acid (GABA), is responsible for producing changes in the dopamine-releasing neurons.[40] Inhibitory interneurons damp down the action of primary neurons and prevent the brain being overwhelmed by sensory input. GABA release is decreased in the brains of people with schizophrenia, suggesting that they may be at greater risk of brain overload from environmental stimuli.

The dopamine hypothesis (which will be dealt with in detail in Chapter 10) is supported in large part by the observation that the standard antipsychotic drugs achieve their effect by blocking the dopamine-2 receptor. With the introduction of the modern "atypical" or "novel" antipsychotic drugs in the past decade, however, researchers have begun to realize that many more receptors are implicated in the illness. Besides the dopamine-2 receptor, the atypical antipsychotic drugs (like clozapine and olanzapine) block the action of a number of other neurotransmitters, such as serotonin, 5-HT$_2$, NMDA and other dopamine receptors, suggesting that these neurochemicals also play a role in schizophrenia.[41]

Brain structure

That there *are* biochemical differences in schizophrenia is certain – just as certain as that there are biochemical correlates in the brain to rage, anxiety and learning Spanish. That there are *anatomical* differences in the brains of people with schizophrenia (as in some organic brain disorders) is not a foregone conclusion, however, and in fact the evidence for such abnormalities in the structure of the brain has been slow in accumulating. Decades of post-mortem study of the brains of schizophrenics failed to produce agreement on any neuroanatomical changes specific to the illness. The application of more advanced research techniques, however, has shown indications of injury in an area of the brain known as the limbic system. Several researchers have identified such degenerative changes in people with schizophrenia, which were not evident in those who were free of the illness.[42] These findings are of interest as they point to abnormalities in the same area of the brain (the limbic system) that neurochemical research has incriminated as functioning abnormally in schizophrenia. This interconnecting network of terminals and tracts is believed to be central to the regulation of emotion and to the individual's response to stress.

Important evidence for anatomical changes in the brain in schizophrenia has been provided by computed tomographic (CT) scans and magnetic resonance imaging (MRI). Scores of studies using CT scans and MRI have found evidence of mild cerebral atrophy in a proportion of people with schizophrenia.[43] The changes, which include enlargement of the fluid-containing ventricles of the brain and widening of the fissures between folds of brain tissue, can also occur in degenerative brain conditions and in some other psychiatric patients.[44]

The cause of such cerebral atrophy in schizophrenia is not known. Since the abnormalities are found equally in people with first-break, acute schizophrenia and in those with chronic illness, it is unlikely that the changes are due to treatment.[45] The atrophy does not indicate that schizophrenia is a degenerative brain disease; it is not progressive, it is not specific to schizophrenia, nor is it present in all cases.[46] The changes occur in only about a quarter of people with schizophrenia, but there is not a well-defined group with enlarged cerebral ventricles and another with normal-size ventricles; the CT-scan and MRI changes are distributed along a smooth gradient from normal to large.[47] The most probable explanation is that the cerebral atrophy found in some people with schizophrenia is an indicator of some earlier non-specific brain injury that increases the vulnerability to developing the illness. Such brain damage might result, for example, from intrauterine oxygen deprivation or infection, birth trauma or one of a number of similar assaults.

It is likely that inheritance and early brain damage are both risk factors for schizophrenia and that the two together create double jeopardy. Studies of identical twins show that if one twin has schizophrenia and the other does not, the one with the illness is more likely to have a history of obstetric complications at birth[48] and, with brain-imaging techniques such as CT-scans, to show evidence of brain damage.[49]

CT-scan and MRI changes are not restricted to one clinical subtype of the illness, but people with schizophrenia who show these signs of brain damage have some characteristic clinical features. Patients with evidence of cerebral atrophy have more severe "negative" symptoms of schizophrenia, such as apathy, withdrawal and poverty of ideas; "positive" symptoms such as hallucinations and delusions are less prominent. They also are more likely to have functioned poorly through childhood and adolescence before the onset of illness, and more likely to show signs of neurological impairment, to respond poorly to treatment with medication and to have an unfavorable outcome.[50]

Viral infection

Evidence of early brain damage in some people with schizophrenia suggests that the fetus may have been harmed in the uterus. The risk of intrauterine brain damage is increased if the mother contracts a viral illness in pregnancy. Interest in the possibility of such damage in schizophrenia has been generated by the discovery that more people with schizophrenia are born in the late winter or spring than at other times of year;[51] the proportion born at this time is approximately ten per cent higher than in other seasons of the year.[52] Many possible reasons have been suggested for this finding,[53] maternal infection during pregnancy being one. Fetal brain damage might be caused by a virus or, equally, by medicines taken by the mother to combat symptoms of the illness.[54] Studies from countries as widely dispersed as Denmark, the United States, Finland and England have shown that the proportion of people with schizophrenia born in winter and spring increases after epidemics of such viral illnesses as influenza, measles and chickenpox.[55] A smaller number of studies have failed to find a connection with viral epidemics.[56] A 1992 report from the United Kingdom found that maternal influenza between the third and seventh month of pregnancy is associated with an increased risk of schizophrenia to the child in adult life.[57]

A study from Milan, Italy, indicates that people with schizophrenia born between December and April are more likely to show signs of ventricular enlargement. These brain abnormalities, moreover, were more common in winter-born schizophrenics with no family history for the disorder than in those with a positive family history.[58] Again the evidence suggests that either inheritance or early brain damage (in this case, an intrauterine effect) may put someone at risk for developing schizophrenia.

Brain functioning

Vulnerability to schizophrenia, then, may have a number of biological sources. How it is expressed as abnormal brain *functioning* has also been studied. Researchers in Colorado have detected a functional abnormality in the limbic system. They have measured differences between people from the general population, people with schizophrenia and their relatives in their response to such stimuli as audible clicks and flashing lights. Computerized averaging of multiple electroencephalograph tracings of subjects' responses to these stimuli (evoked potentials) has been used in this work. The research has shown that most people with schizophrenia, as well as half of their close relatives, have an abnormal pattern of response to environmental stimuli. They appear to be overly responsive to pieces of sensory information – sights, sounds, smells and touch – and more limited in their ability to blot out irrelevant material.[59]

It is essential to our capacity to concentrate on what is happening to us that we be able to attend to one aspect of our environment at a time and screen out the multiplicity of other sensory data with which we are constantly bombarded. This capacity to discriminate stimuli and to focus attention may be disrupted in those who are vulnerable to schizophrenia. Such a "sensory gating" deficit would be a possible result of abnormal functioning in the limbic system. Given sufficient stress the affected individual will become overwhelmed and highly aroused. Withdrawal into an isolated, inner world may thus be a useful maneuver against the effects of the person's excessive vigilance towards irrelevant stimuli.[60]

The knowledge that half of the first-degree relatives of people with schizophrenia share a neurophysiological abnormality with those who themselves suffer from the illness suggests that the defect is transmitted by a single dominant gene. This raises another question, however: why do only some of those with the defect develop schizophrenia? Using MRI studies, the Colorado team has found that people with schizophrenia have a smaller area in the hippocampus (part of the limbic system) than their healthy siblings who have the same sensory gating abnormality. It is possible that early damage to this brain area, combined with an inherited sensory gating defect, is sufficient to produce schizophrenia.[61]

An interesting wrinkle to this research is the discovery that abnormal sensory gating in schizophrenia is linked to the function of brain nicotine receptors and to the gene that controls them. The gene in question has been located on chromosome 15. The sensory gating defect is transiently improved by high doses of nicotine. This finding raises the possibility that some people with schizophrenia may use tobacco as self-medication, and helps to explain why cigarette smoking is heavier and twice as common among people with schizophrenia than in the general population.[62]

Some research workers, using radioactive tracer substances and brain-imaging techniques such as single photon emission tomography (SPECT) and positron emission tomography (PET), have demonstrated that blood flow through the frontal lobes of the brain does not increase in people with schizophrenia, as it does in other people, when they undertake tasks requiring attention and effort. People with schizophrenia may not be able to turn on a specific region of their frontal lobes, the prefrontal cortex, when needed – a problem that could explain the withdrawal, apathy and thinking difficulties in schizophrenia.[63] The prefrontal cortex and the limbic system are linked; an abnormality in one can affect the other, though it is not certain which area is primarily disturbed.[64]

Step by step, links are being forged between inheritance patterns, biochemical and anatomical abnormalities and the symptoms of schizophrenia. We can begin to understand how early biological factors, development and environmental stresses may interact with an individual's physiological response pattern to precipitate an episode of schizophrenia.

The family

"In my own very self," wrote D. H. Lawrence in his last work, "I am part of my family."[65] Psychiatrists since Sigmund Freud have regarded the family as crucial to the development of human personality and mental disorder. Antipsychiatrist David Cooper saw Western family life as a form of imperialism crushing individual autonomy.[66] It is to be expected, therefore, that many will have looked to the family for dynamic forces capable of creating schizophrenia.

In 1948 psychoanalyst Frieda Fromm-Reichmann proposed that some mothers fostered schizophrenia in their offspring through cold and distant parenting.[67] Others have pointed to parental schisms and power imbalances within the family as important in the genesis of the illness.[68] The double-bind theory, put forward by anthropologist Gregory Bateson and his colleagues, postulated that schizophrenia is promoted by contradictory parental injunctions from which the child is unable to escape.[69] Existential psychoanalysts R. D. Laing and Aaron Esterton offered a similar formula for the production of schizophrenia through the mystification of the child with confusing patterns of communication.[70]

While enjoying broad public recognition, such theories have seldom, if ever, been adequately tested. Some researchers claimed to find abnormalities in the patterns of communication within the families of people with schizophrenia that were not evident in other families.[71] These findings, not confirmed by later research,[72] proved to be controversial.[73] None of the work in this area, furthermore, satisfactorily resolved the question of whether the patterns of deviance alluded to in the families of people with schizophrenia were the *cause* or the *effect* of psychological abnormalities in the psychotic family member.

For example, a Finnish study children who were given up for adoption, and whose mothers had been diagnosed with schizophrenia, found that the children who developed schizophrenia themselves were more likely to have been raised in adoptive families that were rated as being disturbed than in normal families. Although the findings suggest that schizophrenia may be the result of an interaction between genetic factors and the family environment, it is also likely that the higher levels of disturbance in the adoptive families were, at least in part, a consequence of rearing a disturbed child who had pre-morbid symptoms of schizophrenia.[74]

While there may be stresses in the rearing of children that could increase vulnerability to schizophrenia, their nature and existence have not been verified. One thing only is certain in this field: thousands, if not millions, of family members of people with schizophrenia in the West have suffered shame, guilt and stigma as a consequence of the widespread acceptance of such theorizing. Parents have not only suffered the pain of seeing their child's personality change and his or her ambitions destroyed by illness, they have also felt blamed, directly or indirectly, for causing the condition. Family members may carry the burden of living with someone whose actions can be unpredictable and distressing and whose emotional responses are unrewarding, but they may also receive little empathy and support from therapists who are liable to censure and distrust them. The reactions of society to the person with schizophrenia and his or her relatives may be sufficient, of themselves, to produce distorted patterns of family interaction.

Stress – domestic and non-domestic

If we study the family, not for formative influences building a vulnerability to schizophrenia, however, but for current household stresses influencing the course of an already established illness, a far more clear-cut picture emerges. People with schizophrenia living with relatives (by birth or marriage) who are critical or smothering have a much higher relapse rate, according to research from several countries and cultures, than those who live with relatives who are less hostile or intrusive.[75] Further studies have shown that relatives who are less critical and over-involved exert a positive therapeutic effect on the person with schizophrenia – their presence leading to a reduction in the patient's level of arousal.[76] In the same vein, people with schizophrenia who see their parents as being affectionate and undemanding have a low relapse rate if they are in contact with their parents, but tend to do poorly and relapse more often if they are not.[77] The benefits of a low-stress household on the relapse rate of people with schizophrenia appear to be equally as strong as the effect of antipsychotic drugs treatment.[78]

There is no indication that the more critical and over-involved relatives are at all abnormal by everyday Western standards. It appears, in fact, that the households where there is more criticism and intrusiveness are those with patients who have personality attributes that make them difficult to live with.[79] The evidence suggests that the families in which people with schizophrenia do well have adapted to having a mentally ill person in the household by becoming unusually low-key and permissive.[80] In the developing world the picture is different. A study conducted in Chandigarh, India, revealed that few relatives of people with schizophrenia in this Third World city showed the same high levels of criticism and over-involvement found to be common in the West.[81] These Western responses to mentally disordered family members may be a product of emotional isolation engendered by nuclear-family life, or the result of high achievement expectations placed on the mentally ill person. The decline of extended-family living is largely a consequence of industrialization, and educational and occupational achievement standards are higher in our advanced technological society. Through such family dynamics as these, political economy may affect the course of schizophrenia.

It is also clear that other forms of stress in the lives of people with schizophrenia trigger psychotic relapse and influence the course of the illness. In a study conducted in London, 46 per cent of a group of people with schizophrenia experienced a stressful life event that was clearly not a consequence of the illness in the three-week period preceding a psychotic relapse. By contrast, only 12 per cent of a matched group from the general population had experienced such stress. The life events noted included role changes (such as leaving school), change of living arrangements, development of illness, and other disappointments and crises. When life events were included that may not have been independent of the individual's own actions or illness (events such as job loss), nearly two-thirds of the people with schizophrenia reported experiencing such stress compared with less than a fifth of the general population sample.[82]

Subsequent research,[83] including a nine-country WHO study,[84] has confirmed that stress, particularly in the preceding two or three weeks, can precipitate episodes of schizophrenia. The research also shows that severe stress provokes more intense symptoms of schizophrenia, but that even mild stress can precipitate a relapse.[85] A basic problem in schizophrenia is that sufferers are exquisitely sensitive to anxiety-provoking situations. Major life-event stress is likely to precipitate relapse in patients who are taking medication,[86] whereas those who are not using medication are more susceptible to relapse with minor stress. Antipsychotic drugs benefit the patient by raising the threshold of response to all but major stresses.

It is unclear whether stress can create a vulnerability to schizophrenia during an individual's development[87] (levels 1 and 2 of Figure 1.2) but it is clear that stresses of various kinds play a part in triggering psychosis in those who are already vulnerable and in shaping the course of a manifest schizophrenic illness (levels 3 and 4 of Figure 1.2). At these later stages – influencing the vulnerable individual and those already suffering from the illness – we may also perceive the prominent effect of political and economic forces. Much that is stressful in life is not covered by such concepts as family hostility or recent life changes. We all need to have the respect of others, for example. Finding value and meaning in life and having a sense of belonging to one's own kind and community are omnipresent existential concerns. Problems arising from these concerns commonly emerge in the lives of people with schizophrenia – problems (it will be argued here) produced or exacerbated by the political and economic dimensions of the society.

The following chapters will attempt to show that political economy assumes a hitherto underemphasized importance in the production and perpetuation of schizophrenia. Specifically, it not only determines mental health policy and legislation, it also molds public reaction to mental illness and even shapes psychiatric ideology. Political and economic factors influence the social status, social role and social integration of the person with a psychosis – his or her sense of worth, meaning and belonging. Just as the destinies of all in society are shaped by political and economic forces, so too is the course of schizophrenia.

SUMMARY

- Schizophrenia, originally termed dementia praecox, is a functional psychosis with some unifying features but several distinctly different forms.
- In defining dementia praecox, Emil Kraepelin saw poor outcome as a central feature of the condition.
- Although Eugen Bleuler found outcome from the illness to be good in a majority of cases, Kraepelin's original pessimism has been more widely accepted.
- Bleuler's good results may have been a consequence of his enlightened treatment approach.
- Scandinavian psychiatrists have adopted a narrow diagnostic approach to schizophrenia, emphasizing poor outcome.
- Soviet psychiatrists used a broad diagnostic concept that included patients who would not have been considered psychotic elsewhere.
- American psychiatry switched from a similarly broad diagnostic approach to a narrow definition of schizophrenia in 1980.
- The course of schizophrenia is quite variable; the outcome can be mild in half the cases.
- The prevalence of schizophrenia varies widely (partly because of diagnostic differences) but it is often close to 1 person with schizophrenia for every 200 adults in populations in the industrial world.
- Schizophrenia appears to be universally distributed.
- Multiple social and biological factors interact to produce a vulnerability to schizophrenia, to trigger an episode of psychosis and to shape the course of the illness.
- Genetic predisposition contributes to the vulnerability to schizophrenia but does not alone account for its occurrence.
- An over-activity in tracts of neurons in which the neurotransmitter is dopamine may be one of the underlying biochemical deficits in schizophrenia.
- Some people with schizophrenia appear to suffer from mild cerebral atrophy.

- The underlying functional deficit in schizophrenia may be an inability to discriminate relevant from irrelevant environmental stimuli.
- Theories that suggest that family communication patterns produce a vulnerability to schizophrenia remain unverified.
- On the other hand, evidence that domestic stresses trigger relapse in schizophrenia is strong.
- Political economy refers to the part of the social structure that regulates labor, energy, production and reproduction in groups larger in size than the family.
- Political and economic factors, it is argued, are important in influencing the course of schizophrenia.

Chapter 2

Health, illness and the economy

How far do economic factors influence our birth and death, control our health, mold our behavior and identity and affect our sanity? We may look for the answer to these questions by two methods – by studying the differences between social classes and by calculating the human effects of fluctuations in the economy.

SOCIAL CLASS, ILLNESS AND DEATH

Lower-class people in industrial society die younger. This much was clear to the statisticians of the nineteenth century and continues to be true today. In 1842, the average age of death for different classes in various British centers of trade and manufacturing was estimated to be as follows:

	Gentry	Tradesmen	Laborers
Bethnal Green	45	26	16
Leeds	44	27	19
Liverpool	35	22	15
Manchester	38	20	17

The well-to-do classes enjoyed a lease of life more than double that of the working classes.[1] The dramatic difference was largely accounted for by high infant mortality in the poorer classes and by deaths among adults from consumption, pneumonia, infectious diseases and other conditions associated with poverty, malnutrition and overcrowding.[2]

Class differences in life span persist in modern industrial society. According to the British Registrar General's figures, there is a clearly defined social-class gradient in mortality rates. British working-class citizens run a greater risk of death at all ages. In adults the difference in death rates is apparent over a wide range of causes from malignancy to heart disease. Where the cause of death is accidental or from respiratory or infectious disease, lower-class mortality rates are most dramatically elevated – from three to five times greater than for the highest social class.[3]

Throughout the Western world there is a similar relationship between social class and life expectancy. In nineteenth-century America, as in Britain, the ratio of the death rates in the highest and lowest classes was around 2:1. By the 1940s the class gap had closed to 1.4:1 or 1.3:1, but in more recent decades little progress has been made towards narrowing the class difference.[4] The differential is greatest in the middle years of life and includes deaths from stress-related causes. Several studies have shown, for instance, that sudden death from heart attack is more common in people with lower levels of education. Some researchers attribute this finding to the stress of living in or near poverty.[5] The latest American figures reveal that poor middle-aged white men must expect to die 7 years earlier than high-income white men of the same age. Death rates from heart disease, lung cancer and diabetes all increase as income decreases.[6]

Sickness rates follow the same pattern as mortality. British unskilled working men, aged 45–64, report four times the number of days of acute sickness as men of the same age in professional jobs, and twice the rate of chronic sickness.[7] In the United States illness of all kinds is more common among the poor. Whereas only 4 per cent of high-income white American men in 1995 reported their health to be poor or fair, over 30 per cent of poor white American men reported this level of ill health.[8] Multiple studies have reported a close association between high blood pressure and lower-class status,[9] and a county-wide survey of risk factors for illness in Florida found socio-economic status to be the social factor most strongly affecting the incidence of psychosomatic illness.[10]

While material factors such as poor nutrition and poor housing contribute to high rates of illness and death in the lower classes, environmental stress is also important. Migration, unemployment, job turnover, divorce and separation are all more common among the poor.[11] A survey of the Toronto Borough of East York found symptoms of physical and emotional distress to be from three to five times more common among the poorly educated and low-income residents. The presence of these symptoms, in turn, was found to be associated with the person's exposure to a recent stressful life event, particularly demotion or job loss.[12] Two studies conducted in New Haven, Connecticut, and another carried out in Manhattan, New York City, yielded similar results – substantially higher levels of psychological symptoms in working-class subjects than in the upper class. The difference in symptom levels in these studies, as in Toronto, was explained by the larger number of unpleasant life events affecting the working-class members. This finding held true (in the New York City study) when only those life events were counted that were independent of the person's own actions – suggesting that it was indeed the stress that precipitated the symptoms and not the psychological disturbance that led to the stressful events.[13]

A large-scale survey of drinking habits among residents of suburban Chicago offers similar evidence of links between social class, stress and symptoms. Low-income residents and those who reported more economic strain were more likely to have symptoms of anxiety. Lower-class members were also more likely to have low self-esteem and a sense of limited personal control over events. Operating together, these three factors – heightened anxiety, low self-esteem and a limited sense of mastery – were found to increase the individual's inclination to use alcohol to relieve distress.[14] Class status may thus mold personality, coping strategies, emotional symptoms, and alcohol use and indirectly influence physical health.

INCOME INEQUALITY

It is not just low social status, but also the extent of inequality between the richest and the poorest in a society, that is associated with increased mortality and morbidity. Over 15 independent studies in recent years have demonstrated that, in developed and developing countries, the greater the gulf between the rich and the poor, the higher the mortality rate from a variety of causes, even after taking into account such factors as cigarette smoking and obstetric risks.[15] There is a strong correlation, for example, between the level of income inequality in each of the 50 US states and the age-adjusted mortality of residents of the state.[16] Similarly, in districts across Britain, the death rate is associated not just with the absolute level of the index of social deprivation but also with the range of variability of the index within each area.[17]

Various explanations have been promoted to explain how income inequality leads to ill-health and death. Many researchers have concluded that various aspects of psychosocial life, such as the sense of control over one's future, social affiliations and support, self-esteem, stressful events and job security have an impact on health through the effects of stress.[18] Some of this thinking is captured in the concept of "social capital" – those features of social organization, like social networks, reciprocity, and trust in others, that facilitate cooperation between citizens for mutual benefit.[19] High income differences in a community, it is argued, undermine the possibility of such positive communal interaction. Involvement in community life through active group membership and a sense of power in one's local community are lessened by the presence of marked social disparities, impeding individual pathways to health.

SOCIAL CLASS AND MENTAL ILLNESS

The evidence is strong that stresses are greater among the lower classes, especially where disparity of income with the more affluent is evident, and that increased ill health and emotional distress are, to a certain extent, a consequence of these stresses. It is also clear that schizophrenia and other mental disorders are more common in the lower classes. In the Great Depression of the 1930s, sociologists Robert Faris and Warren Dunham found that the highest rates for treated schizophrenia were concentrated in Chicago's slum areas. From a rate of over 7 cases per 1,000 adults in these central districts the prevalence of treated schizophrenia declined gradually through the more prosperous sections of the city to the lowest rates of below 2.5 per 1,000 adults in the most affluent areas.[20] Following the publication of this pioneer work, a number of other epidemiological studies confirmed that high rates of mental disorder, particularly schizophrenia, were concentrated in centrally located, low socio-economic districts in many American and European cities – Peoria, Illinois; Kansas City, Missouri; St Louis, Missouri; Milwaukee, Wisconsin; Omaha, Nebraska;[21] Worcester, Massachusetts;[22] Rochester, New York;[23] Baltimore, Maryland;[24] Oslo, Norway;[25] and Bristol, England.[26]

Sociologist Robert Clark demonstrated in the 1940s that Chicago residents in low-status and low-income occupations had a higher incidence of treated schizophrenia than higher-status workers.[27] This observation has also been confirmed by a number of studies. In their survey of New Haven, Connecticut, in the 1950s, August Hollingshead and Frederick Redlich revealed a gradient of progressively greater prevalence of treated schizophrenia in the lower socio-economic classes. The prevalence of the illness was 11 times greater in the lowest class compared with the highest class.[28] Leo Srole and his associates, in a community survey of midtown Manhattan in New York City, which located both treated and untreated cases, found mental disorder to be more common in the lower classes than in the upper classes and more prevalent in those who remained at the same socio-economic level than in the upwardly mobile.[29] Dorothea Leighton and her colleagues found mental disorder to be most frequent in the lowest social class in their comprehensive survey of a rural area of Nova Scotia.[30] Social psychiatrist Örnulv Ödegard demonstrated that first admissions for schizophrenia to all psychiatric hospitals in Norway were most common among low-status workers, such as ordinary seamen and farm laborers and one-third as frequent among the owners and managers of businesses and others in high-status occupations.[31] In London, Lilli Stein showed that there existed a social-class gradient in the incidence and prevalence of mental illness (with the highest rates in the lowest classes) that was particularly marked for schizophrenia.[32] Reviewing these data, epidemiologist William Eaton concluded that, if we divide the population into three social classes, it is common to find a three-to-one difference in rates of schizophrenia between the lowest and highest classes.[33]

SOCIAL DRIFT OR SOCIAL STRESS?

A reasonable explanation for the social-class gradient in schizophrenia, and one which is commonly given, is that people with the greatest risk of developing the illness drift into lower-status occupations and low-income city areas as a result of their marginal, pre-psychotic levels of functioning. This is known as the social-drift hypothesis. Support for the social drift theory came from a study conducted in Britain in 1963 demonstrating that, although males with schizophrenia were over-represented in the lowest socio-economic class, the social class of their fathers and other male family members was distributed much as in the general population.[34] Similar findings came from the US.[35] An alternative explanation would be that the stresses of lower-class living, including labor-market stresses and class-related effects on fetal development and birth complications, increase the risk of developing schizophrenia. A final, theoretical possibility is that there exists an increased genetic predisposition towards schizophrenia in the lower classes. When we come to look at the prevalence of schizophrenia in the Third World (in Chapter 9), we will find that the relationship between class (and caste) and schizophrenia is reversed. In the developing world it is the *upper*-class, *better*-educated individuals who are more at risk for schizophrenia. As industrialization advances, moreover, this inverted social-class gradient switches around to conform to the pattern found in the West. These phenomena clearly defy explanation by either the social-drift or genetic hypotheses and they invite speculation about possible socio-economic and socially determined obstetric causes.

The shifts in the occurrence of schizophrenia that accompany the advance of industrialization may be a result of class-related changes in nutrition, obstetric complications and survival of the newborn (as we shall see in Chapter 9). To acknowledge that class-related factors provoke the development of schizophrenia is not to deny that social drift is also important. Indeed, it is not unusual to find people with schizophrenia who have had marginal levels of social functioning for some years before their first, clear psychotic break. In such cases, downward mobility is unavoidable, and this, in itself, becomes an additional source of stress.

An interesting observation emerges from the research on the social mobility of people with schizophrenia. While many patients may not show a decline in occupational status to a level lower than that of their fathers, the occupational level of the general population is sometimes found to have risen around them.[36] Relative to the rest of the population the people with schizophrenia have lost ground. What is happening, then, is not exactly social *drift* but social *stagnation*. This is what one might expect to see in a group of people who are not high in drive and ambition. For individuals living in some settings this would not be a great weakness. In modern industrial society, however, where to stay at the same level is to lose status, the pre-schizophrenic person may be at a disadvantage in comparison to more driven individuals and under greater pressure than he or she would experience in a non-industrial setting.

SCHIZOPHRENIA AND URBANIZATION

The link between social class and mental disorders such as schizophrenia, interestingly, has only been conclusively demonstrated for city dwellers. Strongest in large cities, it becomes weaker in smaller cities and most rural areas. In small towns like Hagerstown, Maryland,[37] and Pueblo, Colorado,[38] or suburban areas like Rockland County, in New York state,[39] the prevalence of schizophrenia was not related to social class. Dorothea Leighton and her co-workers did detect a social-class gradient for mental disorder in rural Nova Scotia, but not in rural Sweden.[40] In two British studies, one comparing London women with women in the crofting and fishing community of North Uist in the Outer Hebrides and another comparing women in London with women living in the rural Isle of Wight,[41] the prevalence of mental disorder was found to be highly influenced by class in the urban setting but not at all in the rural communities. On the rural Danish island of Samsö, although mental disorder in general was more frequent among the lower social classes, the prevalence of psychosis in particular was unrelated to class.[42]

In fact, it emerges that the occurrence of schizophrenia is substantially greater in urban areas compared to rural areas. So we have to ask ourselves why the incidence of schizophrenia is elevated specifically in the urban lower classes.

As early as 1852, Isaac Ray noted that insanity was more common in manufacturing and mercantile communities in Massachusetts than in farming areas.[43] In 1903, William White reported that the distribution of insanity across the United States paralleled the proportion of the population living in cities of 8,000 or more. He concluded that insanity was a result of "the stresses incident to active competition."[44] A series of studies conducted in New York state between 1915 and 1935 reported that the first-admission rate for dementia praecox and, later, schizophrenia was two to three times greater in large cities than in rural areas.[45] Other studies revealed an incidence of schizophrenia that was twice as high or more in the cities than the rural areas of Ohio, Texas and Maryland.[46] Psychiatrist Fuller Torrey examined the geographical distribution in the United States of insanity or, more recently, schizophrenia for nine different years between 1880 and 1963 and concluded that, throughout the period, there was a consistent regional correlation between the extent of urbanization and the prevalence of these conditions.[47] Studies in Sweden and Britain also show an association between the occurrence of schizophrenia and city living,[48] and a recent Danish study found urban birth to be the most important factor determining a person's risk of developing schizophrenia; being born in Copenhagen rather than a Danish village accounted for a third of the risk of developing the illness.[49]

What could cause this increase in the occurrence of schizophrenia among the urban working class? The social-drift theory offers the solution that people with schizophrenia or pre-schizophrenic symptoms migrate from the country to the city. This effect, however, cannot explain the Danish finding of a higher risk of schizophrenia among people *born* in urban areas. Other possible explanations are increased exposure to infections during pregnancy and childhood due to more crowded living conditions in the city, nutritional differences between the urban and the rural poor, and a greater risk of poor obstetric care and perinatal complications among the urban lower classes. It is also possible that the social conditions of rural working-class life are less likely to create a vulnerability for schizophrenia than urban lower-class exist-ence. We shall see shortly, when we look at the effects of the business cycle, that there is a rural–urban difference in the effect of fluctuations in the econ-omy on symptoms of mental disorder, just as there is a rural–urban variation in the influence of social class on the occurrence of schizophrenia. The effect might be similar in each case.

This, then, may be a convenient point to begin to examine the effects of the business cycle on health, illness and mortality.

BUSINESS CYCLES

The economy rises and falls with a variety of rhythms. Since the Industrial Revolution, capitalist development has advanced in long phases of growth, interrupted every few decades by great global depressions marked by indus-trial stagnation and high rates of unemployment. Each newly industrialized nation joins in synchrony with the economic pulse of the more developed societies. In Britain, the "hungry forties" of the nineteenth century were followed by the Great Victorian Boom (1850–73). The industrialized econ-omies of Europe and North America all felt the impact of the protracted Great Depression of the late nineteenth century (1873–96) and reeled again in the 1920s and 1930s.[50] Faced with this pattern it hardly seemed surprising that we again struggled with a protracted global economic recession in the 1990s. Superimposed on the long waves are shorter business cycles of varying ampli-tude – about two a decade may be identified, for example, in the period since the Second World War.

The social effects of both the long and short business cycles as well as of briefer economic fluctuations have been studied. Researchers have looked for correlations between economic indicators and illness, mortality rates and such social events as marriage, divorce and crime.

As early as 1893, for example, it was noticed that divorce became less common in the depression and more common in the boom.[51] (This phenomenon, which continues to hold true today, may well be a consequence of the greater degree of individual economic independence that becomes possible when more employment – especially women's employment – is available.) By 1901 another researcher identified an increase in marriage rates with periods of prosperity in trade.[52]

More elaborate social studies of the impact of fluctuations in business were carried out in the 1920s. Statisticians William Ogburn and Dorothy Thomas found that the boom brought with it high rates of marriage, divorce, birth, infant mortality and general mortality. Only suicide and (possibly) criminal convictions were found to increase in the depression.[53] A few years later, Dorothy Thomas confirmed these findings (except for divorce and crime) and expanded on them. She noted that beer and spirits consumption, arrests for drunkenness and alcohol-related deaths, all increased in the boom. The only social phenomenon clearly tied to economic recession was suicide.[54]

More recent studies of the business cycle have applied advanced statistical techniques and have concentrated not just on the effects of the boom or bust but also on the impact of *any* economic change, up or down, reasoning that any change can be stressful.

Every week for 16 months from 1971 to 1973, researchers conducted surveys of samples of the population of Kansas City to gather information on recent events in people's lives and to evaluate their mood and stress symptoms. Ralph Catalano and David Dooley subsequently looked for correlations between these survey results and measures of local economic fluctuations. They found that both the local unemployment rate and absolute economic change (up or down) were linked to increases in the number of life events reported by the respondents and to their physical and emotional symptoms of stress. The unemployment rate alone was most closely associated with an increase in reports of depressed mood. The researchers noted that the changes in mood and stress symptoms were sometimes immediate but usually followed the economic change with a lag of 1–3 months.[55] People with low income responded much more severely to economic change than did city residents in the middle-income bracket. The poor, Catalano and Dooley reason,

> have the smallest economic resources with which to cushion any short-term economic setbacks . . . When the economy improves it may be the low-income group that disproportionately has to pay the psychological price of adapting to new jobs in new locations with new colleagues.[56]

RURAL–URBAN DIFFERENCES

From the large metropolitan area of Kansas City, Catalano and Dooley and their co-workers next turned their attention to small-town Hagerstown,

Maryland, and the surrounding rural Washington County. Hagerstown, it will be recalled, was the site of an earlier study that revealed no association between social class and mental illness. At the time of both studies the town population was close to 36,000. For 32 months from 1971 to 1974, the researchers conducted surveys of the small town and rural residents, collecting the same information as in the Kansas City study. The survey of Hagerstown and district, however, revealed none of the associations between economic change, stress and pathology that had been found in Kansas City.[57] The small-town and rural residents appeared to be protected against the psychological impact of both social class and economic change. Why was this so?

The contrast was not due to differences in economic stress, for the local economy of Hagerstown was *less* stable than that of the large city. The difference, report the researchers, may have been a result of the fact that the small-town residents started from a lower baseline of stress. Respondents from the Hagerstown area reported fewer life events and stress symptoms than Kansas City residents, and showed less fluctuation in these variables. The small-town residents, furthermore, may have enjoyed more social support, which acted as a buffer against stress. The Hagerstown residents were more satisfied with their neighborhoods, friendships and marriages than were big-city dwellers, and they were more likely to have multiple social roles beyond marriage and employment.[58] Being an amateur baseball coach or a volunteer fireman, for example, may have minimized the impact of unemployment or demotion. We saw this concept of "social capital" used earlier in this chapter to explain the decreased health risk found in areas of low income disparity. It may be that income disparity is less evident in small towns than in big cities and that this contributes also to the reduced effect of economic fluctuations in small towns.

Another report confirms that rural residents may be protected by social support from some of the health hazards of economic change. Comparing the impact on manufacturing workers of plant closings in two areas – one rural and one urban – Susan Gore found that rural workers enjoyed more social support than urban employees. Unemployed workers who rated their spouses, relatives and friends as unsupportive had more severe psychological problems and symptoms of ill-health. They blamed themselves more for being unemployed and felt more economically deprived. Those who feel unsupported, argued Gore, are more dependent on their jobs for self-esteem, and when unemployed they are more likely to lose their sense of worth.[59]

BOOM OR BUST?

The early studies of the business cycle, we have seen, implicated the boom in the production of most social pathology, with one clear exception being suicide. Catalano and Dooley's analysis of short-term economic fluctuations in Kansas City points to absolute economic change (up and down) as a source of stress and stress symptoms, and to a link between unemployment and depressed mood. When the news media cite research on the effect of the economy, however, it is always the harmful impact of the depression and deepening unemployment that we hear about – never the boom. Why is this so?

The commonly cited research that links economic *recession* to multiple social problems is the work of Harvey Brenner, an American statistician. Using complex statistical techniques, Dr Brenner has pursued the hypothesis that the increase in problems during the boom is, in fact, a delayed response to the business decline that precedes it. Thus, when the US Congress asked for a report, in 1976, on the *Social Costs of National Economic Policy*, Brenner was able to supply them with a document, more than 200 pages long, that pointed to unemployment as having a profound impact on health and crime.[60] A sustained one per cent increase in unemployment, claimed Brenner, has the following effect:

Social phenomenon	% Increase
Suicide	4.1
State mental hospital admissions	3.4
State prison admissions	4.0
Homicide	5.7
Cirrhosis of the liver mortality	1.9
Cardiovascular-renal disease mortality	1.9
Total mortality	1.9

The figures have since been widely quoted and widely accepted. But can they be taken at face value? At the crux of this issue is Brenner's heavy reliance on the supposed lag between the initial stress of unemployment and the subsequent appearance of social pathology. Cerebral strokes, for example, are linked to the economic recession, Brenner argues, with a lag of 6–9 years; cardiovascular-renal disease, with a lag of 3–6 years.[61] When the length of the business cycle being studied is only 3–5 years, the use of lags such as these becomes difficult to comprehend. So, too, is a lag of two years behind the recession for arrests for drunkenness.[62] "The inclusion of a *minus* one year lag borders on the incredible," protested epidemiologist Stanislav Kasl about one of Brenner's pieces of research. "Surely that must undermine and ridicule the investigator's own efforts to suggest unidirectional causal interpretations."[63]

The problem with Brenner's use of the lag is not merely that a number of absurd and inexplicable correlations is offered (some of the lagged correlations, properly explained, might be reasonable) but that the optimal lag is determined *post hoc* by scanning the data. If a lagged effect is expected, it should be possible to predict in advance roughly what the lag period will be, so that a clear hypothesis may be tested. Brenner did not attempt to do this, however, and little pattern or consistency emerges from the lagged correlations.

Does it matter whether it is the boom or bust that brings more problems? To anyone interested in politics and political theory it does, for it is an issue at the heart of a debate between radicals and liberals. To the Marxist it is capitalism that is pathogenic; the business cycle is an inherent element of the capitalist economic system – an unavoidable consequence of the production of goods for the market and of the resulting crises of overproduction.[64] The liberal economist sees the business cycle as an unfortunate feature of the industrial economy, but one which can be controlled.[65] He or she favors fiscal and monetary policies that will stimulate the economy and turn away the ugly face of unemployment. Sustained economic growth is seen as feasible and necessary to minimize human suffering. The Marxist does not regard the upsurge in commodity production and consumption and the accompanying mobilization of labor that marks the boom as necessarily beneficent. One cannot imagine even the most liberal wing of the US Congress, however, calling for a report on the harmful social effects of the economic recovery.

Congress, for example, would not be likely to call upon Joseph Eyer. Unlike Brenner, radical social analyst Eyer sees much social pathology and mortality as a direct consequence of the boom. Less than two per cent of the death rate in the United States – that for suicide and homicide – he argues, varies directly with unemployment. The general death rate, including such stress-related causes as coronary heart disease, alcoholic cirrhosis and perforated gastric and duodenal ulcers, rises during the boom. Eyer attributes some of the excess mortality of the boom to change in diet, alcohol consumption and cigarette-smoking, but he considers social stress to be the most important cause. Among the stresses of the boom he identifies are social-relationship changes such as rising marriage and divorce rates, fragmentation of the community due to increased migration and such job-related factors as over-work, alienating work processes and industrial disputes. The lag between these stresses and the development of pathology, argues Eyer, pointing to research on the impact of life events, would not be years, as Brenner suggested, but a few days, weeks or months –if the impact were not immediate.[66]

Observing that industrialization brings about an increase in mortality in younger adults at the age of labor-market entry, Eyer sees the development of wage work as central to the disease-producing stresses of our society. He argues, moreover, that the deleterious impact of modern labor conditions may be seen in the high mortality that affects those cohorts of workers who enter the US labor market during the boom to a greater extent than those who enter during the depression.[67]

That this type of cohort analysis may lead to more than one interpretation is evident from economist Alfred Bunn's study of heart-disease mortality in

Australia. Bunn has traced an epidemic increase in coronary heart disease back to a point source in the twentieth-century Great Depression. Each cohort of Australian citizens born in successive decades experienced a dramatic increase in mortality during the 1930s – an increased risk that was sustained throughout the lives of surviving members of these cohorts. The decline in the death rate from heart disease after 1968 – a phenomenon that has not otherwise been adequately explained – is due, Bunn argues, to the eventual death of most of the population who had been of working age during the Great Depression. Immediate and late effects of unemployment and economic stress, suggests Bunn, contribute to heart-disease mortality; the more recent recessions of the early 1960s and late 1970s add their own lesser waves of increased mortality to the epidemic initiated by the Great Depression. Bunn, like Brenner, finds an association between high annual unemployment rates and fluctuations in mortality from coronary heart disease.[68]

Bunn disagrees with Eyer's claim that high mortality is closely related to *low* unemployment and the boom, and there is evidence to support each side of the argument. Regardless of which view is correct, both researchers agree on a principle that will become important later in this book: circumstances early in life prime an individual to respond to environmental stimuli later in a way that can promote ill health. According to Eyer, for example, entering the labor force during the boom increases the individual's susceptibility to the effects of economic stress; according to Bunn, working through the Great Depression produces a permanent increase in the risk of heart disease. When we discuss factors promoting the occurrence of schizophrenia in Chapter 9, this idea will emerge again; there it will be suggested that, if a woman's nutrition changes later in life in response to economic change, migration or class-related factors, her risk of obstetric complications will increase and so will her child's risk of schizophrenia.

Which is more harmful to one's health – the boom or the slump? Both have been incriminated. The case of infant mortality gives us the opportunity to pursue the question further and to see if prosperity may indeed bring undesired consequences.

INFANT MORTALITY

Nowhere is the issue of the pathogenic effect of the boom *versus* the bust better illustrated, and nowhere is the question of the use of the lag as a statistical device more central, than when we look at infant mortality. The early studies of the business cycle, as we have seen, found infant deaths to increase in the boom. Predictably, however, when Brenner studied this relationship he found increases in infant mortality to be a response to economic downturn after a lag of varying numbers of years. The death rate of infants aged one month to one year (post-neonatal mortality), for example, is said to be related to increases in unemployment with a lag of 3–5 years.[69] Figure 2.1, which is taken from Brenner's article on the topic, illustrates this point. In the figure, percentage changes in post-neonatal mortality occurring over five-year intervals are plotted annually for half a century. Brenner has advanced the infant-mortality graph by four years, to match the lag that his statistical analysis reveals, and to show a mirror-image relationship between the lagged graph of infant mortality and an inverted graph of unemployment (i.e., unemployment and lagged infant mortality rise and fall together).

There are problems with this analysis, however. In the first place, if we do away with Brenner's lag and put the graph of post-neonatal mortality back where it started, four years later – as in Figure 2.2 – we see that there is a respectable fit between the mortality graph and the inverted unemployment rate. In other words, it seems that post-neonatal mortality rises when unemployment *falls*. This picture suggests that we should at least look to see if such an inverse correlation is statistically significant – but Brenner does not do so.

In the second place, there is no logical explanation for a four-year lag in post-neonatal mortality. Deaths in this age group – one month to one year – are typically related to the immediate environment and are due to such causes

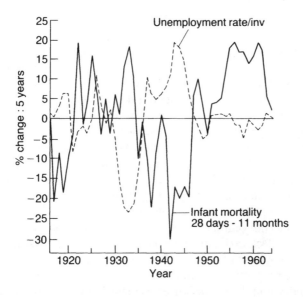

Figure 2.1 Five-year changes in the US unemployment index (inverted) and the neo-natal mortality rate per 1,000 live births. Neonatal mortality is moved forward four years to show the relationship with a four-year lag

Source: Reproduced from Brenner, M. H., "Fetal, infant and maternal mortality during periods of economic instability," *International Journal of Health Services*, 3: 145–59, 1973, by permission of the publisher.

Figure 2.2 Five-year changes in the US employment index and the neonatal mortality rate per 1,000 live births. Neonatal mortality is not lagged

as intestinal and respiratory disease, infections and accidents. One would predict a lag of no more than a month behind an economic change in most cases. Even if one hypothesized that the infant was at increased risk of death due to economic influences working throughout the mother's pregnancy and delivery, then the maximum lag period in those instances would be less than two years. A four-year lag makes no rational sense.

Finally, there exist excellent *a priori* grounds for assuming a direct link between high infant mortality and the boom. Victorian observers were well aware that infant mortality in Britain decreased during crises in trade.[70] Figure 2.3 demonstrates that the contemporary commentators were correct: infant mortality rose and fell with the industrial growth rate through the latter half of the nineteenth century.

The reason for this effect, maintained the philanthropists and physicians of the time, was the employment of mothers. In the industrial areas of Victorian England a very large proportion of young married women were employed in the factories from dawn to dusk – or longer. Female factory hands returned to work within two weeks of the birth of a child, frequently leaving the infant in the care of elderly child-minders or girls as young as seven years of age. Fatal accidents to infants in the care of incompetent minders were not uncommon. Laudanum and other widely available preparations of morphia were freely used to quiet fractious babies. Early weaning was essential and

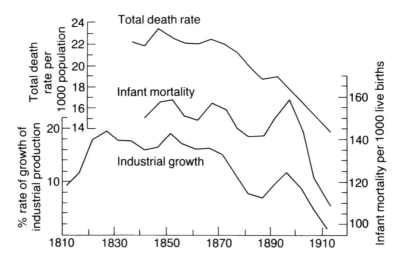

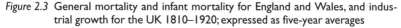

Figure 2.3 General mortality and infant mortality for England and Wales, and industrial growth for the UK 1810–1920; expressed as five-year averages

Source: Mitchell, B. R., *European Historical Statistics 1750–1970*, abridged edn., New York: Columbia University Press, 1978.

infants were routinely fed with watered-down and often contaminated milk. Deaths from intestinal infection were prevalent.[71]

Physicians pointed out that infant mortality was highest where more women were employed in the factories. Around the Lancashire cotton mills the death rate was particularly high, and the Medical Office of Health for Staffordshire offered the following figures for 1880.[72]

Groups of towns	Rate of infant mortality
Many women employed	195
Fewer women employed	166
Practically no women employed	152

There is another reason – one that is particularly relevant to the topic of this book – why infant mortality may increase during the boom. Women who are raised in poverty have poor nutrition in childhood and are consequently small in stature and likely to have small pelvic cavities and birth canals that are malformed by rickets (vitamin D deficiency). During the boom, their nutrition is likely to improve and, when pregnant, the developing fetus will be larger than usual. As a result, labor will be more difficult and rates of brain damage and infant mortality due to obstetric complications will increase. We will return to this issue in Chapter 9. At that point it will be argued that the risk of obstetric complications and infant brain damage – and thus the risk of later development of schizophrenia – increases in different classes at different phases during the advance of industrialization. The result is a curious changing pattern of occurrence of schizophrenia.

WORK STRESS AND ALIENATION

One source of interest in the debate over the harmful effects of the boom versus the bust is the attempt to evaluate the relative importance of two potential health hazards – the stresses of working and of unemployment. The direct link between the working environment and ill health and death is evident in the statistics on industrial accidents and disease. One estimate reveals that each year in Britain two thousand workers die from an injury sustained on the job, another thousand die from an industrial disease and a million take sick leave because of an industrial illness.[73] Industrial injuries are a common cause of death in the US, especially among the less well educated.[74] Less commonly recognized, women performing housework have a high injury rate, thousands dying in Britain each year as a result of domestic accidents.[75] Not so straightforward to evaluate, however, is the importance of workplace stress in the production of mental and stress-related illness.

We may find evidence of the hazards of work stress in the research on heart attacks. Psychological stress and significant life changes increase the risk of myocardial infarction and sudden cardiac death.[76] A 30-year follow-up study of healthy Canadian men found that sudden cardiac death was much more common on the first working day of the week. Thirty-five per cent of such deaths in previously healthy men, and 75 per cent of the deaths at work, occurred on a Monday. The researchers point to "reintroductions to occupational stress, activity or pollutants after a weekend respite" as likely precipitants.[77] A study conducted in the United States similarly revealed a higher death rate from coronary heart disease on Mondays than on other days of the week.[78]

Pointing to the same source of stress, one earlier study demonstrated that overwork increases the risk of heart attack in young men more than any of the standard risk factors.[79] Several other pieces of research have shown overtime and increased work load to be correlated with changes in serum cholesterol, cardiac arrhythmias and an elevated frequency of myocardial infarction.[80] American tax accountants, for example, approaching the tax deadline of April 15, showed changes in blood-clotting and serum cholesterol that increased their risk of heart attacks and strokes.[81] A study comparing heart-attack victims and a matched control group of healthy people, all of whom were employed in the same Swedish nationwide chain, found that workers suffering heart attacks had experienced many more stressful life events before falling ill – but the events that were more common in the heart-attack victims were all job-related. The stressful events included major changes in working schedule or conditions, undertaking more responsibility at work or having trouble with the boss.[82] The same research group studying members of the Swedish construction workers' trade union found that increased responsibility at work was the only life-change measure among dozens examined that predicted an increased risk of heart attack in this sample.[83]

One important piece of research, the Framingham (Massachusetts) study of risk factors in coronary heart disease, found no correlation between job-related stress and the presence of angina pectoris and other indications of heart disease. This finding may well be due to the fact that all of the heart patients in this study suffered from relatively chronic illness and were heart-attack survivors; sudden-death victims were automatically excluded.[84] On balance, the evidence is strong that the stresses of working are important precipitants of heart attack.

One of the most widely embraced of Karl Marx's theories is his concept of alienation. The concept is well enough accepted, in fact, that the US Senate in 1972, concerned about the apparent spread of job dissatisfaction among workers and the threat of falling productivity, commissioned a study of alienation in the workplace.[85] Illustrated in the popular imagination by the assembly-line worker who is so disgusted and bored that he willfully damages the car on which he is working, Marx's theory of alienation covers this phenomenon and more. Marx described the estrangement of the worker from the creative process and from the product of his or her labor, an alienation from his or her essentially human characteristics, and from his or her fellow human beings. This condition, argued Marx, is the inevitable consequence of commodity production, wage work and the division of labor – a result of converting labor into a commodity.[86]

The experience of working-class men and women offers numerous examples of what Marx meant. Many auto workers despise the cars they build. " 'What'd you buy this piece of shit for?' " demands a young General Motors worker of author Barbara Garson, kicking her car – a machine he might have helped build himself.[87] The work process may be regarded with derision. " 'There's a lot of variety in the paint shop,' " reports another Lordstown worker. " 'You clip on the color hose, bleed out the old color, and squirt. Clip, bleed, squirt, think; clip, bleed, squirt, yawn; clip, bleed, squirt, scratch your nose.' "[88] The boredom can be dehumanizing – " 'You forget you're not a machine,' "[89] says a copy typist. The close supervision is oppressive – a steelworker complains, " 'I would rather work my ass off for eight hours a day with nobody watching me than five minutes with a guy watching me.' "[90] Job-status differences estrange co-workers. " 'What is this "*Yes, sir*" bullshit?' " yells the same steelworker at his foreman. " 'I came here to work, I didn't come here to crawl.' "[91]

The problems, moreover, are not only to be found in the industrial workplace. Lillian Breslow Rubin wrote:

There is, perhaps, no greater testimony to the deadening and deadly quality of the tasks of the housewife than the fact that so many women find pleasure in working at jobs that by almost any definition would be called alienated labor – low status, low-paying, dead-end work made up of dull, routine tasks; work that often is considered too menial for men who are less educated than these women.[92]

The issue of household labor may distort domestic relations. A working-class husband insists angrily,

"A wife's got to learn to be number two. That's the way it is, and that's what she better learn. She's going to stay home and take care of the family like a wife's supposed to do."[93]

How widespread is worker alienation? A large majority of workers in many industrialized countries express satisfaction with their work when polled; the size of this majority is always greater in higher-status jobs and older age groups. When asked whether they would prefer another occupation, however, as many as 60 per cent of American workers say yes.[94] Arthur Kornhauser, in his study *Mental Health of the Industrial Worker*, saw the expression of satisfaction with fundamentally unfulfilling jobs as an adaptive response on the part of the workers – a consequence "of their dwarfed desires and deadened initiative, reduction of their goals and restriction of their efforts to a point where life is relatively empty and only half meaningful."[95] The extent of alienation, therefore, is hard to measure. Reviewing the research, Marie Jahoda and Harold Rush can only conclude that:

there exists a stratum of society – its size is hard to determine – of degraded, frustrated, unhappy, psychologically unhealthy people in employment whose personal morale is as low as their productivity, who are unable to provide a constructive environment for their families, [and] whose lack of commitment in employment colors their total life experience.[96]

Can we estimate the psychological impact of alienating work? In his study of Detroit factory workers, Arthur Kornhauser found a clear correlation between the mental health of the worker and the skill of his job. Feelings of inadequacy, anxiety, depression and hostility were greater in those who performed the most routine, repetitive work. These symptoms, Kornhauser demonstrated, were not related to the worker's pre-employment characteristics but were a product of the job itself.[97] More than one study has shown that restricted independence at work is related to poor mental health. A large survey of American men representing a broad range of civilian occupations found low work complexity and close supervision to be associated with the worker's low job satisfaction, low self-esteem and raised level of anxiety.[98] A more recent survey of adults living in Oslo, Norway, extended these findings. The degree of close supervision on the job was found to be correlated with a variety of psychiatric symptoms – a link that was not explained independently by social and demographic factors.[99]

Reviewing the literature widely, Stanislav Kasl concludes that the correlation between measures of mental health and job satisfaction is not a particularly powerful one, though, as we have seen, expressed job satisfaction may not be a good reflection of the actual qualities of the work environment. Kasl finds that the evidence is clearest for the heightened prevalence of mental disorder amongst those performing the most routine, unskilled factory work.[100] For some workers, it is clear, we should not necessarily expect unemployment to be psychologically damaging – it may be a welcome release for those in the most alienating occupations.

UNEMPLOYMENT

Though the majority of the research points to serious adverse consequences from unemployment, there are indications that job loss for some workers under certain circumstances may not be distressing and may even be a positive experience. Blue-collar workers laid off by plant closings showed few lasting psychological or stress-related problems over the two-year period of displacement, unemployment and re-hiring through which they were followed by research workers Stanislav Kasl and Sidney Cobb. The working men in this study generally showed brief, initial responses to stress – increased depression, anxiety and raised blood pressure – most evident during the phase of anticipation prior to unemployment. Kasl suggests that these men showed few damaging effects from unemployment because many had given up the idea that their monotonous jobs were meaningful or important.[101]

Researchers Ramsay Liem and Paula Rayman countered with the suggestion that Kasl and Cobb's findings were undramatic because the unemployment circumstances of the men in their sample were not severe. In his own study of blue-collar and white-collar families in which the husband lost his job, Liem found significant increases in psychiatric symptoms in both the men and their wives and signs of mounting family distress. Symptoms increased as unemployment continued but receded after re-employment. The response to job loss was greater in this sample than in Kasl and Cobb's study, argued Liem, because the period of unemployment was much longer, the local economy was severely depressed and job prospects were poorer. Plant closings such as Kasl and Cobb studied, furthermore, may create a type of unemployment in which self-blame is less prominent.[102]

Liem's interpretation of these findings is borne out by a study of middle-class, unemployed men conducted by sociologist Craig Little. Nearly half of the men in this sample had a somewhat more positive response to unemployment; these were more likely to be the men who were optimistic about re-employment, had not been out of work long and who were in a better financial situation. Kasl's point is also supported, however, since the more positive responses came from men whose prior job satisfaction had been low.[103]

The context in which job loss occurs clearly affects the response of the unemployed. Acknowledging this point, we may also recognize that the consequences of unemployment are usually distinctly harmful. Evidence on the damaging effects of unemployment began to accumulate during the Great Depression. Two researchers reviewing the topic in 1938, after compiling more than a hundred reports, observed that unemployment could lead to emotional instability, depression, hopelessness, distrust, domestic problems, narrowed activities and apathy.[104] More refined modern studies confirm these findings; the introduction of higher levels of financial support for the unemployed does not appear to have reduced the impact of joblessness.

Paula Rayman and Barry Bluestone's study of job loss in the American aircraft industry found unemployment to be linked to serious signs of strain such as alcoholism, raised blood pressure, increased smoking and anxiety.[105] Plant closings in Appalachia brought depression and sickness to the redundant employees.[106] A British study noted increasing general symptomatology in unemployed young men.[107] Older American workers laid off after years of stable employment responded with more ill health than those in a control group, a sense of powerlessness and loss of initiative.[108]

As unemployment spread in the late 1980s and early 1990s, fresh reports came in from around the world. A survey of Finnish manufacturing workers demonstrated a strong link between unemployment and mental ill health.[109] German furniture factory employees who lost their jobs were eight times more likely to report poor psychological health if they remained unemployed for a year.[110] Scottish school-leavers who became unemployed showed intellectual, emotional and behavioral deterioration whereas those who went on to a job or training improved or were stable.[111] A series of British studies indicated that unemployed people were more depressed and anxious and had less self-esteem and self-confidence; the worst affected were middle-aged men, middle-class people, those who lived in low unemployment areas and people with a strong work ethic.[112] A study conducted in Michigan found that unemployment may lead to depression, anxiety and poor physical health via two routes – increased financial strain and an increased vulnerability to life-event stress.[113] A Swedish study revealed a physiological basis for the increased vulnerability to stress; unemployment is associated with changes in the person's immune system and dramatically elevated levels of the hormone cortisol.[114]

Some studies point to harmful effects from both job stress and unemployment. The survey of members of the Swedish construction workers' union, mentioned above, found joblessness and dissatisfaction with work to be associated with an increased accident rate; unemployment and changes at work increased the risk of neurosis.[115] In the study of Toronto residents, job loss and demotion at work combined were major risk factors for ill health.[116] We may safely conclude that modern labor dynamics can be unhealthy for both employed and unemployed workers.

SUICIDE

Analysis of suicide patterns yields more evidence of the destructive effect of labor dynamics and especially of unemployment. All authorities are agreed that suicide rates peak during economic recessions and have done so throughout the century.[117] The unemployment index is the strongest predictor of changes in the suicide rate, having a greater impact on male suicide rates[118] and on older people of working age.[119] One researcher, Albert Pierce, asserted that suicide statistics show an increase whenever the economy fluctuates up or down,[120] but later attempts to replicate his work have found unemployment to be more important than absolute economic change.[121] The view of Emile Durkheim, the early French sociologist, that "fortunate crises . . . affect suicide like economic disasters"[122] has not been borne out. His claim, however, that work protects against suicide does appear to be supported by the data.

Throughout the industrial world suicide is more common in the elderly[123] and is higher in retired men than in working men of the same age.[124] The pattern of increasing suicide with age holds true for white Americans; but for blacks and especially American Indians, who experience high levels of unemployment early in life, the suicide rate shows a peak in the young-adult years (see Figure 2.4). The Indian reservations with the highest suicide rates are those with the most severe problems of unemployment, alcoholism and traditional family disintegration.[125] Suicide is more common among those in the lower-income, lower-status jobs where employment is least secure.[126] Economic stress could account for many of these findings, or the absence of a socially endorsed useful role (in middle-class whites, a problem most common in late life) could be an important precipitant of suicide. That the current picture is a response to changes accompanying the growth of wage work is supported by a study of suicide in Hong Kong. Before industrialization, Chinese suicide was more common in younger adults; industrial development has brought declining prestige, changed roles and a steep rise in suicide to the elderly of the modern city.[127]

The circumstances of individual suicide victims suggest that joblessness, work problems and economic difficulties may all be critical stresses. Studies have generally found around a quarter to a third or more of suicide victims to be unemployed – a substantially higher rate than in the general population or in control groups.[128] For example, a large-scale study of bricklayers and carpenters in Denmark found more unemployment in the recent background of

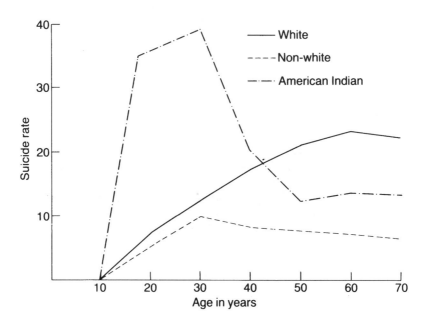

Figure 2.4 Age-specific suicide rates per 100,000 population for white, American Indian and other non-white groups in the USA, 1969 and 1971 average

Source: National Institute of Mental Health, *Suicide, Homicide and Alcoholism among American Indians*, Washington, DC, Department of Health, Education and Welfare, 1973

workers suffering violent deaths from both accident or suicide.[129] In addition, a pattern of frequent job changes, job dissatisfaction and downward mobility can often be uncovered in the history of suicide victims.[130] Which comes first – the emotional problems or the work difficulties? Two controlled studies have tried to tackle this question by examining unemployment rates in psychiatric patients who committed suicide versus those who did not: both studies found an association between unemployment and suicide for men.[131] In many cases it is clear that unemployment and job instability is a result of poor physical or mental health;[132] but we should not expect a simple one-way relationship. Impaired performance or loss of work role may well damage self-esteem and increase hopelessness and depression. The central role of the workplace in this relationship for those who are employed is revealed by the repeated finding that suicide (like sudden cardiac death) is most common on Mondays, declining in frequency as the week progresses.[133]

It is clear that the job market and the economy have a direct and decisive impact on our patterns of living, our view of ourselves and our emotions. Since this is so, we might reasonably expect the economy to influence the onset of serious mental illness and to affect the rate of admission to psychiatric hospital.

MENTAL HOSPITAL ADMISSIONS

The first comprehensive attempt to estimate the effect of the economy on mental hospital admissions was Harvey Brenner's *Mental Illness and the Economy*, published in 1973.[134] Earlier researchers had studied the variations in hospital admissions over relatively short periods of time, and some had pointed out that rising admission rates during the Great Depression appeared to correspond to increasing unemployment figures.[135] Brenner's work went a great deal further, however, and is still the most important study of the topic.

Brenner analyzed admissions to New York state mental hospitals from the mid-nineteenth century to the late 1960s, looking for correlations with measures of economic activity and employment. From 1910 the data included admissions to public and private hospitals; for the earlier period admissions to one state hospital were examined. Admission rates regularly increased during economic decline. This relationship was particularly clear for patients with functional psychosis. For people with schizophrenia from childhood up to the age of around 60 years the relationship was strong, and the finding held true for first admissions and readmissions. The effect of economic change appeared to be more or less immediate; the correlation occurred with no lag but was strengthened by the addition of a (theoretically acceptable) one-year lag.

In select groups of patients the relationship between admission rates and the economy was found to be reversed. Elderly patients with senile brain disease were more commonly admitted during the boom, as were female patients with late-onset involutional psychosis.[136]

Brenner's work on mental hospital admissions has been subject to close scrutiny and has survived the challenge largely undamaged. Statisticians James Marshall and Donna Funch criticized Brenner for his use of statistical detrending procedures and for his failure to make allowances for changes in hospital capacity. Their replication of Brenner's work, taking into account these technical points, essentially confirmed the original findings. The state of the economy, they found, was closely tied to the admission of working-age men and women; but for the young and the aged, hospital capacity was a better predictor of admission rates.[137]

Brenner's principal finding of a link between the recession and mental hospital admissions has since been confirmed by a number of other studies. In Ontario, admissions to a provincial psychiatric hospital for the period from 1960 to 1977 were found to exceed discharges during economic slumps; during the boom the reverse held true.[138] Readmissions to state inpatient and outpatient mental health facilities in Missouri from 1971 to 1979 correlated with the unemployment rate.[139] Community mental health center outpatient admissions in Denver, Colorado, in the 1970s were also linked to the unemployment rate.[140]

What could explain these findings? Brenner examines three theories.

Firstly, the tolerance for the dependent mentally ill might decrease as families encounter greater economic stress. The data do not support this hypothesis, for the most dependent – the young and the aged – tend to be hospitalized in the boom and not the recession. It seems likely, in fact, that increased mobility during the boom and expanding employment opportunities outside of the home for potential care-givers may be stronger factors leading to rejection of the mentally disabled.

A second possibility is that financial destitution may lead patients to seek the shelter of hospital as an almshouse. Again, the explanation is not supported by the statistics. Economically comfortable patients show the same increase in admission rates during the slump as do marginal patients. Admissions to costly private hospitals also increase during recessions – an economic burden rather than a means of support.[141]

We are left with one likely explanation – economic stress and unemployment lead to a true increase in symptoms of psychiatric illness. Much of the research cited in this chapter supports the notion that the economy can lead directly to such changes in psychological symptoms. Why should the impact on hospital admissions occur more in the recession than in the boom? Perhaps because those who are susceptible to serious mental illness are most likely to be functioning marginally on the job and are most likely to be laid off when the economy takes a downturn. The fact that it is principally working-age men and women who show increased hospital admissions during declines in the economy favors this idea. Other research has shown that the admission of unemployed patients and those with job-related difficulties does, in fact, increase during recessions.[142] Overall, we have strong evidence that the onset of episodes of mental illness increases with each setback in the economy and with the reduction in the call for labor.

Physical and mental diseases, including schizophrenia, are more common in the urban lower classes and their occurrence fluctuates with the economy. The effects of economic expansion, economic stress, working conditions and unemployment are involved in the genesis of this ill-health, despair and insanity. In the next chapter we will examine the extent to which the economy and the labor market shape the course of schizophrenia and influence whether it emerges as a benign or a malignant condition.

SUMMARY

- Illness and death rates are higher in the working classes.
- Stressful life events are more common in the lower classes and contribute to the raised prevalence of stress-related physical and mental illness.
- A high rate of inequality between the richest and poorest in society is associated with increased illness and mortality.
- Schizophrenia is concentrated in the lower classes in the industrial world

and in the upper castes and classes in the Third World – a pattern that only a theory of social causation can explain.

- Schizophrenia occurs more frequently in large cities and the incidence of the illness is elevated specifically in the urban lower classes.
- Social causation and social drift may operate together to account for the social-class gradient for schizophrenia in urban-industrial areas.
- In large cities, fluctuations in the economy are associated with increased changes in people's lives and with symptoms of psychological distress.
- Residents of rural areas appear to be protected from the adverse effects on physical and mental health of low socio-economic status and fluctuations in the economy.
- Early studies of the business cycle found that most social pathology increased in the boom, except suicide which became more common in the slump.
- Research tying social pathology to rising unemployment can often be faulted for over-enthusiastic reliance on the notion of lagged effects.
- Infant mortality increases during the boom.
- Both the stresses of working and unemployment can create significant health hazards.
- Work problems, economic stress and unemployment appear to be important in precipitating suicide.
- Mental hospital admissions for working-age people increase during the slump, probably in response to economic and labor-market stresses.

Part II

The political economy of schizophrenia

Chapter 3

Recovery from schizophrenia

Few topics in psychiatry have been researched as frequently over as long a period of time as has recovery from schizophrenia. Ever since Emil Kraepelin focused on the deteriorating course of the illness in defining dementia prae-cox, psychiatrists throughout the Western world have been interested in comparing the recovery rates of their patients with those of other physicians. More than a hundred long-term outcome studies of schizophrenia were published in Europe and America during the twentieth century and several thousand studies of the short-term effect of different treatment methods were carried out. Despite this volume of work, however, a clear picture of long-term outcome in schizophrenia has not emerged.

Many researchers have formed the impression that recovery rates in schizophrenia have improved in comparison with earlier times. Their opti-mistic conclusions have not always been disinterested; often they have attributed the improved outcome to new treatment methods – insulin coma, electro-convulsive therapy and psychosurgery[1] or, more recently, community treatment and the antipsychotic drugs.[2] Heinz Lehmann, a Canadian psych-iatrist, writing in a major textbook, endorsed the widespread opinion that modern psychiatric treatment has improved the outlook in schizophrenia. The chances for a favorable outcome from a schizophrenic psychosis, he argued, are four or five times better than they were in the early years of the twentieth century. He attributed this change to "good follow-up therapy and well controlled maintenance drug treatment."[3] He presented a table of ten follow-up studies of schizophrenia conducted since the 1930s that appeared to support his argument and show improving recovery rates.

In 1994, psychiatrist James Hegarty and his colleagues at Harvard pub-lished a more comprehensive analysis of a hundred years of schizophrenia outcome studies. They too concluded that there had been an improvement in outcome compared to the early years of the twentieth century, which they attributed in large part to the introduction of the antipsychotic drugs in the 1950s, but they also found that there had been a decline in outcome since the 1970s.[4]

A number of researchers have arrived at more pessimistic conclusions than those cited above.[5] Joseph Stephens, a professor of psychiatry at Johns Hopkins University, after reviewing 38 long-term follow-up studies that included data on patients admitted as early as the First World War, was unimpressed with improvements in recovery rates or the long-term benefits of drug treatment.[6] Swiss psychiatrist Manfred Bleuler (son of Eugen Bleuler, who coined the term "schizophrenia") had a particularly interesting perspective. "During the greater part of my life," he wrote, "I have lived in hospitals which cared mostly for severe cases of schizophrenia, and from babyhood on through my whole childhood, gravely sick schizophrenics even lived in my parents' family."[7] Study of the course of illness in his patients over several decades led him to conclude, in 1968, that little change had occurred in the proportion of patients who deteriorated or who recovered. "There still exists the sad chronic evolutions to severe chronic conditions, and it is doubtful whether modern therapy has been able much to increase the number of total, life-long recoveries."[8] The only improvement Manfred Bleuler could detect was a decrease in the severity of chronic schizophrenic deterioration as a result of a reduction in the mishandling and neglect of hospitalized patients that was common earlier in the century. Although not impressed with the results of treatment, Dr Bleuler was less pessimistic about the natural course of the illness. He wrote:

> Generations of psychiatrists felt that schizophrenia was a process psychosis progressing to complete deterioration, if life was long enough to allow the process to come to an end. ... I am certain today that the contrary is true.[9]

Dr Bleuler found that many of his chronically disturbed patients improved later in life, rather than deteriorating, and that another 25–35 per cent of his patients with schizophrenia before the Second World War recovered from their illness after only acute episodes of psychosis.

Which view is correct: that schizophrenia is an inherently catastrophic illness from which only modern psychiatric treatment can afford relief; or that it is a condition with a considerable, spontaneous recovery rate upon which treatment has little long-term effect? The first point of view, without a doubt, is the opinion of the majority of psychiatrists. Taking a deeper look into the storehouse of information on recovery from schizophrenia in the dusty volumes of psychiatric journals going back to the beginning of the twentieth century may help resolve this issue. If we analyze this material according to time periods that reflect the major changes in the state of the economy, we may also throw some light on another question: to what extent have changes in the economy during the century influenced the outlook for people with schizophrenia?

FOLLOW-UP STUDIES

Unfortunately, there are problems involved in comparing the results of the many long-term follow-up studies of people with schizophrenia. As we have seen in Chapter 1, which patients are labeled as having schizophrenia varies from country to country, from time to time and from one psychiatrist to another. The patients chosen to be followed may be male or female, adolescent or adult, experiencing their first psychotic break or more chronically ill, or selected by any other criteria the researcher chooses. Any of these factors may affect the course of the psychosis. The patients may be followed for any period of time: one year, ten years or until death. If the illness is progressive, this factor could clearly affect the results. These follow-up studies are obviously not strictly comparable. Any attempt to get useful information from them, then, makes the assumption that the differences between the studies balance out when a large number of them are collected into groups. If significant changes in outcome are uncovered, it will be necessary to calculate whether the variations may be due to differences in diagnosis, patient characteristics or follow-up methods between the groups.

MEASURES OF RECOVERY

One of the crucial variables in these studies is how the researcher chooses to measure the patients' condition at the time of follow-up. The investigator may be most concerned about whether symptoms of the illness are still present but could focus on either psychotic features, such as hallucinations or delusions, on neurotic symptoms, such as anxiety, or on behavior problems like withdrawal or eccentric habits. The proportion of patients considered to have recovered will depend on how rigorously recovery is defined. If outcome is measured in terms of social functioning, the investigator may look at any combination of a range of features including the following: working ability, capacity to care for basic needs, abnormal behavior causing distress to others, criminal activity, number of friends, or sexual functioning. Social functioning measures are particularly hard to standardize. A fairly unambiguous measure is whether the patient is in or out of hospital at follow-up; but this is not necessarily, as we shall see, a reliable measure of social functioning.

To impose some consistency on the follow-up results, information has been gathered from studies according to predetermined definitions of terms that have been in use throughout the twentieth century:

- *Complete recovery:* Loss of psychotic symptoms and return to the pre-illness level of functioning.
- *Social recovery:* Economic and residential independence and low social disruption. This means working adequately to provide for oneself and

not being dependent on others for basic needs or housing. This term is the one most open to variations in measurement. Since an important part of the definition is employment status, we run a risk of tautological reasoning in correlating social recovery with the unemployment rate.

• *Hospitalization:* In a psychiatric hospital at the time of follow-up.

Every Developed World follow-up study of patients admitted during the hundred-year period beginning in 1885 that was uncovered during a lengthy period of library research and that provided information on one or more of these categories has been included in Table 3.1 A study is included only if it followed a sample of patients selected at the time of admission to treatment; cohorts selected at the time of hospital discharge do not include those who remained in hospital and died there. The list is certainly not complete; the German literature alone probably contains a great many more suitable studies. The 114 studies that are included, however, provide a comprehensive survey giving us a good deal of information about recovery rates for patients admitted in every decade over the course of more than a century.[10]

Recovery rates during various time periods were calculated by the simple method of adding all patients who achieved each level of recovery in one time period and calculating what percentage they formed of the total group of patients followed up in that period. A point of detail: patients who were dead at the time of follow-up, and for whom there was no information about the state of their illness when they died, could either have been included in the analysis or excluded. In this survey they were included in the total of patients followed up but, of course, they never contributed to the proportion of recoveries. This tends to reduce the calculated recovery rates for the earlier decades of the twentieth century, when institutional death rates were substantially higher, and makes the test of the theory that outcome from schizophrenia was good during those years more severe.

PERIODS OF ANALYSIS

Each study was assigned to a time period according to the median date of admission of the group of patients. Unavoidably, several patient groups were admitted during one time period and followed up in another. Assigning the group to the earlier time assumes that the conditions in force earlier in the illness are more important in shaping the ultimate course. This limitation suggests, however, that the trends in recovery rates should be analyzed only over rather long periods of time.

The periods of analysis selected were as follows.

1881–1900: The Great Depression of the late nineteenth century (1873 to 1896 in Britain) ran through most of this period and was a time of severe unemployment throughout the industrial world. Mental institutions were overcrowded and, particularly in Germany, barren and coercive.[11] An aura of pessimism pervaded psychiatry. Kraepelin's patients were admitted at this time, and since only one other study is available for the period, these results are not included in the formal analysis.

1901–1920: The period was characterized by improving employment and included the First World War. More active psychiatric treatment methods were established and, in the United States, the mental hygiene movement developed.

1921–1940: This was a time of severe economic depression, beginning several years earlier in Europe than in the United States, with unemployment rising to around a quarter of the work force throughout the industrial world. Electro-convulsive therapy, insulin coma and psychosurgery were introduced in the treatment of psychosis.

1941–1955: This period saw the Second World War and, particularly in northern Europe, postwar full employment. A postwar social revolution in psychiatric treatment occurred in Northern Europe, resulting in increased rehabilitative efforts for patients with psychosis.

1956–1975: Declining employment and "stagflation" characterized the economies in most industrial countries. The neuroleptic drugs were introduced into widespread use at the beginning of this period and US community mental health centers began to be established in the mid–1960s.

1976–1995: Major industrial countries experienced an economic recession throughout much of this period, with unemployment in Britain rising to substantially greater heights than in the USA. New community treatment models, such as the psychosocial clubhouse and assertive community treatment, diffused across North America and, to a lesser extent, Europe and Australia. The first of the novel antipsychotic agents, clozapine, was introduced towards the end of this period.

RESULTS

The results of the analysis are shown in Figure 3.1 (p. 78). Average figures for unemployment in the United States and the United Kingdom for each time period are also drawn in (inverted) to allow comparison.[12] The figures from the two outcome studies on patients admitted before 1901 are sketched in dotted lines to emphasize that they are not reliable but merely indicative of the general trend.

The picture that emerges is in conflict with some widely held beliefs in psychiatry. In the first place, *recovery rates from schizophrenia were not significantly better at the end of the twentieth century than they were at the beginning.* The arrival of the antipsychotic drugs shortly before 1955 appears to have had little effect on long-term outcome. At the end of the century complete recovery rates remained around 20 per cent and about

Table 3.1 Recovery and hospitalization rates in 114 outcome studies of schizophrenia

Authors	Country	Years of admission	Median year of admission	Follow-up years later	Original cohort size	Number dead and not followed up
Kraepelin (1919)	Germany	late 1880s	late 1880s	up to 29 or until death	c65	−
Kraepelin (1919)	Germany	late 1880s	late 1880s	up to 29 or until death	c45	−
Kraepelin (1919)	Germany	late 1880s	late 1880s	up to 29 or until death	c97	−
Evensen (1904)	Norway	1888–1897	1892	5–15	182	29
1881–1900		Percentages derived from totals				
E.Bleuler (1950)	Switzzerland	1898–1905	1901	3–10	515	0
Stearns (1912)	USA	1901–1905	1903	?	395	75
Rosanoff (1914)	USA	1907–1908	1907	5	169	23
Mayer-Gross (1932)	Germany	1912–1913	1912	16–17	328	125
Bond (1921)	USA	1914	1914	5	47	3
Murdoch (1933)	England	1900–1931	1915	1–31	75	11
Müller (1951)	Switzerland	1917–1918	1917	5–30	100	1
Rennie (1939)	USA	1913–1923	1918	1–26 or until death	500	−
Strecker & Willey (1927)	USA	prior to 1920	prior to 1920	over 5	186	0
Lemke (1935)	Germany	1918–1923	1920	15	255	24
Freyhan (1955)	USA	1920	1920	13	100	11
Otto-Martiensen (1921)	Germany	before 1921	before 1921	?	527	98
1901–1920		Percentages derived from totals				
Jonsson & Jonsson (1992)	Sweden	1925	1925	30 or until death	77	7
Langfeldt (1939)	Norway	1926–1929	1927	7–10	100	0
Braatöy (1936)	Norway	1926–1929	1927	6–7	208	15
Bond & Braceland (1937)	USA	1927–1928	1927	5	116	10
Norton (1961)	England	1928–1930	1929	2	207	−

Complete recovery			Social recovery			Hospitalized			Stage or type of illness	Treatment
Number followed up (+ dead)	Number completely recovered	%	Number followed up (+ dead)	Number socially recovered	%	Number followed up (+ dead)	Number in hospital at follow up	%		
c65	c12	8							Hebephrenic	
c45	0	0							Paranoid	
c97	c13	13							Catatonic	
			182	27	15				Male, first admission	
207	25	12	182	27	15					
			515	307	60				First admission	Early discharge
315	16	5				315	202	64		
						169	99	59	First admission	
294	89	30	294	103	35	294	56	19		
47	1	2	47	9	19	47	31	66	Women, mixed duration	
75	12	16							Criminal	
			100	28	28	100	33	33	First admission	
456	112	25	456	166	36	456	254	56	Mixed duration	
186	38	20								
			126	43	34	126	35	27	Male	
						100	65	65	Mixed duration	ECT, insulin coma, psychosurgery psychotherapy
			312	105	34	312	66	21		
1373	268	20	1850	761	41	1919	841	44		
77	0	0							First admission	
100	17	17	100	21	21	100	46	46	Acute onset	
208	40	19	208	62	30	208	97	47	First admission	
113	12	11							Mixed duration	No specific treatment
						207	122	59	Female, mixed duration	

Table 3.1 – continued

Authors	Country	Years of admission	Median year of admission	Follow-up years later	Original cohort size	Number dead and not followed up
Wootton et al. (1935)	England	1928–1931	1929	2–5	104	–
Fromenty (1937)	France	mid-1920s to mid-1930s	1930	up to 15 or until death	271	–
Cheney & Drewry (1938)	USA	1926–1935	1930	1–12	500	50
Hunt et al. (1938)	USA	1927–1934	1930	3½–10½	677	69
Rupp & Fletcher (1940)	USA	1929–1934	1931	4½–10	641	89
Horwitz & Kleiman (1936)	USA	1930–1933	1931	1–3	193	8
Gerloff (1936)	Germany	1925–1939	1932	7–11	382	52
Malamud & Render (1939)	USA	1929–1936	1933	2–9	344	21
Müller (1951)	Switzerland	1933	1933	5–18 or until death	100	5
Stalker (1939)	Scotland	1932–1937	1934	1–6	133	0
Fröshaug & Ytrehus (1963)	Norway	1933–1935	1934	6–8	95	3
Briner (1939)	Germany	1933–1936	1934	2–5	267	37
Romano & Ebaugh (1938)	USA	1933–1936	1934	1–4	600	46
Guttman et al. (1939)	England	1934–1935	1934	3–4	188	7
Norton (1961)	England	1934–1936	1935	2	224	–
Beck (1968)	Canada	1930–1942	1936	25–35	84	0
Carter (1942)	England	1935–1937	1936	3	47	–
Tsuang et al. (1979)	USA	1934–1944	1939	30–40 or until death	200	–
Coryell & Tsuang (1986)	USA	1934–1945	1939	40 or until death	93	–
Errera (1957)	USA	1932–1948	1940	8–24	59	2
Johanson (1958)	Sweden	1938–1942	1940	10–18	100	16
Freyhan (1955)	USA	1940	1940	13	100	4

Complete recovery			Social recovery			Hospitalized			Stage or type of illness	Treatment
Number followed up (+ dead)	Number completely recovered	%	Number followed up (+ dead)	Number socially recovered	%	Number followed up (+ dead)	Number in hospital at follow up	%		
95	18	19				95	64	67	Mixed duration	
271	41	15							Mixed duration	Heavy sedation, "abcés de fixation" or "sulfoidol"
452	51	11	452	112	25	452	197	44	Mixed duration	No specific treatment
604	82	14							First admission	
608	40	7	608	133	22	608	343	56	First admission	
170	9	5				170	89	52		Radiothermy CO^2 & O^2, and psychotherapy
			341	113	33					
309	53	17	309	94	30	309	155	50	Mixed duration	Psychotherapy or social readjustment
				100	38	38	100	28	First admission	
129	15	12	129	26	20	129	91	71	First admission	"Ordinary" methods
			87	16	18	87	32	37	First admission	
			245	111	45	245	64	26	Early	Continuous narcosis or early discharge
442	1	0	442	152	34	442	247	56	Mixed duration	
184	42	23	184	67	36	184	77	42	Early	No drastic treatment
						224	141	63	Female, mixed duration	
84	6	7	84	11	13	84	54	64	First admission	No insulin coma, ECT or psychotherapy
47	10	21	47	14	30				Adolescent	No specific treatment
186	38	20	186	65	35	186	33	18	Mixed duration	
87	27	31	87	42	48				"Schizophreniform" Brief duration	
			54	14	26	54	13	24	Ages 15 to 21	
98	1	1	98	8	8				Males, first admission	No treatment or lobotomy
						100	42	42		

Table 3.1 – continued

Authors	Country	Years of admission	Median year of admission	Follow-up years later	Original cohort size	Number dead and not followed up
1921–1940		Percentages derived from totals				
Hastings (1958)	USA	1938–1944	1941	6–12	251	9
M. Bleuler (1978)	Switzerland	1942–1943	1942	20–23 or until death	208	–
Masterson (1956)	USA	1936–1950	1943	5–19	83	–
Holmboe & Astrup (1957)	Norway	1938–1950	1944	6–18	255	0
Astrup et al. (1963)	Norway	1938–1950	1944	5–22	721	32
Eitinger et al. (1958)	Norway	1940–1949	1944	5–15	154	–
Harris et al. (1956)	England	1945–1968	1946	5	126	2
Vaillant & Funkenstein (1966)	USA	1948–1950	1949	2–14 or until death	72	–
Leiberman et al. (1957)	England	1948–1950	1949	3	156	2
Norton (1961)	England	1949–1950	1949	2	145	–
Niskanen & Achté (1971)	Finland	1950	1950	5	100	4
Huber et al. (1975)	Germany	1945–1959	1952	22	502	–
Kelly & Sargant (1965)	England	1950–1955	1952	2	39	2
Stephens (1970)	USA	1948–1958	1953	5–16	472	17
Norton (1961)	England	1953	1953	2	129	–
Ackner & Oldham (1962)	England	c1954	1954	3	66	–
Astrup & Noreik (1966)	Norway	1951–1957	1954	5–12 or until death	273	–
1941–1955		Percentages derived from totals				
Brown et al. (1966)	England	1956	1956	5	111	3
Brown et al. (1966)	England	1956	1956	5	228	6
Fröshaug & Ytrehus (1963)	Norway	1953–1959	1956	3–8	103	5

Complete recovery			Social recovery			Hospitalized			Stage or type of illness	Treatment
Number followed up (+ dead)	Number completely recovered	%	Number followed up (+ dead)	Number socially recovered	%	Number followed up (+ dead)	Number in hospital at follow up	%		
4264	503	12	3761	1099	29	3984	1935	49		
247	68	28	247	103	42				Mixed duration	No "modern" therapies
208	30	14	208	64	31	208	93	45	Mixed duration	
83	15	18	83	27	33				Adolescent	
255	97	38	255	147	58	255	89	35	First admission Acute onset	ECT, insulin coma, and psychosurgery
696	131	19	696	248	36	555	118	21	Non-acute	ECT, insulin coma, and psychosurgery
154	18	12								ECT, insulin coma, and lobotomy
125	37	30	125	61	49	125	42	34	Mixed duration	Insulin coma
			70	19	26	70	17	23	Mixed duration	ECT, insulin coma
154	49	32	154	85	55	154	44	29	First admission Early	ECT, insulin coma
						145	53	37	Female, mixed duration	
100	30	30	100	59	59	100	22	22	First admission	
502	111	22	502	281	56	502	67	13		
39	14	36	39	18	46	39	12	31	Selected	Insulin coma
383	97	25							First admission	
						129	26	20	Female, mixed admission	
66	27	41	66	38	58	66	14	21	Early	Insulin and barbiturate coma
273	16	6	273	92	34				First admission	ECT, insulin coma, leucotomy, and psychotropic drugs
3285	740	23	2818	1242	44	2348	597	25		
88	32	36	97	53	55	88	11	12	First admission	Phenothiazines
173	32	18	205	79	39	173	47	27	Previous admissions	Phenothiazines
97	23	24	97	35	36	97	17	18	Female, first admission	

Table 3.1 – continued

Authors	Country	Years of admission	Median year of admission	Follow-up years later	Original cohort size	Number dead and not followed up
*Wirt & Simon (1959)	USA	c1956	1956	1	80	0
Henisz (1966)	Poland	1956	1956	7	249	22
Mandelbrote & Folkard (1961)	England	1856–1958	1957	2–4	288	8
Kelly & Sargant (1965)	England	1956–1958	1957	2	39	0
Norton (1961)	England	1957	1957	2	189	–
Cole et al. (1963)	USA	1957–1959	1958	3	110	0
Hoenig & Hamilton (1966)	England	1958–1960	1959	4	62	0
Kelly & Sargant (1965)	England	1958–1961	1959	2	45	0
Holmboe et al. (1968)	Norway	1958–1961	1959	5–7	169	0
Engelhardt et al. (1982)	USA	1958–1962	1960	15	670	24
Niskanan & Achté (1971)	Finland	1960	1960	5	100	5
Leyberg (1965)	England	1960	1960	3	81	0
Holmboe et al. (1968)	Norway	1959–1962	1960	5–8	42	0
Levenstein et al. (1966)	USA	1959–1961	1960	2	77	1
Vaillant et al. (1964)	USA	1961–1962	1961	1–2	103	0
Kelly & Sargant (1965)	England	1960–1963	1961	2	48	0
Hall et al. (1966)	USA	1961–1962	1961	1	188	0
Bland et al. (1978)	Canada	1963	1963	11–12	92	0
Bland & Orn (1978)	Canada	1963	1963	14	45	2
Niskanen & Achtè (1971)	Finland	1965	1965	5	100	6

Complete recovery			Social recovery			Hospitalized			Stage or type of illness	Treatment
Number followed up (+ dead)	Number completely recovered	%	Number followed up (+ dead)	Number socially recovered	%	Number followed up (+ dead)	Number in hospital at follow up	%		
79	7	9	79	29	37	79	20	25	First admission	Chlorpromazine, reserpine, ECT, insulin coma and psychotherapy
230	30	13	230	73	32				Early	Chlorpromazine, ECT and insulin coma
			230	96	42	288	51	18	Mixed duration	
39	12	31	39	24	61	39	2	5	Selected	Phenothiazines
						189	19	10	Female, mixed duration	
			108	47	43				Male, mixed duration	
62	17	27	53	20	38	62	6	10	First admission mixed duration	Antipsychotic drugs, ECT and psychotherapy
44	14	32	44	32	73	44	3	7	Selected	Phenothiazines
169	12	7	169	35	21				First admission	
						670	75	11	Mixed duration	Outpatient treatment
100	29	29	100	68	68	100	14	14	First admission	Antipsychotic drugs
81	18	26	81	26	32	81	14	17	Mixed duration	Hospital and community treatment
42	6	14	42	15	36				First admission	
77	9	12	77	30	34				Selected	Antipsychotic drugs and psychotherapy
100	25	25	100	64	64	100	13	13	Mixed duration	Phenothiazines and psychotherapy
48	24	48	48	32	67	48	4	8	Selected mixed duration	Phenothiazines, ECT and insulin therapy
188	c38	20	188	72	38				Acute, first admission	
88	29	33	88	61	69				First admission	Antipsychotic drugs and ECT
43	7	16	43	27	63	43	2	5	First admission	Antipsychotic drugs
100	21	21	100	64	64	100	10	10	First admission	Antipsychotic drugs

Table 3.1 – continued

Authors	Country	Years of admission	Median year of admission	Follow-up years later	Original cohort size	Number dead and not followed up
Jonsson & Nyman (1991)	Sweden	1964–1967	1965	14–17	110	18
Salokangas (1983)	Finland	1965–1967	1966	7½	100	8
Helgason (1990)	Iceland	1966–1967	1966	20–21	107	23
Cottman & Mezey (1976)	England	1964–1968	1966	4–9	56	1
Marneros et al. (1992)	Germany	Before 1967	Before 1967	25	148	
W.H.O. (1979)	Denmark	1968–1969	1968	2	48	
W.H.O. (1979)	England	1968–1969	1968	2	57	
W.H.O. (1979)	USA	1968–1969	1968	2	38	
W.H.O. (1979)	Czechoslovakia	1968–1969	1968	2	53	
Prudo & Blum (1987)	England	1968–1969	1968	5	100	6
Salokangas (1983)	Finland	1969	1969	8	75	5
Stone (1986)	USA	1963–1976	1969	10–20	c140	
Harrow et al. (1978)	USA	after 1970	after 1970	2–3	79	4
Munk-Jorgensen & Mortensen (1992)	Denmark	1972	1972			
Möller et al. (1982)	Germany	1972–1974	1973	5–6	103	7
1956–1975		**Percentages derived from totals**				
Johnstone et al. (1979)	England	before 1978	before 1978	1	45	1
Marengo et al. (1991)	USA	c1977	c1977	8	111	
Wiersma et al. (2000)	Bulgaria, Germany, Ireland, Netherlands, Czech Republic, England	1977–1978	1977	13–16	496	45
Biehl et al. (1986)	Germany	1978	1978	5	70	3
Mason et al. (1996)	England	1978–1980	1979	13	67	5

Complete recovery			Social recovery			Hospitalized			Stage or type of illness	Treatment
Number followed up (+ dead)	Number completely recovered	%	Number followed up (+ dead)	Number socially recovered	%	Number followed up (+ dead)	Number in hospital at follow up	%		
			110	26	24	–	–	–	First admission	
100	25	25	100	64	64				First admission	
107	3	3	107	27	25				First episode	Hospital and/or community treatment
42	22	52	42	34	81	42	2	5	First admission	Phenothiazines and community care
148	28	19	148	61	41	148	36	24		
48	5	10							Mixed duration	
57	20	35							Mixed duration	
38	8	21							Mixed duration	
53	14	26							Mixed duration	
88	17	19	71	42	59	100	13	13	Mixed duration	
75	16	21	75	38	51				First admissions	Hospital and community treatment
72	0	0	72	7	10	72	11	15	Mixed duration	Exploratory psychotherapy
79	13	16	79	33	42	79	14	18	Acute and chronic	Phenothiazines and psychotherapy
53	10	19	53	10	19	53	8	15	First admission	
85	16	19	85	42	49				Mixed duration	Neuroleptics and sociotherapy
2893	582	20	3160	1366	43	2695	392	15		
			43	15	35				Acute	
			74	38	51				Mixed duration	Hospital and community treatment
344	42	12	344	120	35	393	21	5	Recent onset, Non-affective psychosis	
						70	3	4	First episode	Hospital and community treatment
63	11	17	63	18	29				First episode	

Table 3.1 – continued

Authors	Country	Years of admission	Median year of admission	Follow-up years later	Original cohort size	Number dead and not followed up
Jablensky et al. (1991)	Denmark	1978–1980	1979	2	80	
Jablensky et al. (1991)	Ireland	1978–1980	1979	2	57	
Jablensky et al. (1991)	USA (Hawaii)	1978–1980	1979	2	29	
Jablensky et al. (1991)	USA (Rochester)	1978–1980	1979	2	31	
Jablensky et al. (1991)	USSR	1978–1980	1979	2	164	
Jablensky et al. (1991)	Japan	1978–1980	1979	2	70	
Jablensky et al. (1991)	England	1978–1980	1979	2	86	
Jablensky et al. (1991)	Czechoslovakia	1978–1980	1979	2	87	
Breier et al. (1991)	USA	1976–1984	1980	2–12	74	4
Johnstone et al. (1995)	England	1975–1985	1980	2–12	532	66
Leary et al. (1991)	England	1975–1985	1980	2–12	532	66
Johnstone et al. (1991)	England	1975–1985	1980	2–12	532	66
Lynge & Jacobsen (1995)	Greenland	1980–1983	1981	7	37	6
Lay et al. (2000)	Germany	1976–1987	1981	over 10	96	4
Shepherd et al. (1989)	England	before 1983	before 1983	over 5	121	9
Salokangas & Stengård (1990)	Finland	1983–1984	1983	2	227	8
Wieselgren & Lindström (1996)	Sweden	1979–1989	1984	5	120	10
Scottish Schizophrenia Research Group (1992)	Scotland	before 1986	before 1986	5	49	1

Complete recovery			Social recovery			Hospitalized			Stage or type of illness	Treatment
Number followed up (+ dead)	Number completely recovered	%	Number followed up (+ dead)	Number socially recovered	%	Number followed up (+ dead)	Number in hospital at follow up	%		
80	22	27							First episode	Hospital and/or community treatment
57	21	37							First episode	Hospital and/or community treatment
31	12	39							First episode	Hospital and/or community treatment
29	7	24							First episode	Hospital and/or community treatment
164	30	18							First episode	Hospital and/or community treatment
70	20	29							First episode	Hospital and/or community treatment
86	52	60							First episode	Hospital and/or community treatment
87	58	67							First episode	Hospital and/or community treatment
62	2	3	62	21	34	62	11	18	Chronic	
408	49	12								
			408	108	26					
						408	31	8		
37	6	16	37	12	32				First admission	
69	8	12	69	13	19	69	21	30	Adolescent onset schizophrenia & schizoaffective disorder	
116	17	15	116	51	44				Mixed duration	Hospital and community treatment
			209	88	40				First contact	Hospital and community treatment
110	10	9	110	30	27				Schizophrenia & schizophreniform	Some treated later with clozapine
40	7	17	43	8	19				First admissions	Antipsychotic drugs and ECT

Table 3.1 – continued

Authors	Country	Years of admission	Median year of admission	Follow-up years later	Original cohort size	Number dead and not followed up
Benazzi (1998)	Italy	1984–1993	1988	5	20	0
Vasquez-Barquero et al. (1999)	Spain	1989–1990	1989	3	86	2
Kurihara et al. (2000)	Japan	1991–1992	1991	5	46	3
1976-present	Percentages derived from totals					

Note: * Year of admission unclear: study included in this section as phenothiazine was used.

35–45 per cent of people with schizophrenia were socially recovered at follow-up.

Second, *the state of the economy appears to be linked to outcome in schizophrenia.* During the Great Depression of the 1920s and 1930s, the rate of complete recovery was halved at 12 per cent; social recovery fell to less than 30 per cent. During the recession of the 1980s and early 1990s, social recovery declined again to 33 per cent. An analysis of variance shows that these changes are greater than would be expected by chance. The little information available for patients admitted during the Great Depression of the late nineteenth century shows the same trend toward low recovery rates. There is a significant correlation between changes in the recovery rates and US and UK average unemployment over the five time periods after 1900 (see Table 3.2). The more important finding is the correlation of complete, symptomatic recovery with unemployment; social recovery may fluctuate with the economy merely because it is itself partly a measure of patient employment.

These variations in recovery rates now allow us to explain the conflicting opinions of how outcome in schizophrenia changed during the twentieth century. If we contrast recent rates of recovery with results from the Great Depression of the 1930s or with Kraepelin's figures for patients admitted in the 1880s then modern outcome will appear superior. On the other hand, if we include recovery statistics from the two decades between the Victorian Depression and the Great Depression, recent results do not benefit from the comparison.

The explanation for Hegarty and colleagues' conclusion, that there was an improvement in outcome during the twentieth century, is more complex. Hegarty and co-worker's conducted an analysis of twentieth-century schizophrenia outcome studies, somewhat similar to the one presented in this chapter, but which had a number of methodological flaws.[13] They mixed together Third World and Western studies, even though outcome in schizophrenia is

Complete recovery			Social recovery			Hospitalized			Stage or type of illness	Treatment
Number followed up (+ dead)	Number completely recovered	%	Number followed up (+ dead)	Number socially recovered	%	Number followed up (+ dead)	Number in hospital at follow up	%		
20	4	20							Schizophreniform	
78	23	29	78	27	36				First episode	
						43	4	9		
1951	401	20	1656	549	33	1045	91	9		

very different in the Third World (see Chapter 7); they included studies with cohorts of patients selected at the time of hospital discharge, even though such samples are biased by the fact that they exclude people who remain in hospital or who die there; and they left out all the true long-term outcome studies with follow-up duration of longer than ten years. Their search methodology led them to discover only half the number of studies of cohorts admitted prior to 1920 that are presented in the analysis above and, thus, they underestimated the recovery rate during this early part of the century.

Finally, it is clear that *people with schizophrenia experienced the impact of deinstitutionalization before the antipsychotic drugs were brought into use.* The claim that is commonly heard, particularly in the United States, that the antipsychotic drugs made community treatment of schizophrenia possible, is brought into dispute. The proportion of people with schizophrenia out of hospital at follow-up increased significantly from around 50 or 55 per cent before 1940 to more than 70 per cent in the immediate postwar period. After the antipsychotic drugs were introduced, the proportion of patients out of hospital continued to increase to 85 per cent between 1956 and 1975 and to more than 90 per cent after 1975. One point stands out with regard to this trend towards community treatment; whereas the decrease in hospital use in the postwar years before 1955 was associated with an improvement in the recovery rates for people with schizophrenia, after the advent of drug treatment deinstitutionalization did not bring any improvement in the symptoms or social functioning for these patients.

Despite the popular view in psychiatry, the antipsychotic drugs have not proved to be a critical factor in either emptying mental hospitals or achieving modern recovery rates in schizophrenia. Other probable causes of the deinstitutionalization movement will be presented in Chapter 4, and political, economic and social explanations for the variations in recovery from schizophrenia will be offered in Chapters 5, 6, 7 and 8. The reasons for the poor

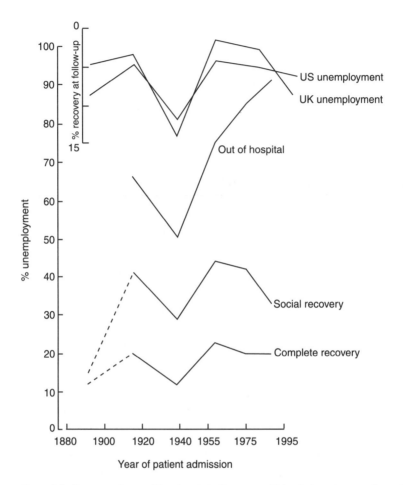

Figure 3.1 Outcome from schizophrenia in Europe and North America as reflected in
114 studies, and average unemployment (inverted) for the USA and the UK
for the same time periods

showing of the antipsychotic drugs will be discussed in Chapter 10. It will be argued that, rather than psychiatric treatment having a big impact on schizophrenia, both the course of the illness and the development of psychiatry itself are governed by political economy.

Before going on to this analysis, however, we should see if there are reasons to doubt the accuracy of the findings of the survey of outcome studies of schizophrenia.

Table 3.2 Correlation of recovery rates in schizophrenia with average unemployment rates in the USA and UK during five periods of the twentieth century

Admission period	Complete recovery %	Social recovery %	US unemployment %	UK unemployment %
1901–20	20	41	4.7	3.5
1921–40	12	29	11.9	14.0
1941–55	23	44	4.1	1.5
1956–75	20	43	5.1	2.3
1976–1995	20	33	6.9	8.2

	Pearson's Correlation Coefficient			
	US unemployment		UK unemployment	
	r	α	r	α
Complete recovery	0.96	0.01	0.91	0.03
Social recovery	0.92	0.03	0.98	0.003

DIFFERENCES IN DIAGNOSIS

Could differences in the diagnosis of schizophrenia between one country or one time period and another have produced these results? We know, for example, that Scandinavian psychiatrists have a narrow concept of schizophrenia that excludes brief illnesses and emphasizes poor outcome. American psychiatry, on the other hand, until the 1970s, employed a broad concept of schizophrenia that included much of what European psychiatrists call manic-depressive illness and also some conditions that would not be considered psychoses elsewhere (see Chapter 1). If the sample of outcome studies included proportionally more Scandinavian studies and fewer American studies during the Great Depression, then this bias might account for the low recovery rates found for that time period. As Table 3.3 shows, however, this is not the case. In fact the largest proportion of Scandinavian studies in the survey appears during the period 1941–55, when the overall outcome was best; and the largest proportion of American studies comes during the Great Depression, when outcome was worse. These variations, theoretically, would tend to minimize the changes in outcome that were found, not inflate them.

If the studies for the three geographic areas, Great Britain, the United States and Scandinavia, are plotted separately, as in Figure 3.2, we find that recovery rates were, in fact, worse in Scandinavia and better in Britain for the most of the twentieth century. If there were a large proportion of British studies during the period 1941–55, this might account for the good outcome noted at that time. Again, this is not the case. The largest proportion of British studies happens to be in the most recent two time periods – a variation that should have biased the results in favor of antipsychotic drugs treatment

Table 3.3 Recovery rates in the USA, Scandinavia and Britain in 114 outcome studies of schizophrenia. The proportion of total subjects from all countries in each time period upon which the regional recovery rate is based is also shown

	1901–20		1921–40		1941–55		1956–75		1976–95	
	Recovery rate %	Proportion of total group %	Recovery rate %	Proportion of total group %	Recovery rate %	Proportion of total group %	Recovery rate %	Proportion of total group %	Recovery rate %	Proportion of total group %
USA										
Complete recovery	17	73	11	70	25	22	16	22	17	6
Social recovery	35	27	29	57	37	14	40	22	43	8
Scandinavia										
Complete recovery	–	0	12	12	20	45	17	31	17	12
Social recovery	–	0	22	13	41	47	40	30	37	21
Britain										
Complete recovery	16	5	19	11	33	12	29	25	19	37
Social recovery	–	0	30	10	53	14	48	29	30	41

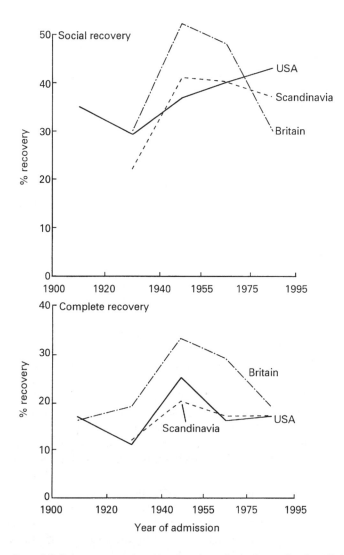

Figure 3.2 Recovery rates in schizophrenia as shown by studies from Britain, the USA and Scandinavia

during the 1955–75 time period. It is true that there were no Scandinavian studies included for the years before 1921, and this fact may have boosted the outcome results for those early decades, but this bias should, in theory, have been offset by the small proportion of British studies during the same period.

The most important conclusion to draw from Figure 3.2, however, is that, with some minor exceptions, the same overall pattern of poor outcome during economic downturns and higher recovery rates during the boom is shown in all three parts of the world. The pattern is not demonstrated for Britain and Scandinavia before 1921, as there is only one British study for that period and none from Scandinavia, but the subsequent relationship to economic fluctuations and the lack of improvement with the arrival of the antipsychotics is clear. The decline of social recovery rates in Britain during the recent economic recession in that country is particularly striking. Social recovery rates did not appear to improve as much in the United States immediately after the Second World War as they did in the European countries; this could well be a reflection of the fact that the postwar social psychiatry revolution occurred several years earlier in northern Europe than it did in the United States. US social recovery rates, however, have surpassed those of Britain and Scandinavia in the most recent time period, perhaps because US unemployment rates have not increased as dramatically in recent decades as they have in Europe.

Diagnostic differences from country to country, then, probably do not account for the observed results. Could the findings be an artifact of changes in diagnostic habits over time? One important historical change was Eugen Bleuler's conception of schizophrenia, introduced in 1911, which attempted to escape Kraepelin's emphasis on inevitable deterioration as a central feature of the illness. Bias from this source is averted in this survey of outcome studies by beginning the formal analysis with Eugen Bleuler's own patients.

Another important historical factor has been the changing American diagnosis of schizophrenia. The broadening of the US concept of schizophrenia may have become most evident after 1950 – this is when the incidence of manic-depressive illness appeared to decline in the United States.[14] American psychiatrists began to separate schizophrenia from manic-depressive illness more rigorously again in the mid-1970s, after lithium carbonate was introduced as an effective treatment for the latter condition. American diagnosis became even more narrow in 1980, when it adopted the Scandinavian practice of excluding from the category of schizophrenia brief, "schizophreniform" psychoses.[15] These developments suggest that American studies between 1950 and the late 1970s might tend to report better outcome and give a false picture of fluctuating recovery rates. Although this is a reasonable concern it does not appear to be a critical factor in shaping the results of this survey in view of the following:

- US results fluctuate according to the same pattern as European results after 1920.
- British outcome figures have been better than US results throughout much of the century despite a narrower British diagnostic approach.
- US studies account for a relatively small proportion of the results in this survey after 1950.

PATIENT SELECTION

If more chronic, poor-prognosis patients were included in the cohorts studied in the Great Depression, this bias could account for the worse outcome noted at that time. This potential problem does not appear to have occurred. More studies included in the series from 1921 to 1940 were, in fact, of patients with good prognostic features than were included in the periods immediately before or after. Good-prognosis patients were considered to be those designated as "first admission," "early," "acute" or "selected" (see Table 3.4). An even larger proportion of patients in the studies after 1956 had good prognostic features; this could conceivably have led to an over-optimistic estimate of recovery rates since antipsychotic drugs were introduced. Any kind of bias due to patient selection seems to be less important when we compare the actual recovery rates for "good-prognosis" patients with the total group. The differences, as shown in Figure 3.3, are not particularly great.

Although we have to use caution in interpreting the findings of this survey of outcome in schizophrenia, particularly for the early years of the twentieth century, the results are by no means invalidated by the limitations of the research material. In fact, most of the possible bias that was detected would

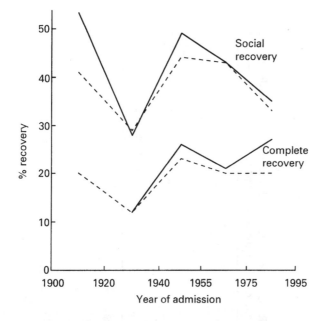

Figure 3.3 Recovery rates for good-prognosis patients designated as "first admission," "early" or "selected" among 114 outcome studies of schizophrenia (solid line). Recovery rates for the total group of patients are added (dotted line) for comparison

Table 3.4 Recovery rates for good-prognosis patients designated as "first admission," "early," "acute" or "selected" among 114 outcome studies of schizophrenia. The proportion of total subjects with these good-prognosis designations is also shown

	1901–20		1921–40		1941–55		1956–75		1976–95	
	Recovery rate %	Proportion of total group %	Recovery rate %	Proportion of total group %	Recovery rate %	Proportion of total group %	Recovery rate %	Proportion of total group %	Recovery rate %	Proportion of total group %
Complete recovery	–	0	12	51	26	39	21	61	27	61
Social recovery	54	33	28	51	49	31	43	59	35	49

tend to downplay the somewhat provocative findings rather than dramatize them.

SUMMARY

An analysis of 114 follow-up studies of outcome in schizophrenia conducted in the Developed World since the beginning of the twentieth century reveals:

- Recovery rates for patients admitted following the introduction of the antipsychotic drugs are no better than for those admitted after the Second World War or during the first two decades of the twentieth century.
- Recovery rates were significantly lower during the Great Depression of the 1920s and 1930s, and have shown a further decline in Britain during the recent economic recession.
- The Great Depression and the recent economic recession excepted, complete recovery occurs in roughly 20–25 per cent of people with schizophrenia and social recovery in 40–45 per cent.
- The proportion of patients with schizophrenia in hospital at follow-up has declined dramatically through the century, most of the decrease having taken place before the advent of the antipsychotic drugs.
- These findings do not appear to be artifacts of variation in diagnosis or selection of patients.

Chapter 4

Deinstitutionalization

What accounts for the finding arrived at in the previous chapter, that the proportion of patients with schizophrenia found to be in hospital at follow-up declined dramatically *before* the advent of the antipsychotic drugs? A widely held belief about modern mental health care is that these drugs, introduced in the mid-1950s, brought a new dawn to psychiatry, making possible effective treatment and community care for psychotic patients. Chlorpromazine, the first of the antipsychotic drugs, initiated a "therapeutic revolution" in the hospital and community treatment of schizophrenia, argued psychiatrist John Davis in the *Comprehensive Textbook of Psychiatry*. He continued:

> Those changes have resulted in a massive reduction in the number of hospitalized schizophrenic patients, a finding all the more remarkable since, up to the introduction of the new drugs, there had been a steady increase in the number of hospitalized mental patients. The shift in the fate of mental patients is the most convincing proof of the efficacy of those agents.[1]

Dr Davis illustrated the point with a graph showing the rise and fall in the number of residents of US state and county mental hospitals during this century. His graph is essentially similar to the broken line in Figure 4.1, with the addition of the letters CPZ and an arrow pointing to the peak of the graph in the mid-1950s indicating the time chlorpromazine began to be widely used. The observation that the antipsychotic drugs made deinstitutionalization possible has become a truism of modern psychiatric practice. But how accurate is it?

A moment's reflection discloses that the figures relevant to this issue are not the *absolute* numbers of mental hospital residents, but the numbers *as a proportion of the general population*. A graph of the *rate* of mental hospitalization – the continuous line in Figure 4.1 – reveals a different picture. Whereas the absolute number of mental hospital residents peaked in 1955, the rate of hospital use peaked in 1945 and never climbed as high again.

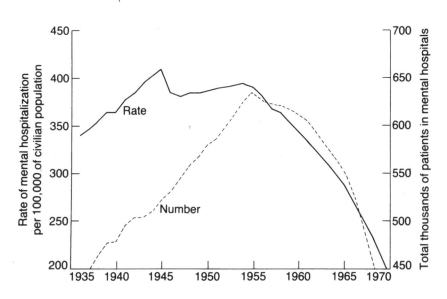

Figure 4.1 Resident patients in US federal, state, county and private hospitals

Source: US Bureau of the Census, *Historical Statistics of the United States: Colonial Times to 1970*, Part I, Washington, DC, 1975, p. 84.

Although there has been a marked decline in the population of mental hospitals since the introduction of the antipsychotic drugs, it is clear that something else was happening in the first postwar decade to alter patterns of psychiatric hospital use.

THE IMPACT OF THE ANTIPSYCHOTICS

Several psychiatrists, especially those practicing in northern Europe before and after the Second World War, remarked that the arrival of the antipsychotic drugs in 1954 had little impact on the discharge rates of many mental hospitals. Örnulv Ödegard studied the figures for patients first admitted to all Norwegian psychiatric hospitals before and after the introduction of the antipsychotics.[2] He found a small increase in discharge rates for patients admitted during 1955–59 compared with those admitted during 1948–52, prior to the use of drugs. But he found a much bigger increase in the discharge rate when he compared the 1948–52 group with patients admitted in the late 1930s. The figures for patients suffering from functional psychosis were:

Admission date	% discharged and not readmitted
1936–40	52
1948–52	63
1955–59	67

In Britain, Alan Norton observed the same pattern at Bexley Hospital in Kent.[3] Although some improvement in discharge rates occurred between 1953 and 1957 with the introduction of drug treatment, a much more dramatic trend of improvement was already under way by the end of the Second World War, as these figures for female patients with schizophrenia show:

Admission date	% in hospital 2 years after admission
1928–30	59
1934–36	63
1949–50	37
1953	20
1957	10

Michael Shepherd and his colleagues, after studying the discharge rate from St John's Hospital in Stone, Buckinghamshire, between 1954 and 1957, concluded that the introduction of drug treatment after 1954 had made no significant change.[4] Their net release-rate figures (discharges expressed as a proportion of the average number of patients in residence) for schizophrenia were as follows:

Year	Net release rate (%)
1954	18.4
1955	19.5
1956	15.4
1957	18.8

At Mapperley Hospital in Nottingham, the patient population began to decline as early as 1948, from 1,310 patients in that year to 1,060 in 1956, and continued to drop at a similar pace after drugs were brought into use.[5]

Similar examples for the United States are harder to find. The number of patients resident in Massachusetts mental hospitals was already declining in 1954, before chlorpromazine was in use;[6] and at Vermont State Hospital the discharge rate for schizophrenia increased steadily after 1948.[7] Looking only at first-admission, white males with schizophrenia entering California state hospitals, psychiatrist Leon Epstein found that the discharge rate for such patients was already increasing between 1951 and 1954 (the year when drug treatment was introduced). Furthermore, patients with schizophrenia first admitted in 1956 and 1957 who were treated with the new drugs showed a *lower* discharge rate than those who were treated without drugs. The discharge rate for this group of patients as a whole (drug-treated and drug-free) nevertheless continued to increase.[8] Erwin Linn demonstrated that the same phenomenon occurred at St Elizabeth's Hospital in Washington, DC. Although the discharge rate for patients with functional psychosis increased at this hospital between 1953 and 1956, the release rate for those treated with drugs was again lower than for those treated without drugs.[9] (Such a result, however, would theoretically occur if only the patients with the worst prognosis were given drug treatment.) Overall it seems probable that some other influence besides a purely pharmacological effect was operating to stimulate American deinstitutionalization.

Much more influential than these studies, however, were the figures for New York State mental hospitals presented by Henry Brill and Robert Patton. They noted that the residential population of the state hospitals was increasing by around 2,000 patients each year until 1955. In that year 30,000 cases received the new type of drug treatment, and in the following year the upward trend was converted into an annual *decrease* in the residential population of the following approximate magnitude:

1956	500
1957	500
1958	1,200
1959	2,000

The authors concluded that "the abrupt population fall was in material degree due to introduction of the new drugs" because "no other explanation for the statistical changes could be found."[10] They were, however, unable to demonstrate a direct cause-and-effect relation between drug treatment and patient discharge although, as sociologist Andrew Scull points out,[11] and as Davis's view at the beginning of this chapter illustrates, their work is often interpreted as having done so. The New York experience was so close to the pattern for the country as a whole that the use of antipsychotic drugs is now inextricably linked in the minds of most American psychiatrists and mental health professionals with the development of community care for psychotic patients and the radical changes associated with the advent of the deinstitutionalization era. The data from northern Europe, however, make it plain that increased discharge rates, shorter hospital stays, and community treatment for people with psychosis were becoming the rule in many areas well before the antipsychotic drugs arrived on the scene.

If not to the new drugs, then to what may we attribute these postwar changes in the management of mental patients?

THE SOCIAL PSYCHIATRY REVOLUTION

A revolution in the treatment of people with psychosis was taking place in many parts of northern Europe before drugs were available – a revolution that went largely unnoticed in the United States until it was well under way. Mainstream opinion in American psychiatry to this day, in fact, has overlooked the significance of the European social psychiatry revolution and continues to emphasize the central importance of drug treatment. As expressed by John Davis, the advent of chlorpromazine

> created an atmosphere that emphasized positive treatment and led to the vigorous application of other therapies, such as milieu therapy, psychotherapy, group therapy and occupational therapy. The greater use of those social therapies was made possible by the effective treatment, through medication, of the disruptive and destructive aspects of the patient's illness.[12]

From the American perspective this association of events appeared to be true, but the evidence from northern Europe demonstrates that social therapies, far from being "made possible" by drug treatment, preceded and rivaled the antipsychotic drugs in their impact on the rehabilitation of psychotic patients.

British psychiatrists at Netherne Hospital, near London, noted a "greatly improved general pattern of care of the severely ill in hospital" during the period from 1945 to 1948 compared with conditions for those admitted a decade earlier. They saw

> the changes for the better being evident from the larger number of open wards, the increased freedom patients are able to enjoy, the abolition of restraint and strong clothing, and the diminution of seclusion, aggression and incontinence.[13]

The psychiatrists associated these improvements with the introduction of physical therapies (insulin coma and electro-convulsive therapy) and with changes in hospital policy and community attitudes.

In 1949 Dr George Bell unlocked the doors of all the wards of Dingleton Hospital in Melrose, Scotland. In earlier decades physician superintendents of other hospitals had made similar attempts – Rutherford at Lenzie Asylum in 1881, for example, and Saxtby Good at Littlemore Hospital, Oxford, in 1935 – but public pressure had always forced the doors closed again. Bell's success, however, heralded an Open Door Movement in psychiatry which swept the Western world in the years that followed. Mapperley Hospital opened its doors in 1953 and Warlingham Park, South London, soon after. Day hospitals for patients suffering from psychosis were used in Great Britain in the 1940s and 1950s, and in Amsterdam, Holland, a comprehensive program was developed for the treatment of the mentally ill in their own homes. Not until 1958, when drug treatment was well established, did St Lawrence Hospital, New York, become fully open door.[14] Within the European hospitals, other changes were taking place.

Beginning in 1946, British psychiatrists developed new patterns of institutional living. Termed "therapeutic communities" by Dr Tom Main, groups of therapists and patients worked together to create a hospital environment where traditional models of institutional authority were broken down, patients participated in the government of their hospital community, staff and patient roles were blurred and open communication was highly valued. Initially, this type of treatment setting was not available for patients with psychosis. Tom Main worked with demoralized ex-soldiers at Northfield Hospital, Birmingham, and Maxwell Jones, foremost in developing the therapeutic community concept, worked with unemployed drifters and, later, patients with character disorders at the Henderson Hospital in South London.[15] In due course the therapeutic community idea was introduced into wards for patients with psychosis. At the Littlemore Hospital, Oxford, throughout the 1960s, there were therapeutic communities in three different treatment units – for the elderly, for brain-damaged patients and for adult psychiatric patients. The programs, radical in concept, were established by Dr Ben Pomryn, who had worked with Maxwell Jones at the Henderson Hospital. On the general adult unit – the Phoenix Unit – staff and some 60 acute and chronic psychiatric patients (i.e. 70 or more people) participated in daily community meetings that established ward policy, evaluated new admissions, held interviews with patients' families, prescribed treatment (including drug treatment and electro-convulsive therapy) and authorized discharges. Maxwell Jones introduced similar changes to Dingleton Hospital and turned it into an innovative model drawing staff and visitors from many parts of the world.

The new hospital activity and therapeutic optimism were geared to early discharge, rehabilitation, and treatment in the community. Chronically institutionalized patients developed social competence and were placed in supervised hostels, returned to their families, or were set up in houses of their own, living together in family-like groups. Psychiatrists and nurses left the wards to see patients in their homes and in outpatient clinics and to consult with family physicians and community mental health workers. Sheltered workshops prospered, especially in Holland and, after 1960, in Britain, and produced goods competitive in the industrial market place. Industrial therapy in the United States, meanwhile, lagged a long way behind.[16]

Such radical changes, in several areas pre-dating the introduction of chlorpromazine, explain why drug treatment appeared to have little effect in many hospitals. Professor Ödegard demonstrated that of the 17 mental hospitals in Norway, those which had previously had a poor discharge record showed the most benefit from the introduction of the antipsychotic drugs; those which already had a higher discharge rate, and were presumably more advanced in social therapeutic techniques, showed no increase in the number of patients discharged and maintained in the community after drugs became available (see Table 4.1). Dr Ödegard concludes that for hospitals where social *milieu* therapy was not well developed "the drugs were a real blessing," but that

> in the more privileged institutions the drugs simply meant that one form of therapy was replaced by another and equally efficient one.[17]

Similarly, Dr N.H. Rathod, a psychiatrist at Cane Hill Hospital in Surrey, demonstrated that the effects of the new "tranquillizers" were very limited on wards where particular attention was paid to the creation of a therapeutic environment.[18]

Antipsychotic drugs, then, appear to be more effective for the patient with psychosis who is living in an inadequate setting, and to be less valuable where the environment is designed for his or her wellbeing. This is an important point and one that we will return to later in the book. It is a point that is not readily apparent to mental health professionals who were not practicing

Table 4.1 Number of patients discharged and not readmitted per 100 admissions for all Norwegian mental hospitals

Hospital	1949–53	1955–9	% Change
1	75.7	71.6	−5.4
2	67.1	65.5	−2.4
3	66.5	62.3	−6.3
4	60.2	57.6	−4.3
5	58.4	44.9	−23.1
6	57.0	49.8	−12.6
7	56.6	59.6	+5.3
8	54.4	49.0	−9.9
9	53.8	63.9	+18.8
10	53.6	53.6	0
11	52.0	51.2	−1.5
12	51.1	51.4	+0.6
13	49.1	65.4	+33.2
14	48.7	50.4	+3.5
15	46.7	46.5	−0.4
16	44.4	51.4	+15.8
17	34.2	41.4	+21.0

Source: Ödegard, Ö., "Pattern of discharge from Norwegian psychiatric hospitals before and after the introduction of the psychotropic drugs," *American Journal of Psychiatry*, 120: 772–8, 1964.

before the antipsychotic drugs were in use; and because of the peculiarities of deinstitutionalization in the United States, it is a point scarcely recognized in American psychiatry. In practice, drug treatment is all too often used as a substitute for adequate psychosocial care. As concern grows over the harmful side effects of the antipsychotic drugs and over the social plight of large numbers of poverty-stricken people with psychotic disorders in the community, this becomes an issue of some consequence.

DEINSTITUTIONALIZATION IN THE UNITED STATES

The antipsychotic drugs had a more revolutionary impact in the United States, where there were relatively more backward asylums in 1955, than in those parts of northern Europe where social therapy prevailed. The subsequent course of deinstitutionalization in America also differed from that in northern Europe. Despite the development in the United States of a network of community mental health centers after 1965, the welfare of the chronically and severely mentally ill was, for decades, largely overlooked. A substantial proportion of those discharged from US mental hospitals were merely transferred to another category of institution – nursing homes.

For many patients the switch was to their disadvantage. Nursing-home staff were generally low-paid and had no training in mental health, wards were often locked and overcrowded, the environment was frequently shabby, there were generally no attractive grounds for recreation, and psychosocial treatment and activity programs were deficient or absent. In general, the only treatment offered was drugs; and it was the advent of the antipsychotic drugs, facilitating control of the florid features of patients' psychosis even when the patients were in grossly inadequate settings, that allowed huge numbers of the mentally ill to be shunted to cheaper nursing-home care. Thus, although the number of patients in US state and county mental hospitals declined from 505,000 in 1963 to 370,000 in 1969, the number of patients with mental disorders in nursing homes increased to such an extent that the total institutionalized population of the mentally ill was actually *higher* in 1969. Mentally ill residents of mental hospitals and nursing homes combined rose from 726,000 in 1963 to 797,000 in 1969. Many patients were elderly but large numbers of younger adults were also transferred to nursing homes. The number of patients under the age of 65 in state and county mental hospitals fell by nearly 100,000 between 1963 and 1969 but the number of mentally ill patients in this age group in nursing home accommodation increased by more than 25,000 during the same period.[19] Ellen Bassuk and Samuel Gerson pointed out, however:

> Untherapeutic though many nursing homes are, living conditions in most of them are at least tolerable. Conditions may be worse for discharged

patients living on their own, without enough money and usually without any possibility of employment. Many of them drift to substandard inner-city housing that is overcrowded, unsafe, dirty and isolated. Often they come together to form a new kind of ghetto subpopulation, a captive market for unscrupulous landlords.[20]

Newspaper reports exposed the impoverished condition of formerly hospitalized patients leading lives of isolation and fear in the community – 100 discharged patients in Washington, DC, without therapeutic rehabilitation programs; 200 ex-patients of Agnews State Hospital in California housed in boarding homes in San Jose with no medical care; 300 to 1,000 patients in rooming houses and hotels in Long Beach, New York, without supervision. A survey of discharged mental patients conducted in 1970 in California's San Mateo County found 32 per cent living in board and care homes.[21] These "small wards in the community" were generally sordid and bare establishments in poor, inner-city areas where theft was rampant. One-third of the chronic mental patients in a large sample of residents of board and care homes in Los Angeles had been robbed or assaulted or both during the previous year.[22] Each such establishment housed more than fifty ex-hospital patients, and sometimes accommodated several hundred.[23] The patients often received no psychiatric treatment other than a supply of drugs and had no employment or worthwhile social activity. A typical boarding home resident, reported California psychiatrists Theodore Van Putten and James Spar,

> spends 8.46 hours of the day in bed, a time limited primarily by the sponsor's continual efforts to keep him out of his bedroom, and 1.46 hours at the dining table. He spends the rest of the day in virtual solitude, either staring vacantly at television (few residents reported having a favorite television show; most were puzzled at the question), or wandering aimlessly around the neighborhood, sometimes stopping for a nap on a lawn or park bench.[24]

Patients who suffered a psychotic relapse were likely to be treated briefly in hospital with drugs and were discharged again to an inadequate setting or to live on the street. As this cycle repeated itself they become known as "revolving-door patients." About half of the patients released from US psychiatric hospitals in the early 1970s were readmitted within a year of discharge.[25] As public mental hospital beds were cut back, it became increasingly difficult for acutely psychotic patients to gain readmission. For example, in 1981 the state hospital in Denver, Colorado – Fort Logan Mental Health Center – had a waiting list for admission of more than 100 adult cases. Since the hospital's discharge rate was around one adult every week or two, patients at the bottom of the waiting list could expect admission within two to four years.

In consequence of the nationwide bed shortage and rapid-discharge policy, many people with psychosis ended up in jail, usually charged with offenses associated with trying to survive on the streets without money – trespass (sleeping in the hallway of a public building) or defrauding an innkeeper (eat and run). Around six to eight per cent of the 147,000 inmates of local jails in the United States in the 1970s were suffering from psychosis.[26] Similarly, eight per cent of a large sample of federal prisoners surveyed in 1969 were diagnosed as suffering from psychosis.[27]

Such was the plight of a substantial proportion of the "deinstitutionalized" mentally ill across the United States. It is scarcely surprising that, as revealed in the last chapter, the overall social functioning of people with schizophrenia did not improve with the introduction of antipsychotic drugs. But in northern Europe, also, the picture changed after the early days of the social psychiatry revolution.

PSYCHIATRIC STAGNATION

In Britain, the number of mental patients admitted to hospital who had "no fixed abode" increased threefold between 1959 and 1964. By 1966, ten per cent of the 30,000 men and women "sleeping rough" in Britain were thought to be suffering from mental illness.[28] More than 20 per cent of the longer-term residents of the Camberwell Reception Centre for the destitute (a converted Victorian workhouse in South London) were considered mentally ill in the early 1970s.[29] At this time, too, concern developed over the increasing numbers of mentally ill criminal offenders who were incarcerated in prison or borstal, though the proportion of prison inmates suffering from schizophrenia was lower in Britain than in the US.[30]

The Social Services Act of 1970 transferred the responsibility for many aspects of community care for the mentally ill away from local health authorities and placed it in the social services departments. Many professionals feel this was not a successful move. In 1976 only 43 per cent of the recommended minimum number of places in hostels and group homes had been established and day facilities were equally scarce. Some local authorities had provided none at all.[31] A survey of the social situation of 190 people with schizophrenia living in the community in Salford in the late 1970s revealed 30 per cent accommodated in slum housing, 16 per cent with inadequate nutrition and 34 per cent who spent all or most of their time doing absolutely nothing. Among more than 100 patients, most suffering from psychosis, in the psychiatric wards and day hospital of the London Borough of Camden on a single day in 1976, one-half were known to have been living alone before admission, nearly a third in transitory accommodation (such as abandoned homes, doss houses and reception centers) or sleeping on the streets; two-thirds were totally unemployed, most of them for more than a year; and more than a third of the inpatients received no visitors. Many of these patients, clearly, had no worthwhile community links, but despite their obvious social deprivation only six per cent of Camden's inpatients were subsequently discharged to any kind of supportive setting, such as a hostel or group home.[32] Such "rehabilitation" was not what the innovative British community psychiatrists of the 1950s had in mind. Hospital conditions also deteriorated in some parts of Britain in the 1970s. Government reports, covering the period from 1976 to 1982, record the widespread existence of overcrowding, understaffing and custodial attitudes to patients throughout mental hospitals in many counties. Instances of cruelty and neglect were documented.[33]

AND NOW

Recent developments in British mental health services still leave room for concern. Only 14 of the 130 hospitals operational in 1975 remain open in 2002.[34] Critics of British community care draw attention to patient neglect and homelessness and point to inadequate funding and poor management. Newspaper reports focus on vagrancy, suicide and the plight of mental patients isolated in bed-sitters, and suggest that community care has turned into community abandonment.[35] The number of homeless people in Britain doubled during the decade leading up to 1992, and the proportion of mentally ill among the swelling homeless population remained constant. Half of the residents of a hostel for homeless women in London in 1991 were found to be suffering from severe mental illness, many exhibiting high levels of active psychotic symptoms.[36] Of the residents of two other hostels for homeless women in inner London in 1986–87, two-thirds were diagnosed as suffering from schizophrenia, few being in contact with treatment services.[37] Nearly a third of the men at a Salvation Army hostel in the late 1980s were suffering from schizophrenia.[38] At two hostels for the homeless in Oxford in the late 1980s, nearly two-thirds of the residents showed evidence of psychosis.[39] The situation may now be improving, however, as the proportion of mentally ill among British homeless men appears to have decreased in the 1990s (see Chapter 8 and Table 8.1).

Few of these homeless mentally ill seem to have spent much time previously in psychiatric hospital.[40] British social psychiatrist Julian Leff concluded, "The answer must lie in the inadequacy of after-care for patients passing through the admission wards."[41] A 1990 study of single homeless people with psychiatric histories revealed that two-thirds had been discharged from the admission ward without any discussion with the staff about where they would live after discharge.[42] The quality of treatment on the admission wards seems to have been compromised. Bed occupancy rates are over 150 per cent in some areas. Violence, sexual harassment and illicit drug and alcohol abuse on the ward are not uncommon. Nurse–patient contact has declined, and rapid staff turnover and low staff morale are frequent problems.[43]

Tom Craig and Philip Timms attribute the increase in the homeless mentally ill to the long-standing failure to provide assertive community care.[44] Though the number of community treatment teams has increased in recent decades, most are too heavily loaded with patients to deliver comprehensive or intensive services. Many teams lack necessary professionals, and most are closed outside office hours and do not provide crisis services or adequate continuity between hospital and community services.[45]

The shortage of acute and medium-term treatment beds coupled with inadequate community services may have led to the dramatic increase in the number of people with mental illness in Britain being incarcerated in prison.[46] In the decades leading up to 1980, the proportion of prisoners suffering from psychosis did not exceed two or three per cent.[47] By 1990 an increase was evident; six per cent of male inmates on remand were determined to suffer from psychosis.[48] "What Sort of Society Offers a Cell, Not Asylum?" intoned the *Guardian* of June 1, 1994.[49] A large government survey of prisoners in England and Wales in 1997 revealed 14 per cent of women prisoners, 7 per cent of sentenced male inmates and 10 per cent of male inmates on pretrial remand to be suffering from psychosis. The proportion of female remand prisoners who were suffering from psychosis was over 20 per cent.[50] Some mentally ill people, it seems, end up in prison because the psychiatric service refuses to provide treatment. Forensic psychiatrist Jeremy Coid reported in the *British Medical Journal* that one in five of the mentally ill men remanded to Winchester prison in 1979–83 was refused treatment by the community service. Most of these men were suffering from schizophrenia.[51] One researcher concluded that "by finding their way into prison, many (mentally ill people) are finding the only care and treatment anyone is prepared to offer them."[52]

Community psychiatric services continue to be grossly inadequate in many parts of the US, especially in the large cities. In Dallas, the caseload for a case manager in a community mental health center is around 300 people with mental illness – nearly ten times the number considered reasonable in better funded areas of the country and 20 times the number established as the standard for adequate treatment of the most severely disturbed patients with psychosis. A 2002 *New York Times* series details the exploitation, neglect and abuse of the thousands of mentally ill people housed in the huge, ill-run, private board and care homes in New York state (see Chapter 8).[53] While there has not been an increase in the proportion of mentally ill among those incarcerated,[54] the massive increase in the total number of people incarcerated in the US means that, overall, more people with mental illness are in jail than before (see Chapter 8).

Nevertheless, while conditions for the mentally ill stagnated or worsened in Britain during the recession of the 1980s, conditions and programs for the mentally ill in the community in the US may have improved overall. The proportion of the mentally ill among the homeless is less now than in the 1970s and early 1980s (see Chapter 8). Federal legislation has been introduced to prevent people with mental illness being placed in nursing homes unless they also suffer from a debilitating physical condition. Other recent federal legislation has curtailed the use of restraints and seclusion in hospitals. Beginning in the late 1970s and early 1980s, the United States developed community treatment approaches that have been adopted as models elsewhere in the world. The American innovations have been driven, to a certain extent, by the development of an important power-bloc – the National Alliance for the Mentally Ill – an advocacy group of relatives of people with mental illness that began to gather strength in the late 1970s. Applying the power-sharing approach implicit in the postwar therapeutic community concept, the psychosocial clubhouse model of rehabilitation (based on Fountain House in New York City) diffused widely in the US and later in other, primarily English-speaking, countries.[55] Assertive community treatment, an approach in which the most disturbed patients with psychosis receive intensive, highly individualized daily attention from case managers who work with small caseloads, had great success in reducing the problem of the revolving-door patient. By 1996, 15 of the 50 US states reported statewide implementation of the assertive community treatment model, and many others were using the model effectively in parts of the state.[56] Since that time, the National Alliance for the Mentally Ill has heavily promoted the further dissemination of the model. Supported employment programs, in which job coaches find jobs in the community for people with mental illness and provide them with on-the-job training and ongoing support, has led, in parts of the United States, to dramatic improvements in the rate of employment.[57] Whereas Britain taught the world how to practice community psychiatry in the 1950s and 1960s, in the last two decades of the twentieth century, the US assumed some of the teaching role.

Why did the deinstitutionalization movement go sour in Britain? Why did it start out so bitter in the United States and turn sweeter later? Or, phrasing the questions differently, why was there a golden era of active social and community psychiatry in northern Europe in the immediate post-war years but little of note in the United States until the last years of the twentieth century?

OUTDOOR RELIEF

Sociologist Andrew Scull in his book, *Decarceration*, attributes the motivating force for the British and American deinsitutionalization movement to the postwar development of welfare programs that enabled the indigent and the disabled to be maintained more cheaply outside an institution.[58] This form of support, known to the Victorians as "outdoor relief," had been drastically reduced in the mid-nineteenth century. The twentieth-century Great Depression increased the pressure for a more comprehensive relief of poverty in the industrial nations, and both Britain and America instituted social-insurance schemes for the totally and permanently disabled in the five years following the Second World War.[59] Scull's analysis has considerable merit. Ödegard made a similar observation concerning Norway's

> new and improved pension system for persons incapacitated by illness, which was introduced in 1960 and which includes psychotic invalids . . . This has made possible the discharge of many psychotic invalids and is probably the main reason why the rates of discharge as 'not cured' did not show any great increase until after 1960.[60]

It is also clear, as Andrew Scull has argued, that the American switch to the use of nursing homes was attributable to the health-insurance structure. The state governments are responsible for the cost of maintaining patients in state mental hospitals, but care provided in a private nursing home may be billed to Medicaid (for the indigent) or Medicare (for the elderly and some indigent). Since the federal government pays a large part of these insurance bills, it rapidly became apparent to state legislators after the inception of these programs in 1965 that they could cut the state budget by transferring mental patients to private-sector care.

Reference to disability pensions and health-insurance schemes, however, does not answer all the questions about the early stages of deinstitutionalization. Looking at disability payments, one would have predicted, for example, a late onset for community care in Norway, and an earlier, roughly simultaneous timing in Britain and America. To understand why the post-war social psychiatry revolution took place in northern Europe and not America, and why it subsequently stagnated in Britain, it is necessary to study other political factors.

POLITICS AND INSTITUTIONS

Broadly speaking one can set down four possible political motives for a deinstitutional trend:

- cost savings;
- a humanitarian concern for the welfare, liberty and human rights of the institutional inmates that outweighs the fear of their liability to the community;
- a need to put the buildings to a new purpose;
- a need to put the inmates to a new purpose.

Which elements are applicable to postwar psychiatric deinstitutionalization?

Cost saving, as discussed above, has clearly been an important factor behind the emptying of psychiatric institutions, but it does not explain the differences in the characteristics of the process between countries.

Humanitarian concerns, while usually part of the rhetoric associated with changes in institutional use, are probably never sufficient cause for such changes. The welfare of the mentally ill was the espoused reason for the nineteenth-century movement to institutionalize massive numbers of the insane and of the reverse trend after the Second World War. The humanitarian concerns of the advocates of deinstitutionalization during the late nineteenth and early twentieth centuries, however, were never sufficient to halt the expansion of hospital care. Why did their views suddenly become effective after the Second World War? Furthermore, humanitarian considerations scarcely account for the widespread practice in the US, after deinstitutionalization, of maintaining people with psychosis in poverty and in degrading housing or institutional environments in the community, largely without proper care and treatment. On the contrary, it seems more probable that the philosophy of care is a secondary phenomenon, itself shaped by the contemporary patterns of institutional use.

The conversion of old institutions to new purposes historically has been very common. Seventeenth-century French leper hospitals became houses of correction,[61] a nineteenth-century British jail was converted into an insane asylum[62] and Victorian infirmaries and workhouses in the twentieth century became general hospitals or reception centers for the destitute. There is no indication, though, that the mentally ill were discharged from mental hospitals after the Second World War to make way for some urgent new function for the buildings. Many of the old hospital wards were closed and left vacant. More urgent, perhaps, was the need to avoid the capital outlay required to keep the old, Victorian institutions functional.

We must look, then to a *change in the perceived value of the institutional inmates* themselves to find the stimulus for deinstitutionalization.

LABOR DYNAMICS

So great was the labor shortage in postwar Britain that *The Times* of January 1947 called for the selective immigration of half a million foreign workers, and economist Lionel Robbins warned that 100,000 foreigners should be recruited to work in the coal mines if the country was not "to lapse into a position of impotence and economic chaos." The government launched an attack on non-productive "spivs and drones," and the *Daily Mail* argued that if Scotland Yard were used "to help to round up the work dodgers" one-and-a-half million workers could be added to the labor force. By September of that year the Cabinet was discussing the possibility of banning the football pools to force the redeployment of the women who processed the coupons into the labor-starved textile industry.[63]

A sustained, peacetime labor shortage of these dimensions had not been seen in Britain, or in those other northern European nations that experienced the phenomenon, since employment records began or, quite probably, since the beginning of the Industrial Revolution. It seems reasonable to suppose that such a demand for labor, extraordinary also by recent Western standards, was a major stimulus to the effective rehabilitation of the mentally ill. Contemporary observers confirm this view. British social psychiatrist David Clark identified as major factors that promoted the European Open Door Movement and deinstitutionalization: "the development of welfare states where the disabled (including the psychiatrically crippled) were supported in their homes, [and] the development of full employment (in northern Europe at least) creating a demand for the labour of impaired people."[64] Similarly, Professor Ödegard reported of Norway: "Since the war there has mostly been a certain degree of over-employment, and it has been possible for hospitals to discharge to an independent existence even patients with a borderline working capacity and a questionable social adjustment."[65] In Massachusetts, one of the few parts of the United States where the mental hospital population began to diminish before antipsychotic drugs were introduced, the decline in hospital use was also seen to be associated with a vigorous demand for labor.[66]

The strategic importance of the rehabilitation of large numbers of the mentally ill should not be underestimated. Between the Great Depression and the 1950s the proportion of people with schizophrenia in Britain who were employed may have increased by as much as 20 percentage points; this estimate is suggested by the improvement in the social recovery rate of people with schizophrenia in Britain as revealed in the previous chapter. Since 34 people in every 10,000 of the population suffered from schizophrenia, according to a postwar prevalence study conducted in London,[67] one can estimate that the rehabilitation of these people alone may have added 30,000 workers to the British labor force.

A number of other reports confirmed that rehabilitation efforts for the disabled are closely related to the demand for labor. The Heller Committee survey of permanently disabled workers in the San Francisco Bay area in 1942 and 1943 found that wartime labor conditions left virtually none of the disabled unemployed.[68] British and American studies show that the employment of the developmentally disabled increased from around 40 per cent in the Great Depression to 80–90 per cent during and after the Second World War.[69] Vocational rehabilitation activities were also very highly developed in the full-employment conditions of the Eastern Bloc countries before the dissolution of communism.[70]

Recent economic changes in the United States can also illustrate the effect of the labor market on the rehabilitation of the mentally ill. When unemployment dropped to less than two per cent (essentially full employment) in Boulder County, Colorado, in 2000, the rate of stable employment of people with psychotic illness increased from around 15 per cent a few years before to 50 per cent. Vocational rehabilitation services for people with mental illness were stepped up to keep pace with the job placement opportunities.[71]

Labor dynamics, then, may explain many features of the deinstitutionalization movement and subsequent developments in community psychiatry. Before the introduction of the antipsychotic drugs, postwar full employment in northern Europe called for the rehabilitation of the marginally employable mentally ill, and stimulated the development of more therapeutic styles of hospital care and a policy of early discharge. The move to milieu therapy and community treatment was delayed in the United States, where full employment did not generally develop. The introduction of disability pension schemes made possible the discharge of patients in the absence of employment opportunities, and the advent of the antipsychotic drugs allowed the control of symptoms in patients placed in inadequate and stressful settings. These changes, particularly in the United States, led to a different style of community management – the transfer of patients to low-cost placements, often without genuine attempts at making patients productive, valued and integrated members of society.

The steep rise in unemployment in Britain after the 1960s may go a long way to explain the subsequent stagnation in British psychiatric rehabilitation. The relatively better-functioning US economy of recent decades, leading to areas of labor shortage in the 1990s, may explain the successful expansion of American psychiatric community treatment and rehabilitation in the later years of the century.

INTERNATIONAL COMPARISONS

The countries that led in the postwar revolution in social psychiatry were, according to Maxwell Jones,[72] Britain, the Netherlands, Norway and Switzerland. Table 4.2 lists postwar unemployment statistics for these countries and other parts of Europe and North America; the unemployment figures have been adjusted[73] to make them reasonably comparable. The four countries that were progressive in psychiatry at that time are among those with low unemployment rates.

Countries, like the United States and Italy, where the rehabilitative movement was delayed, had higher rates of unemployment. Open-door policies and the deinstitutionalization movement did not reach Italian mental hospitals until the 1960s, arriving in the wake of an economic boom that brought many changes in the social and political climate.[74] Italian psychiatrist Franco Basaglia introduced sweeping innovations, after 1961, in the mental hospitals

Table 4.2 Unemployment rates in northern Europe and North America

	High unemployment						Low unemployment					
	Belgium	Denmark	Germany	Italy	Canada	USA	France	Netherlands	Norway	Sweden	Switzerland	UK
1950	6.3	4.1	7.2	8.7	3.6	5.2	1.4	2.0	2.7	1.7	0.5	2.5
1951	5.7	4.5	6.4	9.2	2.4	3.2	1.3	2.4	3.6	1.6	0.2	2.2
1952	6.8	5.9	6.1	9.8	2.9	2.9	1.3	3.5	2.4	1.7	0.3	2.9
1953	6.8	4.4	5.5	10.2	2.9	2.8	1.6	2.5	3.3	1.9	0.3	2.6
1954	6.2	3.8	5.2	8.7	4.5	5.3	1.6	1.8	2.2	1.8	0.2	2.3
1955	4.7	4.7	3.8	7.5	4.3	4.2	1.5	1.3	2.5	1.8	0.1	2.1

Sources: All unemployment statistics, except those for Norway, have been adjusted to render them comparable, and are taken from Maddison, A., *Economic Growth in the West*, New York: Twentieth Century Fund, 1964, p. 220. Unadjusted figures for Norway are taken from Mitchell, B.R., *European Historical Statistics 1750–1970*, abridged edn., New York: Columbia University Press, 1978, p. 68.

in Gorizia and then Trieste, as unemployment dropped to a postwar low. The subsequent national psychiatric reforms embodied in law 180 (enacted with the support of both the Italian communist party and the right wing) led to a dramatic decrease in the numbers of mentally ill people in hospital. The reforms were implemented with most success in the industrial north of the country where the labor shortage was most apparent.[75]

The number of mental hospital beds in use varies substantially from one industrial nation to another. Sweden, in 1974, provided one psychiatric hospital bed for 250 citizens, for example, whereas in Poland one psychiatric bed served more than 800. A number of economic and political factors might be expected to influence mental hospital use and, if the demand for labor was an important stimulus to deinstitutionalization, then unemployment could prove to be one such influence on psychiatric hospital use. In the mid-1960s, in fact, industrial nations with higher unemployment rates tended to use more mental hospital beds (see Table 4.3). A multiple regression analysis shows that the average national unemployment over a five-year period accounted for 40 per cent of the variance in the provision of psychiatric beds in 1965 in the nine Western industrial nations for which comparable statistics are available (see Table 4.4).[76] This relationship was independent of a number of other economic and demographic variables. After taking into account the influence of per capita gross national product, infant mortality (as an indicator of the national level of health and welfare provisions) and the proportion of elderly in the population, unemployment accounted for 47 per cent of the variance in the use of mental hospital beds. Over the next decade, however, the relationship between mental hospital use and unemployment disappeared. As Table 4.4 shows, by 1974 a combination of two factors – the national infant mortality rate and the proportion of the population over age 65 – predicted 71 per cent of the variance in mental hospital beds provided; unemployment accounted for only 1 per cent of the variance.

The link between unemployment and mental hospital use in 1965 suggests that, until that time, the availability of work may have acted as a control on hospital discharge rates. The correlation disappeared after the 1960s because psychiatric hospital populations continued to shrink in Australia, Canada and the United States in the absence of improvements in employment. Elsewhere mental hospital use increased or remained relatively constant. This divergence may be attributed to the degree to which each country exercised the option, offered by disability benefits and drugs, to maintain mentally ill people in the community regardless of the availability of employment. In addition, in the United States the advent of Medicaid in 1965 led to massive reductions in mental hospital beds as patients were transferred to nursing homes. No longer was it essential that mental hospitals control and sustain a large segment of the surplus population. Their use became, to a greater degree, a matter of social policy. The extent of psychiatric institutional care now appeared to be largely a reflection of two factors. One was the national,

Table 4.3 Psychiatric hospital beds per 10,000 of the general population, average annual unemployment rates over five-year periods, infant mortality per 1,000 live births, general population over age 65 and per capita gross national product in 1979 US dollars

	1965					1974				
	Psychiatric hospital beds	Average annual unemployment (%) 1961–5[b]	Infant mortality	Elderly population %	Per capita GNP	Psychiatric hospital beds	Average annual unemployment (%) 1970–4[b]	Infant mortality	Elderly population %	Per capita GNP
Western industrial nations										
Japan	13.3	1.3	18.5	6.4	3,633	18.4	1.3	10.8	8.0	7,425
West Germany	17.7	0.5	23.9	12.0	7,908	17.8	1.0	21.1	14.0	10,681
France	20.5	1.5	21.9	12.2	6,304	–	2.8	14.7	13.0	9,508
Italy	22.4	2.9	35.6	9.9	3,568	20.9	3.2	22.6	12.0	5,243
Australia	27.1	2.1	18.5	8.4	5,801	20.7	2.2	16.1	9.0	7,874
UK	28.5[a]	2.6	19.0[a]	12.3	5,348	31.9[a]	3.3	16.3[a]	14.0	7,874
USA	31.1	5.7	24.7	9.5	7,873	14.2	5.4	16.7	11.0	6,529
Sweden	35.4	1.5	13.3	12.8	9,374	40.5	2.3	9.2	15.0	9,577
Canada	35.9	5.4	23.6	7.6	6,070	21.8	5.8	15.0	8.0	11,835
Centrally planned economies										
Hungary	2.4	–	38.8	10.2	2,335	–	–	34.3	13.0	3,039
Romania	3.1	–	44.1	7.6	1,824	7.0	–	35.0	9.0	2,804
Bulgaria	4.2	–	30.8	8.5	1,866	–	–	25.5	11.0	2,645
USSR	9.9	–	27.6	7.3	3,354	–	–	27.7	9.0	4,913
Czechoslovakia	11.7	–	25.5	9.9	3,567	11.3	–	20.4	12.0	4,692
East Germany	18.2	–	24.8	14.6	3,412	18.9	–	15.9	16.0	4,558
Poland	–	–	41.7	7.0	2,042	12.1	–	23.7	10.0	3,069

Sources: Psychiatric hospital beds (except USSR) and infant mortality: World Health Organisation, *World Health Statistics Annuals, 1964 to 1977*, vols I, III, Geneva: 1967–77; USSR psychiatric hospital beds (1962 figure): Field, M.G. and Aronson, J., "Soviet community mental health services and work therapy," *Community Mental Health Journal*, I: 81–90, 1965; Unemployment: Sorrentino, C., "Unemployment in international perspective," in B. Showler and A. Sinfield (eds), *The Workless State*, Oxford: Martin Robertson, 1980; Elderly population: World Bank, *World Tables*, 2nd edn, Baltimore: Johns Hopkins University Press, 1980; Per capita GNP: CIA National Foreign Assessment Center, *Handbook of Economic Statistics 1980*, Washington, DC: US Government Printing Office, 1980.

Notes: [a] Figure for England and Wales.
[b] Unemployment statistics are adjusted to US concepts to render them comparable.

Table 4.4 Variance in psychiatric hospital beds provided in nine Western industrial countries accounted for by different social indicators

		% of variance accounted for	Cumulative % of variance
1965	(N=9)		
	Unemployment	40	40
	GNP	25	64*
	Infant mortality	5	70
	Elderly in population	6	75
1965:	Entering unemployment as the last step (N=9)		
	GNP	26	26
	Infant mortality	0	26
	Elderly in population	3	28
	Unemployment	47*	75
1968	(N=9)		
	GNP	39	39
	Unemployment	24	63*
	Infant mortality	9	72
	Elderly in population	3	75
1971	(N=9)		
	GNP	37	37
	Unemployment	10	47
	Infant mortality	10	57
	Elderly in population	8	65
1974	(N=8)		
	Elderly in population	34	34
	Infant mortality	36	71*
	GNP	8	79
	Unemployment	1	80

* Significant at the .05 level (two-tailed test).
Note: Variance statistics were obtained by a stepwise multiple-regression method.

political commitment to the quality and universality of health and welfare provisions (of which infant mortality is an indicator). The other, since the antipsychotic drugs are of little benefit in the care of senile organic psychosis, was the proportion of the elderly in the general population.

Deinstitutionalization, in some circumstances a sign of progressive efforts towards community care and rehabilitation of the mentally ill, may elsewhere have indicated the opposite – abrogation of responsibility for the welfare of a segment of the poor. In the United States in the 1970s, where health and welfare provisions for the destitute were not well developed, the small numbers of available mental hospital beds represented a refusal to provide adequate psychiatric treatment for the indigent mentally ill. In Sweden, on the other hand, a political commitment to adequate health and welfare provisions coupled with the existence of a large elderly population led to a substantially greater use of mental hospitals. Each of the other Scandinavian countries, like Sweden, maintained comprehensive health and welfare services, low infant mortality rates and substantial numbers of psychiatric hospital beds. Of these four countries Denmark and Norway, with the greatest labor shortages until the mid-1970s, preserved relatively low rates of mental hospital use and the most highly developed community treatment programs.[77]

It is evident from the figures in Table 4.3 that it was not only the labor shortage in the Eastern Bloc countries in the 1970s that led to their minimal use of psychiatric institutions but also the underdevelopment of their health services in general (witness their high infant mortality rates) and the low proportion of the elderly in the general population. Nevertheless, we know that the labor shortage in these countries, particularly Russia and Poland, at that time led to a very great emphasis on work therapy, intensive community rehabilitation efforts, greater acceptance of the mentally ill in the community and the workplace and efforts to keep the elderly productive.[78]

Full employment, then, may no longer be a major factor determining the size of mental hospital populations but it may be an important influence on the characteristics of community treatment and the adequacy of rehabilitative efforts. Where the surplus population is large, the conditions established for the person with a psychotic illness tend to be least conducive to his or her recovery. Where the labor of the marginally productive is in demand, there shall we find the most highly developed community treatment programs and the most humane hospital conditions. We shall see to what extent these factors influence the course of schizophrenia.

SUMMARY

- The rate of mental hospital occupancy as a proportion of the general United States population was declining before the introduction of the antipsychotic drugs.
- Revolutionary changes in hospital and community psychiatry in northern Europe preceded the introduction of antipsychotic drugs treatment.
- The discharge rates from progressive hospitals, particularly in northern Europe, were not improved by the arrival of the antipsychotic drugs.
- The delay in the introduction of new social and community psychiatry techniques to the United States created the impression there that drug treatment was vital to community care.
- Deinstitutionalization in the United States relied heavily on the use of drugs and led to the placement of large numbers of the mentally ill in low-cost, inadequate settings.
- Community care for the mentally ill in Britain stagnated and declined after the 1960s.

- Community treatment methods in the United States improved in the 1980s and 1990s.
- The main political and economic driving forces to deinstitutionalization were (a) cost-saving and (b) in northern Europe, the postwar demand for labor.
- Comparing Western industrial nations in 1965, the number of mental hospital beds in each country was correlated with the national unemployment rate.
- A decade later, mental hospital use appeared to be less influenced by the labor market and more affected by national health and welfare policy.
- The unemployment rate may still influence the adequacy of community rehabilitative efforts.

Chapter 5

Madness and the Industrial Revolution

In the last decade of the eighteenth century a humane method of treating the mentally ill sprang into being in Europe, within a few years came to be adopted in many parts of the civilized world, and after half a century or so faded away. It left in its place restrictive patterns of institutional care of which few people in psychiatry are proud but which persisted until the latter half of the twentieth century. Many psychiatrists have remarked on the common features of moral treatment (as the early movement was called) and the post-Second World War social psychiatry revolution. Were the two movements indeed similar and, if so, could they have been stimulated by similar political and economic conditions? If not, why did moral treatment come into being when it did? The use of moral management was accompanied by claims of excellent recovery rates in mental illness. Were these claims accurate? If so, why were the methods abandoned and what light does the episode throw on the conventional approach to the history of medicine which shows us always progressing to higher levels of technical achievement through a process of scientific discovery?

THE YORK RETREAT

> This house is situated a mile from York in the midst of a fertile and smiling countryside; it is not at all the idea of a prison that it suggests, but rather that of a large farm; it is surrounded by a great walled garden. No bars, no grilles on the windows.[1]

So runs the description of the York Retreat given by a Swiss visitor in 1798. The name, "Retreat," was significant; not a "hospital" nor an "asylum" but "a quiet haven in which the shattered bark might find the means of reparation or safety."[2] Within this house was developing a mode of care for the mentally ill that was to prove as revolutionary as Pinel's action in striking the chains from the inmates of Bicêtre in 1793.

Like Pinel's work, the York Retreat was a reaction against the inhumanity of the contemporary treatment of the insane. It was founded in 1792 and opened in 1796 by the Society of Friends after one of their members, Hannah Mills, died in the York Asylum under circumstances that suggested neglect or ill treatment. Designed for 30 patients and primarily made available to Quakers, the cost of treatment at the York Retreat ranged from eight to fifteen shillings a week. Accommodation for personal servants was provided at a further fee. The establishment was clearly not intended to be for the poor.

Under the direction of William Tuke, a 60-year-old tea and coffee merchant, a style of non-medical care was developed that, like Pinel's approach, came to be called moral treatment. Believing that most deranged people could be rational if not provoked by harsh treatment or cruelty, the Tukes encouraged the exercise of patients' self-control as an alternative to the use of external restraint. Punishment for inappropriate behavior was avoided, but minor privileges were awarded to those who conformed to the attendants' wishes. Chains were never used and straight waistcoats rarely, and then only to prevent a patient hurting himself or herself or other residents. The iron sashes of the windows were disguised to look like wood. Patients were expected to dress in their best clothes and take part in all usual social activities – tea parties, reading, writing, sewing and gardening. Work was felt to be essential in fostering patients' self-control and self-esteem. Drugs were seldom used, and exercise, warm baths and a generous diet of "meat, bread and good porter" were felt to be most useful in quieting patients and ensuring good sleep.[3]

BEFORE MORAL TREATMENT

The revolutionary nature of moral treatment at the York Retreat becomes evident when it is set against conventional care of the time. At the nearby York Asylum, where Hannah Mills had died, abuses were exposed by investigations conducted some years after the opening of the Retreat. "Flogging and cudgelling" were routine, and patients were "verminous and filthy."[4] Behind a partly hidden door, a visitor in 1814 discovered a series of small cells

> in a very horrid and filthy condition ... the walls were daubed with excrement; the air-holes, of which there was one in each cell, were partly filled with it.

Upstairs he found a room

> twelve feet by seven feet ten inches, in which there were thirteen women who, [the keeper] told me, had all come out of those cells that morning. ... I became very sick, and could not remain longer in the room. I vomited.[5]

Charles Dickens characterized asylum care of this period as follows:

> Coercion for the outward man, and rabid physicking for the inward man, were the specifics for lunacy. Chains, straw, filthy solitude, darkness, and starvation; jalap, syrup of buckthorn, tartarised antimony, and ipecacuanha administered every spring and fall in fabulous doses to every patient, whether well or ill; spinning in whirligigs, corporal punishment, gagging, "continued intoxication"; nothing was too wildly extravagant, nothing too monstrously cruel to be prescribed by mad-doctors.

Lest we should consider that these practices were enforced through malice, he continues:

> In other respects these physicians were grave men, of mild dispositions, and – in their ample-flapped, ample-cuffed coats, with a certain gravity and air of state in the skirts; with their large buttons and gold-headed canes, their hair-powder and ruffles – were men of benevolent aspects.[6]

Frank abuses aside (and psychiatrist William Parry-Jones[7] argues that these may well have been overemphasized by historians), Dickens' point is well taken. We should not assume that the eighteenth-century mad-doctors were morally degenerate; chains and flogging were not necessarily maliciously intended. Even George III during his bouts of insanity was chained, beaten, starved and intimidated with threats.[8] The management techniques were those of animal trainers because the insane were regarded as bestial. At the Bicêtre in Paris and the Bethlem Hospital in London, the inmates were exhibited to the public, for a fee, like zoo creatures.[9] The insane were left naked in the cold and damp because they were believed to possess inhuman resistance to the effects of the elements.[10] Both Andrew Scull and French philosopher Michel Foucault have emphasized that the introduction of moral treatment involved a redefinition of the madman's condition from the essence of bestiality to a degree of human rationality.[11] Now the lunatic becomes a fractious child. As the Swiss doctor commented in the visitors' book at the Retreat:

> In moral treatment, one does not consider the insane to be completely deprived of reason, out of reach of the influence of fear, hope, affection and honour. Rather one regards them, it seems, like children who have too much energy, and who put it to dangerous uses.[12]

In this redefinition lay the revolutionary impact of moral management.

THE ORIGINS OF MORAL TREATMENT

Curiously enough, this fundamentally new approach was not only introduced simultaneously by Pinel and Tuke, but similar humane methods of patient care also sprang into being independently at the same time in other parts of Europe. In Florence, Vicenzo Chiarugi, the physician in charge of the newly open Hospital Bonifacio, published regulations for patient care, in 1789, which eliminated the use of physical force or any type of restraint except for the occasional use of the straightjacket. He specified:

> It is a supreme moral duty and medical obligation to respect the insane individual as a person.[13]

Similarly, Joseph Daquin, the physician in charge of the institution at Chambéry in the Savoy region (an independent duchy situated between France and Italy) published, in 1791, a treatise advocating humane care for the mentally ill.[14] Around the same time, Parisian physician and philosopher Georges Cabanis, who arranged Pinel's appointment to the Bicêtre, proposed improved treatment methods for the insane.[15] Physician John Ferriar at the Manchester Lunatic Hospital, although administering such standard medical remedies as blood-letting, blistering and purging,[16] expressed the opinion, in 1795 (the year before the Retreat opened), that the primary goal of treatment lay in "creating a habit of self-restraint," not through coercion, but by "the management of hope and apprehension, . . . small favours, the show of confidence, and apparent distinction."[17]

For each of these independent innovations, local causes may be found. Psychiatric historian George Mora, for example, suggests that Pinel and the French physicians, in liberating the insane, were reflecting the spirit of freedom and equality of the French Revolution (1789–99); Chiarugi's radical reforms were a product of the revolutionary political economic reforms of the rule of the Grand Duke Peter Leopold (1747–92); the philosophy of the York Retreat was based on the contemporary British bourgeois ideal of the family.[18] But these individual influences fail to explain the simultaneous but independent origin of the same notion within a five-year period in different parts of Europe.

To call the phenomenon "a striking example of *zeitgeist* in the history of psychiatry"[19] is to say nothing about causes. To see it as a reflection of the Enlightenment's eighteenth-century ideals of human dignity, worth and freedom is to provide a unifying concept but still only fits one ideology within the broader framework of another. If we examine the political and economic underpinning of Enlightenment thinking, however, we may be in a better position to understand why moral treatment occurred when and where it did. British historian, Eric Hobsbawn, has this to say about the philosophy of the Age of Reason:

The Great Encyclopaedia of Diderot and d'Alembert was not merely a compendium of progressive social and political thought, but of techno-logical and scientific progress. For indeed the conviction of the progress of human knowledge, rationality, wealth, civilization, and control over nature with which the eighteenth century was deeply imbued, the "Enlightenment," drew its strength primarily from the evident progress of production, trade, and the economic and scientific rationality believed to be associated inevitably with both.[20]

Revolutionary to the old social and political order, the Enlightenment ideas were central to the capitalist transformation of production. Leaving aside, for the moment, the American Revolution (1776–83), the culmin-ation of eighteenth-century Enlightenment philosophy and its associated political, economic and technological changes was (what Hobsbawm refers to as) the "dual revolution."[21] This comprised the French Revolution of 1789 and the contemporaneous British Industrial Revolution (which Hobsbawm dates from the 1780s, when the British economy became "airborne"[22]).

"It is significant," writes Hobsbawm,

> that the two chief centres of the [Enlightenment] ideology were also those of the dual revolution, France and England. . . . A secular, rational-ist and progressive individualism dominated 'enlightened' thought. To set the individual free from the shackles that fettered him was its chief object. . . . Liberty, equality and (it followed) the fraternity of all men were its slogans.[23]

Enlightenment ideas, then, gave the French Revolution its slogan, the deter-mined capitalist his individualism, and the innovators of moral treatment their philosophical base. Beyond France and England, the sites of the origin of the humane treatment methods were also centers of Enlightenment ideo-logy and progressive politics. Savoy, culturally linked to France, instituted enlightened peasant liberation shortly before the French Revolution;[24] and Chiarugi in Florence was under the influence of one of the most remarkable reforming princes of the eighteenth century, Grand Duke Leopold of Tus-cany, a man strongly influenced by Enlightenment ideas. Moral treatment, moreover, was most avidly adopted by another enlightened nation – post-revolutionary, industrializing America.

When moral treatment, then, set the insane "free from the shackles," the movement was a component of the dual revolution that shook the Western world. This is most compellingly revealed in the image of Pinel, at the height of the French revolution, striking the chains from the insane of Bicêtre and La Salpêtrière. But the essential connection between the Industrial Revolution and the new methods of managing the insane can, similarly, be demonstrated. Central to an understanding of the process are the changes that were taking place in the deployment of labor.

THE GROWTH OF WAGE LABOR

In 1780, on the eve of the dual revolution, France and Britain were the two economic giants of Europe. In volume of trade they were nearly equal. France's foreign trade had increased fourfold in 60 years and her colonial system in some areas was stronger than that of the British.[25] Each of these countries, like the rest of Europe, was experiencing staggering population growth. In the half-century after 1750 the population of France rose by 22 per cent, from 22 million to nearly 27 million; in the United Kingdom population increased 36 per cent, from 10 million to 16 million.[26] In each of the two countries the conditions of the rural poor were harsh and worsening. The great majority of French peasants were landless or had insufficient holdings, oppressed by feudal dues, tithes, taxes and inflation.[27] In Britain, the enclosure of common lands in the eighteenth century deprived cottagers of their subsistence and drove increasing numbers into agricultural wage labor that provided meager and intermittent compensation. The result was destitution for many and an increase in applications for poor relief. Taxes for relief – the poor rate – more than tripled between 1760 and 1801 in Britain, and nearly equaled the entire cost of English national government, excluding the army and navy.[28]

Holding back the onset of the Industrial Revolution, argues British historian T.S. Ashton, were social resistance to change and the lack of skill and adaptability of the workers.[29] But as the population grew, the mass of the landless poor swelled and the ranks of beggars, vagrants and unemployed increased, the diversion of laboring men, women and children into industrial wage work became possible. "It was not the least of the achievements of the Industrial Revolution," writes Ashton, "that it drew into the economic system part of that legion of the lost, and that it turned many of the irregulars into efficient, if over-regimented, members of an industrial army."[30] In France, by way of contrast, the Revolution so far improved the condition of the peasants that the flow of "landless free labourers merely trickled into the cities" and the "capitalist transformation . . . was slowed to a crawl."[31]

Some of the "irregulars" in Britain, were less readily "regimented" than others – the insane among them. What was to be done with those who would not, or could not, work? In striving to hold down the cost of poor relief the policy makers of the early Industrial Revolution became obsessed with the need to force "the very great number of lazy People to maintain themselves by their own Industry." Obligating applicants for relief "to submit to the Confinement and Labour of the Workhouse."[32] was one such measure. The number of psychotic and mentally deficient people confined in poorhouses in

England and Wales, however, became considerable – 4,000–5,000 by 1789, estimates Kathleen Jones.[33] Many more were confined for vagrancy in jails and Bridewells (houses of correction), and others were maintained on outdoor relief.[34] Hospitals and asylums were few. Bethlem in London had existed since the twelfth century, and two hospitals were opened through voluntary public subscription in the 1750s – the Manchester Lunatic Hospital and St Luke's in London. In most areas, however, those lunatics who were unmanageable in workhouses and jails were transferred, at public expense, to private madhouses. The number of these private establishments was increasing, and 30–40 licensed houses existed at the end of the eighteenth century.[35] The York Retreat was one such.

THE ASYLUM MOVEMENT

Public responsibility for the care of pauper lunatics could not be avoided, and indeed it became a basic requisite in shaping the new wage labor force (as Andrew Scull pointed out in his book on this theme, *Museums of Madness*[36]). To separate the employable from the unemployable was essential to the rationalization of poor relief. The able-bodied should not be encouraged to be idle, but the incapacitated had to be accommodated. In an effort to reduce the bill for the care of pauper lunatics in private madhouses, the British County Asylum Act of 1808 recommended the establishment of public specialty hospitals for the insane. The first county asylums to open were in rural districts where pauperism was severe and subsistence farming declining.[37]

Throughout Europe, moral treatment was intimately tied to the development of the new specialty establishments for lunatics. The York Retreat was one of a growing number of private madhouses, and its methods were copied, to a limited degree, by the new county asylums. Bicêtre had become a central institution for the insane alone, only one year before Pinel struck off the fetters. La Salpêtrière was converted to that purpose in the same year. The miscellany of the poor, who had previously been confined there, was released by the revolutionary government "in order to distribute it to the points where the labor force was rarest."[38] Criminals, henceforth, were to be housed separately from lunatics.[39] Chiarugi's humane methods were introduced in a newly erected hospital for the insane in Florence. And in the United States, as the first wave of hospitals for the insane began to be opened, moral treatment was the style of management that the new superintendents studied and aimed to establish in their institutions.

REHABILITATION AND INSTITUTIONALIZATION

One of the attractions of moral treatment was its curative and rehabilitative emphasis. If patients could be cured and discharged to support themselves, they would cease to be a drain on the public purse. The proprietor of the private Whitchurch Asylum in Herefordshire, for example, played up this point in an advertising handbill. Arguing that patients admitted to his establishment recovered in a matter of days, compared with months and years for a cure in the local county asylums, he estimated that the cost of a cure in his private licensed house was a fraction of the cost in the public asylums.[40] Furthermore, the emphasis in moral management on hard work and self-discipline, as Scull has pointed out, reflected the same attitudes required in shaping the new industrial labor force.[41]

Despite the rehabilitative emphasis in moral treatment, however, the increase in asylum care was rapid. With the growth of wage work and the existence of a large, cheap supply of labor, the marginally functional insane were at a considerable disadvantage. Many of those who might have been fairly productive in working subsistence smallholdings were now unemployable. Labor mobility, long working hours and poverty made it harder for families to support their disabled members at home.[42]

When outdoor relief expenditure was severely restricted in the mid-nineteenth century there was a commensurate increase in the outlay on lunatic asylums and workhouses.[43] The proportion of the population of England and Wales officially identified as insane (including those in workhouses and the community, but largely comprising asylum inmates) grew dramatically during the moral treatment era and the period of establishment of county asylums. In 1807, the official count was 2.3 insane people per 10,000 population; by the time moral treatment had faded away in 1870, there were officially 24.3 per 10,000. Nearly all of the increase (at least after 1844 when the available figures allow a distinction to be made) is in the number of pauper lunatics; the number of private patients remained remarkably small and constant throughout the nineteenth century.[44]

There was clearly a growth in the recognition and confinement of the insane, but did the Industrial Revolution also spawn an actual increase in the occurrence of insanity? Contemporary opinion was divided on this question, the majority arguing that the increase was more apparent than real. As we shall see in Chapter 9, however, there is a distinct possibility that psychosis, and particularly schizophrenia, was indeed becoming more prevalent as the nineteenth century advanced.

MORAL TREATMENT FOR THE POOR

The treatment methods of the moral-management advocates and of the twentieth-century pioneers of social psychiatry were very similar (see Table 5.1); so, too, was the political function of the movements they created. Just as the post-Second World War social psychiatry revolution legitimized deinstitutionalization, so moral treatment legitimized the growth of institutional care in the nineteenth century. In each case, the ideology of a treatment approach, initially humane and directed towards the patients' benefit, became subtly distorted and was used to serve political ends that were not necessarily in the patients' interests. After the Second World War, the effort to rehabilitate patients to decent living conditions and a useful role in the community became translated into a rush to dump patients on the street and in nursing homes in order to save money. Similarly, Samuel Tuke's *Description of the Retreat*, published in 1813, encouraged reformers in the belief that asylums could be curative and hastened the expansion of the county asylum system. Moral treatment, as it was offered to paupers in the public asylums, however, bore relatively little resemblance to moral treatment as it was developed for the middle-class clientele of the York Retreat.

At the Retreat, seven staff cared for thirty patients, and, in addition, personal servants lived on the premises. In the county asylums, the generally accepted ratio was one keeper to thirty patients.[45] The early asylums were overcrowded and staffed by unqualified and untrained keepers. Despite the

Table 5.1 Moral treatment and the post-Second World War social psychiatry revolution compared

Moral treatment	Post-Second World War social psychiatry revolution
Non-restraint	Non-restraint
Non-confinement	Open door
Self-control emphasized	Therapeutic community
Privileges – not punishment	Positive reinforcement
Small treatment settings	Small units
Homelike environment	Less barren wards
Warm baths and generous diet	Patient comforts improved
Work therapy	Vocational rehabilitation
Patients are human	Patients are to be respected
Patient seen as child	Patient seen as adult
Social activities	Social retraining
Drugs seldom used	Drug treatment valued
Early discharge	Early discharge
Community involvement	Community involvement
Legitimized institutional expansion	Legitimized institutional decline
Supposed cost savings	Supposed cost savings

superintendents' promises of improved cure rates, local authorities were unwilling to pay for a decent standard of care. Consequently, many patients slept on straw, mechanical restraints were commonly used and opportunities for patients to work or enjoy social diversion were restricted.[46] The high annual mortality rates at the asylums of Lancaster and the West Riding of Yorkshire (17 per cent and 18 per cent, respectively, of the resident population) were the result, argued John Thurnam, a physician at the York Retreat, of poor nutrition and hygiene. Even greater mortality rates at the Norfolk County Asylum (19 per cent) and at St Peter's Hospital for paupers in Bristol (20 per cent) were the consequence of lack of adequate medical care and "the want of a proper amount of land for the exercise and employment of the patients."[47]

By the mid-1840s only five of the seventeen county asylums had abandoned mechanical restraint. Foremost amongst them were Lincoln Asylum, under the direction of Robert Gardiner Hill, and the massive new asylum at Hanwell, Middlesex, where John Conolly was the superintendent. The limited acceptance of moral treatment at that time is illustrated by the fact that Hill was forced to resign his post owing to public opposition; and Conolly was unable to persuade his governing committee to meet the expense of two of his innovative ideas – basic education classes for patients and professional training for the staff. With the restriction of outdoor relief and the great expansion of the asylum system during the next decade, the situation was reversed. By the mid-1850s, nearly all the 30 county asylums had discarded mechanical restraints and adopted some features of moral management.[48] Staffing patterns, at least in some asylums, improved. At Lancaster Asylum in 1846, on the "tranquil" wards, there was one attendant for 25 patients, and on the more disturbed wards, one attendant to 15 refractory patients.[49] The value of moral treatment in legitimizing social policy is illustrated here – legitimizing the Poor Law Commission policy of categorizing the destitute, providing poor relief in specialized institutions and cutting back on outdoor relief. The task accomplished, the cost of care per patient was soon reduced through progressive cheeseparing and expansion of the size of the institutions. Mechanical restraints and solitary confinement returned, and by the late 1860s moral treatment in the public asylums had again become a mere facade.[50]

In his description of nineteenth-century private madhouses, *The Trade in Lunacy*, William Parry-Jones highlights the differences in treatment for the poor (paid out of the public purse) and for private patients. He remarks:

> With regard to the maltreatment of lunatics in madhouses, confined under bad, often appalling, physical conditions, the evidence is . . . substantial and refers, especially to pauper departments during the first half of the nineteenth century.[51]

Again:

> The various factors which operated to keep the charge for paupers as low as possible . . . served to delay the introduction of the non-restraint system and to foster the continuance of the merely custodial confinement of lunatics.[52]

Mechanical restraint was rarely seen in licensed houses receiving only private patients, but was freely used in those houses taking paupers.[53] Some proprietors felt that restraints should not be used on patients from the "respectable class: their feelings are more acute than those of the humbler grade."[54] But the fact that non-restraint treatment required more and better trained staff and led to higher charges was generally recognized.[55] Whereas in the pauper establishments one keeper might care for ten or fifteen patients, in the houses for the wealthy the ratio was one attendant or servant for every one or two patients.[56] Moral treatment in Britain, it is clear, was not generally for the poor. As we have seen, for a few years, from the 1850s to the 1860s, during the expansion of the asylum system, a form of moral treatment was made available to paupers in county asylums; but otherwise, humane care was for those who could afford it.

CURE RATES

Did the class bias in quality of care influence the outcome of insanity? In attempting to answer this question, we have to be very cautious about using the published cure rates of the time. Where one madhouse proprietor talked of patients being "cured" or "discharged recovered" another might have used the term "relieved" or "improved." Again, patients admitted to one establishment might have included more who were young and early in the course of a functional psychosis; on the other hand, many of those admitted to county asylums were chronic patients transferred from workhouses or were elderly people with dementia. Bearing these considerations in mind, the statistics published in 1845 by Dr John Thurnam (see Table 5.2) are among the most useful. The figures show that institutions receiving paupers consistently reported lower recovery rates and higher mortality rates. Dr Thurnam argued that these results were not entirely due to the condition of the patients on admission but were, in part, a consequence of the differences in their management.[57]

The size of the institution may have been an important factor; asylums and licensed houses receiving private patients were generally a good deal smaller. Metropolitan licensed houses for paupers held an average of 400 patients; those for private patients had an average capacity of 23 residents.[58] For this reason, perhaps, at the model pauper asylum of Hanwell in Middlesex – with a thousand beds, far and away the largest mental institution in the country –

Table 5.2 Recovery and mortality rates for British mental institutions, comparing private and pauper establishments before 1845

	Recovery as % of admissions	Mortality as % of number resident
County asylums		
Receiving both private and pauper patients (average of 6 asylums, 1812–44)	46.87	10.46
Receiving paupers only (average of 9 asylums, 1812–44)	36.95	13.88
Metropolitan licensed houses		
Receiving principally private patients (average of 27 houses, 1839–43)	30.87	6.80
Receiving principally paupers (average of 3 houses, 1838–43)	23.74	18.10
Provincial licensed houses		
Receiving principally private patients (average of 41 houses, 1839–43)	43.50	6.57
Receiving principally paupers (average of 44 houses, 1839–43)	41.50	10.56

Source: Thurnam, J., *Observations and Essays on the Statistics of Insanity*, London: Simpkin, Marshall, 1845, Table 12.

the recovery rate was well below average, despite the emphasis on moral management and non-restraint. Daniel Hack Tuke's figures show the recovery rate at Hanwell fluctuating between 25 per cent and 32 per cent of admissions during the first 45 years of the hospital's operation.[59] At Lancaster Asylum, Britain's rapidly expanding, second-largest mental hospital, the introduction of more progressive treatment methods in the early 1840s reduced mortality rates but failed to improve discharge and cure rates; the percentage of recoveries, in fact, declined after the introduction of moral treatment.[60] The social policy that established large, cost-effective asylums and limited expenditure on patient care, reduced the possibility of rehabilitation for the insane poor. The improvements in public mental hospital care made during the expansion of the asylum system in the 1850s and 1860s cannot be shown to have improved cure rates. The smaller size of the private establishments, on the other hand, and the much higher ratio of staff to residents, may well have enhanced the possibility of recovery for wealthier patients.

LABOR IN NINETEENTH-CENTURY BRITAIN

What was the effect of the labor market on policy and practice in nineteenth-century British psychiatry? As we have seen, at no time was there a particularly strong rehabilitative emphasis to public psychiatry. This observation is understandable in view of the exceptionally high levels of unemployment that existed throughout the century. A famous dispute has raged among social historians as to whether living conditions for the working class worsened or improved during the early decades of the British Industrial Revolution.[61] Over one fact, however, there can be little room for debate – prior to 1850 unemployment was substantial. Vagrancy was increasing dramatically, ten per cent of the population were paupers in the 1840s and, at times, cyclical unemployment reached colossal heights. In the business slumps of 1826 and 1841–2, unemployment in the region of 75 per cent was not uncommon in the hard-hit areas of the industrial North and Midlands.[62] A contemporary observer, Henry Mayhew, writing of Londoners in the early nineteenth century, concludes: "In almost all occupations there is . . . a *superfluity of labourers* . . . In the generality of trades the calculation is that one-third of the hands are fully employed, one-third partially, and one-third unemployed throughout the year."[63] Although the availability of employment increased after 1850,[64] unemployment continued to be considerable throughout the Great Victorian Boom (1850–73) and may well have been only moderately better than during the subsequent Great Depression (1873–96).[65] That the heyday of moral treatment in the county asylums occurred in the boom years of the 1850s and 1860s is perhaps not especially relevant (except insofar as improved institutional conditions allowed an increased strictness in the limitation of outdoor relief[66]). There is no evidence, on the one hand, of a labor shortage at that time or, on the other hand, of a stronger rehabilitative effort or increase in discharge rates from the institutions. What is relevant is that the one clearly rehabilitative movement in psychiatry in Britain since the beginning of industrialization and the development of asylums occurred during the only period of significant labor shortage in two centuries – the years immediately following the Second World War.

The labor history of nineteenth-century America is substantially different from that of Britain. How did it influence psychiatry in the United States?

INDUSTRIALIZING AMERICA

Labor was in short supply in industrializing and expanding America during the first half of the nineteenth century.[67] "English observers in the mid-nineteenth century," writes historian Daniel Boorstin, "admired the ease with which American labourers moved about the country, from one job to another. They were amazed at the general freedom from fear of unemployment. . . ."[68] Real wages, in consequence, were higher in the United States than Europe.[69] The members of the Yates Committee to the New York legislature in 1824, reported:

> In this country the labour of three days will readily supply the wants of seven, while in Europe the labour of the whole week will barely suffice for

the maintenance and support of the family of an industrious labourer or peasant.[70]

Pauperism was exceedingly rare by European standards, and what there was existed largely in the maritime cities, where newly arrived immigrants congregated. Less than one per cent of the population of Philadelphia were paupers in the 1820s and less than two per cent of the population of New York State.[71] Unemployment remained low during much of the antebellum period, becoming more significant from the 1850s onward.[72] Population increase and the late Victorian depressions of 1873, 1884 and 1893, however, brought high unemployment and poverty.[73] Peacetime labor shortage of early nineteenth-century dimensions has not been seen since in the United States until the short-lived boom of 1999–2000.

Was American psychiatry more rehabilitative in its emphasis in the early nineteenth century, in response to the heavy demand for labor? It is certainly true that moral treatment was vigorously adopted by the first corporate asylums that were established (by public subscription) in those years. The founders of these New England hospitals were much influenced by the examples and writing of Tuke and Pinel and applied their methods from the moment the doors were opened – at the Friends' Asylum, Frankford, Pennsylvania (1817), Bloomingdale Asylum, New York (1821), McLean Hospital, Boston, Massachusetts (1818), and the Retreat at Hartford, Connecticut (1824). The independent Pennsylvania Hospital in Philadelphia, which established a separate branch for the insane in 1841, was also a model of progressive care. These hospitals, many of them established by Quakers, were, like the York Retreat, primarily intended for the treatment of private patients. Some, however, like the Hartford Retreat and the Bloomingdale Asylum, took substantial numbers of paupers in return for public funding. As in the best British private establishments, staffing was comfortably high – one attendant to two patients was common. Restraints were very rarely used, and a full, if somewhat over-regimented, schedule of social and work activities was established for all inmates. Such was the success and public good favor of these progressive institutions that they were a major influence in the development of public hospitals for the insane.[74]

AMERICAN PUBLIC HOSPITALS

Discussions of this era in American psychiatry often make the point that moral treatment was not generally made available to the poor or that it existed more in the pious mouthings of hospital superintendents than in the actual condition of patients in the public institutions.[75] This point of view deserves some debate, however, especially if we restrict ourselves to a study of the earliest decades of operation of the public hospitals. George Mora writes, in the *Comprehensive Textbook of Psychiatry*, for instance:

> Among the earliest state-supported institutions were the Eastern State Hospital at Lexington, Kentucky, opened in 1824; the Manhattan State Hospital in New York City, opened in 1825; the Western State Hospital in Staunton, Virginia, opened in 1828; and the South Carolina State Hospital in Columbia, South Carolina, opened in 1828. In contrast with the private or corporate hospitals, in which moral treatment was applied, those state institutions remained largely custodial.[76]

Of the four examples chosen by Dr Mora, two might reasonably be described as "largely custodial." The performance of the state asylum in Lexington, Kentucky, was less than creditable. Historian David Rothman considers that it "had . . . become a custodial institution" by 1845;[77] the figures supplied by Gerald Grob in his review of *Mental Institutions in America* suggest that this may have been true as early as 1840 (see Table 5.3). Yet even this institution had high ideals in the early years – the directors insisted, for example, that no restraints be used.[78] In using Manhattan State Hospital as an example, Mora is presumably referring to the New York City Asylum on Blackwell's Island which actually opened in 1839. This institution, as we shall see later, was also clearly custodial, but for special reasons. At the Western Virginia State Hospital, however (according to Norman Dain's study of that state's mental hospitals), moral treatment *was* introduced in 1836 by an enthusiastic young superintendent who so upgraded the quality of the hospital that he was able to attract private, upper-class, white patients, who accounted for a third of the admissions.[79] Social reformers visiting the hospital in 1842 regarded it as excellent, and reported:

> The employments, recreations, amusements, instructions, and influences are very various, and well fitted to soothe the excited, cheer the desponding, guide the erring, check the vicious, raise the fallen, and restore the insane. The restraints are very few.[80]

Treatment at each of the two Virginia state hospitals was reportedly comparable, and benefited from an exceptionally good level of staffing – one staff member (including slave attendants) for every three patients.[81] South Carolina State Hospital, the last of Dr Mora's examples, far from being custodial had a high patient turnover. From data provided by Gerald Grob, we can calculate that from 1845 (when records became available) to 1865 the number of patients discharged as recovered (and not merely improved) was regularly around 50 per cent of admissions (as shown in Table 5.3) or 20 per cent of the total hospital population.[82]

As we survey the 14 or so public hospitals that were in operation in the

Table 5.3 Patients discharged "recovered" expressed as a percentage of admissions in selected years for American asylums open before 1845[a]

	1820	1825	1830	1835	1840	1845	1850	1855	1860	1865	1870	1875
Corporate and private hospitals												
Hartford Retreat, Connecticut	—	23	55	50	60	43	47	43	41	37	33	40
McLean Asylum, Massachusetts	22	36	41	54	48	62	45	46	32	43	42	19
Bloomingdale Asylum, New York	—	46	43	42	53	44	51	49	33	43	39	30
Friends' Asylum, Pennsylvania	20	—[b]	44	22	46	52	52	40	40	28	42	32
Pennsylvania Hospital	—	—	—	—	—	45	51	57	46	44	36	42
State and city hospitals (northern)												
Maine Insane Hospital	—	—	—	—	28	39	60	32	46	33	37	36
Boston Insane Hospital, Mass.	—	—	—	—	7	24	51	29	41	25	26	30
Worcester State Hospital, Mass.	—	—	—	46	51	42	52	55	60	48	41	25
New Hampshire Asylum	—	—	—	—	—[b]	42	44	53	45	39	28	44
New York City Asylum, Blackwell's Is.	—	—	—	—	—[b]	—[b]	—[b]	—[b]	—[b]	—[b]	27	31
Utica State Asylum, New York	—	—	—	—	—	46	47	47	31	32	32	31
Central Ohio Asylum	—	—	—	—	52	29	51	63	49	41	—	—
Vermont Asylum	—	—	—	—	45	29	53	48	41	38	29	25
State hospitals (southern)												
Kentucky Eastern Asylum	—	44	—[b]	—[b]	8	37	34	35	46	44	28	60
Maryland State Hospital	—	—	—	9	38	44	35	37	50	65	83	16
Tennessee State Hospital	—	—	—	—	—	—[b]	34	46	47	—[b]	41	44
South Carolina Asylum	—	—	—	—	—	57	50	31	54	70	29	29
Virginia Eastern Asylum	—[b]	—[b]	—[b]	—[b]	—[b]	—[b]	—[b]	—[b]	—[b]	—[b]	—[b]	46
Virginia Western Asylum	—	—	—[b]	—[b]	—[b]	—[b]	—[b]	—[b]	—[b]	—[b]	44	40

Source: Percentages calculated from data in Grob, G.N.I, *Mental Institutions in America*, New York: Free Press, 1973, pp. 374–93.

Notes: [a] These figures, being calculated on statistics for a single year, are substantially less accurate and more subject to fluctuation than if based on longer time periods.
[b] Hospital open but figures not available.

United States by 1845, and recall that non-restraint management had established itself in fewer than a third of the ill-staffed, British county asylums by the mid-1840s, it appears possible that the pauper lunatic in America at this time was the more fortunate. Unsatisfactory hospital conditions were primarily to be found in New York City and in some institutions in the non-industrial South. Besides the two state hospitals in Virginia, we know that progressive and humane measures were practiced in Worcester State Hospital, in Massachusetts; at Utica, in upstate New York; and at the Vermont Asylum, in Brattleboro. The Maine Insane Asylum was in the hands of Isaac Ray, a prominent psychiatrist and moral-treatment advocate.[83] If Worcester State Hospital is a fair illustration, staffing patterns were excellent by contemporary British asylum standards – one attendant to twelve or fifteen patients during the 1830s and 1840s.[84]

Mortality rates (the measure that Dr Thurnam considered the best standard of comparison of the quality of asylum care) were considerably better in American state hospitals than in British county asylums in the 1840s (see Table 5.4). These differences were not due to the admission of more elderly patients to British hospitals – the age distribution of admissions to British and American asylums was quite similar.[85] Since acutely ill patients tended to have a higher death rate, the low mortality might theoretically have been a

Table 5.4 Mortality rates in British and American pauper asylums as a percentage of the number resident

British county asylums		American state and city hospitals		
	Mean annual mortality % 1839–44		Annual mortality %	
			1840	1845
Receiving paupers only		Northern states		
Bedford	10.5	Maine	10.4	8.7
Dorset	12.2	Boston, Mass.	6.2	5.8
Kent	10.7	Worcester, Mass	6.6	7.6
Lancaster	13.2	New Hampshire	–	7.9
Middlesex	9.1	Utica, New York	–	7.9
Norfolk	19.1	Central Ohio	10.7	10.8
Suffolk	10.8	Vermont	7.4	7.6
York	13.6			
Receiving private and pauper patients		Southern states		
Chester	11.8	Maryland	10.0	9.3
Cornwall	7.7	South Carolina	–	8.4
Gloucester	10.7	Virginia Eastern	–	9.4
Leicester	11.3			
Nottingham	9.2			
Stafford	13.7			

Source: British asylums: Thurnam, Observations and Essays on the Statistics of Insanity. Table 13. American asylums: mortality rates calculated from statistics in Grob, Mental Institutions in America, pp. 374–93.

result of the admission of more chronic patients to the American hospitals. Equally, the lower death rate in the American institutions may well have reflected better conditions for American insane paupers.

In general, David Rothman feels the American public asylums tried to emulate the private institutions but were not able to achieve quite the same standards.

> There were lapses and failures, but in the first few years of the asylums they were not gross ones. Most mental hospitals in the 1830s and 1840s abolished the whip and the chain and did away with confinement. . . . And often they accomplished more, treating patients with thoughtfulness and humanity.[86]

Charles Dickens, in his *American Notes*, though critical of much that he saw in the New World of 1842, was very favorably impressed by the Boston Insane Hospital for paupers, and devotes several pages to a description of his visit. He was particularly struck by the dignity with which the patients were treated, their freedom from restraint or restrictions in the use of potentially dangerous instruments, their provisions for work and social activity (including sewing circles, balls and carriage rides) and the intimate involvement of the superintendent and his wife in the daily life of the hospital:

> It is obvious that one great feature of the system, is the inculcation and encouragement, even among such unhappy persons, of a decent self-respect.[87]

The Boston Hospital, aside from this report, has never been heralded as an outstandingly progressive hospital by the standards of the times. Dickens also found the private Hartford Retreat to be "admirably conducted,"[88] but he was severely critical of the recently opened New York City Asylum on Blackwell's Island. At the latter institution:

> I saw nothing of that salutary system which had impressed me so favourably elsewhere; and everything had a lounging, listless, madhouse air.[89]

At last Dickens had come upon an American asylum as depressing as he was to find St Luke's in London a few years later.[90] And the reason for the melancholy conditions at the New York City Asylum? Perhaps, as he says,

> New York, as a great emporium of commerce, and as a place of general resort, not only from all parts of the States, but from most parts of the world, has always a large pauper population to provide for; and labours, therefore, under peculiar difficulties in this respect.[91]

The New York *State* Hospital, over 200 miles north at Utica, escaped the problem of overcrowding with foreign-born paupers from which the city hospital suffered,[92] and became recognized as a model state institution. The rare instance of unenlightened hospital conditions was to be found where poverty and unemployment were beginning to appear within the shores of the United States.

REHABILITATION

Not only were conditions generally humane in the public institutions, they were also genuinely rehabilitative. Work therapy was strongly emphasized at such state hospitals as Worcester, Massachusetts; Utica, New York; and Brattleboro, Vermont.[93] Patients were released on parole from the Eastern Virginia Asylum to seek work in local towns, and some were also boarded out with families in order that "the accustomed life of the lunatic shall be less essentially at variance with that pertaining to persons generally of sound mind."[94] Several hospitals, including Utica, instituted the measure for which Conolly in England was unable to obtain funding – classes for patients. A variety of subjects was taught, including music and drama. Most hospitals had libraries for the patients. In addition, links with the community at large were strengthened by encouraging the participation of teachers, ministers and other visitors in the day-to-day operation of the hospitals.[95]

The rehabilitative emphasis appears to have been associated with reasonably high discharge rates. As Table 5.3 shows, the proportion of patients discharged "recovered" from public hospitals in different years compared quite well with figures for private hospitals. (No doubt, of course, hospital superintendents attached different meanings to "recovered," but there is no reason to believe that public-hospital doctors were particularly optimistic in this respect.) We see very respectable recovery rates not only at South Carolina Asylum, as previously noted, and at such hospitals of repute as Worcester and Utica, but also at the New Hampshire Asylum, the Central Ohio Asylum and the Vermont Asylum. Recovery rates at these hospitals through the 1850s were at least equal to those (given by Thurnam) for the best British county asylums. Table 5.5, drawn from Thurnam's statistics, shows that recovery rates at the American corporate hospitals and at the Worcester Asylum (admittedly the best of the state hospitals) all exceeded average cure rates at British institutions through the mid-1840s. Such direct comparison of overall recovery rates, however, can only yield very crude impressions in view of the probable differences in the patient populations and in measures of recovery. Cure rates in the United States, for example, might have been boosted if many people with chronic psychosis (especially those who were black) were not admitted to the state hospitals but languished in jails and workhouses. It is not apparent, however, that this occurred more in the

Table 5.5 Recovery and mortality rates in British and American mental institutions before 1845

	Recovery as % of admissions	Mortality as % of number resident
Britain		
Private and Charitable Asylums (average of 8 asylums, 1766–1843)	40.94	8.93
Metropolitan Licensed Houses (average of 30 houses, 1839–43)	25.65	14.68
Provincial Licensed Houses (average of 85 houses, 1838–43)	42.24	9.85
County Asylums (average of 15 asylums, 1812–44)	40.25	12.79
United States		
Corporate Hospitals		
Bloomingdale Asylum, New York, 1821–41	46.18	10.32
Friends' Asylum, Frankford, Penn., 1817–42	44.38	10.64
Hartford Retreat, Conn., 1824–43	56.29	–
McLean Asylum, Boston, Mass., 1818–43	44.95	11.07
Average of 4 corporate asylums	47.41	10.65
State Hospitals		
Worcester State Hospital, Mass., 1833–43	44.56	6.76

Source: Thurnam, *Observations and Essays on the Statistics of Insanity,* Table 12.

United States than in Britain (and, as we have seen, the lower mortality rates in American institutions suggest that the American hospitals were receiving their fair share of chronic patients). Higher discharge rates from American institutions might partly have reflected a policy of early discharge rather than a real difference in patient outcome. Nevertheless, such figures would still have been an accurate reflection of a greater rehabilitative emphasis in American psychiatry of the period.

THE "CULT OF CURABILITY"

Some contemporary observers formed the impression that American mental hospital treatment and cure rates were superior to those which existed in Britain. Like Dickens, Captain Basil Hall was a British visitor whose impressions of America were generally somewhat uncomplimentary. In the published account of his travels, however, he waxed lyrical over the patient management at the Hartford Retreat, which he witnessed in 1827, and contrasted the high recovery rates at that hospital with current British results. During the previous year, 25 of the 28 "recent" cases admitted to the Hartford Retreat – 89.2 per cent – had recovered, he reported, but "at two most ancient and celebrated institutions" of the same type in Britain only

25.5 per cent of "recent" (acute) cases were cured.[96] Hall's claims attracted a great deal of attention on both sides of the Atlantic and were widely quoted in the press. Soon, other American hospital superintendents reported similar rates of success. Samuel Woodward at the Worcester State Hospital claimed recovery rates for "recent" (acute) cases of 82–91 per cent for the early years of the hospital's operation between 1833 and 1840. John Galt, superintendent at the Eastern Virginia Asylum, announced 92 per cent recovery in acute cases and 53 per cent recovery overall in new admissions in his report of 1842. Around the same time, William Awl, superintendent of the Ohio State Asylum, reported cure rates of 80–100 per cent for cases of recent onset, and 48 per cent recovery for all cases of up to ten years duration admitted over a four-year period.[97] Heads of corporate and public asylums alike argued that recovery from insanity was the rule, incurability the exception. As stated by Amariah Brigham of Utica State Hospital: "No fact relating to insanity appears better established than the general certainty of curing it in its early state."[98]

It is easy to dismiss such claims as American bombast and typical of the entrepreneurial audacity of the New Republic. The claims were, indeed, extravagant and clearly motivated, in part, by a wish to impress state legislators with the value of investment in hospital care. Dorothea Dix used these reports of the benefits of modern treatment in her successful campaign to establish public mental hospitals throughout the United States. The episode in American psychiatry has subsequently been disparaged as the "Cult of Curability."[99] Obviously, statistics may have been molded somewhat to improve the effect. Galt's 92 per cent recovery figure was, like many other reports, based on a small sample – 13 admissions. Criteria for defining "recent" cases and "recovery" were subject to manipulation; and patients who relapsed, were readmitted and subsequently discharged again, might be counted as "recovered" more than once.[100] Despite such statistical flaws, nevertheless, we cannot rule out the possibility that cure rates were outstandingly good at the time. Indeed, it seems quite possible that recovery rates for acutely ill patients admitted to American public and private mental hospitals throughout the first half of the nineteenth century were distinctly better than in the decades that followed or in contemporary Britain. Two points emerge clearly from the reports of the period. The emphasis on curability was largely an American phenomenon, and it pervaded public psychiatry as extensively as it did the private institutions. In Britain, George Burrows reported similarly high recovery rates in 1820 for "recent" cases admitted to his madhouse, as did the proprietors of other private establishments.[101] The same degree of universal optimism, however, did not develop in British public hospitals of the period.

The enthusiasm of the American hospital superintendents was, in fact, based upon the observation of distinctly superior rates of recovery. Table 5.6 allows us to compare separately the cure rates for acute and chronic patients admitted to several British and American hospitals before 1842. The American recovery rates for acute patients were substantially better than the British. It may reasonably be assumed that these figures for recent cases are more comparable than those for total admissions. Undetermined numbers of chronically psychotic and demented patients, epileptics and mentally retarded amongst the general admissions largely determined the overall recovery rate, which, as we may see in Table 5.6, bore little relationship to the cure rate in acute illness. Significant differences in the causes of acute mental illness, however, could conceivably have accounted for the disparity in recovery rates. Thurnam argued, for example, that more of the American hospital admissions were suffering from alcohol-related psychoses and delirium tremens, which ended either in early recovery or death.[102] If this opinion were correct, we would expect to find higher death rates in the American asylums (in fact, as we have seen, they were lower) and higher recovery rates in male patients (which was true at Bloomingdale Asylum, but not at Worcester[103]). Whatever the causes, it is clear that there was a distinctly better

Table 5.6 Percentage of admissions discharged "recovered" from British and American asylums according to duration of illness

	Less than 12 months duration	More than 12 months duration	All cases
Britain			
Private Hospitals			
York Retreat, 1796–1843	61.87	18.88	46.94
Asylums for Private and Pauper Patients			
Bethlem Hospital, 1827–39	52.38	12.50	50.96
Dundee Asylum, 1820–40	59.06	13.71	42.36
Lincoln Asylum	50.95	9.62	40.10
St Luke's Hospital, 1751–1834	39.71	–	–
County Asylums for Paupers Only			
Maidstone Asylum, Kent	49.26	4.84	20.68
Wakefield Asylum, Yorkshire	53.74	11.50	44.18
United States			
Corporate Hospitals			
Bloomingdale Asylum, New York, 1882–41[a]	74.85	11.57	47.19
Friends' Asylum, Frankford, Penn., 1817–38[b]	58.23	25.20	45.11
State Hospitals			
Worcester State Hospital, Mass., 1833–40	82.78	14.40	42.30
Central Ohio Asylum, 1838–42	79.53	20.20[c]	47.70[d]

Source: Thurnam, *Observations and Essays on the Statistics of Insanity*, p. 57. Statistics for Ohio Asylum are added from Grob, *Mental Institutions in America*, p. 182.

Notes: [a] Private patients only.
[b] Private and pauper patients.
[c] Cases of 1–10 years duration.
[d] Cases of up to 10 years duration.

course and outcome to acute mental illnesses in early nineteenth-century America, which needs to be explained.

THE COVER-UP

Few physicians care to believe that their methods are not as successful as those of others and, still less, that the achievements of their profession are following a progressively downhill course. Such concerns may well explain the intensity and somewhat derisory air with which later American psychiatrists have attempted to refute the curability claims of the moral-treatment era. They have been anxious to see the errors in these reports but less keen to validate any truth within them. Most vigorous and influential of these critics was Pliny Earle, and his work *The Curability of Insanity*, published in 1876, is frequently cited as the definitive debunking of the "myth of curability."[104] Dr Earle contended that the excellent recovery rates recorded by Samuel Woodward during the earliest years of the Worcester State Hospital were grossly exaggerated by statistical juggling. He made much of the fact that the same patient might be counted as "recovered" after every relapse and that percentages of recoveries were calculated on the basis of those discharged, not on the numbers admitted. His conclusion, much more in keeping with the figures for his own institution, late in the century, was that insanity was, in fact, far less curable than had been supposed.

Pliny Earle's attempt to rewrite psychiatric history, however, has itself been exposed as a cover-up. Dr Sanbourne Bockoven, who has reanalyzed Dr Earle's figures and uncovered more material on Samuel Woodward's patients,[105] concludes that Earle himself was guilty of statistical juggling. Dr Earle knew, for example, that the counting of repeated recoveries, which he so criticized and which has been raised by every critic since, made almost no difference to the overall recovery rate of Worcester State Hospital patients – a difference of less than a quarter of a percentage point. Dr Earle also knew of the existence of a comprehensive follow-up study of Samuel Woodward's discharged patients, conducted by Dr John Park, a later superintendent of Worcester State Hospital – a study that showed that outcome was, indeed, so superior in the early decades of the hospital's operation that Dr Park judiciously withheld the results from publication.

At Dr Earle's suggestion, Dr Park had compiled a retroactive review of admissions and discharges since the opening of the hospital in 1833, employing his own criteria for "recovery," not Dr Woodward's. His results (continued up to 1950 with modern data), showing the changes in the percentage of admissions discharged as recovered from Worcester State Hospital, are displayed in Figure 5.1 (taken from Dr Bockoven's book). Dr Park, who was as keen as Dr Earle to demonstrate that the early recovery rates were

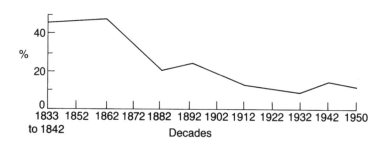

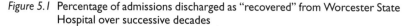

Figure 5.1 Percentage of admissions discharged as "recovered" from Worcester State Hospital over successive decades

Note: Reprinted by permission of the author. From Bockoven, J. S., *Moral Treatment in Community Mental Health*; New York: Springer, 1972, p. 56, © J. Sanbourne Bockoven.

artificially inflated, was unable to reduce Dr Woodward's figures by more than two or three per cent. Overall recovery rates of 45 per cent in the moral-treatment era, as we can see, fell to 20 per cent in the late Victorian Great Depression and to 10 per cent in the 1930s.

David Rothman has criticized Dr Bockoven's work on two counts. Rothman argues, in the first place, that the revised recovery rates for Dr Woodward's patients "are considerably lower than the claims for the 1830's and 1840's." Here Rothman makes the error of confusing the claimed recovery rates for "recent" (acute) cases (which were over 80 per cent) with general admissions (45 per cent recovery). Secondly, Rothman claims that Bockoven "makes no attempt to question just what 'recovery' meant in the original records."[106] But Rothman is incorrect here, also. Bockoven demonstrates exactly what "recovery" meant for Woodward's patients by presenting the results of Dr Park's follow-up, 36–60 years after discharge, of all of Woodward's patients who left the hospital, "recovered," prior to 1847. There were 1,173 such patients, and information was collected on the condition of 984 of them. This project was both ambitious and successful, and took Dr Park ten years to complete. The study showed that an extraordinary 58 per cent of the patients followed-up never had another relapse in the rest of their lives or until the time of follow-up. Another eight per cent had relapsed but were well at follow-up. Dr Bockoven draws the conclusion that, during the moral-treatment era,

> the natural history of psychosis in general (including cases due to organic changes of the central nervous system) was such that a large proportion of patients were able to leave the mental hospital, and only a small proportion, perhaps 20–30 per cent, were destined to die in a mental hospital. Favourable outcome was, of course, even more frequent in the functional psychoses considered alone.[107]

A contemporary of Pliny Earle, Isaac Ray, a psychiatrist of equal stature and experience, rebutted Earle's views in 1879. Dr Ray argued that the early statistical reports were no more biased than recent figures and that recoveries had, in fact, become less frequent. The reasons, he believed, for the decline in recovery rates included a failure to provide an adequate trial of moral treatment for many patients. Latter-day psychiatric historians, however, have generally ignored Dr Ray and repeated Pliny Earle's rather self-serving opinions as accurate.[108] They have, thereby, buried important information – the course of functional psychoses in patients admitted to early nineteenth-century American hospitals was more benign than in the hundred years that followed.

THE DEMISE OF MORAL TREATMENT

It is possible, then, that the labor shortage in the first half of the nineteenth century in America influenced rehabilitative efforts for the insane and elevated recovery rates in psychosis. This notion, however, reverses some of the orthodox explanations for the demise of moral management in the latter part of the century. Thus, it was not so much that the failure of promises of curability led legislators to demand cost-cutting in the institutions; it may have been the diminished need for manpower that reduced the incentive to fund vigorous treatment programs and caused a reduction in cure rates. It was not just a build-up of chronic patients and an increase in hospital size and overcrowding that caused the deteriorating institutional conditions; it was the decline in rehabilitative efforts that created the build-up of chronic patients. And the foreign paupers who filled the asylums and so outraged the sensibilities of the psychiatrists and middle-class clientele – the Irish "clodhoppers" with their "filthy habits" – were not incurable because they had "scarcely an idea beyond that of . . . manual employment," as Isaac Ray claimed.[109] They were stuck because there was no employment outside the hospital, and no longer any work therapy within the hospital.[110] (Inmates' work had become too competitive to be tolerated by the unemployed beyond the institutions' walls.) If funding cuts and overcrowding with chronic patients and paupers were the problems, then the affluent private hospitals that selected more "recent" cases and excluded paupers – Pennsylvania Hospital, the Friends' Asylum, McLean Hospital, Bloomingdale Asylum (which excluded paupers after 1857) and the Hartford Retreat (after 1866)[111] – should have experienced few difficulties. As Table 5.3 shows, however, recovery rates deteriorated in these institutions also after 1870. Public and private asylums alike declined from curative to custodial institutions.[112]

Moral treatment reached its zenith in labor-starved, early nineteenth-century America for two reasons. Firstly, given a demand for labor, moral management was a truly rehabilitative measure that could restore the maximum level of functioning to the marginal psychotic patient. Secondly, as in contemporary Britain, it legitimized the establishment of specialized institutions for confining the unemployable insane. With the inevitable disappearance of the labor shortage, the social-control functions of the institutions overcame their rehabilitative purpose. Where environmental factors had previously been seen as important in causing psychosis, the emphasis now was on heredity. Prevailing concepts of prognosis were pessimistic.[113] At this point in history, in the coercive, prison-like environment of a German asylum[114] during the universal, late nineteenth-century Great Depression, dementia praecox was defined as a progressively deteriorating and all but incurable illness.

When moral treatment returned, a century and a half after its original appearance, its objectives and ideology were similar but the locations were switched. This time it was in labor-short northern Europe that it served (at least initially) a genuinely rehabilitative purpose, but in America it was largely used merely to legitimize the deinstitutionalization movement – the transfer of the indigent mentally ill from indoor to outdoor relief, and from state budget to federal. Both the concept and management of psychosis appear to have been influenced by political and economic factors. Ideology and practice in psychiatry, to a significant extent are at the mercy of material conditions.

SUMMARY

- Moral treatment was a humane and non-restrictive method of management for people with psychosis that came into being simultaneously in several parts of Europe in reaction to the eighteenth-century concept of madness as bestial.
- The origins of moral treatment were also those of the French Revolution and the English Industrial Revolution – Enlightenment thinking, dramatic changes in population and labor patterns, and the capitalist transformation of production.
- The treatment method was inextricably tied to the development of mental institutions, and it helped legitimize the public asylum movement.
- A function of the new asylums was to enact the social policy of providing poor relief to the unemployable in institutions and the cutting back on outdoor relief to the employable.
- Moral treatment was little used in British public asylums except for a brief spell during the boom years of the 1850s and 1860s when the asylum system was being expanded.
- Private patients in Britain enjoyed more humane care and better recovery rates than paupers.
- The high levels of unemployment in Britain throughout the nineteenth century may well have limited rehabilitative efforts for the insane poor.

- The labor shortage in early nineteenth-century America was associated with more intense rehabilitative efforts and higher cure rates, especially in acute mental illness, in public asylums.
- Later American psychiatrists attempted to obscure the fact that recovery rates were higher during the moral-treatment era.

Chapter 6

Labor, poverty and schizophrenia

Why did fewer people with schizophrenia recover during the twentieth-century Great Depression? It is worth examining this question in depth as the answer may help us understand why outcome from schizophrenia deteriorated during the recent, late twentieth-century economic downturn in Britain.

It is scarcely surprising that social recovery rates in schizophrenia declined during the Great Depression since employment is a large part of the measure of social functioning; but why was there a drop in the rate of complete, symptom-free recovery at that time (as revealed by the analysis of follow-up studies in Chapter 3) from an average of 20 per cent to 12 per cent? Which of the following possible explanations is most applicable?

- Government spending on psychiatric treatment decreases during hard times, resulting in hospital overcrowding and poor-quality care.
- The stresses of the Depression, including economic hardship and unemployment, affected patients and their families and prevented recovery or precipitated psychotic relapse.
- The reduced demand for labor led to diminished rehabilitative and reintegrative efforts for people with schizophrenia, resulting in changes in mental health policy, psychiatric ideology and social tolerance for people with mental illness.

GOVERNMENT SPENDING

Mental hospital admissions, especially for people with schizophrenia and other forms of functional psychosis, increase during an economic recession (as Harvey Brenner's work, *Mental Illness and the Economy*, has shown). If legislators cut back on funding during the Great Depression, at a time of increasing demand, the result would, presumably, have been overcrowding, deteriorating care and non-therapeutic hospital conditions. Is this what happened? The evidence suggests it is not.

The annual expenditure on psychiatric hospitals in the state of Colorado,

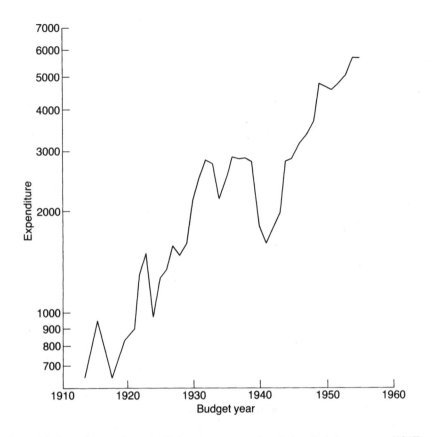

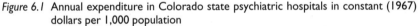

Figure 6.1 Annual expenditure in Colorado state psychiatric hospitals in constant (1967) dollars per 1,000 population

Source: Expenditure: "State of Colorado Budget Reports, 1923–24 to 1955–56;" inflation factor: "Bureau of Labor Statistics Wholesale Price Index, All Commodities;" population of Colorado: Decennial US Census with interval year estimates.

Note: Capital outlay is included.

for example (as can be seen in Figure 6.1), increased considerably between 1913 and 1955, even after allowance is made for inflation and state population growth. During the decade of the Great Depression, however, expenditure was consistently well *above* the general trend. Before the 1930s, two other spikes of increased spending are evident during the recessions of 1914–15 and 1920–22. Hospital spending was less than usual during the Second World War, but returned to the general trend after the war. In this state of the union, at least, psychiatric funding did not decrease during the Depression but, rather, increased at a faster rate than usual in an effort to meet the increased demand for care.

The same spending pattern held true for England and Wales during the

Figure 6.2 Annual expenditure on "lunacy" and lunatic asylums in England and Wales in constant (1871) pounds per 100 population; annual unemployment for comparison

decades following the late Victorian era, as Figure 6.2 shows. Here the rate of expenditure on "lunacy" and lunatic asylums increased during the nineteenth- and twentieth-century Great Depressions, decreased slowly during the relatively full employment years after the turn of the century and after the Second World War, and dropped sharply during the two world wars.

It is possible, of course, that the increased use of mental institutions in the Depression outstripped even these inflated hospital expenditures, in which case overcrowding and poor care would still have occurred. This does not seem to have happened, however. Brenner reports, for example, greatly increased capacity at New York state public hospitals during the Great Depression – a 73 per cent increase in available beds between 1929 and 1938. Overcrowding was common at these hospitals before, during and after the Great Depression, but was apparently no worse during the early years of the economic downturn than in the late 1920s and mid-1950s.[1] Figures for the percentage occupancy of Canadian mental hospitals between 1934 and 1960

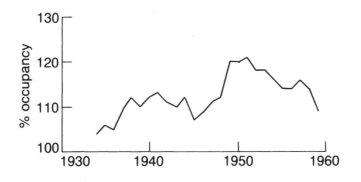

Figure 6.3 Percentage occupancy of Canadian mental institutions

Source: Urquhart, M. C. and Buckley, K. A. H., *Historial Statistics of Canada*, Cambridge: Cambridge University Press, 1965.

draw the same picture (see Figure 6.3). Overcrowding in these hospitals was at its lowest in the 1930s and at its highest in the 1950s.

Decreased government spending and hospital overcrowding, it seems, are not the explanation for the poor outcome in schizophrenia during the Great Depression. Similarly, there is no sign of increased spending after the Second World War to account for the improved recovery rates at that time. The switch to community care was, in fact, considered to be a cost-saving measure. Whether, in actuality, community treatment was cheaper is hard to determine. An analysis of the real cost of such care would have to include the expense of social services provided through several agencies, and of supportive accommodation and disability payments. No such study appears to have been done in Britain. Some American cost and benefit studies of deinstitutionalization were made available in the 1970s. Their value for our purpose is somewhat reduced by unsophisticated analytic methods, small sample size or the inclusion of unrealistic projections of savings and benefits attributed to the patients' employability. All of these studies, however, show community treatment to be cheaper than state hospital care.[2]

It seems that, during the Great Depression, more money was spent on buying more hospital care for people with schizophrenia and the result was, for whatever reasons, lower recovery rates.

LATE TWENTIETH-CENTURY BRITISH ECONOMIC DOWNTURN

Does this lack of connection between government spending on psychiatric care and outcome in schizophrenia continue at the present time? Apparently so.

The analysis of outcome studies in Chapter 3 demonstrates that outcome from schizophrenia in Britain took a downturn during the last two decades of the twentieth century, matching the decline in the British economy at that time. Figure 6.4 shows us, however, that National Health Service spending on psychiatric treatment services did not decline between the late 1950s and the end of the century. The methods of analyzing the data and presenting them in health service publications changed from time to time, so the graph is not continuous. Nevertheless, it is clear that inflation-adjusted, *per capita* spending did not decline in any of the data series and it appears to have increased towards the end of the century. Other sources of information reveal that local authority spending on community and residential care was also not reduced over this period.

As in the case of the Great Depression, decreasing government spending on mental health care does not explain the deterioration in outcome from schizophrenia. What does?

ECONOMIC STRESS AND UNEMPLOYMENT

Stress may provoke a psychotic relapse in someone with schizophrenia (as discussed in Chapter 1). Both the boom and bust parts of the business cycle bring their own varieties of stress. In the depression they include loss of status, self-worth and independence for the unemployed, a sense of failure for those who slip down the social ladder, and economic hardship for many. People with schizophrenia living in the community are exposed to all these possible stresses and those with marginal levels of functioning are particularly at risk when jobs are in short supply.

Clinical experience shows us that economic uncertainty is a serious stress for many patients. As social security regulations were tightened during the

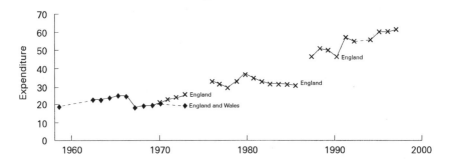

Figure 6.4 Annual *per capita* National Health Service expenditure on mental illness (before 1987) and mental health services (after 1987) in England and Wales (first series) and England (last three series) in constant (1998) pounds

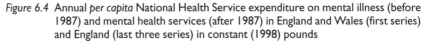

Source: The raw data were gathered from health service publications by Gyles Glover, University of Durham, and subsequently adjusted for annual inflation and population growth.

early years of the Reagan administration, for example, many people with a stable psychotic disorder whose disability payments were abruptly terminated suffered relapses of their illness. The mental condition of many people with psychosis similarly becomes worse when their most basic needs are not provided for. In the United States, homeless male patients with schizophrenia are frequently admitted to hospital, hungry, dirty, sleepless and floridly psychotic. When, after some meals and a good night's sleep, their mental state dramatically improves, hospital staff may claim that the patient has "manipulated" his way into free board and accommodation. More benign observers argue that the patient's improvement is evidence of the efficacy of the dose of the antipsychotic medication that he received on admission. In fact, such patients often improve as readily without medication. The florid features of their psychosis on admission are an acute response to the stress of their poverty and deprivation.

We can estimate from the social recovery rates in Chapter 3 that 70 per cent of people with schizophrenia were unemployed at follow-up during the Great Depression – significantly more than after the Second World War. In recent years, again, it has become so common for people with schizophrenia living in the community to be out of work that mental health professionals rarely consider unemployment a significant stress for their patients. For many of these people with psychotic illness, however, the dreary round of days without purposeful activity, lives devoid of meaning and a social existence stripped of status are a constant strain. British unemployed men complain:

"You're a drag on everybody else really."
"Sometimes I get to walking up and down on the carpet."
". . . cannot be bothered to dae nowt, just feel like stopping in bed all day."
"When you're out of work you worry and don't feel like eating."
"I go for a walk and try to do some reading if I can, but it's very hard for me to get the brain functioning properly."
"I'm so *moody* you know."
"I thought, 'What's the bloody point of it all, anyway? What's the reason for it all?' Then you start to become, well, deranged."
"I think you start to lose your identity in yourself. . . . There's times when, well 'What's . . . what am I?' "[3]

Such responses are those of unemployed men who are not particularly susceptible to psychosis. The impact on people with schizophrenia can scarcely be less severe, and could well affect their recovery and relapse rates.

Indeed, the similarity of many features of chronic schizophrenia to the psychological effects of extended unemployment is striking. Anxiety, depression, apathy, irritability, negativity, emotional overdependence, social withdrawal, isolation and loneliness, and a loss of self-respect, identity and a sense of time – all these are common amongst the long-term unemployed.[4] Compare these features, and the words of the British unemployed quoted above, with this description of schizophrenia:

> Anergy, or disturbances of volition, have at times been incorrectly described as apathy. . . . Patients may be abnormally tired, fatigue easily, and experience clinical depression. The chronic schizophrenic may sit blankly for long periods, unaware of the passage of time. . . . He may remain in bed when he intended to look for a job, avoid or put off without reason any activity that is new, unfamiliar or outside of his routine. . . . Life is routine, constricted, empty. He may sleep most of the day, be awake most of the night. The chronic schizophrenic in the community may fear contact with strangers. . . . He may be unable to cope with . . . the complex demands of welfare departments.[5]

Although many of these "negative" features of schizophrenia are known to be made worse by the social deprivation of institutional care, they are nevertheless seen by psychiatrists as inherent aspects of the illness. (Hence the emphasis on the biological concept of "anergy" rather than the psychological attribute of "apathy.") Mental health professionals become frustrated by, and sometimes critical of, their patients' dependency, incompetence and unreliability. To label such problems as biological deficits helps the professional cope with his or her frustrations, but it also increases the pessimism regarding treatment and the stigma that attaches to the patient. That such deficits are, to an extent, socially induced becomes apparent, however, when we read the words of this unemployed (non-psychotic) teenager:

> "I feel outside of it . . . [unemployment] just makes me feel different. I really admire these guys who can get up and shave, and have breakfast, and make a journey to work, and come home again, and have meals – guys who can do all that in one day! I don't know how they can manage it. When I've got to sign on, or anything like that, just do the one thing, it bugs me all day. . . . Or if I've got anything to do . . . say to catch a bus to go somewhere, it's a real drag. We can't seem to get with it."[6]

The similarity in the emotional reactions of the unemployed and of people with psychosis was highlighted by a study conducted in the Great Depression. The level of negativity and pessimism about the future in large samples of the Scottish and Lancashire unemployed was found to be greater than that of groups of patients with psychotic depression and schizophrenia.[7] If the unemployed are as distressed as hospitalized people suffering from psychosis, how can we hope that the unemployed people with psychosis will return to normal during hard times? In fact we may ask, as did the author of the study

of the Scottish and Lancashire jobless, "why mentally distressed unemployed
. . . do not become psychotic."[8]

The answer is, of course, they may well do so. Brenner found that it was
precisely that segment of the population that suffers the greatest relative
economic loss during a depression – young and middle-aged males with moderate levels of education – that showed the greatest increase in rates of admission to New York mental hospitals for functional psychosis during an economic downturn. Prominent among these patients were people admitted for
the first time with schizophrenia.[9] We saw in Chapter 2 that the likeliest
explanation for this effect was a true increase in the occurrence of psychosis
secondary to the stresses of the economic recession and unemployment. In
Chapter 9 we shall explore in more detail whether labor dynamics significantly affect the rate of occurrence of schizophrenia. Here we shall concentrate on how far the labor market influences the course and outcome of the
illness.

Unemployment may exert an indirect influence on some people suffering
from psychosis in the community. One stress factor known to be associated
with poor outcome in schizophrenia is the effect of living with hostile, critical
or emotionally over-involved relatives. The greater the proportion of time a
person with schizophrenia spends in the company of such a relative, the
greater is his or her chance of relapse.[10] During an economic depression, both
the relative and the patient are more likely to be unemployed and at home
together. For the minority of people with schizophrenia who live with such a
relative, this may be a serious stress. A successful treatment program that has
been developed to reduce the high risk of relapse for such patients uses as one
of its techniques efforts to increase the separation of patient and relative by
getting one of them out of the house and at work.[11]

On the other hand, the home environment for the unemployed patient may
be too under-stimulating. It was found in one five-year follow-up study of
people with schizophrenia in London that for patients who were unemployed
and living at home, the length of time spent doing absolutely nothing was
similar to that of patients in backward asylums.[12] Such poverty of daily
existence is known to be closely allied to the clinical poverty of institutionalism and the negative features of schizophrenia.[13]

To emphasize, thus, the stresses of unemployment for people with schizophrenia is not to overlook the fact that, for many of these individuals, the
stress of employment is also a major difficulty. People with schizophrenia
experience severe problems, argues psychiatrist Hans Huessy, as a consequence of the "fabulously highly developed division of labor in industrial
society."[14] Work-related stress is certainly important for these patients. In one
group of people with schizophrenia, for example, 60 per cent had experienced
a stressful life event in the three weeks before their psychotic breakdown; of
these, the stress for one-third had been related to stopping or starting work,
completing job training or changing hours of employment.[15] Starting work,

however, is an acute stress that, if weathered, may lead the person with psychosis to higher functioning. Unemployment, on the other hand, brings the chronic strain of low status and purposelessness, which may prevent recovery. Whichever part of the picture we study, nevertheless, it seems likely that the labor market is closely involved in the social production and perpetuation of psychosis.

THE INDUSTRIAL RESERVE ARMY

Unemployment, argued Friedrich Engels, is not an aberration but an unavoidable component of capitalist production.

> It is clear that English manufacture must have at all times save the brief periods of highest prosperity, an unemployed reserve army of workers, in order to be able to produce the masses of goods required by the market in the liveliest months.[16]

Karl Marx, like Engels, not only maintained that "a surplus labouring population is a necessary product of accumulation . . . on a capitalist basis" but also that it is a condition of existence of the capitalist mode of production. It forms a disposable industrial reserve army, that belongs to capital quite as absolutely as if the latter had bred it at its own cost.[17]

Marx developed this concept in some detail in *Capital* and distinguished various components of the reserve army of labor. The segment that he labeled the "stagnant" category of the "relative surplus population" would these days be called the secondary labor force. It is characterized by

> extremely irregular employment. Hence it furnishes to capital an inexhaustible reservoir of disposable labour-power. Its conditions of life sink below the average normal level of the working class.[18]

Even the most poverty-stricken among them are "in times of great prosperity . . . speedily and in large numbers enrolled in the active army of labourers."[19] Many of the marginally functional mentally ill are to be found in this group and in the related category of

> those unable to work, chiefly people who succumb to their incapacity for adaptation, due to the division of labour; . . . the victims of industry, . . . the mutilated, the sickly, the widows, &c.[20]

The size of the industrial reserve army in modern times is considerable. The ranks of the officially unemployed have to be multiplied several times to include discouraged workers, housewives who wish to work, the underemployed and the disabled (who could be rehabilitated).[21] The true United States unemployment rate during the early 1970s, according to political scientist Charles Anderson, could be realistically estimated at 25 per cent.[22] Subsequently it became considerably greater. In the next two decades official unemployment in the United States exceeded 10 per cent, and in Britain ran close to 14 per cent. These figures conceal even more massive wastage of human power in certain segments of the population. Official unemployment among adult black men in the United States rose to 45 per cent in the 1980s; and if black men not counted by the census-takers were included, the figures would indicate that fewer than half of adult black males were employed. Increasingly, US workers are employed in low-paid jobs – in 1990 a fifth of American workers, a third of Hispanic-Americans, earned too little, working full-time, to keep a family out of poverty. With the definition of "full employment" being adjusted upwards with some regularity – most recently to 6.5 per cent in the United States; with poverty increasing – nearly a sixth of American families, a third of black families, living in poverty in 1992; it cannot be argued that the industrial reserve army has been demobilized.[23]

REHABILITATION AND REINTEGRATION

Marx's analysis suggests that the treatment of the great majority of the mentally ill will reflect the condition of the poorest classes of society. In the absence of a powerful political counter-force the outlook in schizophrenia is unlikely to get better. Despite the fact that an improvement in conditions of living and employment for people with psychotic disorders may yield higher rates of recovery, this consideration will remain secondary. Significant treatment efforts will only be expended on those skilled workers who are acutely mentally ill and whose disappearance from the work force involves the loss of a substantial investment in training. Efforts to rehabilitate and reintegrate the chronically mentally ill will only be seen at times of extreme shortage of labor (such as in the boom years of the late 1990s in the US) – after the other battalions of the industrial reserve army have been mobilized. At other times, the primary emphasis will be one of social control. The rate of recovery of those who have an "incapacity for adaptation" will, then, be a barometer of the extent of general unemployment.

There is evidence to support this interpretation. In an earlier chapter, for example, we have seen that successful rehabilitation and social reintegration of the mentally ill are related to the demand for labor and, in many instances, this success appears to be a reflection of the intensity of the rehabilitative efforts. To recapitulate:

- Rehabilitation of the mentally and physically disabled is more successful in wartime and during periods of labor shortage.

- Deinstitutionalization began, before the introduction of the antipsychotic drugs, in those northern European countries that had low unemployment rates.
- The number of mental hospital beds provided in the industrial nations in 1965 was related to the national unemployment rate.
- The proportion of people with schizophrenia confined to hospital at follow-up increased during the Great Depression.
- Discharge and recovery rates in labor-starved, early nineteenth-century America may have been higher because of the availability of moral treatment in the public asylums.
- Recovery rates and treatment efforts declined as pauperism and unemployment became more common in the new republic.

Just how does the labor market influence approaches to the mentally ill? Rehabilitative and reintegrative efforts for psychiatric patients are comprised of three inter-related elements:

(1)   political consensus, or state mental health policy;
(2)   professional consensus, or psychiatric ideology; and
(3)   social consensus, or tolerance of the mentally ill.

A speculative attempt to illustrate how these components may vary with the business cycle is set out in Table 6.1. At any one time, opposing sets of attitudes may be encountered, but as the economic climate changes so does the balance of opinion.

It becomes clear from this formulation that psychiatric ideology may be influenced by changes in the economy – a notion that implies a rejection of the conventional concept of scientific progress inherent in mainstream medical history. There are certainly grounds for this position. As we have seen, when recovery rates and treatment standards declined at the end of the moral-management era, and at the onset of the Great Victorian Depression, psychiatric philosophy became pessimistic and turned from an interest in social causes of illness to biological and hereditary factors. Kraepelin defined schizophrenia as an incurable disease. Early discharge was considered dangerous. Eugen Bleuler reformulated the concept of schizophrenia as a condition from which many recovered without defect in the sunnier economic climate of Switzerland before the First World War. At this time, he and his colleagues at Burghölzli Hospital in Zurich – Carl Jung and Adolf Meyer – developed psychodynamic theories of schizophrenia. Bleuler encouraged the early discharge of his patients to avoid the dangers of institutionalism. During the twentieth-century Great Depression, physical treatment methods and psychosurgery were emphasized. Psychosis was neglected and psychiatry, especially in America, concentrated upon the long-term, dynamic treatment of less severely disturbed, middle-class and upper-class, neurotic patients.

Table 6.1 Differences in rehabilitative and reintegrative efforts for the mentally ill during the depression and the boom

Depression	Boom
Political Consensus	
Custodial care is necessary to protect the community	Community care is preferable
Hospital expansion is required	A cost-benefit analysis of psychiatric rehabilitation must include savings resulting from patients' increased productivity
Professional Consensus	
Schizophrenia is incurable	Schizophrenia is curable
Genetic and biological factors are important causes of psychosis	Social factors are important causes of psychosis
Hospitals are therapeutic	Mental institutions are harmful
Early discharge is dangerous	
Physical, surgical and pharmaceutical treatment methods are most valuable	Psychosocial treatment is valuable in psychosis
Neurotic patients are more treatable than patients with psychosis	Treatment efforts should be directed towards the severely mentally ill
Social Consensus	
The mentally ill are dangerous and should be locked up	Anybody can become mentally ill
I would not want to work with/live next to/ marry a mental patient	

Widespread interest in social factors in mental illness, in the understanding of psychosis and in community care were not to return until 80 or 90 years after moral treatment disappeared – until the boom decades after the Second World War. By contrast, psychiatry in post-revolutionary Russia during the early twentieth century pursued a different course – a method of psychological and social reintegration that evolved from the work of Ivan Pavlov.[24]

Ideological views that emerge counter to the mainstream of psychiatric thought make no headway in the face of a contrary political and social consensus. Critics, in the mid-Victorian era, who objected to the expansion of asylums into mammoth institutions where individual treatment was impossible were ignored by local authorities and a tax-conscious populace concerned to maximize cost-efficiency.[25] Hospital superintendents who attempted to establish open-door policies before the advent of the postwar social psychiatry revolution were defeated by public opinion.[26] Alfred Adler, in the 1930s, gained little recognition for his views on the importance of social factors in psychopathology; and the work of American social scientists in the 1930s on the interaction of culture and mental disorder did not influence psychiatric theory or practice to an appreciable degree.[27]

A fairly recent example further illustrates how psychiatric philosophy is molded by the politics of the period. In 1981, as part of a nationwide trend towards budgetary cuts in human services, the City and County of Denver, Colorado, sharply reduced its allocation to Denver General Hospital. The administrators of the community mental health center, which formed a part of the hospital, responded by drastically cutting their services to their most severely disturbed clients – money-losing outreach services to hundreds of ex-state hospital clients in boarding homes, including a day-care program, alternative supportive housing, sheltered employment and vocational training. A number of these chronically ill clients brought a class action suit against the hospital and its funding agencies, demanding reinstatement of these essential services. The psychiatrists and administrators of the mental health center entered the following defense: there was no evidence to show that the type of community services they had been providing to the chronic psychotic patients were at all effective.[28] Their view was incorrect,[29] but this is incidental. The point of interest here is that less than a decade earlier the Colorado state legislators had been assured that such community-treatment methods were so superior that the state hospitals could be run down and the funds diverted to community mental health centers. From buoyant optimism to the depths of pessimism in less than ten years – from legitimizing the last stages of deinstitutionalization to legitimizing the final abandonment of the same patients to poverty and neglect in their inner-city ghetto. The story of moral treatment is, here, being repeated under similar economic conditions. The cause for mounting pessimism appears the same in each case – governmental indifference leaves the patients stranded in sordid environments, without adequate treatment and without a purpose in life. The victims are blamed each time, however; it is, supposedly, the inherently incurable nature of the patients' condition that indicates that we should not waste time and money treating them.

SOCIAL TOLERANCE

Can it be shown that public tolerance of the mentally ill is similarly affected by the economic climate? In general, discrimination, prejudice and negative stereotyping are known to increase sharply as competition for scarce jobs increases. Negative attitudes towards ethnic minority groups become more common during hard times.[30] But information about the effect of the economy on attitudes towards the mentally ill is limited. In Britain, many observers noted an improvement in public attitudes towards mental patients at the time of the postwar social psychiatry revolution.[31] As Professor Morris Carstairs wrote in 1961: "Few would claim that our current 'wonder drugs' exercise more than a palliative influence on psychiatric disorders. The big change has been rather one of public opinion."[32] In America, in line with the higher unemployment, the later onset of deinstitutionalization and the less intense rehabilitative and reintegrative thrust of that movement, public attitudes were slower to change. Community studies from the 1950s reported that attitudes towards the mentally ill were characteristically negative and rejecting.[33] By the 1960s there were indications that the general public was becoming more accepting,[34] but there was no subsequent demonstrable improvement in the status of the mentally ill during the economic stagnation of the 1970s.[35] Not until the improved economic conditions of the late 1990s do we see a renewed interest in the US in combating the stigma of schizophrenia.[36]

REHABILITATION EFFORTS – CAUSE OR EFFECT?

Having seen that both recovery rates in schizophrenia and rehabilitative efforts expended on the mentally ill tend to diminish during the depression, the question of cause and effect remains to be addressed. Do the patients fail to get better because nobody bothers to treat them, or does nobody bother to treat them because they fail to get better? Earlier in this chapter it was suggested that unemployment has a direct psychological impact on those who are out of work, including the mentally ill, and could thus stand in the way of recovery from psychosis. Can we rule out the additional possibility, implicit in Marxist theory, that a labor glut so diminishes the political incentive to rehabilitate the mentally ill that treatment efforts and community integration are discouraged, thereby worsening recovery rates?

Like most "chicken and egg" questions, this one is probably unanswerable. The events occurring at times of major policy change are so tightly intertwined that no one factor can be recognized as causative. Kathleen Jones, for example, sees three components to the postwar British social psychiatry revolution – the Open-Door Movement, the introduction of the antipsychotic drugs and legislative developments.

> From the point of view of the therapy or of public policy, the coincidence of these three movements was fortunate, since each reinforced the other. From the point of view of social analysis, it was less so, since it made it impossible to trace cause and effect with any confidence. The three strands of development crossed and re-crossed, becoming so interwoven that it will probably never be possible to determine what influence each had.[37]

Certainly there is no indication, in the case of postwar Britain, that psychiatrists, noting greater success rates, dragged politicians unwillingly along. As early as 1948, the National Health Service Act established local authority mental health departments that assumed responsibility for community care for the mentally ill; in 1954 a parliamentary debate pushed for further modernization of mental health services and hospitals; and, in the same year, a

Royal Commission was formed to consider legislative reforms that would facilitate community care.[38] All this occurred before the widespread introduction of the antipsychotic drugs and contemporaneous with the earliest moves to open the doors of the psychiatric wards. It seems probable that the political incentive to put into practice advances in psychiatric care and to increase the rehabilitation of the mentally ill was already there – stimulated by the urgent need for labor.

The question of cause and effect has a practical aspect. If it were possible artificially to maintain employment for the mentally disabled during hard times, would recovery rates improve (and admission rates and treatment costs decline), or would the social and political consensus existing during the depression limit the potential for improvement in the course of psychosis? It seems quite possible, in fact, that the effect of the social and political forces would be to obstruct the development of preferential employment for mental patients. Since the earliest days of institutions, workers in the regular labor force have objected to the unfair competition of inmates' labor during periods of unemployment. Charles Dickens illustrates this point by contrasting the prisons of labor-starved America in the 1840s with those of Britain, where a surplus of workers existed.

> America, as a new and not over-populated country, has, in all her prisons, the one great advantage, of being able to find useful and profitable work for the inmates; whereas, with us, the prejudice against prison labour is naturally very strong, and almost insurmountable, when honest men who have not offended against the laws are frequently doomed to seek employment in vain. Even in the United States, the principle of bringing convict labour and free labour into a competition which must obviously be to the disadvantage of the latter, has already found many opponents, whose number is not likely to diminish with access of years.[39]

Here, in a nutshell, is the antagonism between unemployment and rehabilitation and recovery in mental illness.

More recent examples may readily be found. In the 1930s, efforts were made to introduce into British psychiatric hospitals methods of work therapy designed (by Dr Herman Simon of Gütersloh, Germany) to discourage "idleness or fatuous madness." The failure of these efforts is explained by David Clark:

> The world-wide depression of the 1930s may have made it difficult to justify diverting work to hospital patients when fit men outside were unemployed.[40]

In modern times, sheltered workshops in the United States, which generally provide employment for the disabled by contracting for piece-work with industry, face similar difficulties. During a business recession, fewer contracts are available and disabled workers have to be laid off. Alternatively, the workshops can bid to complete contracts for less than the actual cost. This makes them reliant upon government subsidies that are liable to be cut back as the depression deepens. Some workshops go bankrupt, others find that their attempts to subsidize their programs and under-bid for contracts are opposed by labor unions. Government sponsored job programs, furthermore, tend to concentrate on finding work for higher-functioning workers as unemployment mounts. All in all, it seems likely that, despite the best efforts and intentions of mental health professionals, it may not be possible completely to overcome the negative effects of the business slump on the course of schizophrenia.

LABOR DYNAMICS

Recovery from schizophrenia may worsen in the depression, it seems, because unemployment directly affects people with schizophrenia and because the reduced demand for labor results in a deterioration of rehabilitation and reintegration efforts. Economic hardship in the depression may also affect people who suffer from psychosis. We can explore just how powerful is the effect of labor dynamics on the course of schizophrenia by looking beyond the effects of the business cycle to broader relationships between the utilization of labor and outcome in schizophrenia. Specifically, we may predict:

- If one gender is less severely affected by labor market forces, members of that gender will tend to achieve better outcome in schizophrenia.
- If one social class is more affected by the rigors of the labor market, that class should experience poorer outcome in schizophrenia.
- Outcome from schizophrenia will be better in industrial nations with continuous full employment unaffected by cyclical changes.
- The course of schizophrenia will be more benign in non-industrial societies where wage labor and unemployment are uncommon.

These predictions allow us to discriminate, to a certain extent, between the effects of the labor market and of economic hardship – only in some of these instances can we expect economic hardship to produce the same direction of change in the course of schizophrenia. Let us see how accurate are these predictions.

GENDER DIFFERENCES IN RECOVERY FROM SCHIZOPHRENIA

Despite the fact that the level of female unemployment is often higher than for males in the United States, for most of the past century men have suffered more from the fluctuations of the labor market than have women. In general, substantially fewer women have been involved in wage work than men, and women are more likely to have a valued social role when not earning a wage. One could argue that patients who return to an assured role as a homemaker will experience less difficulty than those who must re-enter the competitive labor market. Furthermore, as Brenner[41] has pointed out, men are more adversely influenced by a recession than women. During the Great Depression and subsequent business downturns, male unemployment increased more than female unemployment and often surpassed it. From this, one might reasonably predict that the course of schizophrenia in women in Western industrial society will be milder than in men.

"That the probability of recovery is greater in women than in men . . . may now be regarded as established,"[42] wrote Dr Thurnam in his *Observations and Essays on the Statistics of Insanity*, as early as 1845. His analysis showed that the proportion of patients discharged as recovered from the asylums of his day was consistently higher for female than for male admissions. In more recent times Professor Ödegard, in studying all first admissions to Norwegian psychiatric hospitals from 1936 to 1945, found a higher early discharge rate for females with schizophrenia than for males.[43] Two follow-up studies of patients with schizophrenia who entered hospital in Finland in the 1960s showed that women patients were more likely to be symptom-free, working and functioning independently.[44] Psychiatrist James Beck has noted that outcome studies often demonstrate that males suffering from schizophrenia do worse than females but that women are never found to fare worse than men.[45] Similarly, in two different WHO international follow-up studies of schizophrenia, proportionally fewer women subjects were in the worst outcome group at follow-up, and more were in the best outcome category. In the industrial countries, in particular, women tended to have shorter episodes of schizophrenic psychosis.[46] In addition, Brenner's data show that female patients with functional psychosis are less likely than men to be admitted or readmitted to psychiatric hospital when unemployment increases.[47] These gender differences confirm the impression that labor dynamics may influence outcome in schizophrenia, though other factors, such as the neuroprotective effect of female hormones, may also contribute to the observed findings.[48]

SOCIAL CLASS

Some social scientists have argued that the social groups that suffer the most stress during the depression are those which suffer the greatest *relative* decline in status – the unemployed amongst the middle classes, for example.[49] On this basis Brenner has explained the particularly heavy impact of the depression on the mental hospital admission rate of more highly educated male patients.[50] This is as may be; but the business cycle aside, the social classes that come off worst in the competition for jobs are, clearly, the poorest. Black unemployment in the United States, for example, is regularly twice that of whites, in good times or bad. Unskilled workers in the secondary labor force have the least job security of any group, and the lowest status. Their work is often casual, menial, highly routine and, always, poorly paid. Alienation from the creative process is greatest, in general, in the working class. Clearly, if any group were to experience constant difficulty in gaining and holding wage work and in deriving self-esteem and gratification from their employment it would be those in the lowest social classes.

It comes as no surprise to find that recovery from psychosis is worst in the lower socio-economic groups. Admission rates were higher for pauper lunatics in Victorian Britain and, as we saw in Chapter 5, their recovery rates were lower. Similarly, in modern times, not only is the incidence of serious mental disorder greater in the lower classes (as we saw in Chapter 2), but the outcome from psychosis is distinctly worse. A study conducted in Bristol, England, of males with schizophrenia first admitted in the early 1950s found that patients from the lower social classes had longer hospital stays, were much less likely to be improved or recovered at the time of discharge, were liable to be readmitted earlier and were very much more likely to become chronically institutionalized than were upper-class patients. The lower-class patients in the community, moreover, were less likely to be employed and showed worse overall social adjustment.[51] The author of this study, Dr B. Cooper, concludes:

> It seems most likely that clinical condition and economic status are mutually related and interacting, and that the patient who fails to return to useful work is more prone to schizophrenic relapses.[52]

Other investigations have produced similar results. Another British study of males with schizophrenia from the 1950s found that lower-class patients had longer admissions.[53] In New Haven, Connecticut, August Hollingshead and Frederick Redlich in the 1950s showed that lower-class patients spent longer in hospital and were more likely to be readmitted.[54] Repeating that study a decade later, Jerome Myers and L.L. Bean also found that lower-class patients were more likely to be kept in hospital and more likely to be readmitted. In the community, the patient of low social class had a worse work record (except for homemakers, where ex-patients performed as well as never-hospitalized women), and was more socially isolated and stigmatized.[55] A 1974 follow-up study of people with schizophrenia from the eastern United States demonstrated that social class was strongly related to symptomatic outcome. Lower-class patients had more psychotic symptoms when interviewed 2–3 years after discharge from hospital.[56] Finally, the WHO international follow-up study of schizophrenia found that having a higher-status occupation was one of the best predictors of good outcome for patients living in cities in the Developed World (London, Moscow, Prague, Washington, DC and Aarhus, Denmark).[57]

Three studies do *not* show a significantly longer duration of hospital stay for lower-class people with schizophrenia. Two of these, however, were conducted in Britain during the early 1950s, when there was full employment.[58] Under such conditions, one might expect some improvement in outcome from schizophrenia in the lower classes (although Cooper's contrary findings for people with schizophrenia in Bristol were also from this period). Ödegard's study of Norwegian hospital admissions from 1936 to 1945 failed to show a consistent pattern of longer hospital stay for patients from lower-status occupations. Ödegard recognized that his results did not conform to the usual pattern found in other countries, and he attributed the findings to the fact that some of the lower-status occupations in Norway, such as public service employment, carried better economic job security, which resulted in the unusually high discharge rates for patients from these groups.[59]

Overall, it is apparent that the majority of studies, and the more comprehensive among them, point to worse outcome in schizophrenia for the lower classes. A number of factors might explain this phenomenon – economic hardship, different levels of tolerance in the family or in the community, or even, as some American researchers have argued, "more limited and rigid concepts of social reality" and poorer "drug compliance" in the lower-class patients.[60] In conjunction with the other material in this chapter, however, the finding may be taken as further support for a link between labor dynamics and the course of schizophrenia.

FULL EMPLOYMENT

Professor Luc Ciompi has argued that the benign course of schizophrenia in twentieth-century Switzerland may have been a result of the "exceptionally favorable socioeconomic conditions" that prevailed in that country throughout much of the century. He followed up more than 1,600 people with schizophrenia admitted throughout the century to the University Psychiatric Clinic in Lausanne until they passed the age of 65. Twenty-seven per cent had completely recovered and a further 22 per cent were only mildly disturbed. Thus, about half of the patients had a favorable ultimate course of their illness.[61] Such results are better than average for the Western nations at that time or since. Were they a result of the full employment that had long existed in Switzerland? Unemployment there rarely reached one per cent in the decades following the Second World War, and through the 1960s and early 1970s was generally around a tenth of that figure. Even during the Great Depression Swiss unemployment did not scale the heights common throughout the rest of Europe.[62] As Professor Ciompi remarks:

> If the socioeconomic condition in Switzerland did indeed exert a favorable influence on outcome, that would certainly be a highly significant finding. It would suggest that under favorable circumstances schizophrenia may run a predominantly favorable course.[63]

It would be equally significant if it could be shown that a benign course to schizophrenia was a by-product of the full employment that used to exist in planned socialist economies. The job security and the lower-intensity, slower-paced labor process that were usual under socialist central planning[64] could have been particularly suitable for the rehabilitation of people with schizophrenia. In the USSR, continuous full employment existed from 1930 until the collapse of the communist regime. A right to work was recognized, and workers could expect jobs to be found for them even if they were barely productive.[65] As the mayor of Moscow pointed out on a visit to London in 1983, "It might be difficult for you to understand, . . . but one of the main issues we face in Moscow is the lack of labor hands in the city."[66] In Moscow, Leningrad and other large cities at that time, vocational rehabilitation programs for the mentally disabled were highly developed and psychiatrists gave a great deal of attention to patients' optimal work placement.[67]

In fact, outcome from schizophrenia in Moscow in the late 1960s was shown to be better than for patients in Western industrial countries. The WHO International Pilot Study of Schizophrenia is a large-scale, cross-national, collaborative project that was conducted simultaneously in nine countries in the West, in the Eastern Bloc and in the Third World. (This study will be discussed in more detail in the next chapter.) Patients with schizophrenia were selected from among those admitted to psychiatric centers in 1968 and 1969. On initial evaluation (as mentioned in Chapter 1) the groups of patients in most centers appeared to be comparable, but a standardized evaluation procedure showed that psychiatrists in Moscow and Washington, DC were using a broader, more inclusive diagnostic concept of schizophrenia. At two-year follow-up, overall outcome for the people with schizophrenia in Moscow was found to be better than for those admitted to the Western centers in London, Washington, DC and Aarhus (Denmark). Although relatively few of the Russian patients made a rapid and complete recovery (as can be seen in Table 7.2 in the next chapter), nearly half of these patients had a favorable outcome – that is, they had been non-psychotic for less than a year or had, at least, shown no serious social impairment for longer than four months during the two-year follow-up period. By the same standardized follow-up criteria, only slightly more than a third of the patients in the centers in Britain, America and Denmark showed as great a degree of overall improvement. Substantially fewer of the Russian patients, furthermore, were in the worst outcome category at follow-up.[68] The superior recovery rates for people with schizophrenia in Moscow may have been an artifact of the broader diagnostic approach there; yet a similarly inclusive diagnostic concept in Washington, DC, does not seen to have led to better outcome for the Americans with schizophrenia.

Recovery from schizophrenia in the WHO study was, however, no better in Prague (Czechoslovakia) than in the West, despite a labor shortage in Prague at that time. This difference between outcome in Moscow and Prague is difficult to explain. It may have been a result of the broader Russian diagnostic approach to schizophrenia. The year these patients were admitted to the study (1968) is the same year that the Warsaw Pact countries occupied Czechoslovakia, but it is not clear that this had an impact on the rehabilitation of people with schizophrenia. We can only say that the data so far available from full-employment societies are ambiguous, but that there is some evidence that such societies benefit from a more benign course to schizophrenia than is found in industrial nations with significant levels of unemployment.

We have gone a long way towards demonstrating that socio-economic conditions shape the course of schizophrenia. Outcome data on schizophrenia in the Depression, in the two sexes, in different social classes and in different political-economic systems all tend to support the notion that the effects of the labor market and, possibly, economic hardship are critical. In all of these instances the observed differences in the course of schizophrenia may be explained by both a direct effect of unemployment on the individual suffering from psychosis or by the influence of the demand for labor on rehabilitative and reintegrative efforts. In all these instances except one – the difference in recovery patterns for men and women – economic hardship may also be an important stress leading to relapse or poor outcome.

One further prediction remains to be examined – that if labor-market conditions can adversely affect the course of schizophrenia, the illness should be more benign in non-wage-labor settings. In the next chapter we will examine this possibility and, also, use the opportunity to study how major differences in political and domestic economy may affect the person with schizophrenia.

SUMMARY

- Spending on psychiatric hospital care increased during the Great Depression.

- Spending on mental health services in Britain did not decline in the late twentieth-century economic downturn when outcome from schizophrenia was worsening.
- The effect of both economic stress and unemployment on patients in the community could account for the decreased recovery rate from schizophrenia during the twentieth-century Great Depression.
- Many of the negative symptoms of long-term schizophrenia are identical with the psychological sequelae of long-term unemployment.
- Rehabilitative and reintegrative efforts for the mentally ill fluctuate with the business cycle and may contribute to changes in outcome in schizophrenia.
- Females with schizophrenia achieve better outcome than men.
- People with schizophrenia from the lower social classes achieve worse outcome than higher-class patients.
- Outcome from schizophrenia in full-employment societies may be better than in other industrial nations.

Chapter 7

Schizophrenia in the Third World

Sixteen billion dollars was spent on the treatment of schizophrenia in the United States in 1990[1] – about 0.3 per cent of the gross domestic product. This figure excludes social security benefits paid to people with schizophrenia and other indirect costs. Such a substantial investment should surely have yielded Americans significantly better rates of recovery than in less affluent parts of the world. By contrast, psychiatric care is very low on the list of priorities in developing countries. Despite this fact, the evidence points overwhelmingly to much better outcome from schizophrenia in the Third World. It is worth looking at this evidence in some detail.

BRIEF PSYCHOSES IN THE THIRD WORLD

There are numerous reports that psychoses have a briefer duration in the Third World, and virtually none to indicate that such illnesses have a worse outcome anywhere outside the Western world. Transitory delusional states (*boufées délirantes*) in Senegal, for example, with such schizophrenia-like features as "derealization, hallucinations, and ideas of reference dominated by themes of persecution and megalomania"[2] occasionally develop the classic, chronic course of schizophrenia, but generally recover spontaneously within a short period of time. Acute paranoid reactions with a favorable course and outcome are common in the Grande Kabylie of northern Algeria[3] and throughout East Africa.[4] Acute psychotic episodes with high rates of spontaneous remission are frequent in Nigeria,[5] and brief schizophrenia-like psychoses have been reported to account for four-fifths of the admissions to one psychiatric hospital in Uganda.[6] Indistinguishable from schizophrenia, acute "fear and guilt psychoses" in Ghana manifest hallucinations, inappropriate emotional reactions, grotesque delusions and bizarre behavior. Under treatment at local healing shrines, such illnesses are generally cured within a week or so, although they may occasionally progress to chronic schizophrenia.[7] Doris Mayer, a psychiatrist, also found typical schizophrenic states to be more readily reversible in the Tallensi of northern Ghana.[8] Many more examples could be given of the prevalence of such brief psychoses in Singapore, Papua and other developing countries.[9] "Acute, short lasting psychoses," according to Dr H. B. M. Murphy, a Canadian psychiatrist with much research experience in cross-cultural psychiatry, "form a major part of all recognized mental disorders . . ." in the Third World.[10]

NOT REALLY SCHIZOPHRENIA

But are they schizophrenia? Some psychiatrists would argue that these acute psychoses are indeed schizophrenia in view of the typical schizophrenic features such as hallucinations, delusions, bizarre behavior and emotional disturbances. They would also point to the minority of cases, initially indistinguishable, which develop the chronic schizophrenic picture. Others would deny that any brief psychosis can be schizophrenia precisely because schizophrenia, by definition, is a long-lasting illness. According to the American Psychiatric Association's *Diagnostic and Statistical Manual (DSM-IV)*,[11] a psychosis must last six months to be labeled schizophrenia. This is a terminological issue that must not be allowed to obscure the point of logic. If schizophrenia has a more benign course in the developing world (and there is considerable evidence to show that this is the case), then we might well find many schizophrenia-like episodes in these societies that are of a shorter duration than six months. To argue that these are not schizophrenia is to prejudge the issue.

Could these be cases of organic psychosis? Certainly, some could be. There is a high prevalence in Third World countries of trypanosomiasis, pellagra and related parasitic, nutritional and infectious disorders that may develop into psychotic states. Malaria, in particular, is often associated with acute psychotic episodes.[12] It is unlikely, however, that all brief episodes in the Third World are organic in origin. In conducting their social psychiatric survey of four aboriginal tribes in Taiwan, two psychiatrists, Hsien Rin and Tsung-Yi Lin, were particularly concerned about the diagnosis of organic and functional psychoses. They carefully separated schizophrenia from malarial psychosis, drug-induced psychosis and unclassifiable cases. Although skeptical at the outset of the study, after cross-checking their information and cross-validating their diagnoses they were forced to conclude that psychoses in general, and schizophrenia in particular, had a particularly benign course among these Formosan farmers and hunters. Of ten confirmed cases of schizophrenia only two had been active for more than two years and five had been ill for less than a year.[13] More recent data, presented below, from the WHO ten-country study confirm the impression that the superior outcome in Third World cases is not due to the inclusion of acute psychotic episodes of organic origin.

CONFLICTING REPORTS

Some reports fail to show better outcome for schizophrenia and other psych-oses in the Third World. They are relatively few and deserve a closer analysis. Dr J. De Wet, the assistant physician superintendent of a South African mental hospital, concluded that the recovery rate from schizophrenia was no greater in his Bantu patients than was reported for Europeans. His observa-tions were made, however, on patients treated in what appears to have been a particularly traditional and restrictive Western-style hospital setting, which we now know can have a profoundly deteriorating effect on the course of schizophrenia. Only a handful of patients in his 1943 sample were ever dis-charged from hospital, and these only after several months confinement. Those who were discharged were the patients who "completely recovered"; ten years later they were still doing well at home. None of the patients who remained in hospital regained anything but an indifferent functioning level or worse. The patients in De Wet's 1953 sample all received 15–30 electro-convulsive treatments and none "was discharged until two months after E.C.T. in order that sudden relapses did not take place at home."[14] Again the results were not good. By contrast, others who are familiar with the Bantu have described excellent recovery from schizophrenia-like psychoses in their own communities.[15] Dr De Wet's report demonstrates what happens to the usually excellent course of schizophrenia in African villages when people with the illness are managed in a traditional European hospital setting. The report is not evidence, despite De Wet's claims, of generally poor outcome from psychosis among the Bantu.

Another study that found poor outcome from schizophrenia in a Third World peasant society came from psychiatrist Joseph Westermeyer. Dr Westermeyer published a series of articles on 35 people with psychosis whom he located in 27 villages of Ventiane province, Laos. The cases were selected by asking villagers if any of their neighbors were considered *baa* or insane. Nine of the subjects so identified were rated as suffering from organic psychoses and 24 as having functional psychoses, mostly schizophrenia. Only two teenagers were considered to be no longer suffering from psychosis. The group of subjects was clearly very actively disturbed; only two were working and only five were lucid enough to provide useful information about themselves. Dr Westermeyer compared the current functioning of these dis-turbed people with their pre-illness state and concluded, not unreasonably, "that severe social dysfunction was associated with psychosis in a peasant society."[16] He went on to argue, however:

> These findings are in contrast to the social functioning of psychotic patients who are receiving psychiatric care. Follow-up studies of psychotic persons receiving psychiatric care in North America and Europe have shown that many return to economic productivity (about

half of schizophrenics do so) and make a fair to good social adjustment.[17]

A problem with this conclusion is not difficult to detect. Dr Westermeyer was comparing Lao cases who were, by virtue of the selection technique, currently highly disturbed, with Westerners suffering from psychosis who were followed up some time after their acute episode. Later in this chapter we shall see that many people suffering from psychosis in Third World societies are never labeled insane. Dr Westermeyer himself, in an earlier paper, emphasized that "folk criteria for mental illness are determined primarily by the persistence of social dysfunctional behavior rather than by disturbances in thought and affect."[18] People suffering from psychosis but not disruptive were overlooked by this study, as well as those who were psychotic and who recovered. Drs Rin and Lin, in their community survey, located subjects who had been psychotic previously and had become well. They found three times as many of these individuals as active cases. Rin and Lin's technique provided something close to lifetime prevalence data; Westermeyer, whose method detected only those who had been psychotic in the past year, provides period prevalence data. As Dr Westermeyer confirmed when questioned about this issue, his method has "a built-in bias for prolonged cases." [19] It gives us no indication of true recovery rates.

Follow-up studies can give us a more definitive picture of recovery from schizophrenia in the Third World. Several such reports are available, and only two, the first two listed here, fail to reveal substantially better recovery rates for people with schizophrenia in the developing world.

Chandigarh, India

Drs P. Kulhara and N.N. Wig, British-trained psychiatrists, reported that the outcome for patients with schizophrenia treated by the Department of Psychiatry in the Postgraduate Institute of Medical Education and Research of Chandigarh, India, was no better than for similar patients in a previous study in London.[20] Modern inpatient and outpatient services were offered to the Indian patients admitted in 1966 and 1967 and followed up four to six years later. A criticism of this study is that of 174 cases admitted, only 100 could be found for follow-up. These included, of course, all the patients who remained in hospital but excluded those who had moved away and others who might have been expected to show a good outcome.[21] This problem may explain why these researchers reported a much less impressive recovery rate for India than that found in the WHO study to be described later.

Sichuan, China

Chinese researchers attempted to identify all the people with schizophrenia who had never received any treatment in a rural county of Sichuan, China, in 1994, offered them treatment, and evaluated them again two years later. Of the 510 people they identified, only six per cent took antipsychotic medication, and 31 per cent received no treatment at all. The remainder were treated by traditional Chinese healers. Thirty-eight per cent of the group progressed to complete or partial remission of symptoms and the remainder continued to suffer from marked symptoms of the illness. It was striking, however, that more than three-quarters of the total group were working full-time or part-time at follow-up. The reason that overall outcome was not better for this group is probably because it was a *point prevalence* sample, not an *incidence* sample (see Chapter 9). That is, the sample encompassed all the cases of the illness that existed in the community at a single point in time – including those who had been ill for years (who would have been in the majority) as well as those who had fallen ill recently. Most of the outcome studies we examined in Chapter 3 were, in contrast, of people who had just been admitted to hospital for the first time. The outcome for such first-time admissions will be much better on average than for those who have been ill for a long time. A prevalence sample of the type selected in Sichuan will contain many more people who have failed to recover and who will have a poor outcome at follow-up.[22]

Two Indian studies

The different outcomes to be expected from incidence and point prevalence studies may be illustrated by two reports from India. One study, conducted at several sites, recruited people with schizophrenia *at first contact* with a mental health facility. Most of these people had been ill for less than a year. In this group, nearly 60 per cent were completely recovered after one year and three-quarters showed no continuing social impairment.[23] The second study selected people with *never-treated long-term schizophrenia detected by a door-to-door survey* in the city of Chennai in southern India.[24] Less than 30 per cent of this group recovered completely after one year of treatment and two-thirds showed no social impairment. By Western standards the results are good for both groups.

Mauritius

A follow-up study of African and Indian people with schizophrenia 12 years after their first admission to hospital was carried out in Mauritius, an island in the Indian Ocean, by the Canadian social psychiatrist Dr H. B. M. Murphy and the superintendent of the hospital, Dr A. C. Raman. They found that, although the incidence of schizophrenia was close to the British rate, the recovery rate was outstandingly better. Sixty-four per cent of the patients had maintained a complete, symptom-free recovery, and over 70 per cent were functioning independently. The patients were initially treated in hospital without the use of antipsychotic drugs. Strenuous efforts were made to trace as many as possible for follow-up, with the result that all but two per cent were found.[25]

Sri Lanka

Very similar results were obtained in Sri Lanka by anthropologist Nancy Waxler, who followed up patients five years after their first admission to hospital in 1970 with schizophrenic episodes. Some of these patients had been ill for as long as five or ten years before admission. Most of the sample came from rural areas, generally from families of farmers and laborers. All but one of the 44 patients with schizophrenia were traced. At follow-up, 45 per cent of the patients reported no symptoms at all and 69 per cent had no psychotic symptoms; half of the patients were rated by a psychiatrist as having made a normal adjustment and 58 per cent were considered normal by their families. Clearly, these people were well not merely by virtue of the tolerance of their family members, they were well by a number of standards.[26]

Hong Kong

Psychiatrists W. H. Lo and T. Lo attempted to follow up, after an interval of ten years, all of the patients with schizophrenia who lived on Hong Kong Island and had first attended the Hong Kong Psychiatric Centre in 1965. They were able to evaluate only 82 out of the original 133 patients. Their outcome results for this densely urbanized manufacturing center are intermediate between those for European patients and those for people with schizophrenia in Mauritius and Sri Lanka. A substantial number of their subjects had a relapsing course to their illness, but at follow-up 65 per cent were free of psychotic symptoms and a similar proportion had achieved good social recovery.[27] The outcome for these patients compares favorably with the estimated 45 per cent social recovery rate for Westerners with schizophrenia (see Chapter 3).

Singapore

In a study conducted by three British-trained psychiatrists, Drs Tsoi, Kok and Chew, an effort was made to trace all 637 patients with a diagnosis of schizophrenia who were admitted for the first time to Woodbridge hospital in Singapore during 1975. Five years after admission, 424 were located and re-examined. Despite the fact that many cases could not be traced, and that those who were reassessed included the patients who fared poorly and required readmission to hospital, the outcome results were very favorable. Complete recovery was observed in 35 per cent of cases and only minimal illness in a further 28 per cent. A later study of the same patients showed 15-year outcome to be very similar. These results are very similar to those for Hong Kong, both sites being densely populated cities. Nearly two thirds of the patients in the Singapore study were working at five-year follow-up. At that time labor was in short supply and jobs for patients were easy to come by.[28]

Three Indian cities

A team of psychiatrists, headed by Dr Verghese, conducted a five-year follow-up study of all of the patients attending three Indian clinics, in Lucknow, Vellore and Madras, in 1981–82 who suffered from schizophrenia of less than two years duration. Out of 386 patients identified, 323 were successfully traced and interviewed. Sixty-six per cent of the patients displayed a favorable overall outcome on a combination of measures; 64 per cent were free of psychotic symptoms and 40 per cent showed no deficits in working ability. The patients from rural areas did better than those from the cities.[29] Followed up after ten years, the people in the Madras sample were still doing as well as five years earlier.[30]

Nigeria

One hundred and sixteen patients with schizophrenia and schizophreniform disorder newly admitted to a psychiatric unit in Oyo State, Nigeria, in 1982–83 were followed up after two to three years by psychiatrist Roger Makanjuola and social worker Sunday Adedapo. Nearly half had recovered completely and three-quarters had a good clinical outcome. Sixty per cent were back at work.[31]

Bali

A comparative study of five-year outcome for patients with schizophrenia admitted to hospitals in Bali, Indonesia, and Tokyo, Japan, in 1990–92 found interesting differences between the two small cohorts of patients. Average levels of psychopathology were similar in the two groups, but the duration of hospital stay in Bali was less than a quarter of the duration in Tokyo, the proportion of the sample taking medication at follow-up was only 25 per cent in Bali versus 85 per cent in Tokyo, and hospital readmission rates were lower on the Indonesian island. The Balinese patients were admitted to Bangli State Mental Hospital which contained nearly all the psychiatric beds on the island. Despite the very small number of available beds, the hospital was less than two-thirds full, suggesting that it was a place of last resort for difficult patients who could no longer be managed in the community. This observation may explain why the outcome for the Balinese patients was not as clearly superior as it was for some of the other Third World studies described here.[32]

WHO INTERNATIONAL PILOT STUDY OF SCHIZOPHRENIA

A problem with attempts to compare recovery rates in different parts of the world is that research studies vary in the way patients are selected and diagnosed and in the criteria used for measuring outcome. To clarify this picture the World Health Organization international, collaborative follow-up study of schizophrenia[33] brought standardized methods of diagnosis and follow-up to the analysis of outcome for psychotic patients from nine countries in the industrial and non-industrial world. Patients admitted to psychiatric centers in Aarhus (Denmark), Agra (India), Cali (Colombia), Ibadan (Nigeria), London (UK), Moscow (USSR), Prague (Czechoslovakia), Taipei (Taiwan), and Washington, DC (USA) were evaluated according to a standardized procedure and categorized by a computerized diagnostic scheme – the CAT-EGO system. By this method, groups of very similar cases of acute and chronic schizophrenia were selected in each of the nine centers from among those patients applying for treatment during 1968 and 1969. In seven of the centers (as mentioned in previous chapters) the patients diagnosed as suffering from schizophrenia were found to be essentially similar, but in Moscow and Washington, DC, the diagnosis of schizophrenia was distinctly broader. At two-year follow-up the researchers were taken by surprise at the marked variability in the course and outcome of schizophrenia in the different centers. Patients in the developing world showed strikingly better results.

Combining various factors, patients were categorized into five groups according to overall outcome. As may be seen from Table 7.1, the best-outcome category includes 35 per cent of patients from centers in the Third World by comparison with only 15 per cent from centers in the industrialized world. These patients were suffering from psychosis for less than four months of the two-year follow-up period and developed a full remission with no social impairment. The two best-outcome categories combined embrace 59 per cent of patients from the developing world but only 39 per cent of those from industrial nations. More than a quarter of patients from the Developed World were in the worst-outcome category at follow-up, twice the proportion of those from the developing nations. These patients were suffering from psychosis for more than 18 months of the follow-up period and were severely socially impaired. Nigeria and India, where the catchment areas were largely rural and most of the population was engaged in agriculture, recorded the best overall outcome. Urbanized Cali, where unemployment was significant, showed somewhat less satisfactory outcome. In Taipei, the most

Table 7.1 Percentage of patients with schizophrenia in different overall outcome groups in the WHO International Pilot Study

Centers	Best-outcome group %	Two best-outcome groups combined %	Two worst-outcome groups combined %	Worst-outcome group %
Aarhus	6	35	48	31
Agra	48	66	21	15
Cali	21	53	28	15
Ibadan	57	86	7	5
London	24	36	41	31
Moscow	9	48	20	11
Taipei	15	38	35	15
Washington	23	39	45	19
Prague	14	34	39	30
Developed nations	15	39	37	28
Developing nations	35	59	23	13

industrially developed of the Third World centers and with serious levels of unemployment, the outcome was little better than in the industrial West and less good than in Moscow. Although few patients in Moscow were in the best-outcome group, a large proportion was in the best two groups combined, and few were in the worst categories; these results place Moscow in an intermediate position between centers in the developed and developing worlds.

Could patient selection have influenced these results? It is possible that the people presenting for treatment of schizophrenia at Third World centers, while appearing comparable with those in the Western samples, were in fact not representative of all those with schizophrenia in the community. It seems unlikely, however, that those who were admitted to treatment would be predominantly people with less severe forms of the illness, and a more recent WHO study allows us to be certain about this point.

WHO TEN-COUNTRY STUDY

Beginning in 1978, the WHO conducted another international follow-up study of people suffering from psychosis,[34] using the same standardized diagnostic procedure as the earlier research. The study, conducted at twelve locations in ten countries around the world, aimed to include every person at each location who made contact with any helping agency because of psychotic symptoms for the first time in his or her life during the study period. The sites for the study were Aarhus, Denmark; Agra and Chandigarh, India; Cali, Colombia; Dublin, Ireland; Honolulu and Rochester, USA; Ibadan, Nigeria; Moscow, USSR; Nagasaki, Japan; Nottingham, UK; and Prague,

Czechoslovakia. At the Third World sites, a variety of traditional and religious healers was contacted to identify subjects – herbalists, Ayurvedic practitioners and yoga teachers in India, for example, and *babalawo* and *aladura* healers in Nigeria. This wide-ranging effort to identify every new case of psychotic illness at each location virtually eliminated the chance that the cases in any area were biased by the selection procedure.

Again, the outcome for Third World cases was substantially better, indicating that the results in the earlier WHO study were probably not a result of a selection bias. Nearly two-thirds (63 per cent) of the subjects in the developing-world sites experienced a more benign course leading to full remission compared to little more than a third (37 per cent) in the Developed World. Similarly, a smaller proportion of Third World cases suffered the worst type of outcome; only 16 per cent of developing-world cases were impaired in their social functioning throughout the follow-up period compared to 42 per cent in the Developed World. The superior outcome for Third World subjects was certainly not a result of more intensive treatment; more than half (55 per cent) of the developing-world cases were never hospitalized, in contrast to a mere eight per cent in the Developed World; and only 16 per cent of developing-world subjects versus 61 per cent of cases in the Developed World were taking antipsychotic medication throughout the follow-up period.

Did the Third World cases experience a milder course because more of them were, in reality, suffering from some good-prognosis condition that mimics schizophrenia – an acute atypical psychosis or an organic disorder caused by an infectious agent? If this were the case, we would expect there to have been more acute atypical psychoses in the Third World sample and for the good-outcome cases to be clustered among these subjects. In fact, this was not the case. The proportion of acute illnesses and of the more atypical, broadly defined cases, it is true, was greater among the Third World subjects; but outcome was better in Third World subjects regardless of whether the illness was acute or insidious in onset, or whether it was of the "core" variety, diagnosed according to the most restrictive criteria, or diagnosed by broad criteria.

In 2000, medical anthropologist Kim Hopper and researcher Joseph Wanderling revisited the data from two WHO outcome studies asking two questions. Followed-up decades after the studies were initiated, are the patients in the developing world still doing better than those from the industrial world? And are the results due to some artifact in research methodology? They examined the outcome for 809 people in both the WHO outcome studies described above, 13 to 26 years later, and in some similar studies, and concluded that the results for people with schizophrenia in the developing world were still consistently better. They looked at six potential sources of research bias: differences in follow-up methodology, arbitrary grouping of centers into developed/developing world categories, diagnostic ambiguities, selective outcome measures, gender and age. They concluded that none of these possible confounding factors explained the observed differences.[35]

The general conclusion is unavoidable. Schizophrenia in the Third World has a course and prognosis quite unlike the condition as we recognize it in the West. The progressive deterioration that Kraepelin considered central to his definition of the disease is a rare event in non-industrial societies, except perhaps under the dehumanizing restrictions of a traditional asylum. The majority of people with schizophrenia in the Third World achieve a favorable outcome. The more urbanized and industrialized the setting, the more malignant becomes the illness. Why should this be so?

WORK

It was argued in earlier chapters that the dwindling cure rates for insanity during the growth of industrialism in Britain and America, and the low recovery rates in schizophrenia during the Great Depression, were possibly related to labor-force dynamics. The apparently superior outcome for schizophrenia in the USSR in the WHO Pilot Study, if it was not a consequence of diagnostic bias, may have been a result of full employment and an emphasis on work rehabilitation in the country at that time. The picture that has now been drawn of schizophrenia in the Third World gives more support to the notion that the work role may be an important factor shaping the course of schizophrenia.

In non-industrial societies that are not based upon a wage economy, the term "unemployment" is meaningless. Even where colonial wage systems have been developed, they frequently preserve the subsistence base of tribal or peasant communities, drawing workers for temporary labor only.[36] In these circumstances, underemployment and landlessness may become common but unemployment is rare. Unemployment, however, may reach high levels in the urbanized and industrial areas of the Third World.

The return of a person suffering from psychosis to a productive role in a non-industrial setting is not contingent upon his or her actively seeking a job, impressing an employer with his or her worth or functioning at a consistently adequate level. In a non-wage, subsistence economy, people with mental illness may perform any of those available tasks that match their level of functioning at a given time. Whatever constructive contributions they can make are likely to be valued by the community and their level of disability will not be considered absolute. Dr Adeoye Lambo, a psychiatrist well known for developing a village-based treatment and rehabilitation program in Nigeria, reports that social attitudes in Nigerian rural communities permit the majority of those with mental disorders to find an appropriate level of functioning and thus to avoid disability and deterioration.[37] In India, research workers for the WHO follow-up study of schizophrenia encountered difficulty in interviewing their cases as the ex-patients were so busy – the men in the fields and the women in domestic work.[38] In rural Sichuan, China, more than three-quarters of people with schizophrenia who had never been treated were working; even people with significant psychotic symptoms were doing housework or farm work.[39] The more complete use of labor in pre-industrial societies may encourage high rates of recovery from psychosis.

But what of the nature of the work itself? John Wing, a British social psychiatrist who undertook a great deal of research on schizophrenia, identified two critical environmental factors that lead to optimal outcome from the illness. The first of these, which we will return to later, is freedom from emotional over-involvement – smothering or criticism – from others in the household. His second criterion, which is relevant here, is that there should be stable expectations precisely geared to the level of performance that the individual can actually achieve.[40] Industrial society gives relatively little leeway for adapting a job to the abilities of the worker. High productivity requirements and competitive performance ratings may be particularly unsuitable for a person recovering from schizophrenia. In a peasant culture he or she is more likely to find an appropriate role among such tasks of subsistence farming as livestock management, food- and fuel-gathering or child-minding. As the authors of the WHO Pilot Study of Schizophrenia comment about life in the countryside of India:

> work in the rural setting is mostly collective, agricultural, and often does not require particular skills. Many occupations are passed from father to son. Thus, competitive situations seldom exist. The occupational pursuits do not usually require fine skill and adaptability and often do not demand much effort or strain. . . . Employment conditions in the country usually do not have any untoward effects on most patients.[41]

Many clinicians in the West have noticed that the demands of a 40-hour week are often overly taxing for patients suffering from psychosis. In hunter-gatherer and peasant societies, the distinction between work and non-work may be hard to make (in some cultures it is not linguistically possible to differentiate "work" from "ritual" or from "play"[42]), but the demands of subsistence are unlikely to be burdensome. !Kung Bushmen work no more than two to three (six-hour) days a week in hunting and food-gathering for themselves and their dependants, and about two hours further each day is spent on food preparation and "housework."[43] Slash-and-burn agriculture, for example among the Bemba of north Zimbabwe or the Toupouri of north Cameroon, calls for only three or four (five-hour) working days a week.[44] Plough agriculture commonly requires a 30–35-hour work week.[45] Estimates of labor requirements for irrigation agriculture vary. In Yunnan Province in pre-revolutionary China, the working day was seldom longer than seven to eight hours, including frequent rest periods, even at the busiest time of year; during the slack months, there was virtually no farm work to be done. Elsewhere a demanding 50–70-hour work week has been recorded, but both of these examples of irrigation agriculture involve market production, not just local subsistence needs.[46] Where production is for use and not for exchange, labor needs tend to be low.[47]

In each setting there is wide individual variation. In pre-revolutionary Russia, for example, peasant farmers in Volokolamsk worked between 79 days a year in the least industrious households and 216 in the most industrious.[48] This compares with an expectation of around 230 to 240 working days a year for employees in modern industrial society. Work demands in many cultures are particularly low for young, unmarried adults[49] (who may be at higher risk for developing schizophrenia), but whatever the usual pattern, workload expectations are more readily adjusted to meet the capacities of the marginally functional individual in a village setting than in the industrial labor market. There can be little doubt that it is simpler for a person with schizophrenia to return to a productive role in a non-industrial community than in the industrial world. The merits of tribal and peasant labor systems are apparent. As in the West during a period of labor shortage, it is easier for family and community members to reintegrate the sick person into the society, and the sufferer is better able to retain his or her self-esteem. The result may well be not only better social functioning of the sick person but also more complete remission of the symptoms of the illness.

OCCUPATION AND OUTCOME

In searching for predictors of good outcome in schizophrenia, the WHO Pilot Study examined a number of patient characteristics. We may look at these data for evidence of an association between occupation and outcome in schizophrenia but, in so doing, we encounter difficulties presented by the variety and complexity of work and subsistence patterns in the developing world. Poverty can be extreme in the urban slums of the Third World, where many eke out an existence by self-employment in street-vending and similar activities or with low and irregular earnings from work in the formal and informal segments of the urban labor market. Outright unemployment, however, is often most severe in the upwardly striving, urban middle classes. In rural areas, this reversal of the usual Western pattern is even more marked, with unemployment among the aspiring educated at times being severe, while those working the land are largely outside the labor market.[50]

In rural districts, therefore, we should look for a reversal of the usual Western pattern of outcome from schizophrenia and for superior outcome in the less educated – the subsistence farmers with limited exposure to Western acculturative forces. A mixed recovery picture might be expected to occur in those urban areas where economic development is incomplete and is creating stresses for the new managerial and professional classes. In the most highly developed cities of the Third World we should expect a pattern of recovery similar to the West with the best outcome in the high-status occupations. In general, we might anticipate outcome to be better in villages, where more of the population is outside the wage-labor market, than in the cities.

In fact the WHO data show neither rural nor urban living to be strong predictors of good outcome.[51] The information on residence, however, was gathered at intake rather than at follow-up. The lack of association between residence and outcome, therefore, may merely reflect what several authors have noted – that migrant laborers who fall ill while working in the industrial areas return to the village to recuperate.[52] City-dwellers with psychosis may benefit from this return to traditional village roles.

Other WHO Pilot Study data more clearly document an association between occupation and outcome. Farmers were more likely than patients of any other occupation to experience the most benign pattern of illness – full remission with no relapses – and the unemployed were least likely to experience such a mild course to the psychosis. In urbanized Cali and Taipei patients from high-status professional and managerial occupations were found to achieve good overall outcome, while this was not the case in the largely rural catchment area around Agra, India.[53] This pattern confirms the impression that schizophrenia may be more benign in the successful upper classes in the industrialized setting, but more malignant among the better educated in India who are known to suffer rates of unemployment several times greater than the poorly educated and illiterate.[54] The data from Nigeria do not fit as neatly. Even though many patients in the sample appear to have come from rural districts, Nigerians with schizophrenia in managerial jobs experienced good overall outcome.[55] This could be explained by a strong local demand for educated labor at that time or, again, the high mobility of the migrant labor force may confuse the picture; patients who were unable to continue in managerial positions could return to a less demanding role in their farming community.

Migrant-labor practices allow people with schizophrenia in the Third World to change occupation and residence after developing psychotic symptoms. Level of education, however, is less easily changed. It is therefore interesting to note that a *high* level of education is one of the few strong and consistent indicators of *poor* outcome in the Third World,[56] thus standing in contrast to Western patterns of recovery. This point, then, may be one of the most useful pieces of evidence in the WHO study, pointing to a link between good outcome for schizophrenia in the Third World and the maintenance of traditional occupational roles.

STRESS

Unemployment on the one hand and intensified work demands on the other are special stresses of modern industrial society. Are there other increased stresses of life in the fast-paced industrial world that might account for the poor prognosis for schizophrenia in the West? It depends what we mean by stress. Urban overcrowding, job insecurity, productivity pressure and alienation from the creative process are all chronically stressful facets of industrial life. Those who live in peasant communities, however, must face equal levels of domestic discord and often suffer problems of poor health, high infant mortality and inadequate housing, clothing, food and water. With the development of state-level societies and colonialism come increasing difficulties with authority, status disparity, poverty and starvation. To passing tourists, the palm-studded fishing village near Mazatlan on the west coast of Mexico might seem a subtropical paradise; but when Russell McGoodwin, an anthropologist, asked the inhabitants what caused them most suffering they listed many complaints including poverty, family problems, the burden of work, inadequate water supplies and poor clothing. In response to the question, "What do you enjoy?" nearly half answered, "Nothing."[57] Life in non-industrial societies is not low in stress. Rousseau's "noble savage" leading a life of peace and perfect order in "the state of nature" cannot be found. But some features of tribal and peasant life might well improve the social integration and the outlook for those who suffer from a psychotic episode.

A PSYCHOTIC EPISODE IN GUATEMALA

Maria, a young Indian woman living in a village on Lake Atitlan in Guatemala, alienates her close relatives and the people of the community by her irresponsible behavior before finally suffering a full-blown psychotic episode. She hallucinates, believing that spirits are surrounding her to take her to the realm of the dead, and she walks about the house arguing with ghosts. A local shaman perceives that she is *loca* (crazy) and diagnoses her as suffering the effect of supernatural forces unleashed by the improper behavior of certain relatives. He prescribes a healing ritual that calls for the active participation of most of her extended family. Her condition requires her to move back to her father's house, where she recovers within a week. Benjamin Paul, the anthropologist who describes Maria's case, points out several features of interest. Maria is never blamed for her psychotic behavior or stigmatized by her illness, because her hallucinations of ghosts are credible supernatural events and she is innocently suffering the magical consequences of the wrongdoing of others. The communal healing activities lead to a dramatic reversal of Maria's course of alienation from family and community. In the West, a psychotic episode is likely to lead to increased alienation. In the case of Maria, conflict resolution and social reintegration are central to her recovery and result from the folk diagnosis and treatment of her symptoms.[58]

THE FOLK DIAGNOSIS OF PSYCHOSIS

Throughout the non-industrial world, the features of psychosis are likely to be given a supernatural explanation. The Shona of southern Rhodesia, for example, believe visual and auditory hallucinations to be real and sent by spirits.[59] In Dakar, Senegal:

> one can have hallucinations without being thought to be sick. A magical explanation is usually resorted to and native specialists are consulted. There is no rejection or alienation by society. The patient remains integrated within his group. As a result, the level of anxiety is low . . .[60]

The psychiatrist who gives this report claims that 90 per cent of the acute psychoses in Dakar are cured because the patient's delusions and hallucinations have an obvious culturally relevant content, and he or she is not rejected by the group.

Similarly, in the slums of San Juan, Puerto Rico:

> If an individual reports hallucinations, it clearly indicates to the believer in spiritualism that he is being visited by spirits who manifest themselves visually and audibly. If he has delusions . . . his thoughts are being distorted by interfering bad spirits, or through development of his psychic faculties spirits have informed him of the true enemies in his environment. Incoherent ramblings, and cryptic verbalizations indicate that he is undergoing a test, an experiment engineered by the spirits. If he wanders aimlessly through the neighborhood, he is being pursued by ambulatory spirits who are tormenting him unmercifully.[61]

In many cases where a supernatural explanation for psychotic features is used, the label "crazy" or "insane" may never be applied. I once remarked to a Sioux mental health worker from the Pine Ridge Reservation in South Dakota that most Americans who heard voices would be diagnosed as suffering from psychosis. Her response was simple. "That's terrible."

Nigerian attitudes to mental illness

Urban and rural Yoruba with no formal education, from the area of Abeokuta in southwestern Nigeria, were asked their opinions about descriptions of typical mentally ill people. Only 40 per cent of those questioned thought that the person described as having the features of paranoid schizophrenia was mentally ill.[62] (Some 90–100 per cent of Americans label the subject of this vignette as mentally ill.[63]) Only 21 per cent of the uneducated Yoruba considered the description of the person with simple schizophrenia to have a

mental illness. (Some 70–80 per cent of American respondents call this hypo-
thetical case mentally ill.[64])

What is perhaps even more impressive than the details about labeling
psychosis in this Nigerian study is the very high level of tolerance revealed.
More than 30 per cent of the uneducated Yoruba would have been willing to
marry the person described as having paranoid schizophrenia and 55 per cent
would have married the person with simple schizophrenia. In contrast, when
skilled workers from the area of Benin in midwestern Nigeria were asked
their opinions about someone specifically labeled a "nervous or mad person,"
16 per cent thought that all such people should be shot and 31 per cent
believed that they should be expelled from the country. These educated
Nigerians conceived of mad people as "senseless, unkempt, aggressive and
irresponsible."[65]

Malaya

In Nigeria it appears that the label "mad," "crazy" or "mentally ill" is only
applied to highly disruptive individuals and brings with it harsher treatment.
The same pattern has been observed in a Malay village in Pahang state. Here
the term for madness, *gila*, is only applied to violent people. "Madmen" are
always handed over to authorities outside the village for permanent banish-
ment. Within the community of over 400 people, however, are many people
who probably suffer from psychosis who have never been labeled mad –
twelve who are "eccentric," including senile elderly people and marginally
functional hermits; and one "person with less than healthy brains" who
spends a good deal of time praying and reading in solitude. Five people
exhibiting *latah* – a so-called culture-bound psychosis – were also identified;[66]
but this condition may not be a psychosis in the proper sense of the term.[67]

Laos

Although Dr Westermeyer in some of his publications disputes that people
with psychosis often escape being labeled *baa* (insane) in Laos, his own
observations are very close to the findings in Nigeria and Malaya. Lao villagers are apparently slow to apply the term *baa*, and a person so labeled
tends to have a chronic illness, usually of several years' duration, and to be
highly disruptive, assaultive or bizarre. Hallucinations are never mentioned
by the villagers as a feature of insanity. Unless there are local conditions
restricting the development of brief psychoses so common elsewhere in the
Third World, then one must assume that the reason there are so few acute
cases in Dr Westermeyer's Lao sample is that they are not considered by the
villagers to be *baa*. Interestingly, the severely psychotic *baa* individuals in
Laos are not exiled or assassinated but continue to receive food, shelter,
clothing and humane care and are restrained and incarcerated only as long as

their violent behavior requires.[68] It is apparent that labeling is an important issue only insofar as it affects management. As we shall see in the next example, it is the concept of illness that lies behind the label that is also critical in determining care and treatment.

Four East African societies

Anthropologist Robert Edgerton, describing attitudes to psychosis among tribesmen of four East African pastoral and farming societies, confirms that violence and destructiveness are emphasized in descriptions of psychosis (*kichaa*) and hallucinations are virtually never mentioned.[69] Most commonly reported features of psychosis include murder, assault, arson, abuse, stealing and nakedness. The pastoralists whose homesteads are more widely dispersed and who are more free to move away from disagreeable circumstances are less concerned than the farmers about the social disruption caused by people suffering from psychosis.[70] The intriguing conclusion of Edgerton's survey is that the tribal view of the cause of psychosis determines not only the manner of treatment but also the level of optimism about recovery.[71] The Pokot of northwest Kenya and the Sebei of southeast Uganda have a naturalistic conception of the cause of psychosis. They implicate a worm in the frontal portion of the brain and are very pessimistic about the possibilities of cure. The Kamba of south-central Kenya and the Hehe of southwest Tanzania, on the other hand, attribute the cause of psychosis to witchcraft or stress and are optimistic about curing such disorders. The two tribes that are most unsure about their respective theories of causation, the Pokot and the Hehe, also tend to be more ambivalent about the curability of the condition. The Kamba and the Hehe, holding a supernatural theory for the cause of psychosis, favor the use of tranquilizing herbs and ritual in treatment. The pessimistic Sebei and Pokot, with the naturalistic belief system, are much more inclined to treat people with psychotic disorders harshly, as illustrated by the remarks of a Pokot shaman: "I am able to cure mads. I order the patient tied and placed upon the ground. I then take a large rock and pound the patient on the head for a long time. This calms them and they are better."[72] The Pokot and Sebei recommend that people suffering from psychosis should be tied up forever, allowed to starve, driven away to die or killed outright.

NEGATIVE CONSEQUENCES

We have to recognize that many people with psychotic illness in the developing world, especially those who do not recover, can suffer bad consequences. Follow-up studies of people with psychosis in the Third World reveal an unusually high number of deaths. A study of 94 people with schizophrenia in Nigeria reported that nine had died within two to three years. One had been beaten to death by night guards who found him wandering and five had died in the homes of traditional healers.[73] In a sample of people with schizophrenia in Chandigarh, India, less than ten per cent experienced the worst course of illness, but, of these, nearly half died within the 15-year follow-up period, most within five years of their first admission. The causes of death were usually natural and not uncommonly secondary to malnutrition.[74]

Life can be very hard for some people with psychosis in the developing world, especially those who are most severely and continuously disturbed. But we should not allow reports of harsh treatment of some individuals to obscure the central facts. Many people who would be considered to be psychotic in the West are not so labeled in the Third World, especially if their condition is brief or not disruptive. Many more, though labeled "crazy" like Maria the Guatemalan Indian woman, are treated vigorously and optimistically with every effort to reintegrate them rather than reject them.

Stigma

Psychiatrists working in the Third World have repeatedly noted the low level of stigma that attaches to mental disorder. Among the Formosan tribesmen studied by Rin and Lin, mental illness is free of stigma.[75] Sinhalese families freely refer to their psychotic family members as *pissu* (crazy) and show no shame about it. Tuberculosis in Sri Lanka is more stigmatizing than mental illness.[76] The authors of the WHO follow-up study suggest that one of the factors contributing to the good outcome for people with schizophrenia in Cali, Colombia, is the "high level of tolerance of relatives and friends for symptoms of mental disorder" – a factor that can help the "readjustment to family life and work after discharge."[77]

The possibility that the stigma attached to an illness may influence its course is illustrated by research on Navajos who suffer from epilepsy conducted by anthropologist Jerrold Levy in cooperation with the Indian Health Service. Sibling incest is regarded as the cause of generalized seizures, or Moth Sickness, in Navajo society, and those who suffer from the condition are highly stigmatized for supposed transgressions of a major taboo. It is interesting to learn that these individuals are often found to lead chaotic lives characterized by alcoholism, promiscuity, incest, rape, violence and early death. Levy and his co-workers attribute the career of the Navajo epileptic to the disdain and lack of social support that he or she is offered by the community.[78] To what extent, we may wonder, can features of schizophrenia in the West be attributed to similar treatment?

HIGH STATUS IN PSYCHOSIS

It seems strange in retrospect that tuberculosis should have been such a romantic and genteel illness to eighteenth- and nineteenth-century society that people of fashion chose to copy the consumptive appearance.[79] Equally curious, the features of psychosis in the Third World can, at times, lead to considerable elevation in social status. In non-industrial cultures throughout the world, the hallucinations and altered states of consciousness produced by psychosis, fasting, sleep deprivation, social isolation and contemplation, and hallucinogenic drug use are often a prerequisite for gaining shamanic power.[80] The psychotic features are interpreted as an initiatory experience. For example, whereas poor Puerto Ricans who go to a psychiatric clinic or insane asylum are likely to be highly stigmatized as *locos* (madmen), people who suffer from schizophrenia who consult a spiritualist may rise in status. Sociologists Lloyd Rogler and August Hollingshead report: "The spiritualist may announce to the sick person, his family, and friends that the afflicted person is endowed with *facultades* (psychic faculties), a matter of prestige at this level of the social structure . . ."[81]

The study indicates that Puerto Ricans with schizophrenia who consult spiritualists may not only lose their symptoms, they may also achieve the status of mediums themselves. So successful is the social reintegration of the male Puerto Ricans with schizophrenia that, after some readjustment of family roles, their wives found them *more* acceptable as husbands than did the wives of normal men.

Similar folk beliefs exist in Turkey. Dr Orhan Ozturk, a psychiatrist in Ankara, writes:

A person may be hallucinated or delusional, but as long as he is not destructive or very unstable he may not be considered insane. . . . Such a person may sometimes be considered to have a supernatural capacity for communication with the spirit world and may therefore be regarded with reverence and awe.[82]

Ruth Benedict tells us that Siberian shamans who dominate the life of their communities

are individuals who by submission to the will of the spirits have been cured of a grievous illness. . . . Some, during the period of the call, are violently insane for several years; others irresponsible to the point where they have to be constantly watched lest they wander off in the snow and freeze to death. . . . It is the shamanistic practice which constitutes their cure.[83]

Several other writers have suggested that indigenous healers who have suffered psychotic episodes may find their elevated status and well-defined curing role to be a valuable defense against relapse.[84] Psychiatrist Fuller Torrey argues, however, that few shamans can be psychotic. The role is too responsible and demanding, he claims, for a person with schizophrenia to manage.[85] While, no doubt, many healers have never suffered from psychosis, Dr Torrey underestimates the importance of psychotic features as an initiatory experience. He neglects on the one hand, the heightened possibility of complete remission from psychosis for people in the Third World and, on the other hand, the capacity of individuals with schizophrenia to be completely functional in some areas of their lives despite islands of illogical thinking. One well-known North American Indian medicine man with whom I am familiar would doubtless be diagnosed as suffering from schizophrenia by a Western psychiatrist by virtue of his extremely tangential and symbolic speech, which is often incomprehensible, his inappropriate emotional responses and his hallucinations. This man, however, is highly respected by his community and travels the country on speaking engagements. The person suffering from psychosis may be able to function well as a shaman, argues anthropologist Julian Silverman of the US National Institute of Mental Health, because "the emotional supports . . . available to the shaman greatly alleviate the strain of an otherwise excruciatingly painful [schizophrenic] existence. Such supports are all too often completely unavailable to the schizophrenic in our culture."[86]

HEALING CEREMONIES

Being thought of as a spiritualist or healer is not the only way a person with a psychotic illness in the Third World may gain status. Curing rituals for those with mental disorders may also enable the individual to increase his or her social status and redefine his or her social role. Anthropologist Ralph Linton observed that low-status individuals among the Tanala of Madagascar, such as second sons and childless wives, may rise in status as a result of the elaborate healing rite for mental illness.[87] Patients who participate in the curing possession cults in Trinidad[88] among the Yoruba of Nigeria[89] and in the Zar cult of northern Ethiopia[90] have all been observed to achieve an elevation of social status as a consequence of their membership.

Initiation into these cults also provides new friends, ongoing group support and the opportunity for social involvement, and similar benefits appear to result from other healing rites. Robin Fox, a British anthropologist, gives a detailed account of a clan cure for a 40-year-old woman with a chronic mental disorder in the Pueblo Indian community of Cochiti in New Mexico. The woman is a member of the Oak clan by birth, but by undergoing a healing ritual that entails adoption also into the Water clan, she acquires additional supportive relatives, a new social role and a new home. She subsequently shows complete recovery.[91]

GROUP PARTICIPATION

The process of curing in pre-industrial societies, it is clear, is very much a communal phenomenon tending not only to reintegrate the deviant individual into the group but also to reaffirm the solidarity of the community. Thus, the N'jayei secret society of the Mende tribe in Sierra Leone, which aims to treat mental illness by applying sanctions to those who are presumed to have committed a breach of social rules, provides members with a mechanism for social reintegration and, simultaneously, reinforces the integrity and standards of the culture.[92] Such a dual process of unification of the group and integration of the individual is seen to result from the great public healing ceremonies of the Zuni medicine societies[93] or from the intense communal involvement and dramatic grandeur of a Navajo healing ceremony. The Navajo patient, relatives and other participants alike take medicine and submit to ritual procedures in a symbolic recognition that illness is a problem for the community as a whole.[94]

Nancy Waxler, in her research on people suffering from psychosis in Sri Lanka, was impressed with the way in which the intense community involvement in treating mental illness prevents the patient from developing secondary symptoms from alienation and stigma and results in the sick person being reintegrated into society. She writes:

> Mental illness is basically a problem of and for the family, not the sick person. Thus we find among the Sinhalese that almost all treatment of mental illness involves groups meeting with groups. When a mad person is believed to have been possessed by a demon the whole family, their relatives and neighbours, sometimes the whole village, join together to plan, carry out and pay for the appropriate exorcism ceremony. The sick person is usually the central focus, but often only as the vehicle for the demon, and during some parts of these ceremonies the patient is largely ignored.[95]

The importance of this process of social reintegration is confirmed by data from the two WHO outcome studies. In both the developed and developing worlds, social isolation was found to be one of the strongest predictors of poor outcome in schizophrenia.[96] Several other researchers have found this factor to be important in the genesis and outcome of schizophrenia.[97]

SOCIAL CONSENSUS

There is some anthropological evidence that broad group participation in healing not only aids the reintegration of the patient but is also a necessary and powerfully effective element in the treatment of emotional illness. The French anthropologist Claude Levi-Strauss, for example, analyzed the effectiveness of a highly respected Kwakiutl shaman from British Columbia who was skeptical of his own healing powers. Levi-Strauss concluded that the shaman was effective despite his cynicism because "the attitude of the group" endorsed his treatment. The social consensus is more important than the attitude of the healer or even of the patient.[98]

A related example of the importance of social consensus in the outcome of mental illness is provided by anthropologist Lloyd Warner's discussion of the role played in the voodoo death of an Australian aborigine by his own social group after he has been "boned" by an enemy. First the victim's kin withdraw their support and he becomes an isolated and taboo person. Then the community conducts a mourning ritual to protect the group from the soul of the "half dead" man. Unless the group attitude is reversed by the performance of a counter-ritual, the victim shortly dies.[99] These examples illustrate, on the one hand, the powerful effect of social rejection and stigma on the course of emotional illness and the importance of social acceptance and reintegration. On the other hand, they suggest that any form of treatment that does not receive full community endorsement (and much of institutional psychiatry in the West falls into this category) has a limited chance of success. This analysis, for example, would predict that the Kamba and the Hehe of East Africa who are optimistic about the treatment of mental illness would have better recovery rates from psychosis than the Pokot and Sebei who have no confidence in the ability of their doctors to effect a cure. Edgerton's study presents no evidence, unfortunately, to indicate whether or not this is the case.

Understanding the potential of social consensus to affect outcome allows us to explain why even those individuals who are treated in modern Western-style hospitals and clinics in the developing world rather than by indigenous therapists may experience a higher recovery rate from psychosis. It is not the specific treatment technique that is crucial (as long as it is not too regressive) but the social expectations that are generated around the episode of illness. The treatment approaches of the psychiatric clinic may well be supplemented by community diagnosis, rediagnosis and indigenous healing ceremonies that facilitate social reintegration of the sick person. Even among relatively Westernized city-dwellers, according to a report from Senegal, traditional cultural beliefs persist that help to alleviate psychological distress and mental disorder.[100] The existence of a social consensus for recovery and the willingness and capacity of the community to reintegrate the psychotic person are, no doubt, strongly influenced by whether he or she can serve a useful social role. The benefits of traditional community life for the person suffering from psychosis are less likely to persist in the face of changing patterns of labor use that increase the risks of unemployment and dependency.

THE FAMILY

One of John Wing's criteria for good outcome in schizophrenia mentioned earlier in the chapter was freedom for the patient from excessive emotional demands or criticism within the family. His recommendation is backed up by a good deal of social psychiatric research from the Medical Research Council in London and from other research centers, that was outlined in Chapter 1 and will be discussed further in Chapter 10. The family environment for people with schizophrenia in the Third World is different from the West. In India, spouses, parents or siblings are willing to provide for a relative, however disabled.[101] The multiple caregivers in an Indian extended family will handle most of the problems presented by a family member with schizophrenia without seeking outside assistance – self-neglect and dirtiness seem to be of the greatest concern.[102] At the end of the twentieth century, however, with urbanization, increased female employment and the break-up of the extended family, the level of tolerance was declining.[103] Increased acceptance, nevertheless, can bring better outcomes. In Qatar, on the Persian Gulf, people with schizophrenia in extended families have been reported to show better outcome at follow-up than those who return to nuclear family households.[104] The extended family structure, which is more common in the Third World, allows a diffusion of emotional over-involvement and interdependence among family members.

The emphasis on community involvement in the treatment of mental illness in non-industrial societies similarly tends to reduce family tensions. Responsibility is shared broadly and the patient often escapes blame and criticism, allowing the family to be more supportive. According to one study, for example, relatives of people with schizophrenia in Chandigarh, north India, are much less likely to be demanding or critical of their psychotic family member than are the relatives of people with schizophrenia in the industrial world. In London, nearly a half of patients with schizophrenia have such emotionally stressful relatives; in Rochester, New York, the proportion is similar; but in north India, fewer than a fifth of subjects with schizophrenia were found to have critical and demanding relatives.[105] As mentioned in Chapter 1, this difference might be a consequence of the higher achievement expectations placed on Westerners suffering from psychosis or of the emotional isolation so common for families of people with schizophrenia in the West but so much rarer in the developing world.

In the Third World, it appears, the person with a psychotic disorder is more likely to retain his or her self-esteem, a feeling of value to the community and a sense of belonging. These are things that, as we shall see, sixteen billion dollars does not buy the person with schizophrenia in the United States or elsewhere in the Western world.

SUMMARY

- Brief psychoses clinically indistinguishable from schizophrenia are a common occurrence in the Third World.
- Outcome from schizophrenia is better in the non-industrial world than in the West.
- Intermediate levels of outcome from schizophrenia are found in the more industrialized parts of the Third World and in the pre-*peristroika* USSR.
- People with schizophrenia in the Third World are more readily returned to a useful working role.
- In the developing world, outcome from schizophrenia is worse among the better educated – a finding that may be explained by the greater labor market stresses affecting the educated.
- The folk diagnosis of insanity stresses violence and disruption, and many people suffering from psychosis in the developing world escape this label.
- Many of those with psychosis in the Third World are not stigmatized and some may even rise in status.
- Although some people suffering from psychosis in non-industrial societies may be brutally treated, in the majority of cases vigorous and optimistic efforts are made to achieve a cure.
- Curing rituals encourage broad community involvement and aid the social reintegration of those who suffer from mental illness.
- The optimistic social consensus mobilized by the curing ceremony may aid recovery from emotional disorders.
- Family patterns of support in the Third World are better suited to the rehabilitation of people with schizophrenia.

Chapter 8

The person with schizophrenia in Western society

What is it like to suffer from schizophrenia in Western industrial society? For Mary Byrd in New York City, according to a 1982 newspaper report, it is an unbelievably bitter experience.

> One night last week . . . when the air felt like ice and half a foot of snow sent thousands of New Yorkers home early . . . Charlie, Mary Byrd and Frank Jarnot went home to a cluster of IBM cartons, covered with mailing labels and stamped: "Handle With Care." . . . By day, Mary huddles outside a subway entrance. There she stays until Frank comes to lead her the 50 paces to a choice spot alongside the bank building. . . . Taking care of Mary is almost a full-time job for the men, who call the 23-year-old "just a baby," and who take turns leaving hamburgers, coffee and cakes outside her box. . . . "She's living in a fantasy world," Frank says.[1]

An extreme case? Not at all. According to estimates, roughly half of New York City's 36,000 homeless were thought to be mentally disabled in the early 1980s.[2] A total of 25,000 chronically mentally ill New Yorkers were thought to be living on the street, in missions, public shelters, flophouses and cheap hotels.[3] Of 1,235 men sleeping at a public shelter on New York's Bowery on a night in 1976, half showed signs of obvious mental illness, excluding alcoholism; many of these men were former state hospital residents. At the Women's Shelter in New York City more than three-quarters of the women admitted in 1971 were suffering from a psychosis.[4] The degree of mental disturbance amongst such down and out New Yorkers was by no means slight. Mental health professionals who interviewed 100 long-time residents at the same Men's Shelter on the Bowery in 1965 found 50 per cent of the men to be psychotic and diagnosed 36 per cent of the whole group as suffering from schizophrenia. They compared this group of 100 Bowery men with a large sample of recently admitted inpatients at five local psychiatric hospitals. Startlingly enough, the residents of the Men's Shelter were found to be *more* disturbed than the inpatients according to several measures in a standardized evaluation procedure.[5]

Researchers who conducted an ethnographic survey of New York City's homeless in 1981 concluded that the ranks of the destitute on Skid Row had been greatly swollen over the prior 15 years by large numbers of former state hospital patients. They reported:

> By a stroke of grim irony some of these ex-patients had come full circle back to the institution that had originally discharged them – this time for shelter not treatment.[6]

As the result of a class action suit filed on behalf of the city's homeless, the municipal government had been forced to open an empty state hospital building on Ward's Island as an emergency shelter. This time around, though, conditions were far worse than when the facility had been staffed as a hospital. Now the building was crammed full of cots and there was no type of treatment or recreational activity. Infestation, disease, violence and fear were pervasive. In consequence, staff pushed and prodded the residents with nightsticks to avoid contact and to maintain order. They dealt with the men in rough language and through barked orders. One feature had not changed since the days when the building was a hospital, however – the characteristics of the residents. Eighty-four per cent of the men seeking shelter there in May 1980 were mentally ill; 60 per cent were found to be moderately or severely disturbed – mostly suffering from psychosis.[7]

There was little doubt that patients were ending up on the streets because of the deficient aftercare planning and services of the mental health system. Nearly a quarter of the patients discharged from New York State psychiatric centers in the early 1980s were released to "unknown" living arrangements. From one hospital, nearly 60 per cent of patients were released to an "unknown" address.[8]

This state of affairs was not confined to New York. In a random sample of 50 men on Chicago's Skid Row in the late 1960s, Robert Priest, a British psychiatrist, found 25 per cent to be certainly or probably suffering from schizophrenia.[9] Only a decade earlier, however, in 1957 and 1958, before deinstitutionalization was far advanced, an American researcher, Donald Bogue, found a mere nine per cent of men on Skid Row in the same city to have mental illness. At that time, Bogue reported, "mentally unsound persons . . . are picked up rather promptly by the police, and . . . institutionalized."[10] A survey conducted in Los Angeles in the early 1980s found half of the 7,000–15,000 people living on Skid Row to be incapacitated by chronic mental illness – 40 per cent of the men and 90 per cent of the women.[11] Around the same time, in Philadelphia, 44 per cent of the Skid Row homeless, and at least a quarter of the people living on the streets and in the shelters of Washington, DC, were suffering from schizophrenia.[12] In Boston, 40 per cent of those staying at an emergency shelter were suffering from a psychosis in 1983.[13] Forty-seven per cent of the emergency shelter users in St Louis in the mid 1980s suffered from a functional psychosis.[14] In Denver in 1981, the judge who heard most of the cases related to the mental illness statute remarked that the primary residential care provider for mental patients was the city bus company. When they stopped offering free rides on the buses "the mentally disabled people who had found a home on the Ride (the bus system) hit the streets again."[15]

Since the early 1980s the reported frequency of mental illness among the American homeless has decreased. The studies of the homeless listed in Table 8.1[16] reveal that the average proportion of homeless men suffering from psychosis has dropped to about 25 per cent since 1982, half of the earlier rate; and the proportion with schizophrenia has fallen to less than 10 per cent. A 1996 source reported that 20–25 per cent of the adult homeless population suffered from a long-term severe mental illness,[17] but only five to seven per cent of the mentally ill homeless, it argued, were disturbed enough to be hospitalized.[18] The number of homeless Americans appears to have held fairly constant at about 500,000–600,000 people over the past 20 years. Advocates for the homeless population emphasize the economic factors that inflate the proportion of disabled among the population. The National Coalition for the Homeless points out that the low level of disability benefits forces many Americans into poverty and homelessness.[19] In most states the monthly pension amount barely covers rent; in 14 states and 69 cities the pension is actually less than the fair market rent for a one-bedroom apartment.[20] If we accept the recent estimates that around 10 per cent of this population are suffering from schizophrenia, it is still clear that lives such as Mary's (p. 103) are to be counted in the tens of thousands (see Table 8.3).

The dimensions of the problem have also varied over time in Britain. A survey of the Camberwell Reception Centre in London on a night in the 1960s found 22 per cent of the longer-term residents to be mentally ill, mostly with schizophrenia. It was apparent that their destitution was a consequence of their illness – 90 per cent had been living in settled homes before they fell ill.[21] In two Salvation Army hostels in Central London in the late 1960s, 15 per cent of a sample of residents were "gross and unequivocal cases" of schizophrenia.[22] Robert Priest found that 32 per cent of the men in his random sample of residents of Edinburgh doss houses in the late 1960s were definitely or probably suffering from schizophrenia.[23] The situation worsened as the economy declined. A tenth of all the people with schizophrenia seen at the emergency psychiatric clinic of the Maudsley Hospital in south London during six months in 1978 and 1979 were homeless; few were offered any ongoing treatment.[24] The number of homeless in Britain doubled during the 1980s but the proportion of mentally ill among them did not decrease. Observers complained that the expansion of community services had failed to keep pace with hospital closures. Hospital units appeared to have given up on the task of finding housing for patients with psychotic illness. A 1990 study of homeless mentally ill people in Britain revealed that a large majority

Table 8.1 Proportion of homeless suffering from schizophrenia or psychosis in the United States and the United Kingdom: 1965–1994

United States

		Percentage affected	
	Year	Schizophrenia	Psychosis
Men and mixed gender			
Spitzer et al. (1969)	1965	36	50
Priest (1970)	1968	25	
Baxter & Hopper (1982)	1981		60
Arce et al. (1983)	1981–2	37	40
Bassuck et al. (1984)	c1982	29	38
Fischer et al. (1986)	c1983	2	
Sacks et al. (1987)	1985	10	16
Gelberg et al. (1988)	1985		40
Koegel et al. (1988)	c1985	14	28
Vernez et al. (1988)	c1985	11	
Susser et al. (1989)	1985	8	17
Morse et al. (1986)	c1986		47
Breakey et al. (1989)	1986–7	12	19
Toro & Wall (1991)	1987–8	1	
North & Smith (1992)	c1989	5	
Leda et al. (1992)	1988–91	12	19
Culhane et al. (1998)	1990–2	7	
Haugland et al. (1997)	1993	10	
Women			
Reich & Siegel (1973)	1971		75
Breakey et al. (1989)	1986–7	17	25
Leda et al. (1992)	1988–91	17	27
Culhane et al. (1998)	1990–2	11	

United Kingdom	Year	Schizophrenia	Psychosis
Men and mixed gender			
Lodge Patch (1971)	c1968	15	
Priest (1971)	c1968	32	
Tidmarsh & Wood (1972)	c1968		22
Marshall (1989)	c1986		42
Weller et al. (1989)	1985–8		22
Timms & Fry (1989)	1986–7	31	31
Stark et al. (1989)	1988	25	
Sclare (1997)	1989–90	5	8
Hamid et al. (1995)	c1990		13
Geddes et al. (1996)	1992	9	10
Women			
Marshall & Reed (1992)	1986–7	64	
Adams et al. (1996)	1991	42	

See Footnote 16 for references

Table 8.2 Proportion of jail inmates suffering from psychosis in the United Kingdom and the United States: 1965–1997

United States

	Year	Men	Women
Bolton (1976)	c1975	7	–
Swank & Winer (1976)	c1975	5	–
Schuckit et al. (1977)	1976	2	–
Kreftt & Brittain (1983)	c1982	10	6
Teplin (1990)	1983–4	4	–
Guy et al. (1985)	1984	15	–
Teplin et al. (1996)	1991–3	–	5
Powell et al. (1996)	c1995	9	–

United Kingdom

	Year	Men	Women
Gibbens (1966)	c1965	2	–
Blugrass (1966)	c1965	2	–
Gunn et al. (1978)	1972	2	–
Faulk (1976)	c1975	3	–
Gunn et al. (1991)	1988	2	–
Maden et al. (1994)	1988–9	2	2
Watt et al. (1993)	1991	3	–
Brooke et al. (1996)	1992–3	5	–
Birmingham et al. (1996)	1995–6	6	–
Singleton et al. (1998)	1997	7–10	14

See Footnote 28 for references

Table 8.3 Crude estimates of the location of people with schizophrenia in the USA around 2000

Location	Total population	% with schizophrenia	Number with schizophrenia	% of all Americans with schizophrenia
Homeless	500,000–600,000	13	50,000–60,000	4–5
Jails	620,000	6	37,200	3
Prisons	1,300,000	5	65,000	5
Board & care homes:				
licensed	574,000	20	115,000	9
unlicensed	400,000	20	80,000	6
Nursing homes	1,720,000	2–3	34,400–51,600	3–4
Hospitals	260,000	17–25	44,200–65,000	3–5
Total in non-domestic setting			425,800–473,800	33–37

Note: See the text for an explanation of the derivation of these estimates.

had been discharged from hospital without any discussion of their housing needs.[25] Some improvement in the proportion of mentally ill among homeless men was noted in the 1990s,[26] though the proportion among homeless women remained very high.[27] It seems that the problem of homelessness for the mentally ill is as great in Britain as it is in the US.

JAILS AND PRISONS

To escape hunger many of the destitute and homeless people with psychosis steal or eat meals for which they cannot pay; to avoid cold, damp and the discomforts of homelessness many sleep in public buildings or empty houses and are arrested. As Table 8.2 shows,[28] in the 1980s, an average of around eight per cent of the inmates of local jails in the United States were found to suffer from schizophrenia. More recent figures show the proportion in jail to be similar. In Britain, the number of incarcerated mentally ill has been increasingly dramatically in recent years – from two to three per cent of male inmates in the decades leading up to 1980,[29] to six per cent of male inmates in the early 1990s,[30] to seven to ten per cent of male inmates and 14–20 per cent of women prisoners in 1997[31] (see Table 8.2), The problem of incarcerating the mentally ill, like the problem of homelessness, has become as bad in Britain as in the US in recent years.

Some of the people with psychosis in jail are being held on serious charges, such as burglary, assault and arson – their crimes often a product of their mental illness.[32] Substantial numbers of these inmates have proven too dangerous to be treated effectively in the community, but no long-term hospital care can be found for them.[33] Whatever the type of crime, in fact, many people suffering from psychosis remain in jail because hospital care or effective community care is not available. In 1991, the jail in Flathead County, Montana, held 82 mentally ill people because local psychiatric hospitals would not take them.[34] Even non-criminal psychiatric patients are housed in jail for the sake of mere convenience. In Kentucky in 1987, 1417 people were jailed, merely awaiting a court hearing for involuntary hospitalization,[35] and three-quarters of a random sample of admissions to Bryce Hospital, Alabama, in 1978 were confined in jail while awaiting admission.[36]

In US state and federal prisons a similarly large proportion of the inmates suffer from psychosis.[37] In one study, five per cent of Oklahoma state prisoners were found to be suffering from schizophrenia;[38] ten per cent of admissions to the Washington state prison system were suffering from psychosis, in another;[39] and seven per cent of Michigan prison inmates were suffering from psychosis, in a third.[40] A study of New York state prisons in 1987 detected severe psychiatric disability among five per cent of the inmates.[41] A 1989 review concluded that six to eight per cent of people in US prisons were seriously mentally ill and that the number was increasing.[42] The 1991

Epidemiologic Catchment Area Study determined the prevalence of schizophrenia in US prisons to be five per cent.[43]

In some states, patients with psychosis are even sent from mental hospitals to prison for treatment. In Massachusetts in 1979 approximately one patient every four days was transferred to prison because mental hospital staff considered the person unmanageable. Judges, furthermore, send severely mentally ill offenders to prison in preference to hospital because they find that mental health facilities frequently fail to provide adequate long-term hospital or community care for dangerous and highly disruptive patients.[44] The number of inmates of US jails and prisons in 1999 was more than 1.9 million,[45] and a modest estimate would allow that six out of every hundred of these jail inmates and five out of every hundred prison inmates is suffering from schizophrenia. Thus, there may be as many as 100,000 prisoners with schizophrenia in the US. But if only two per cent of the 11.4 million US jail *admissions* a year[46] were suffering from schizophrenia, then hundreds of thousands of people with schizophrenia spend some time behind bars annually (even allowing for the repeated admission of many).

Under the ever-present threat of litigation, services for the mentally ill in US jails have improved in recent years. Intake screening to detect mental illness and case management services for mentally ill inmates are now provided in four-fifths of the jails in the country.[47] While conditions have improved, they are still often disgraceful. Large jails in the US generally have so many mentally ill inmates, often acutely disturbed, that they establish cell blocks as "hospital units." In such units mental patients may be seen sitting on their beds in bare cells gazing blankly into space. In the old asylums, conditions as bankrupt and deadening as these were rare. Mentally ill inmates may be found nude and agitated in isolation cells. The disruptive behavior of the mentally ill in jail is often regarded as a "disciplinary problem;" such individuals are often held in bare cells of solitary confinement, shackled to the wall if necessary.[48] Only 40 per cent of the mentally ill in US jails received mental health treatment in 1998 – usually medication, rarely counseling.[49]

An administrator of the US Department of Justice has stated that "Jails are without question, brutal, filthy cesspools of crime – institutions which serve to brutalize and embitter men to prevent them from returning to a useful role in society."[50] Open toilets in overcrowded cells, vermin, filth, dilapidation, brutality, homosexual rape and lack of medical care, of hygiene or of constructive programs have all been documented as existing widely in US jails and prisons.[51] To attempt to treat patients with psychosis in such settings by the mere addition of antipsychotic drugs is scarcely calculated to improve their chances of recovery.

What accounts for such treatment of the mentally ill in a civilized society? In a word, money. State governments have drastically cut back the funding for psychiatric hospitals and have failed to maintain community mental health services at an adequate level. Police and judges have responded as they feel they must to protect the community from the crime, disruption and violence that result from the lack of support and treatment of people with psychosis. State legislators do not counter this problem by boosting mental health funding because, in the first place, prison care is cheaper than hospital treatment (about four times cheaper in Colorado) and, in the second place, the expense of law enforcement and the upkeep of local jails is borne, not by the state government, but by the counties and municipalities.

In the broadest sense, however, the mentally ill are incarcerated in these degrading conditions because, where there exists a massive reserve army of unemployed, the concern to establish social control over the deviant takes precedence over the concern to provide effective rehabilitation. The same is true of sane offenders – incarceration rates rise during an economic recession (but are unrelated to crime or conviction rates),[52] and jail and prison populations tend to be greater in those Western industrial nations with the highest rates of unemployment.[53] The larger the surplus population, the greater the extent of confinement and the worse the conditions of the poor – the mentally ill among them.

WHERE ARE AMERICANS WITH SCHIZOPHRENIA?

The plight of the long-term mentally ill discharged from hospital to a barren existence in America's boarding homes and nursing homes during the early years of deinstutionalization has been described in Chapter 4. How many people with schizophrenia live in these institutions? A report of a committee of the Department of Health and Human Services estimated that some 300,000–400,000 people with long-term mental illness were residing in board and care homes in the United States in 1981,[54] the majority suffering from schizophrenia.[55] A Congressional report estimated that there were nearly a million residents of licensed and unlicensed board and care homes in the US in 1986, and suggested that about half, many of them elderly, were mentally ill.[56] There is no indication that the number of mentally ill in board and care homes has decreased since the mid-1980s, and if we conservatively estimate that 20 per cent of the residents of licensed and unlicensed board and care homes suffer from schizophrenia, then nearly 200,000 people with this illness must be housed in these, often squalid, conditions.

The living conditions in board and care homes – which often house hundreds of people – have not improved since they were first called into service for ex-hospital patients. The 1986 Congressional Report detailed fraud, exploitation, neglect, physical and sexual abuse, malnutrition, overcrowding and overmedication as being common.[57] A series of front-page articles in the *New York Times* in 2002 described the same conditions as being prevalent for thousands of mentally ill people housed in homes in New York State. In a predatory atmosphere, prostitution and drug abuse are common, rooms are fetid, clothing is dirty, residents are unwashed, and dead cockroaches are found in medication boxes. Minimum-wage workers beat patients to subdue them and forge treatment records of contact with fake psychiatrists. Premature death of residents from illness, suicide, or stifling summer heat is not uncommon, but may passed unnoticed until the stench of rotting flesh attracts attention. Operators of the homes steal from residents and refer them for unnecessary eye and prostate surgery in return for kickbacks from surgeons. Defending the state supervisory system, the health commissioner told lawmakers that her department was "doing miracles" in its regulation of the homes.[58]

A 1981 government report indicated that there were 250,000 patients in nursing homes with a primary diagnosis of mental illness, excluding elderly patients with non-psychotic, senile mental disorder. One hundred thousand of these patients were transferred directly into nursing home care from state mental hospitals; more were admitted there after an interim period in another nursing home, in hospital or in the community.[59] In 1987 the US Congress mandated that states screen potential residents to ensure that they were not being inappropriately placed in nursing homes. In most states this has resulted in the reduction of the placement of the mentally ill in such units – only those with concomitant physical disability are now being admitted.[60] In at least one US state, however, the state government has skirted the Congressional mandate and has encouraged nursing homes to admit young, physically healthy, mentally ill people. A 2002 *New York Times* article revealed that as many as 100,000 people with mental illness may be housed in such units in New York state with the approval of Governor Pataki's administration. The *Times* reporter described these unregulated wards as "reminiscent of old-style institutions."[61] Patients are rarely allowed outside; they sit idle or pace, do jigsaw puzzles, and crowd round the locked elevator doors whenever anyone leaves or enters. In the Orwellian language of the state bureaucrats, these nursing home wards are termed "neurobiological units," and administrators claim that they are not locked but "key-operated."[62]

Many people with schizophrenia are elderly or in poor health and so, in those parts of the country where the states have followed the Congressional mandate, they still constitute two to three per cent of the US nursing home population.[63] With this population having expanded greatly in recent decades, this means that at least 40,000–50,000 people with schizophrenia are housed in these settings.

If we add to these numbers another 45,000–65,000 people with schizophrenia resident in state, county, private and Veterans Administration hospitals,[64] and if we accept the estimate that there are around 1,275,000 people with schizophrenia in the United States,[65] we are forced to the discomforting conclusion that at least a third of Americans with schizophrenia are to be found in institutions, in inadequate community settings, in jail, prison or on the streets (see Table 8.3). On the positive side, because the number of mentally ill people among the homeless, in hospital and in nursing homes has decreased, this proportion is smaller than in the early 1980s. Nevertheless, fewer than seven out of ten people with schizophrenia in the United States are likely to be living in anything resembling a family home or domestic environment. We need to increase this number if we are to see an improvement in outcome from schizophrenia in America.

RESTRAINTS AND SECLUSION

We should not assume that the patients who are in hospital are necessarily in ideal therapeutic environments. Their conditions of confinement may be quite harsh. Although both restraints and seclusion, for example, have proved to be largely unnecessary in British practice, their use has been commonplace in hospitals in the United States. A 1979 report indicated that 44 per cent of patients on an acute admission unit in California were locked up in seclusion for varying periods of time.[66] The seclusion room experience often colors and dominates the patient's view of his or her illness. When patients at a major US psychiatric hospital were asked to draw pictures of themselves and their psychosis, over a third spontaneously drew a picture of the seclusion room. Even a year after the hospital stay, the experience of seclusion, with its associated feelings of fear and bitterness, symbolized for many patients the entire psychiatric illness.[67]

It has also been common for patients to be strapped down to their beds with restraints in US hospitals. During one month in the 1980s, a quarter of all patients evaluated in a psychiatric emergency room in Cincinnati, Ohio, were placed in restraints.[68] Mechanical restraints have frequently been used on psychiatric wards, the commonest reasons being not violence but "nonconformity to community rules"[69] and "behavior disruptive to the therapeutic environment."[70] Under-staffing and overcrowding may also force the use of such measures. The Colorado Foundation for Medical Care found that the overuse of both restraints and seclusion at Fort Logan Mental Health Center in Denver, Colorado, in the 1980s was the result of a shortage of staff. At the Colorado State Hospital around the same time, overcrowding on the forensic unit was so severe that patients were transferred to the surgical ward and shackled to their beds in order to accommodate the overflow.[71] Such are the human consequences of cost-cutting in public psychiatric services.

Recent federal regulations have imposed restrictions on the use of restraints and seclusion in psychiatric inpatient units with the result that the use of these measures has been reduced. The regulations have imposed such a burden on the inpatient psychiatrists, however – they are obliged to see a patient within an hour of ordering the use of restraints or seclusion, even in the middle of the night – that many have quit doing inpatient work and a staffing crisis has arisen.

STIGMA

There is more to the degradation of suffering from schizophrenia in Western society, however, than harsh treatment and inadequate living conditions. As an American woman with schizophrenia explains:

> Let's just say I have a case of shame – I really do. When I look at some of the things I've really gone through – some of the things I've done, some of the things I've said – my father's feeling of shame for me does not equal my own."[72]

Another patient writes:

> I have often been fraught with a profound guilt over my diagnosis of schizophrenia. . . . I had little idea how dehumanizing and humiliating the hospital would be for me. . . . I felt that I had partly lost my right to stand among humanity . . . and that for some people I would be forever-more something of a subhuman creature. . . . Mental health professionals often treated me . . . as if I were a stranger or alien of sorts, set apart from others by reason of my label.[73]

In contrast to Maria, the Guatemalan Indian woman whose episode of psychosis was described in the last chapter, these Americans with schizophrenia must accept blame, and must blame themselves, for their condition. They feel estranged from others; the stigma of their illness obstructs their social reintegration.

With the growth of interest in community psychiatry, considerable attention was focused on the question of the stigma of mental illness in the 1950s and 1960s. Shirley Star, using a series of vignettes depicting people with psychiatric symptoms, conducted a nationwide survey of members of the American public in 1950 and found the general reaction to the mentally ill to be negative and poorly informed.[74] Elaine and John Cumming, using the same techniques, uncovered essentially similar attitudes among residents of a rural town (which they called Blackfoot) in Saskatchewan, Canada, in 1951, and found that the negative attitudes towards the mentally ill were untouched after a six-month psychiatric educational campaign.[75] After a six-year survey of residents of the Champaign-Urbana area of Illinois in the 1950s, J.C. Nunally concluded that the insane are viewed by the general public with "fear, distrust, and dislike."[76] "Old people and young people," reported Nunally, "highly educated people and people with little formal training – all tend to regard the mentally ill as relatively dangerous, dirty, unpredictable and worthless."[77] They are considered, in short, "all things bad."[78]

In more recent years a dispute has arisen over whether the initial impressions of high levels of stigma attached to mental illness continue to hold true.

A number of researchers in the 1960s concluded that the public tolerance of the mentally ill had improved.[79] In the late 1970s, 20 years after Nunally's original survey, William Cockerham again analyzed public attitudes towards the mentally ill in Champaign-Urbana and found them to be somewhat more tolerant.[80] But other researchers found no improvement in popular mental health attitudes between the 1960s and 1970s;[81] and a second survey of public tolerance of the mentally ill in Blackfoot, Saskatchewan, 23 years after the Cummings' original study, revealed that virtually no change had occurred.[82]

As recently as 1993, public surveys conducted in two English communities revealed a similar failure to identify someone as being mentally ill as in Star's 1950 US study; the authors argued that there was a reluctance to label someone mentally ill because of the negative associations of the term.[83] Some British studies, in fact, suggest that certain types of discrimination increased in the 1990s.[84] Misconceptions continue to abound. In Britain, half of the respondents to a survey in the mid-1990s believed that setting fire to public buildings was a "very likely "consequence of mental illness[85] and, in an American survey, 58 per cent blamed "lack of discipline" as a cause while 93 per cent blamed drug and alcohol abuse.[86] People with mental illness are more likely to be seen as being responsible for their condition than AIDS patients, the obese or other stigmatized groups.[87]

It is possible that gains were made in the public acceptance of the mentally ill in the 1960s but that, as the consequences of the abandonment of people with psychotic disorders in the community have become apparent, no further progress has taken place. Whatever the truth of the matter, it is obvious that people with mental illness are still highly stigmatized and the targets of discrimination. Branded as "psychos" in popular parlance, they encounter hardship in finding accommodation[88] and employment[89] and generate fear as to their dangerousness. Citizens fight to exclude psychiatric treatment facilities and living quarters for the mentally ill from residential neighborhoods,[90] even though group homes for the mentally ill have not been shown to have adverse effects on communities.[91] According to a recent survey of the American public, the "Not in My Backyard" phenomenon is a widespread obstacle to the community integration of people with mental illness.[92] Over two-thirds of a sample of key mental health service providers in Britain reported confronting "Not in My Backyard" campaigns; most thought that these had increased in the 1990s and reported delays in the opening of at least one facility due to community opposition.[93] Another British study documented that half of the mentally ill people surveyed reported unfair treatment by general health care services and a similar number reported being subjected to verbal and physical harassment in the community.[94] An American study conducted in 1990 found that 40 per cent of landlords immediately reject applicants with a known psychiatric disorder.[95] Other researchers have demonstrated a similar effect of the label of mental illness on job-seeking.[96] Forty-two per cent of the Greek general public would refuse to employ a person with mental illness (although over 90 per cent would employ a physically disabled person).[97]

The status afforded the mentally ill is the very lowest – lower than that of ex-convicts or people with learning disabilities.[98] Even after five years of normal living and good work, according to one survey, an ex-mental patient is rated as less acceptable than an ex-convict.[99] Usually indigent and unemployed, the person with long-term mental illness does not have a valued social role. He or she rarely possesses any of the indicators of mainstream social status; if working, the job is likely to be the most menial available; he or she generally has no decent housing, no yard, no family, and no car. Such people rarely have social or sexual contact with any but other mental patients. The person with long-standing mental illness in our society truly has pariah status.

Even the agencies serving the mentally ill are tainted by association. Mental health professionals may disdain patients with chronic psychosis, preferring to work with "good therapy cases" closer to their own class and interests.[100] Psychiatrists may avoid such patients – in one sample, only five per cent of private psychiatric patients were suffering from schizophrenia[101] – and community mental health centers often fail to address their needs. Mental health professionals are likely to hold attitudes towards mental patients that are similar to those of the general public; they may even be *more* rejecting. In one study, mental hospital staff were considerably less likely than members of the public to take the trouble to mail a sealed, addressed letter that they believed to have been accidentally lost by a mental hospital patient.[102]

Most tragic of all, the mentally ill themselves accept the stereotype of their own condition. Young patients in rural Ireland viewed their "spending time in the 'madhouse' . . . as a permanent 'fall from grace' similar to a loss of virginity."[103] A number of studies have shown that psychiatric patients are as negative in their opinions of mental illness as the general public.[104] Some reports, indeed, have indicated that psychiatric patients were *more* rejecting of the mentally ill than were their family members or the hospital staff.[105]

LABELING THEORY

Research on the stigma of mental illness has been fueled by interest in labeling theory. Once a deviant person has been labeled "mentally ill," argued sociologist Thomas Scheff, society responds in accordance with a pre-determined stereotype and the individual is launched on a career of chronic mental illness from which there is little opportunity for escape.[106] There is evidence to support Scheff's position. A study of the attitudes of residents of a small New England town, published in 1963 by Derek Phillips, shows that a normal person of an "ideal type" who is described as having been in a mental hospital is socially rejected to a much greater degree than is a person with simple schizophrenia who seeks no help or who instead consults a clergyman.[107]

In David Rosenhan's well-known study, normal volunteers presented themselves for voluntary admission to a dozen different psychiatric hospitals with complaints of auditory hallucinations. Every pseudo-patient was admitted, and although they reverted to normal behavior and denied psychotic symptoms immediately upon admission, each one was labeled schizophrenic at the time of discharge. Staff described the reasonable actions of the pseudo-patients as if they were pathological. None was discharged in less than a week – one was detained for almost two months.[108] One might reasonably conclude from studies such as these that pressures to conform to stereotypic expectations may well influence hope of recovery and the features of schizophrenia.

Critics of labeling theory argue that the approach understates the importance of the initial deviance and of the inherent pathology of mental illness in causing a label to be attached, and that it minimizes the capacity of mental patients to shake off the harmful effects of stigma.[109] Of a dozen studies conducted after 1963 assessing the relative importance of the mental illness label versus the person's behavior in determining public attitudes, most found the effect of labeling to be significant but nearly all found the person's behavior to be a more potent factor.[110] Similarly, in a more recent study, knowledge of the symptoms of a person's acute psychotic episode created more stigma than the label "schizophrenia."[111] Both symptoms and label appear to be important, and labeling may have a significant effect on shaping the features of mental illness once established. John Strauss and William Carpenter, American psychiatrists who are authorities on the outcome of schizophrenic illness, conclude that:

> Labeling is an important variable affecting the course, and perhaps the onset of schizophrenia. . . . Who can doubt the devastating impact on a fragile person of perceiving that the entire social milieu regards him (wittingly or not) as subhuman, incurable, unmotivated, or incompetent to pursue ordinary expectations . . .? Can we doubt that a deteriorating course of disorder is fostered when fundamental roles are changed by social stigma and employment opportunities become limited?[112]

HOW STIGMA INFLUENCES THE COURSE OF ILLNESS

Exactly how could the stigma and degradation of mental illness affect the symptoms of schizophrenia and shape the course of the illness? Cognitive dissonance theory helps explain this process. In outline this social psychological theory states that:

(a) pieces of knowledge or ideas (cognitions) are dissonant if one contradicts the other;

(b) dissonance is psychologically uncomfortable and motivates a person to resolve the contradiction; and

(c) the person will actively avoid situations that increase the dissonance.

For example, if a woman smokes two packs of cigarettes a day, believes herself to be reasonably strong-willed and sensible but knows that cigarettes cause lung cancer, she may reduce the level of dissonance between these ideas by either quitting cigarettes, coming to see herself as weak-willed and foolish, or minimizing the evidence that links smoking with cancer.

Experiments have shown the following consequences of cognitive dissonance theory to hold true:

(a) After a change in opinion has been made with the aim of reducing dissonance, the person will select from available information evidence to confirm his or her decision, and will tend to overvalue this evidence.

(b) In the face of contradictory evidence that increases dissonance the individual will become *more* active in defense of his or her belief.

(c) If a person is obliged to state a public opinion that is contrary to his or her privately held opinion (thus creating dissonance), there is a tendency for the opinion to change to conform more closely with the public statement; the smaller the external pressure to make the public statement, the greater is the opinion change.[113]

Faced with the need to accept a diagnosis of major mental illness (and its associated stigma and debased status), anyone with an internal sense of relative worth and competence will experience dissonance (see Figure 8.1). In fact, those who accept a diagnosis of mental illness tend to be people with a sense of ill-being (dysphoria) and a poor self-image; the grandiose and euphoric reject the illness label.[114] Cognitive dissonance theory predicts that those who choose to accept the diagnosis of mental illness will attempt to resolve their sense of dissonance by conforming to their new outcast status and to the stereotype of worthlessness; they will become more socially withdrawn and adopt a disabled role. In seeking to confirm the incurable and incapable features of their role, their symptoms of psychosis will tend to persist and they are likely to become dependent on the treatment agency and others in their lives.

Such patterns will be even more exaggerated if the patient's stigmatized status is made evident by discernible physical traits; at worst these may be the shuffle, rigid facial expression and drooling secondary to the use of high doses of antipsychotic drugs; at the least they may include the slow gait of the unemployed, devalued individual with nowhere to go and nothing to do.

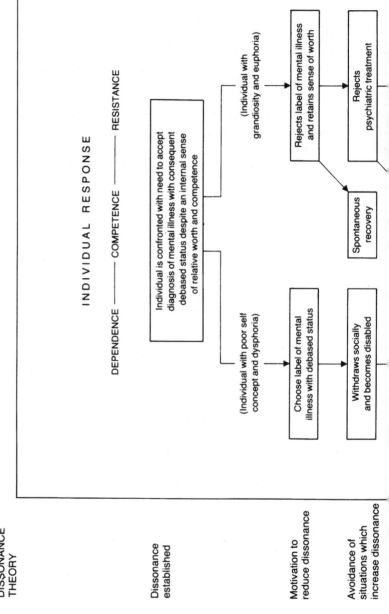

FEATURES OF
COGNITIVE
DISSONANCE
THEORY

Dissonance
established

Motivation to
reduce dissonance

Avoidance of
situations which
increase dissonance

INDIVIDUAL RESPONSE

DEPENDENCE ——— COMPETENCE ——— RESISTANCE

Individual is confronted with need to accept
diagnosis of mental illness with consequent
debased status despite an internal sense
of relative worth and competence

(Individual with poor self
concept and dysphoria)

Choose label of mental
illness with debased status

Withdraws socially
and becomes disabled

(Individual with
grandiosity and euphoria)

Rejects label of mental illness
and retains sense of worth

Rejects
psychiatric treatment

Spontaneous
recovery

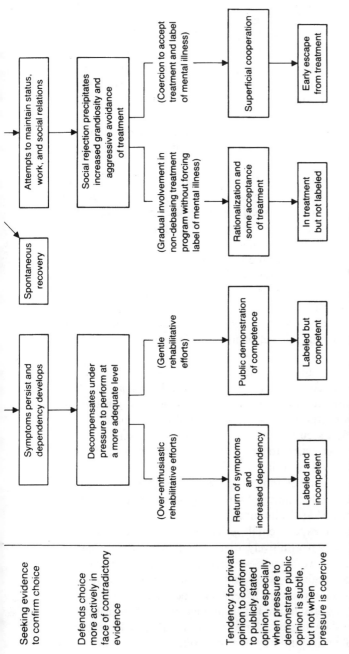

Figure 8.1 Impact of labeling individual "mentally ill" as predicted by cognitive dissonance theory

Under pressure to return to adequate functioning, symptoms of illness will tend to recur as a defense against mounting dissonance. However, gentle and gradual efforts that lead such individuals to demonstrate publicly that they can function at a more adequate level, may result in a change in their self-concept and a movement towards labeled but competent status. Cognitive dissonance theory thus helps explain the precarious balance of functioning that is found in rehabilitating the person with mental illness. High expectations for his or her level of achievement can lead the patient to a higher level of functioning and decreased segregation and stigma, but they can also increase the risk of exacerbating psychotic symptoms and of hospitalization.[115] We may now see why success is so often frightening and stressful to people with psychosis.

In contrast, those who initially reject the label and status of mental illness (and psychiatric treatment) will usually attempt to maintain their previous occupational and social status. Any social rejection they experience is likely to result in an increase in grandiosity and even more aggressive avoidance of treatment. Strong efforts to compel such individuals to accept a diagnosis of mental illness may result in superficial compliance but little genuine change in their privately held opinion; consequently they are likely to attempt to evade treatment at every opportunity. However, gradually increasing involvement in a non-debasing treatment program, coupled with a high degree of rationalization, may lead these people to a limited compliance with treatment, provided a dissonant label of mental illness is not forced upon them.

Thus, the patient with "insight" will tend to function less well than expected and may become excessively dependent, while the patient who functions well will be inclined to reject treatment. Cognitive dissonance theory gives the mental health professional an explanation of the common observation that he or she often seems to be encouraging each patient to do the opposite of what the person wants to do – a situation that can lead to "burnout" among staff and punitive attitudes towards patients. A reduction in stigma should reduce this conflict and, more directly, result in improved outcome in schizophrenia. If schizophrenia were a high-status illness (as it is in some cultures), it would be less debilitating.

If we were looking for experimental verification of this viewpoint, we would expect to find, counter-intuitively, that patients who accept that they are mentally ill will have the worst course to their illness, that those who reject the label from the outset might do better and that the patients who show the most improvement will be those who accept the label of mental illness but subsequently are able to shake if off. This is, in fact, the finding of Edmund Doherty's study of self-labeling by 43 psychiatric inpatients. Patients who accepted throughout their hospital stay that they were mentally ill were rated as showing the least improvement; those who consistently denied that they were mentally ill did slightly better; and the patients who began by accepting that they were mentally ill but subsequently rejected that notion showed the greatest gains. All three groups were equally disturbed at admission.[116]

My colleagues and I tested the same hypothesis – that labeling and stereotyping are so damaging that patients who accept that they are mentally ill have a worse outcome than those who deny it – in a study of 54 people with psychosis living in the community in Boulder, Colorado. Our results provide some support for this view but do not fully confirm Doherty's findings. Patients who accept that they are mentally ill, we found, have worse self-esteem and lack a sense of control over their lives. Those who find mental illness most stigmatizing have the worst self-esteem and the weakest sense of mastery. Neither rejecting the label of mental illness nor accepting it, by itself, leads to good outcome, it emerges; patients can only benefit from accepting they are ill if they also have a sense of control over their lives. Such patients are few and far between, however, since a consequence of accepting the illness label is loss of a sense of mastery. This is the Catch 22 of being mentally ill in Western society – one loses the very psychological strength that is necessary for recovery in the process of gaining insight.[117]

A conclusion we can draw from this research is that it is equally important for therapists to assist patients in developing a sense of mastery as it is to help them find insight into their illness. This is not what conventional treatment programs do, however. Ordinarily, a good deal more effort is expended on persuading patients that they are ill than on finding ways to put them in charge of their illness. Some of the programs that are most successful at keeping patients out of hospital are unfortunately quite controlling rather than empowering (see "Intensive Community Support" in Chapter 12). To achieve real empowerment we have to turn to programs that are run or co-run by consumers of mental health services themselves. Some ventures of this type will be described in Chapter 12.

SOCIAL ISOLATION

As might be expected from the humiliating living conditions of the majority of mentally ill people and from their pariah status, people with schizophrenia in the West lead lives of social isolation. Many studies have shown that such patients have networks of social contacts that are much more restricted than is usual in our society. People with schizophrenia are found to have close contacts with a third to a fifth of the number of people that is average for other members of the community. A third of those with long-standing mental illness have no friends at all. The relationships of people with schizophrenia tend to be more one-sided, dependent and lacking in complexity of content and diversity of interconnections. Although family relationships deteriorate less than contact with friends, a considerable disintegration of family ties does occur.[118] The collapse of the patient's social network appears to be a consequence of the illness, for it occurs after the first hospital admission.[119]

The social isolation of the person with schizophrenia in the West stands in contrast to the effective social reintegration of the person with psychosis in the Third World. Although disruptive and violent individuals living in peasant villages who have been designated "mad" do have restricted social networks,[120] the same problem does not apply, as we saw in Chapter 7, to less chronically and severely disturbed people with psychosis in the Third World. It was pointed out in that chapter, furthermore, that social isolation in both the developed and developing world has been repeatedly shown to be associated with poor outcome. The reports on the social networks of people with schizophrenia confirm this pattern. One study of people with schizophrenia housed in New York hotels demonstrated that, regardless of the severity of the patients' symptoms, those with broader and more complex social networks were less likely to be readmitted to hospital.[121]

FAMILIES OF PEOPLE WITH SCHIZOPHRENIA

The contrast between the social reintegration of people with psychosis in the developing world and the isolation of the mentally ill in Western society is highlighted by the plight of the families of people with schizophrenia in the West. The stigma that attaches to mental illness also taints the relatives. Some react by talking to no one about the illness for years, not even to close friends. Those who do discuss the matter openly may find themselves snubbed by acquaintances. "Some old friends quit talking to us," described the mother of a young man with schizophrenia. "They absolutely dropped us." Other families respond by withdrawing socially. "We haven't done much entertaining because of this," commented the parent of another youth with schizophrenia. "I'm never quite sure . . . he's so up and down." One-third of the wives in an American study followed a course of aggressive concealment including dropping and avoiding friends or even moving to a new residence. Another third of the wives discussed their husbands' illness with only a select few friends or relatives.[122] Although there is a marked tendency for family members to deny the stigma, their concealment and withdrawal point to an underlying sense of shame and lead them into social isolation.[123]

In a survey of relatives of people with schizophrenia in Washington, DC, Agnes Hatfield observed "a picture of unremittingly disturbed family life marked by almost constant stress"[124] as the consequence of caring for a patient at home. She noted that marital disruption, blame, grief and helplessness were common results. In a study of British families in which a person with schizophrenia was living at home, half of the family members reported severe or very severe impairment of their own health as a consequence of their relative's psychiatric condition.[125]

All of the parents of the mentally ill in a discussion group at the Massachusetts Mental Health Center "to a greater or lesser extent saw themselves and the others as ogres responsible for the misfortune that befell their children."[126] The burden of guilt that such relatives carry is the result of the popular conception that mental illness is a product of faulty upbringing. Mental health professionals, adopting this same attitude, may see the family members as adversaries and add to their estrangement. Carried to its logical extreme the notion of the "schizophrenogenic" family led to the bizarre occurrence in a Colorado court of a 24-year-old man, with the support of his psychiatrist, suing his parents for "malpractice" that supposedly caused his schizophrenia.[127]

The stigma perceived by families is not decreasing. American researchers found concealment among family members in 1982 to be higher than in a similar study conducted in 1961.[128] Half of the family members of hospitalized psychiatric patients in a more recent US study reported some degree of concealment, more frequently when the family member was well-educated.[129] Perceived stigma and misconceptions among family members can influence the course of the illness. Isolated and guilt-ridden as they are, it is not surprising that the families of people with schizophrenia sometimes become overinvolved with their sick relatives.[130] Seeing this interaction, mental health professionals may try to separate them, encouraging the patient to move away from home and minimize contact with his or her relatives. This step completes a process of social disintegration; the patient is separated from almost everyone except other stigmatized patients; the family members are socially isolated and feel banished not only from the social mainstream but also from their affected relatives.

ALIENATION

Where pre-industrial cultures offer social reintegration with maintenance of social status and provision of a valued social role for many of those suffering from psychosis, Western society leaves people with schizophrenia in a state of social disintegration with pariah status and a disabled role. In the non-industrial world, communal healing processes operate within a social consensus that predicts recovery and minimizes blame, guilt and stigma; whereas in Western society schizophrenia is treated through marginal institutions with a social expectation that all concerned are to blame and that the condition is incurable. These differences in the status, integration and role of the mentally ill may well account for the distinctly worse outcome for schizophrenia in industrial societies.

This constellation of problems has been described before, however; it is encompassed by the concept of alienation. Marx writes of people in industrial society becoming alienated from the process of working and the product of their work, from other people and from their own human qualities.[131] Modern psychologists emphasize that alienation includes a profound sense of meaninglessness and powerlessness.[132]

How does this apply to the person with schizophrenia? In the stigma of mental illness, the most debased status in our society, we see the utmost in painful estrangement of one human from another; and in the person with schizophrenia's own acceptance of this same dehumanized stereotype we witness the loss of his or her sense of fully belonging to humankind. It is in the menial jobs that the mentally ill are most likely to find – dishwashing, envelope-stuffing, day-laboring – that work is most dehumanizing and alienation is most severe. But the more common fate of the person with schizophrenia – unemployment – is even worse. To stand bored and idle, to be unable to provide for oneself, to fulfill no useful social function, to be of little value to oneself or others – these are the ultimate in alienation – a confrontation with the existential concern of meaninglessness.

In one study, when people in community treatment for psychosis in Boulder, Colorado, were interviewed about their lives, their principal complaints were of boredom and (among the men) unemployment – both rated as much more problematic than symptoms of mental illness.[133] People with psychosis, in fact, score lower than any other group on the Purpose-in-Life Test[134] – a psychological measure used to detect alienation and meaninglessness. Many professionals suspect that the high prevalence of drug and alcohol abuse among the mentally ill – 30–40 per cent of most samples[135] – is in part a consequence of the empty lives that many patients lead. In a study of substance use among the mentally ill in the Boulder community, we found that those with the fewest planned activities were the heaviest marijuana users, giving "boredom" as the primary reason for drug use.[136]

Decades ago, when we were shifting the locus of care from the hospital to the community, we found ways to combat what we called at that time the institutional neurosis – the posturing, the restless pacing, incontinence and unpredictable violence that were bred by the restrictions, regimentation and emptiness of hospital life. Humanizing the hospital wards and establishing "therapeutic communities," which changed the power relationships between staff and patients and involved patients in ward management (as described in Chapter 4), led to a reversal of this institutionally ingrained behavior. It now appears that we have traded the earlier *institutional* neurosis for a new *existential* neurosis that may similarly stand in the way of recovery from the original psychotic illness. It seems likely, however, (and I will discuss this in greater detail in Chapter 12) that the same active ingredients that proved successful in reversing the institutional syndrome – normalizing the environment and engaging the patient in his or her own treatment – are also effective in relieving the effect of the existential neurosis.

ORIGINS OF ALIENATION

The person with schizophrenia, it appears, is among the most alienated of industrial society, and it is in this condition that one may perceive the causes of the malignancy of the illness. Looking beyond this, the origins of the mentally ill person's alienation are to be found in the political and economic structure of society – in the division of labor and development of wage work. For it is these aspects of production that have rendered the person with schizophrenia – with his or her limited ability to withstand stress, limited productive capacity and limited drive – marginal to the industrial work force, marginal members of (what anthropologist Jules Henry terms) "the driven society."[137]

Caste systems do not perpetuate themselves. Continued enforcement of discriminatory economic and physical sanctions is necessary to maintain the existence of a pariah group.[138] Similar political and economic pressures are necessary to restrict the interclass mobility of members of US ethnic minority groups.[139] The same is true of the low status of the mentally ill in the West. The postwar drive to influence public opinion and increase the community acceptance of mental patients was equivalent to earnest attempts to adjust the status of a caste. The political motivation at that time, in some areas, was to bring the mentally ill into the work force, in other areas, to transfer the responsibility for their care from the state to the community. These efforts decreased as the political motivation receded. The recent growth in strength and solidarity of advocacy groups for the mentally ill, such as the National Alliance of the Mentally Ill, however, has led to a resurgence of interest in combating the stigma of schizophrenia (see Chapter 12). It takes a power differential to erect the barriers of stigma and discrimination and it takes the creation of a power bloc to knock them down.

SUMMARY

- A third of the people with schizophrenia in the US are living in boarding homes or nursing homes, in hospital, on Skid Row or in jail or prison.
- The stigma of mental illness in Western society continues to be great.
- A combination of labeling theory and cognitive dissonance theory allows us to explain how the stigma of mental illness can lead to poor outcome from psychosis.
- People with schizophrenia in Western society have restricted social networks and they and their families become relatively estranged from society.
- The social plight of the person with schizophrenia in the West is encompassed by the single concept of alienation, and has its roots in the division of labor and the development of wage work.

Chapter 9

The incidence of schizophrenia

Does political economy influence the rate of occurrence of schizophrenia? Could industrialization, migration, social class and caste, or the factors governing production and reproduction determine how many people develop the vulnerability to schizophrenia? Could labor conditions, unemployment and other socioeconomic stresses trigger the onset of the disorder? Up to this point we have concentrated upon the *course* of schizophrenia – recovery from the illness and the level of functioning achieved by chronic sufferers. The course of schizophrenia, it has been argued, is strongly influenced by the utilization of labor, a factor that affects the social role, status and integration of people suffering from psychosis. At this juncture it may be valuable to make a diversion and to examine the *frequency of occurrence* of the illness and the extent to which it is affected by social, political and economic factors. We will also examine what efforts to prevent schizophrenia are likely to be effective and safe.

For social factors to affect a person's vulnerability to illness or the course of the disorder there must be a mediating biological mechanism that converts the social influence into a bodily response. Stressful labor dynamics, for example, can have an impact on the course of schizophrenia because increased stress worsens the dopamine supersensitivity that is believed to underlie the disease (see Chapters 1 and 10). Influences on the occurrence of schizophrenia are likely to be different from those affecting the course of the illness. If social factors are to have an impact on the individual's vulnerability to schizophrenia they might do so by influencing the development of the fetal brain or the occurrence of brain damage later in life – they might affect such factors as maternal and fetal nutrition, maternal drug and alcohol use, infections during pregnancy, delivery complications and childhood infections and head trauma.

INDUSTRIALIZATION AND ILLNESS

Patterns of interaction between socio-economic factors and the occurrence of illness over time can be complex. Some diseases are worsened by affluence and tend to grow in frequency with industrial progress; others are a response to poverty and tend to decrease in incidence with the advance of industrialization. A number of diseases associated with Western industrial growth, however, are influenced both by affluence *and* poverty, and have been found to rise in incidence early in the process of development and to fall in frequency later. These illnesses are initially more common among the rich and, later, become more common among the poor. Such diseases include thyrotoxicosis, peptic ulcer, poliomyelitis, appendicitis and coronary artery disease.[1] The reasons for the rise and fall in incidence vary from condition to condition but, in general, they are related to a change in hygiene or diet that acts in childhood to modify individual susceptibility to the same factor, or a different one, exerting an effect later in life to produce illness. For example, people whose dietary iodine is deficient in youth are less able to adapt to an increase in iodine intake later in life and tend to develop thyrotoxicosis.[2]

The frequency of a mental disorder can vary in a similar way. Emil Kraepelin, in 1926, described a pattern of changing occurrence for a brain disease caused by syphilitic infection, general paralysis of the insane, pointing out that it "was formerly uncommon, underwent a progressively rapid increase from the beginning of the last century and for some time now has been gradually diminishing."[3] Has schizophrenia undergone a similar increase in prevalence followed by a decline? Does the illness first become more common among the upper classes and then among the lower? There is some evidence, in fact, for each element of this pattern. We can look at this evidence in detail shortly, and examine what these curious changes in the occurrence of the schizophrenia tell us about the origins of the illness. First, however, it is necessary to define some of the terms that will be used.

INCIDENCE AND PREVALENCE

The *incidence* of an illness is the rate at which new cases occur in a given period of time (usually a year). The *prevalence* of an illness is the total number of cases, new and old, known to exist. The number in existence at any one point in time is the *point prevalence*; the number observed in a given period (say a year) is the *period prevalence*; and the number of people in the population who have suffered from the illness at any time in their lives gives us the *lifetime prevalence*. Whereas the lifetime prevalence is unaffected by the rate at which people recover, the point prevalence for schizophrenia will tend to be lower in those areas, such as parts of the Third World, where outcome from the illness is better.

Incidence data are difficult to gather by any method other than by counting the number of referrals to treatment agencies. Such information on schizophrenia is therefore hard to obtain in much of the Third World, where health services are not comprehensively available. The mean age-corrected incidence of schizophrenia, computed from studies conducted primarily in Europe and North America and excluding very narrow or very broad diagnostic approaches, is 0.24 per 1,000 of the general population, with a range from 0.07 to 0.52 per 1,000.[4]

True *prevalence* may be assessed by conducting a community survey of all the households in a given area and detecting all current cases, treated and untreated. In carrying out such a survey the researchers may plan to interview every person in the community or, to save time and expense, they may evaluate only those people who are identified by key informants (such as tribal chiefs or general practitioners) as possibly suffering from the illness. An approximation to prevalence can also be calculated from the number of cases in treatment at hospitals and clinics during a given period. Again this method, which assumes that virtually all cases of a disorder are in treatment, is inapplicable to the study of schizophrenia in most of the Third World. Prevalence data for schizophrenia vary more widely than incidence data – from 0.3 to 5 per 1,000 of the population in studies of the United States, from 2 to 17 per 1,000 in Europe, from 2 to 18 per 1,000 in Japan and from 0.4 to 7 per 1,000 in the developing world.[5]

While we may use incidence data to draw conclusions about what causes the appearance of an illness, strictly speaking, we should not use prevalence data in the same way. Prevalence figures for schizophrenia are the product of three processes – the rate of appearance of the illness (the incidence), the death rate of people with schizophrenia (which is greater in the Third World), and (except in the case of lifetime prevalence) the rate of recovery.

A problem with comparing different studies of the occurrence of schizophrenia, especially for Third World peoples, is that to draw an accurate picture it is necessary to know the age distribution of each population. Where a large proportion of the population is below age 15, for example, and not at significant risk of developing schizophrenia, one must expect a spuriously low prevalence of the illness. This source of error would be particularly evident in the Third World, where birth rates tend to be higher and life expectancy shorter than in the West, or in assessing changes in the same culture over a long period of time. In order to correct for this effect it is necessary to calculate a standardized, age-corrected prevalence figure.

Clearly, there are difficulties associated with assessing changes in the frequency of an illness over time or comparing rates between different parts of the world – incidence versus prevalence, point prevalence versus lifetime prevalence, community survey versus treatment statistics, narrow versus broad diagnosis and age-correction differences. It is not surprising that the statistics vary substantially and it is clear that we have to be cautious in interpreting the available data.

Bearing this point in mind, we may return to the issue of variations in the occurrence of schizophrenia over time and what they tell us about links between the illness and society.

WAS SCHIZOPHRENIA RARE BEFORE THE EIGHTEENTH CENTURY?

Is schizophrenia, like death and taxes, an unavoidable part of human existence? Psychiatrist Fuller Torrey argues that it is not; he suggests that schizophrenia may not have existed prior to the eighteenth century.[6] Several other authors disagree, however.[7] There is evidence, for example, that the inhabitants of ancient India and Rome distinguished conditions like schizophrenia from those resembling mania, depression, catatonic stupor and delirium.[8] It is an open question, however, whether schizophrenia was *less common* before the eighteenth century.

The records of Richard Napier, an English mediaeval physician who specialized in the care of the mentally ill, suggest that the condition closest to our modern category of schizophrenia, "mopishness," was not common in his day.[9] British psychiatrist Edward Hare argues that there was a real increase in the occurrence of schizophrenia during the nineteenth century. Not only did the total number of the insane occupying the asylums increase throughout the Victorian era, but so did admission and first-admission rates. First admissions more than tripled between 1869 and 1900.[10] As an editorial in the London *Times* of 1877 quipped,

> "if lunacy continues to increase as at present, the insane will be in the majority, and, freeing themselves, will put the sane in asylums."[11]

Many of the Victorian asylum superintendents, caught, as it seemed, in an upward spiral of lunacy, were at pains to point out that this trend was an artifact of increasing recognition of those in need of treatment, and not an indictment of their attempts at prevention. Others, like Daniel Hack Tuke, believed that there was an actual increase in mental disorder brought about by the spread of poverty.[12] Dr Hare, like Dr Tuke before him, argues that increased recognition of insanity cannot explain a sustained growth rate on such a scale over several decades. If increasing numbers of mild cases were being admitted to the asylums, he contends, one would expect to find decreasing death rates and increasing recovery rates, and this was not the case. Hare points out, moreover, that the greatest increase was in "melancholia," the nineteenth century condition that most closely matches the modern diagnosis of schizophrenia.[13]

Dr Hare argues that it was primarily the early-onset type of schizophrenia that increased during the nineteenth century. He suggests that some new biological factor, such as the mutation of a virus or a change in the immunological defenses of the general population, occurred and caused an increase in schizophrenia around 1800.[14]

Even at the end of the nineteenth century, schizophrenia appears to have been relatively rare. Psychiatrist Assen Jablensky reports that only nine per cent of men and seven per cent of women first admitted to the University Psychiatric Clinic in Munich in 1908 were diagnosed as suffering from dementia praecox (the contemporary term for schizophrenia). Since Emil Kraepelin himself (the psychiatrist who defined dementia praecox) evaluated some of these cases, it is unlikely that missed diagnosis accounts for the low prevalence of the disorder among the admissions. The occurrence rate for the diagnostic categories most likely to have included schizophrenia was low among other nineteenth century asylum populations, also. The greatest increase in institutionalized cases of schizophrenia, Dr Jablensky suggests, may well have occurred in the twentieth century.[15]

We have to be cautious, however. Historical information faces the same problem as present-day Third World data – the low incidence rates, in each instance, may be a result of restricted access to treatment, and the low prevalence rates may be due to the same problem and to higher death rates and more rapid recovery of people with the illness. They may bear relatively little relationship to the actual occurrence of new cases during the period in question. On balance, it seems quite probable that schizophrenia did become more prevalent during the nineteenth century, presumably in response to socio-environmental changes associated with the Industrial Revolution; possible biological mediating mechanisms include nutritional, immunological and infectious causes.

IS THE INCIDENCE OF SCHIZOPHRENIA ON THE DECLINE?

A number of researchers have pointed out that the incidence of schizophrenia now appears to be on the decline. The studies that examine changes in the incidence of schizophrenia since 1960 are listed in Table 9.1.[16] About three-quarters of these studies indicate a decrease in the incidence of the illness since 1960, and about a quarter reveal no change or an increase. All of the studies rely upon data gathered from treatment services, counting patients diagnosed as suffering from schizophrenia who are admitted or making treatment contact for the first time; the figures are age-standardized in only a few instances. The observed changes could be artifacts, therefore, rather than true changes in the occurrence of schizophrenia.

It is possible, for example, that a diagnostic shift from schizophrenia to

Table 9.1 Changes in the incidence of schizophrenia since 1960

Author(s) and year	Country	Period	Measure	Change in frequency
Eagles & Whalley (1985)	Scotland, UK	1969–78	Age-standardized rate	40% decrease
Parker et al. (1985)	New South Wales, Australia	1967–77	Number of first admissions	9% decrease
Dickson & Kendell (1986)	Scotland, UK	1970–81	Number of first admissions	48% decrease
Häfner & an der Heiden (1986)	Mannheim, Germany	1963–80	First-contact rates	18% increase
Munk-Jørgensen (1986)	Denmark	1970–84	Age-standardized	37% decrease
Munk-Jørgensen & Jørgensen (1986)	Denmark	1970–84	Age-standardized	44% decrease (females)
Joyce (1987)	New Zealand	1974–84	Number of first admissions	37% decrease
Eagles et al. (1988)	Aberdeen, UK	1969–84	Age-standardized first-contact rates	54% decrease
de Alarcon et al. (1990)	Oxford, UK	1975–86	Age-standardized first-contact rates and first-ever diagnosis rate	50% decrease (males & females)
Der et al. (1990)	UK	1970–86	First-admission rates	40% decrease (males) 50% decrease (females)
Folnevogić et al. (1990)	Croatia	1965–84	First-admission rates	No change
Bamrah et al. (1991)	Salford, UK	1974–84	Age-standardized first-contact rates	64% increase
Castle et al. (1991)	Camberwell, UK	1965–84	Age-standardized first-contact rates	25% increase (ICD diagnosis) 40% increase (RDC diagnosis) 38% increase (DSM-III)
Harrison et al. (1991)	Nottingham, UK	1975–87	Age-specific first-contact rates	No change
Munk-Jørgensen & Mortensen (1992)	Denmark	1969–88	First-ever admission rates	50% decrease
D'Arcy et al. (1993)	Saskatchewan, Canada	1979–90	First contact rates	66% decrease
Oldehinkel & Geil (1995)	Groningen, Holland	1976–90	First admission rates	13% decrease
Takei et al. (1996)	Scotland, UK	1966–90	First admission birth cohort study	55% decrease (males) 39% decrease (females)
Brewin et al. (1997)	Nottingham, UK	1978–94	Age-standardized first contact for narrowly defined schizophrenia	38% decrease
Suvisaari et al. (1999)	Finland	1970–91	Case register birth cohort study	33% decrease (males) 29% decrease (females)
Allardyce et al. (2000)	Southwest Scotland	1979–98	First contact, standardized diagnosis	No change

Note: The references cited in this table are listed in Note 16.

another diagnostic category could account for a decrease in the observed occurrence of schizophrenia.[17] Australian psychiatrist Gordon Parker and his co-workers, found that the decrease in the treated incidence of schizophrenia in New South Wales was accompanied by an increase in the diagnosis of manic-depressive illness following the introduction of lithium carbonate.[18] Some other studies show a similar increase in the prevalence of affective psychoses,[19] but many do not. One study provides quite strong evidence that the changing incidence of schizophrenia is an artifact resulting from a diagnostic shift. Researchers in Edinburgh, Scotland, have found that the proportion of patients who were diagnosed as suffering from schizophrenia by hospital psychiatrists at the time of first admission decreased by 22 per cent between 1971 and 1989. When diagnoses for these patients were made according to a computer algorithm, however, there was no such decline; in fact there was a small increase in the proportion diagnosed with schizophrenia.[20]

Another source of error may arise from an increase in the number of cases missed by traditional treatment-based statistics.[21] It is likely that the increased use of antipsychotic drugs treatment has led to a greater number of people with psychotic disorders in Europe and elsewhere being treated successfully by general practitioners. These people, consequently, may never be referred to any type of psychiatric treatment agency or included in service-based incidence statistics.[22] Similarly, more people with psychotic illness these days may escape any kind of treatment and, instead, lead eccentric, reclusive lives, live as vagrants, stay in shelters for the homeless or get arrested and jailed. An incidence study of schizophrenia in Nottingham, England,[23] for instance, found that ten per cent of the sample of cases that were ultimately detected were missed by the original screening procedure as they were only fleetingly in contact with the treatment facilities; further cases with no contact at all with the formal psychiatric treatment system would have escaped detection altogether.

If there is, in fact, any true decrease in the incidence of schizophrenia, the finding could give us important clues as to the causes of the illness. Possible biological mechanisms would include a decrease in the fertility of people with schizophrenia, a change in the population's immunity to an infectious agent, and a decrease in brain damage resulting from improvements in obstetric care.

It is not likely that there has been a recent decrease in the fertility of people with schizophrenia. For the incidence of schizophrenia to decrease throughout the 1970s, it would have been necessary for a change in fertility in schizophrenia to have been in effect through the 1950s. The decrease in the use of hospital confinement for people with mental illness, which began in many countries in the mid-1950s, makes it more likely that fertility has been increasing rather than decreasing among people with schizophrenia. The fertility of patients with schizophrenia, moreover, is unlikely to have a major impact on the incidence of the illness because only 11 per cent of people with schizophrenia have a parent with the illness.[24]

Changes in hygiene have produced changes in the general population immunity to various infectious agents. Poliomyelitis is an example of an illness whose prevalence increased with industrialization as a result of changes in hygiene; improvements in sanitation delayed exposure to the poliovirus until later in life, when the virus is more dangerous.[25] Similar changes in immunity or exposure to viral infection might account for the reported changes in the prevalence of schizophrenia.

Developments in obstetric practice may similarly account for the observed changes in the incidence of schizophrenia. The postwar decline in early neo-natal mortality rates in England and Wales is paralleled by the subsequent fall – 20 years later – in the first-admission rate for schizophrenia in the 1960s and 1970s.[26] This possibility is discussed at greater length below.

In summary, schizophrenia may or may not be on the decline in Western industrial countries. If it is, possible underlying biological mechanisms would include changes in immunity to an infectious agent or improvements in obstetric care. Next we should look at the remaining element of the complex pattern of changing occurrence of the illness over time – changes in the rate of occurrence of the illness in different social classes.

CASTE AND CLASS

As with thyrotoxicosis, poliomyelitis, coronary artery disease, and certain other illnesses, schizophrenia may initially increase in incidence among the upper classes as industrialization progresses and then switch to being pre-dominantly a lower-class disease.

The evidence for the increased rate of schizophrenia in the lower classes in cities of the industrial world was presented in Chapter 2. At that juncture it was pointed out that the social-class gradient for schizophrenia was rarely found in rural areas, a fact which eliminated the likelihood of a selective, genetic cause. The drift of people with schizophrenia or those at increased risk for the illness into lower-status occupations might partly explain the concentration of schizophrenia in the poorer classes, but there is an import-ant observation which forces the conclusion that some class-specific stress must additionally be at work – the social-class gradient for schizophrenia appears to slope in the reverse direction in peasant cultures and in non-industrialized parts of the world.

The province of Lazio in Italy in the early 1950s, for example, although it included the city of Rome, sustained a largely rural population many of whom were peasant farmers. An analysis of all reported cases of mental illness in the province between 1951 and 1955 revealed that schizophrenia was most commonly reported in the better educated, clerical workers and profes-sionals.[27] One must expect, however, significant under-reporting of psychosis in peasant communities and this factor may account for the observed findings in Lazio. A similar pattern, though, has been noted in other economically underdeveloped areas.

Several studies from India have made the observation that schizophrenia is more common among high-caste members than among the lower castes. First admissions for schizophrenia to the only public mental hospital in Bihar state in 1959 and 1960, according to psychologist Sharadamba Rao, were much higher among the rich Bania merchant caste, the urbanized and upwardly mobile Kayasthas (many of whom are in managerial and government jobs) and the educated Brahmin and Rajput landowners than among the lower-caste peasants who work the land themselves – the Kurmis, Goalas and Koiris – or among the low-caste Telis and the untouchable scheduled castes. The incidence of treated schizophrenia was nearly 50 times greater among the Banias in this study and more than ten times greater among the Kayasthas than in the lowest castes.[28]

These differences might be explained by a greater tendency for the more educated castes to refer their relatives for Western-style psychiatric treatment. That this explanation is not sufficient is shown by three door-to-door psychiatric surveys that confirm the greater prevalence of schizophrenia among the higher castes in India. The field survey of villages in West Bengal conducted by D.N. Nandi and his colleagues found the prevalence of schizophrenia among Brahmins (at 7.2 per 1,000) to be four times greater than among the untouchable scheduled castes (1.8 per 1,000) or the non-stratified Munda and Lodha tribesmen (1.3 per 1,000).[29] In a house-to-house survey of rural, semi-rural and urban inhabitants of the Agra region of Uttar Pradesh, conducted by K.C. Dube and Narendra Kumar, schizophrenia was shown to be three or four times more prevalent among the high-caste Brahmins and Vaishes than among the lowest castes.[30] The field survey of M.N. Elnagar and his co-workers in rural West Bengal revealed that schizophrenia was more common in the high-caste *paras* (neighborhoods) of the village. The *para* occupied by high-caste Singha Roys, where a large proportion of the residents were well educated and worked in business and professional occupations, had the highest prevalence of schizophrenia. In the *para* for low-caste Mahisyas, where the proportion of people working in agriculture was highest, no people with schizophrenia could be found.[31]

The Third World inverted social-class gradient appears to switch to the usual Western pattern of occurrence as the society becomes industrialized. In studies of the Chinese in Taiwan conducted between 1946 and 1948 by psychiatrist Tsung-Yi Lin and his associates the prevalence of schizophrenia was high in the upper classes and merchants and increasingly prevalent with higher levels of education. By 1961–63, however, after a period of dramatic growth in urbanization, industrialization and education and during a spell of economic prosperity, the patterns of illness had switched to mirror those of the West.[32] These changes are detailed in Table 9.2.

The high prevalence rates among higher-caste Indians and the well-

Table 9.2 Prevalence of schizophrenia per 1,000 of the Taiwanese Chinese population in 1946–8 and in 1961–3

	1946–8	*1961–3*
Social class		
Upper	3.5	0.8
Middle	1.2	1.1
Lower	4.5	2.1
Occupation		
Professional	0	0
Merchant	3.6	0.9
Salaried worker	0.9	0.4
Laborer	1.7	1.9
Farmer and fisherman	1.7	1.1
Unemployed	3.8	5.5
Education		
College	18.2	0.0
Senior high school	13.0	1.9
Junior high school	5.7	0.0
Elementary education	1.1	1.2
No formal education	3.8	3.7

Source: Lin, R., Rin, H., Yeh, E. et al., "Mental disorders in Taiwan, fifteen years later: A preliminary report," in W. Caudill and T. Lin (eds), *Mental Health Research in Asia and the Pacific*, Honolulu: East-West Center Press, 1969, pp. 66–91.

educated in the earlier Taiwanese study could be due to a number of factors, but they cannot be due to the drift of people with schizophrenia or at risk for schizophrenia into a different social stratum. People cannot change their caste, nor would they drift into higher education. Many of the studies are field surveys and, therefore, would not be influenced by differences between groups in treatment-seeking behavior. As we shall see shortly, however, changes in maternal nutrition and fetal and neonatal health in response to changing social conditions could produce this pattern through a neurodevelopmental effect.

It seems likely that the occurrence of schizophrenia in the West increased during the nineteenth century and possible that it has peaked and has been decreasing during the past four decades. In preindustrial settings the illness is more prevalent in the upper castes and classes, but in the post-industrial West the illness is more common in the poorer classes. Can we explain this pattern of occurrence?

INDUSTRIALIZATION AND THE HAZARDS OF CHILDBIRTH

Obstetric complications are one of the contributory causes of schizophrenia.[33] The risk of schizophrenia in people who suffer obstetric complications at birth has been variously estimated to be in the range of one-and-a-half to three times greater than those who have normal deliveries.[34] Some researchers argue that those who develop schizophrenia following obstetric trauma tend to be people without a genetic vulnerability to the illness.[35] Others suggest the reverse – that people with a genetic predisposition to schizophrenia inherit a nervous-system fragility that renders brain tissue more sensitive to the effects of oxygen deprivation or intracranial bleeding. In the latter case, the combination of genetically based neural developmental abnormality and subsequent nerve tissue damage leads to the development of the illness.[36] It is likely, in fact, that obstetric complications are a risk factor for people with or without a genetic vulnerability to the illness.

In the general population, obstetric complications occur in up to 40 per cent of births (the precise rate of occurrence depending on how they are defined).[37] Because they are so common, they are responsible for a large proportion of cases of schizophrenia. According to one analysis complications of pregnancy and delivery increase the prevalence of schizophrenia by 20 per cent.[38]

Changes associated with industrialization alter the risk of obstetric complications differentially in the various classes. For example, obstetric complications include problems with delivery caused by narrowing of the pelvic canal. A significant proportion of women with poor nutrition suffer from pelvic contraction due to childhood rickets caused by vitamin D deficiency. Improvements in nutrition during industrial development reach the upper classes first, but the first generation of women who gain this benefit are relatively small in stature and at risk for bony deformities because, as children, their nutrition was inferior. Their children, however – the first generation to have better nutrition from the outset – are bigger. Consequently, this first generation of more affluent women will have relatively small pelvic dimensions and, when pregnant, will carry large, well-nourished fetuses. The result will be more difficult deliveries and more brain damage in the new generation of infants.

The result may also be increased infant mortality. As we saw in Chapter 2, even though infant mortality has decreased with industrialization, it rises during the *boom* (see Figure 2.3), confirming that it can be a complication of affluence. Increased obstetric difficulties, then, are likely to lead to increased numbers of neonatal deaths as well as increasing numbers of surviving brain-damaged infants. If neonatal care improves, the proportion of brain-damaged infants that survive will increase; infant mortality, however, may continue to be above average.

Improvements in neonatal care, in the early phase of industrialization, become available sooner to the upper classes. This bias increases the tendency for children born with obstetric complications to higher-class women to survive infancy with brain damage and for similar lower-class children to die earlier in life. Both the increased rate of brain damage and the increased survival rate could, in turn, lead to higher rates of schizophrenia in the upper classes.

In the later phases of industrial development upper-class women with good nutrition from birth will have relatively large and well-formed pelvic cavities. Further advances in obstetric care, such as Cesarean section, which decrease the risk of fetal brain trauma, are also selectively available to the upper classes; both of these factors will eventually lead to *lower* brain-damage rates and a subsequent decrease in the incidence of schizophrenia in the upper classes. Lower-class women will not realize these benefits as soon. At the present time, for example, low birthweight, an indicator of obstetric complications, is more common in black infants in the United States than among white newborn infants.[39] These infants are at greater risk for schizophrenia; studies have found that low-birthweight infants have more damage around the ventricles of the brain (characteristically found in schizophrenia)[40] and that people with schizophrenia tend to have lower birthweights than their healthy siblings.[41] The risk of schizophrenia in the lower classes is no longer moderated by poor survival rates, moreover. The low-birthweight black infants have higher survival rates than white low-birthweight infants.

This analysis helps explain why the recent apparent decrease in the incidence of schizophrenia has been greatest in the most prosperous regions of the United Kingdom,[42] why the districts that show no decrease in schizophrenia have large immigrant populations with high rates of poverty[43] and why Western schizophrenia rates are higher among the poor. Differences in intrauterine development, delivery and infant survival may contribute to the increased risk of schizophrenia in the upper classes in the industrializing world and, conversely, to the high risk in lower social classes and (as we shall see shortly) among the children of immigrants in the post-industrial world.

IMMIGRANTS

Information about the occurrence of schizophrenia in immigrants provides a test of the theory that obstetric complications arising from social change affect the rates of the illness. Immigrants to the industrial world from less developed parts of the globe have a higher incidence of schizophrenia than native-born citizens. Some studies demonstrate that the high rates of the illness are also greater than in the immigrants' countries of origin. The common explanations for these observations are that (a) there is a selective tendency for individuals to emigrate who are constitutionally predisposed to develop schizophrenia and (b) the stress of migration or living in an alien culture increases the risk of developing the illness.[44]

Another possibility is that the pattern of occurrence is a response to the same factors that appear to explain the fluctuation in occurrence with the advance of industrialization – immigrants from poorer countries entering the Developed World encounter greater obstetric difficulties due to changes in nutrition but their infants receive better perinatal care, resulting in the survival of increased numbers of offspring with increased risk for schizophrenia. If this explanation is accurate:

- The frequency of schizophrenia will be elevated only in immigrants from countries where nutrition and perinatal care are worse than in the new country.
- The incidence of schizophrenia will be greater in immigrants than in the population of their country of origin.
- The rate of obstetric complications will be elevated among immigrants but neonatal survival rates will also be high.
- The incidence of the illness will be greater in second-generation immigrants than the first generation.

There is no shortage of evidence to demonstrate that immigrants from poor countries to rich show high rates of schizophrenia; the data on this point are clear. In the United States and Canada, numerous studies have shown that successive waves of poor migrants in the first half of the twentieth century, many of them fleeing starvation at home, exhibited first-admission rates for schizophrenia considerably higher than those of the general population – these included Greeks, Poles, Irish, Russians and Swedes.[45] Refugees entering Norway were ten times more likely than the native population to suffer from psychosis.[46] Afro-Caribbean immigrants living in the London boroughs of Lambeth and Camberwell in 1961 were three times more likely (after a correction for the age distribution of the population) than native-born residents to be admitted to hospital with schizophrenia,[47] and many studies since that time have confirmed that the Afro-Caribbean rate of the illness is substantially elevated in Britain.[48] Hospital statistics for England and Wales show that Afro-Caribbean immigrants and (to a lesser degree) Asian immigrants from India and Pakistan had higher rates of admission for schizophrenia than the general population.[49]

Reports of immigrant groups from more affluent countries stand in contrast. British immigrants to Victoria, Australia, in 1959 and 1960, for example, demonstrated an incidence of treated schizophrenia that was similar to the native-born rate but only a quarter of the incidence among immigrants from southern and eastern Europe.[50] European Jews settling in Israel in the 1950s had a lower incidence of schizophrenia than Jewish immigrants from the Middle East.[51] American-born residents of England and Wales experienced rates of hospitalization for schizophrenia in 1971 that were lower than those for most other immigrants and close to those for native-born residents.[52] English-born immigrants to New York State between 1949 and 1951 exhibited a strikingly lower first-admission rate for schizophrenia than immigrants from other nations or even native-born, white Americans.[53]

Immigrants were not over-represented in one sample of Canadians with schizophrenia unless they were coming from Eastern Europe and entering a disadvantaged minority population.[54] When Irish-born patients admitted to treatment from Camberwell in 1966–7 and in 1970 were compared with a class-matched group of English-born patients the prevalence of schizophrenia was found to be no greater in the Irish.[55] These observations confirm the impression that the occurrence of schizophrenia among immigrants from countries with similar nutritional and health care standards is not elevated.

Many of these studies may be faulted for their use of hospital statistics as the measure of incidence. More low-class immigrants might be admitted to public health facilities than affluent citizens, leading to a statistical bias. Community surveys that distinguish immigrants from non-immigrants would theoretically be more accurate, but such studies are rare.

Many researchers have emphasized that the elevated incidence of schizophrenia among immigrants from poor countries is greater than among the population of their countries of origin. Psychiatrist Silvano Arieti points out that in 1949 the treated incidence rate among Italian immigrants to New York was three times greater than the highest incidence in Italy.[56] (Diagnostic variations may account for part of this difference.) Örnulv Ödegard found that treated schizophrenia among Norwegian immigrants to Minnesota, prior to the 1930s, was twice as common as among native-born Americans or among the general population of Norway.[57] A series of studies have demonstrated that the incidence of schizophrenia in Jamaica, Trinidad and Barbados is substantially lower than among Afro-Caribbeans in Britain.[58] On the other hand, immigrants to London from Ireland, where nutrition and obstetric care are no worse, do not show an increased prevalence of illness when compared to the Irish who remain in Eire.[59]

If obstetric complications account for the elevated incidence of schizophrenia among poor immigrants, we should expect to find high rates of these complications of pregnancy and delivery among immigrant women. This is, in fact, the case. Afro-Caribbean and Asian women in England and Wales are much more likely to die from complications of childbirth than women in the general population;[60] Asian-born women in Bradford, England, receive less prenatal care and suffer more complications of pregnancy than British-born women;[61] and Afro-Caribbean babies are two or three times more likely than European infants to have a very low birthweight (indicating obstetric complications).[62]

The infants of immigrants, nevertheless, have high rates of survival because of advanced obstetric care. The children of black women in one British study did not have higher perinatal mortality rates than those born to white mothers, but the black mothers required more emergency Cesarean sections.[63] Although perinatal mortality in the Caribbean is several times greater than in Britain,[64] perinatal death rates are no higher for the Afro-Caribbean infants in Britain than for European babies.[65] As with black low-birthweight infants in the US, neonatal survival for Afro-Caribbean low-birthweight infants in the UK is actually *higher* than for white low-birthweight infants.[66]

An increase in obstetric complications and infant survival in immigrant women would explain an elevation in the occurrence of schizophrenia among *second-generation* immigrants, but would not contribute at all to the rate of the illness among the first generation to arrive. The theory that obstetric complications are implicated in the occurrence of the illness, therefore, is strongly supported by the finding that the rates of the illness are higher in the second generation than the first. A number of studies have shown that second-generation Afro-Caribbean immigrants have higher rates of schizophrenia than those who emigrated from the home country. One study that demonstrated the incidence of carefully diagnosed schizophrenia among Afro-Caribbeans in Nottingham, England, to be at least six times greater than among the indigenous population found that the vast majority of these cases were second generation.[67] A study in Birmingham, England, showed that the schizophrenia rate was substantially greater in *British-born* Afro-Caribbeans than among first-generation immigrants or non-Caribbeans.[68] A study of Afro-Caribbeans in south London[69] confirms that the risk of schizophrenia is substantially greater in second-generation immigrants.

One study that takes particular care to differentiate between first- and second-generation immigrants has established important findings: (1) the rate of first-admission for schizophrenia for young, second-generation Afro-Caribbean immigrants in Manchester was nine times greater than among Europeans, and (2) the rate of first-admission for mental disorder in the same age-group of *first-generation* Afro-Caribbeans was no greater than among the native British population – in fact the rate was a quarter of that found for Europeans.[70] The implication of these observations is that immigration itself may not increase the risk of schizophrenia, but, rather, the process of being born in the new country presents increased hazards.

Another curious finding increases the likelihood that the elevated risk of schizophrenia in second-generation Afro-Caribbean immigrants to Britain is due to an increased risk of obstetric complications among immigrant women. Two studies, one in Manchester[71] and one in London,[72] have shown that siblings of second-generation Afro-Caribbean immigrants with schizophrenia are at a much elevated risk of developing schizophrenia – four to eight times higher than for the siblings of white people with schizophrenia. Since siblings pass through the same birth canal, the finding suggests that obstetric complications may have led to the elevated risk of schizophrenia for the second-generation immigrants. One small study failed to find an increased risk of obstetric complications among second-generation Afro-Caribbean immigrants with psychosis.[73] Clearly more and larger studies of this issue looking specifically at schizophrenia are called for.

Some of the studies described above have found an increase in the rate of occurrence of schizophrenia in the first generation of Afro-Caribbean immigrants over the local population while others have not. It will be important to see which proves to be true in future studies that make careful efforts to distinguish between first- and second-generation immigrants. If there proves to be an increased risk for first-generation immigrants we will need to locate a cause other than obstetric difficulties. Some researchers have argued that such a cause might be exposure to a novel virus in the host country;[74] a similar explanation has been advanced for the elevated rates of infantile autism[75] and multiple sclerosis[76] in immigrant groups.

Others argue that social stress increases the risk of new immigrants developing the illness. The data presented above make it clear that it is only immigrants who come from poor countries and enter the lowest classes of society in the host country who experience elevated rates of schizophrenia. Do the stresses of urban poverty, menial employment and unemployment provoke the development of the illness? The main problem with this explanation is that, although we know that stress can influence the *course* of schizophrenia, we cannot explain how it can *cause* the illness. Stress increases the release of dopamine and, by exacerbating dopamine supersensitivity, could increase the symptoms of schizophrenia; but there is no known biological mechanism that would allow stress to cause new cases of the illness. While there is good evidence that stress can trigger the onset of an episode of schizophrenia and influence the *timing* of its onset, there is no good reason to believe that it will bring on the illness in someone who would otherwise have stayed healthy.

CROSS-CULTURAL COMPARISONS OF INCIDENCE AND PREVALENCE

If, for example, the stresses of unemployment and wage labor could precipitate a schizophrenic illness in predisposed individuals who would not otherwise have fallen ill we would expect the incidence of schizophrenia to be lower in those parts of the Third World where patterns of wage labor have not developed. In fact, this is not the case.

It is true that the *prevalence* of schizophrenia is significantly lower in the Third World. Age-corrected point prevalence or one-year prevalence rates for studies with comparable research characteristics from the developing world average 3.4 per 1,000 (ranging from 0.9 to 8.0 per 1,000) compared to an average of 6.3 per 1,000 (1.3 to 17.4 per 1,000) in Europe and North America.[77] The *incidence* of schizophrenia, however, is not lower in the Third World.

The recently published WHO study of the incidence of schizophrenia conducted at twelve sites in ten different countries was described in Chapter 7. The findings of the study are quite striking. The rate of occurrence of narrowly defined "core" schizophrenia, it emerges, is extremely similar at all the sites studied, varying from a low figure of 0.07 per 1,000 in Aarhus, Denmark, to a high of 0.14 in Nottingham, England. More variation is apparent when a broader diagnostic approach is used, from 0.16 per 1,000 in Honolulu, Hawaii, to 0.42 per 1,000 in the rural area around Chandigarh, India.[78] Even so, this range of variation is far less than would be expected based on the earlier, non-standardized prevalence studies. The gradient of occurrence – from the highest rate in a rural Third World setting to the lowest rate in a large American city – is the exact opposite of what would be expected if labor market stress directly influenced the occurrence of schizophrenia.

Other studies conducted in Ireland[79] and Germany[80] using the same standardized approach applied in the WHO study, have found narrowly defined schizophrenia to occur with incidence rates that are very close to those identified in the WHO report. It is difficult to explain why new cases of schizophrenia should occur at such similar rates around the world. One thing is clear, however – that the wide range in prevalence rates identified in the earlier studies is probably not due to variations in the rate of development of the disorder; it is better explained by differences in case finding, diagnostic approaches, research methodology and death and recovery rates of people with schizophrenia. The apparently lower prevalence of schizophrenia in the Third World is almost certainly due to the fact that people suffering from schizophrenia are more likely to recover quickly or to die young in developing countries than they are in the Developed World.

DOES LABOR MARKET STRESS TRIGGER THE ONSET OF SCHIZOPHRENIA?

It seems unlikely that the stresses of the labor market directly affect the rate of occurrence of schizophrenia. If such stress affects the *timing* of onset of schizophrenia, however, we would predict:

- First-time admissions to hospital for schizophrenia will increase in times of high unemployment.
- The age of onset of the illness will be earlier in the sex that is most adversely affected by the labor market.

The first of these predictions has been shown to be true – the evidence was presented towards the end of Chapter 2 – so we may examine the issue of gender differences.

GENDER DIFFERENCES

In Chapter 6 it was argued that the more benign course of schizophrenia in women when compared with men may be a result of the fact that fewer women participate in the labor force and that, overall, women are less severely affected by labor-market forces. There are no significant differences, however, in the rate of occurrence of schizophrenia in the two sexes in the industrial world. As the age-specific incidence rates for schizophrenia in Monroe County, New York, indicate (see Figure 9.1), however, this overall similarity in the rates masks the fact that there are wide differences between the sexes in the incidence of the illness at different ages.

The incidence of schizophrenia is roughly twice as great for men aged 15–24 years as for women of the same age. As psychiatrist John Strauss argues, this peak may reflect the intense career and work-related stress upon men at this stage of their lives.[81] Unemployment among adolescents is generally three times the rate for adults[82] and more severely affects males, whose participation in the labor force has traditionally been substantially greater than females at all ages.[83]

In the next decade of life, from ages 25 to 34 years, the incidence of schizophrenia in women peaks. For black women the rate substantially exceeds that of black men. While labor-market stresses may play a part in shaping this pattern (the rank ordering of the incidence of schizophrenia at this age, with black women highest and white males lowest, precisely matches the unemployment rates for these groups), it is likely that other life stresses are important. These are years of child-bearing and child-rearing, when women are called upon to make stressful role adjustments equivalent to the occupational demands placed upon men. They are also years when many women are required to make major career changes, to enter the labor force for the first time or to re-enter after a long absence. Other researchers have suggested that female hormones exert a neuroprotective effect that delays the onset of schizophrenia in women.[84]

The relationship between the changing dimensions of society and the occurrence of schizophrenia is not straightforward. Labor-market stress probably does not affect the occurrence of schizophrenia directly except, perhaps, to influence the timing of episodes and the age of onset. The changes in daily life that accompany industrialization, on the other hand, may affect the rate of occurrence of schizophrenia by bringing about changes in maternal nutrition, the birth process and the survival of infants. These same influences may well explain the elevated incidence of schizophrenia in second-generation immigrants. For more than a hundred years the industrial world witnessed a tidal wave of schizophrenia which now, fortunately, may be receding. Given this situation, what are the prospects for preventing schizophrenia?

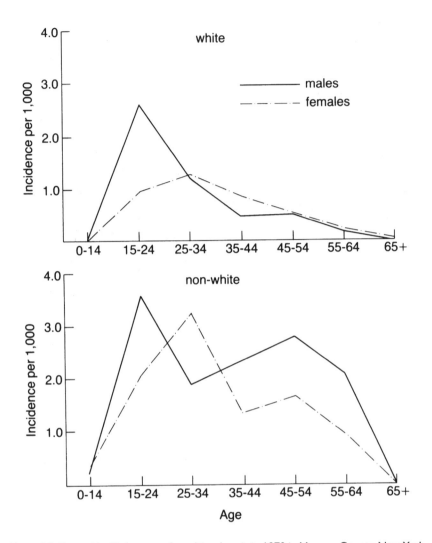

Figure 9.1 Treated incidence rates for schizophrenia in 1970 in Monroe County, New York

Source of statistics: Barfigian, H. M., "Schizophrenia: Epidemiology," in H. I. Kaplan, A. M. Freedman and B. J. Sadock (eds), *Comprehensive Textbook of Psychiatry – III*, Baltimore: Williams & Wilkins, 1980, pp. 1113–21.

IS PREVENTION POSSIBLE?

It is possible that minimizing obstetric complications will lead to reductions in the occurrence of schizophrenia, particularly if we target those who are at greatest risk for bearing children who will develop the illness.

Ironically, obstetric complications are particularly common among infants who already have a high risk for developing schizophrenia – the children of people who themselves suffer from the illness. For people with schizophrenia, the risk that any one of their children will develop schizophrenia approaches ten per cent, and, where both parents suffer from the illness, the risk for each child is close to 50 per cent.[85] But this hazard is compounded by the fact that women with schizophrenia are more likely than other women to experience complications of pregnancy. For women with schizophrenia in the US, the risk of premature delivery and of bearing low-birthweight children is increased by as much as 50 per cent.[86] This is to a great extent a result of the fact that women with schizophrenia (and other psychiatric illnesses) receive less adequate prenatal care than others in the general population.[87] In Oregon, for example, the rate of inadequate prenatal care is five times greater for women with mental illness than for women in the general population.[88]

The increased risk of complications for pregnant women with schizophrenia could also be due to their higher rates of smoking, to their use of alcohol and other substances, or to poverty. It might, theoretically, also be caused by a gene that increases the risk of both schizophrenia and obstetric complications, but this does not appear to be the case. One group of researchers points out that the increased risk of obstetric complications occurs when the mother, but not the father, suffers from schizophrenia; a genetically determined risk of obstetric complications and schizophrenia would not be confined to the mother.[89] Another group points out that a genetic link between obstetric complications and schizophrenia is unlikely because there is no increase in the risk of obstetric complications for those who have a family history of schizophrenia (and, therefore, a greater likelihood of carrying a gene for the illness).[90]

Since the advent of deinstitutionalization in the 1950s, fertility rates for people with schizophrenia have increased and women with schizophrenia bear as many children as women in the general population.[91] Based on this information, it would be reasonable to attempt to decrease the incidence of schizophrenia by educating people with schizophrenia, their blood relatives (particularly those in or approaching child-bearing years) and their treatment providers about the added risk of schizophrenia from complications of pregnancy and delivery that contribute to prenatal and perinatal brain injury. High-risk prospective mothers should be cautioned that smoking in pregnancy or maternal illnesses such as diabetes and heart disease may contribute to chronic fetal oxygen deprivation and increase the risk of schizophrenia in the offspring. Where one or both parents has a family history of schizophrenia, obstetricians should be aware that fetal oxygen deprivation, prolonged labor, placental complications and conditions of pregnancy leading to early delivery and low birthweight may present an added risk of schizophrenia to the newborn later in life. In such cases it would be appropriate to perform Cesarian sections earlier rather than later and to take aggressive precautions to prevent early delivery and low birthweight.

One of the most effective interventions would be to ensure that all women with schizophrenia get adequate prenatal care.[92] Several studies have shown that the provision of adequate prenatal care leads to better obstetric outcomes and fewer low-birthweight babies. The babies of cocaine-using women in New York who attended four or more prenatal appointments, for example, were half a pound (0.25 kg) heavier, on average, than those whose mothers attended three appointments or fewer.[93] Similarly, the birthweight of babies of cocaine users who were enrolled in a comprehensive program of prenatal care in Chicago was more than a pound and a half (0.75 kg) greater than that of babies of women who had made two or fewer prenatal visits.[94] Some studies show that the same benefits of prenatal care accrue to the infants of mothers who are not cocaine users.[95] Many professionals feel that the provision of good prenatal care to women with schizophrenia regardless of the effect on birthweight, is a clinically and ethically important element of health service provision.

To provide the necessary education, one could (1) distribute brochures summarizing recommendations on obstetric counseling and practice to waiting rooms of mental health agencies; (2) emphasize the provision of prenatal care among case-management services for women with schizophrenia; and (3) train residents in primary care, psychiatry and obstetrics to provide genetic and obstetric counseling to people with schizophrenia and their families. Such an educational program could be conducted by an international or national professional group or foundation.

The impact of such a program at a population level is not likely to be great, however. Obstetric complications account for fewer than a fifth of all cases of schizophrenia[96] and no more than a third of people with schizophrenia have a family history of the disorder.[97] Preventing the excess risk of obstetric complications in all relatives of people with schizophrenia, therefore, would reduce the incidence of the illness by less than $1/5 \times 1/3$ or less than seven per cent. This fraction would be substantially reduced, perhaps to less than one per cent, by various other imponderable factors:

- What proportion of the target population would the education reach?
- What impact would the educational intervention have on obstetric care?
- What effect do improvements in prenatal and perinatal care have upon obstetric outcome?

On the other hand, the total direct and indirect costs for a person with schizophrenia (in California) are $35,000 (£23,000) a year,[98] which over a 30-year period amounts to a million dollars (£670,000). At this rate, a five-year educational program on schizophrenia and obstetric complications costing, say, $2.5 million (£1.7 million) could pay for itself if it prevented just three cases of schizophrenia. The intervention, moreover, might have a greater effect on incidence in the developing world where obstetric complications are more common and the potential for their reduction is proportionately greater.

The potential for causing harm by educating people about obstetric complications and increasing access to prenatal care appears very limited. Maternal and infant health and survival should only be improved, regardless of whether the infant was at increased risk for schizophrenia or not. To avoid creating undue personal concern or stigma, educational efforts should make it clear that the risk to a person who is a first-degree relative of someone with schizophrenia of bearing a child who will develop the illness is not frighteningly high. The risk is increased from the general population rate of one per cent to around four or five per cent.[99]

INTERVENTION WITH THOSE "AT-RISK" FOR SCHIZOPHRENIA

There is current interest in the possibility of reducing the incidence of schizophrenia by treating people who have some premorbid features of the illness or other risk indicators prior to developing the full syndrome. The excitement has been generated, in large part, by the work of Australian psychiatrist Patrick McGorry and colleagues at the Early Psychosis Prevention and Intervention Center (EPPIC) in Melbourne and by a project pursuing the same line of research launched by American psychiatrist Thomas McGlashan at Yale University. Articles in the *New York Times*,[100] research newsletters[101] and other media sources have publicized the approach, and the governments of Great Britain and Australia and health regions in Italy and Canada have listed it as a public health priority. Is such enthusiasm supported by the research and epidemiological data? Unfortunately not.

According to psychiatric epidemiologist Assen Jablensky,[102] if a screening and early treatment program for any illness is to do more good than harm, the answer to each of the following questions must be "Yes."

- Does the burden of disease warrant screening?
- Is there a good screening test?
- Is there an effective preventive intervention?
- Will the program reach those who would benefit?
- Can the health-care system handle the screening?
- Will the screen-positive individuals comply with the proposed intervention?

In the case of schizophrenia, the answer to the first question is a resounding "Yes," but to the remainder the answers are "No" or, at best, "Doubtfully."

Adequate screening measures and effective interventions are not yet available. The most promising current screening measure – one devised by Joachim Klosterkötter and co-workers in Bonn, Germany,[103] which detects prodromal symptoms of disturbance in thought, perception, and other areas of functioning – if applied to the general population, would be accurate a mere two per cent of the time.[104] This means that 98 of 100 people labeled as likely to develop schizophrenia by the Bonn measure would be false positives – not in fact at risk for the illness. The accuracy of these measures can be improved by screening only those patients who have already been referred to a clinic. Patrick McGorry reports achieving 80 per cent accuracy in predicting schizophrenia among patients referred to his Personal Assistance and Crisis Evaluation (PACE) clinic in Melbourne using a screening device that selects patients with already present, low-grade or transient psychotic symptoms and such factors as a recent decline in functioning or a first-degree relative with a psychotic illness.[105] This strategy, however, will result in many at-risk cases in the population-at-large who have not been referred to a clinic being overlooked, and, as a result, it will have little broad public health impact on the incidence of schizophrenia. An additional problem is that when other Australian researchers in Newcastle, New South Wales, used the same screening instrument in their clinic it proved accurate, not 80 per cent, but 9 per cent of the time.[106]

Patrick McGorry and colleagues speculate that a variety of treatment interventions may be effective in preventing the onset of schizophrenia in high-risk cases.[107] They suggest using low-dose antipsychotic medication; stress-reduction measures such as social skills training; instruction in problem-solving techniques; family education, support and therapy; "lifestyle restructuring;" and training to enhance coping skills. All these approaches, however, were developed to help people with schizophrenia and their family members cope better with the illness and to reduce relapse rates. Their effectiveness in individuals who are not yet suffering from psychosis is unknown and, on the face of it, not particularly likely to be effective. How does one assess the benefit of antipsychotic medication, for example, before full-blown psychotic symptoms are apparent? How does one teach social skills before they have declined? What support and therapy is to be given to the family before significant problems have emerged?

The potential for harm with these interventions is significant, given the number of false positives expected. Is it appropriate to prescribe antipsychotic medications for someone with no positive symptoms of the illness and, if so, for how long? How much harm will be done to people who will never, in fact, develop the illness to tell them they are at risk for schizophrenia, that they need treatment and must adjust their future expectations? Critics are concerned that the "lifestyle restructuring" proposed by Dr McGorry may lead people who are labeled "pre-schizophrenic" to believe that they should downgrade their life expectations, avoid marriage, and not attend college.[108]

There are two published research reports of prevention attempts with people who have not yet developed full-blown schizophrenia. The first is New Zealand psychiatrist Ian Falloon's program established in a semi-rural catchment area of 35,000 in Buckinghamshire, England.[109] Falloon's team worked with family doctors to screen the population for the prodromal symptoms of schizophrenia. Possible cases were evaluated by the mental health team. People suspected of being in the prodrome of schizophrenia were provided individual and family education about schizophrenia, a stress management program and, in some cases, low doses of antipsychotic medication. These measures were continued until several months after all of the presenting features had resolved. During the four-year period of the program, only one resident of the area progressed to display the full features of schizophrenia. Falloon suggests that the observed incidence of schizophrenia during the period of the program was ten times less than in the same area a decade before. It is difficult to conclude, however, that the program reduced the incidence of schizophrenia, since it is very possible that a number of young people vulnerable to schizophrenia migrated out of the area to seek training and education in urban areas. Given the small size of the catchment area, a handful of cases lost to migration would produce a large apparent decrease in incidence.

A second pre-illness detection and treatment study was conducted by Patrick McGorry's team at the PACE clinic.[110] Thirty-one pre-illness subjects were assigned to preventive treatment with low doses of an antipsychotic drug, risperidone, and cognitive therapy, and 28 were assigned to supportive psychotherapy alone. Only 3 of 31 preventive treatment subjects developed psychosis after six months compared to 10 of the 28 in the control group. We could conclude that the onset of psychosis was delayed in about seven of the experimental group. This is a positive outcome, but we have to set it against some negative aspects. These are: (a) three patients took risperidone without benefit; (b) 21 patients were told they were at high risk for schizophrenia, when they were not; and (c) the same 21 took risperidone unnecessarily. How does one decide, moreover, how long the 28 patients who took risperidone and didn't develop psychosis should continue to take medication? For about three-quarters of the group the medication is unnecessary, but one doesn't know which those are. Should they continue taking medication for six months or six years or longer?

To summarize: educating providers of psychiatric and obstetric care and people with schizophrenia and their relatives about the risk of obstetric complications increasing the risk of schizophrenia could bring about a small decrease in the incidence of the illness, safely and at low cost. On the other hand, the positive aspects of preventive intervention with those considered to be at risk for schizophrenia are limited to the hope for preventing a disabling and costly illness; the negative aspects are substantial and include the likelihood that the accurate detection rate will be extremely low when targeted at the general population, a paucity of interventions of proven effectiveness in non-symptomatic individuals, a considerable risk of harm to those wrongly labeled, and the diversion of scarce health service funds from the treatment of established cases of the illness where the interventions are known to be effective.

We may be grateful that the increase in the incidence of schizophrenia that accompanied industrialization appears to be on the decline, and it is possible that we can hasten this process by improving access to good obstetric care, but efforts to reduce the incidence of schizophrenia by treating those who are at high risk for developing the disorder are premature.

SUMMARY

- Some diseases rise in incidence early in the process of industrial development and fall in frequency later; they are initially more common among the rich and, later, become more common among the poor. Schizophrenia seems to fit this pattern.
- The Industrial Revolution appears to have been accompanied by an increase in the occurrence of schizophrenia.
- Schizophrenia may be becoming less prevalent in recent decades in the industrial countries.
- In pre-industrial settings schizophrenia is more prevalent in the upper castes and classes, but in the West the illness is more common in the poorer classes.
- These shifts in the occurrence of schizophrenia may be a result of changes in nutrition, obstetric complications and neonatal care that accompany the advance of industrialization.
- The risk of developing schizophrenia is greatest for the children of people who migrate from poor countries to rich.
- Labor-market stress may influence the timing of the onset of schizophrenia but probably does not affect the incidence.
- Although the prevalence of schizophrenia is lower in the Third World than in the West, the incidence is not.
- Women in the industrial world show a peak incidence of schizophrenia a decade later in life than men.
- An educational program on the risk of obstetric complications as a cause of schizophrenia could bring about a small decrease in the incidence of the illness.
- Attempts to prevent schizophrenia by treating people at high risk prior to developing the illness offer little chance of success and carry a high probability of unintended negative consequences.

Part III

Treatment

Chapter 10

Antipsychotic drugs: use, abuse and non-use

Hundreds of double-blind studies of the efficacy of the various antipsychotic (or neuroleptic) drugs have now been conducted. The large majority of these studies suggest that these drugs are significantly more effective than inactive placebos in improving the condition of people with acute and chronic schizophrenia.[1] Time after time, in many thousands of treatment settings, clinical experience has shown that the different antipsychotic drugs can bring dramatic relief from psychotic symptoms in most people with schizophrenia. Long-term use of these medications appears to help forestall relapse. Twice as many patients with schizophrenia will relapse if placebos are substituted for their active medication than if they continue to take an antipsychotic drug.[2] Yet the overall outcome in schizophrenia, as shown by the analysis of dozens of follow-up studies in Chapter 3, has not improved since the introduction of the antipsychotic drugs in 1954. How can this be?

There are two probable answers:

- Although the antipsychotic drugs usually have a positive short-term effect on the symptoms of schizophrenia they may have had in some cases – particularly in good-prognosis cases – a negative effect on the long-term course of the illness.
- The emphasis on treatment of acute symptoms with medication has often led to a neglect of patients' community treatment and rehabilitation needs and to their exposure to high levels of symptom-provoking stress.

We should examine these two issues in detail, but, in doing so, we need to recognize that in the past decade and a half there have been major changes in the drug treatment of schizophrenia. Clozapine, a new type of antipsychotic medication with a novel mechanism of action, was introduced in the US in 1989, and has proven effective in cases of schizophrenia that were unresponsive to the standard drugs.[3] Like the standard antipsychotic drugs clozapine probably exerts its effect by blocking the effect of the neurotransmitter dopamine in a part of the brain known as the mesolimbic system.

Clozapine, however, blocks the effect of dopamine for much briefer periods of time than the standard antipsychotic drugs[4] and also has a blocking action on the effect of the neurotransmitter serotonin.[5] More recently other medications with a somewhat similar mode of action to that of clozapine have been introduced and have become widely prescribed for patients with schizophrenia. The patients in all but one of the studies on outcome from schizophrenia reported in Chapter 3, however, entered treatment before the introduction of these novel antipsychotic drugs, so it is the action of the standard drugs that must be considered in explaining why long-term outcome has not improved since the advent of drug treatment.

GOOD-PROGNOSIS SCHIZOPHRENIA

There is a subgroup of people with schizophrenia for which there are grounds to believe that drug treatment may be unnecessary or even harmful in the long run. These are the people with good-prognosis schizophrenia – the patients who show some indication that the course of their illness will be benign. Generally speaking, these are people whose psychotic illness began with sudden onset later in life than is usual in schizophrenia, whose previous work history and social functioning have been good and whose illness has not yet become long-lasting. To understand why standard antipsychotic drugs may have a negative effect on such patients, however, we must review some of what is known of the neurochemistry of schizophrenia and of the action of the drugs.

DOPAMINE ACTIVITY IN SCHIZOPHRENIA

Messages flow through the central nervous system as impulses in the nerve cells, or neurons. Where neurons link up, at the synapse, a chemical mediator is released from one cell that transmits the impulse to the next cell by its influence on a specific receptor. A number of these neurotransmitters have been identified; some, because of their particular importance in areas of the brain concerned with the emotions, have been quite intensively studied and have been implicated in the origin of various neurological and psychiatric disorders. Deficiencies of serotonin at brain synapses, for example, are thought to underlie the development of depressive illness. The neurochemical disturbances in schizophrenia are various, but a link in the chain of brain events appears to be a relative over-activity of certain tracts of neurons in which the chemical mediator is dopamine (dopaminergic tracts).

The importance of dopamine in schizophrenia[6] is based upon two main pieces of evidence:

(1) The standard antipsychotic drugs block the ability of dopamine receptors in the synapse to respond to dopamine and thus reduce the activity in dopaminergic tracts. The relative antipsychotic potency of the different standard antipsychotic drugs, furthermore, appears to be directly proportional to the capacity of each drug to block dopamine receptors – specifically, the dopamine-2 receptor. Observable reduction in psychotic symptoms occurs when 65 per cent or more of the dopamine-2 receptors are blocked.[7]

(2) The stimulant drug, amphetamine, which increases the release of dopamine and other catecholamines in the brain, will produce in humans an acute psychosis that is very similar to schizophrenia if it is taken in sufficient amounts. The drug can also bring about an exacerbation of psychotic symptoms in people with schizophrenia.

Dopaminergic fibers are to be found in a number of major tracts in the central nervous system. Two of these pathways, the mesolimbic and the mesocortical tracts, are considered to be possible sites of defective dopamine activity in schizophrenia. A disturbance in the mesolimbic system, in particular, can result in an inability to filter out multiple environmental stimuli – a characteristic disorder in schizophrenia.[8] Damage to the limbic system, or electrical stimulation of this pathway, can result in a number of other schizophrenia-like symptoms, including hallucinations, disturbances in thinking and emotion, paranoia, depersonalization and perceptual distortion.[9]

DOPAMINE SUPERSENSITIVITY

Researchers refer to "dopamine dysregulation" as being an underlying problem in schizophrenia. They use this term because, while it is clear that dopamine activity is elevated in the mesolimbic system, it is not clear whether this is all a result of an increased synthesis and release of dopamine or if it is partly due to an increased sensitivity of the dopamine-2 receptors to the effects of stimulation.[10] For example, it is possible that there is an excess of the type of dopamine-2 receptors with a high affinity for this neurotransmitter. Regardless of whether or not dopamine supersensitivity proves to be an important underlying problem in schizophrenia, it is clear that treatment with the standard antipsychotic drugs produces such a supersensitivity. Continuous use of these drugs leads to a tolerance to their effect, so that bigger doses have to be used to achieve the same degree of dopamine blockade – a phenomenon which researchers refer to as "up-regulation" of the dopamine system.[11] This is how it happens. Dopamine release is stimulated by stress and exposure to new situations.[12] Ordinarily the effect of dopamine activity is damped down by means of a negative feedback

process in which the neuronal system attempts to prevent overload by minimizing the effect of the neurotransmitter through a reduction in dopamine
turnover.[13] Malfunctioning of the interneurons that bring about this
negative feedback is believed to be one of the problems leading to dopamine
dysregulation in schizophrenia. By blocking dopamine receptors the
standard antipsychotic drugs diminish the activity of dopaminergic neurons
and reduce the symptoms of psychosis. The dopamine-blocking action, however, eliminates the feedback process that has been keeping dopamine
turnover at a low level. With the administration of these drugs dopamine
turnover promptly increases.[14] This is not an immediate problem, as the
receptors are blocked by the neuroleptic drugs and the increase in neurotransmitter can have little effect. There is a potential, however, for serious
long-term effects.

Chronic dopamine receptor blockade by the administration of the standard neuroleptic drugs, and the consequent elevation in dopamine turnover,
have been found to produce a substantial increase in the number of binding
sites for dopamine in the brains of rats and humans.[15] That is, the drugs create
an artificial dopamine supersensitivity. Tardive dyskinesia – the delayed
neurological side effect of chronic neuroleptic drug use that occurs in a proportion of patients – is a dopamine supersensitivity phenomenon. Dopamine
receptors in the nigrostriatal tract overcompensate for the chronic blockade
by becoming hypersensitive. The symptoms of tardive dyskinesia (involuntary muscle movements) usually appear after a reduction in the dose of the
neuroleptic drug, as this change exposes some of the previously blocked
receptors to the action of the neurotransmitter. An increase in drug dosage,
on the other hand, will block the receptors and mask the symptoms of the
disorder.

In the mesolimbic system, chronic dopamine blockade by antipsychotic
drugs leads to an increase in the number of dopamine-2 receptors and a
worsening of the dopamine dysregulation that is one of the underlying problems in schizophrenia.[16] As in tardive dyskinesia the supersensitivity effect
may be temporary, gradually disappearing over the course of weeks or
months after drug withdrawal, or – if drug treatment continues long enough
– it may become permanent. Herein may lie one reason for the failure of
the standard antipsychotic drugs to produce improvements in the long-term
outlook in schizophrenia.

We may predict that certain consequences will flow from the tendency of
the standard antipsychotic drugs to produce dopamine supersensitivity.
These include:

- Psychotic symptoms will rebound, after the withdrawal of standard
  antipsychotic drug treatment, to a higher level than would have been the
  case without treatment. Drug-withdrawal studies that evaluate the efficacy of antipsychotic drugs by substituting a placebo for the active drug

will therefore give an over-optimistic impression of the value of the drugs.

• The adverse long-term effects of the standard antipsychotic drugs will be most evident in the case of people with schizophrenia who would otherwise have had a good prognosis. As illustrated in Figure 10.1, the outcome for people with *poor-prognosis* schizophrenia is likely to be so serious that a worsening due to drug withdrawal would be difficult to detect and the continuous use of drugs will still offer distinct advantages for these patients. In the case of people with *good-prognosis* schizophrenia, on the other hand, drug withdrawal may worsen the course of

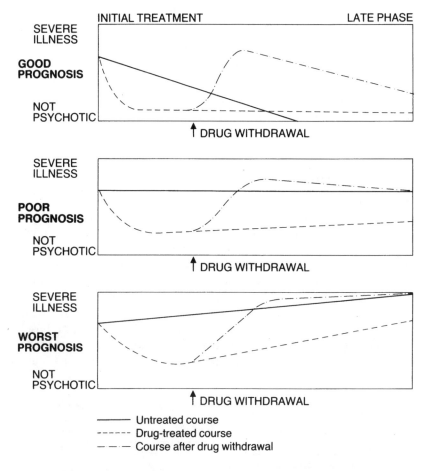

Figure 10.1 Postulated course of illness in good-, poor- and worst-prognosis cases of schizophrenia with and without neuroleptic drug treatment and after drug withdrawal

an otherwise benign condition and drug maintenance therapy may increase the risk of psychosis, cause side effects or, at best, prove worthless.

We may examine the evidence relating to these predictions in turn.

IMMEDIATE ASSIGNMENT STUDIES

Drug-withdrawal (placebo substitution) studies may exaggerate the long-term benefits of the standard antipsychotic drugs on the course of schizophrenia. In particular, they may give a spurious impression of the value of drug treatment for good-prognosis patients that is the reverse of their real long-term effect (see Figure 10.1). Accordingly, the only drug studies that would be expected to give an accurate reflection of the efficacy of the antipsychotic drugs in schizophrenia are those that:

(a)   assign patients to drug or placebo treatment at the beginning of the study (immediate assignment studies) and do not withdraw antipsychotic treatment part-way through the study; and
(b)   also distinguish between good-prognosis and poor-prognosis patients.

Such studies are few.

Rosen and associates

Psychopharmacology researchers Bernard Rosen and David Engelhardt and their co-workers at a New York clinic followed a group of over 400 out-patients with schizophrenia for between four and eight years. They divided the group into good- and poor-prognosis categories on the basis of their own "Hospital Proneness Scale" which measured the patients' prior social attainment, the extent of their previous treatment and their performance in psychological tests. The patients were randomly assigned at the very outset of the study to treatment with either a placebo or one of two standard antipsychotic drugs, chlorpromazine or promazine. The subsequent hospital admission rate indicated that the antipsychotic neuroleptic drugs were effective in keeping the patients with poor-prognosis schizophrenia out of hospital:

	Hospital admission rate of poor-prognosis patients
Patients taking chlorpromazine	35.7%
Patients taking promazine	29.4%
Patients taking placebo	61.5%

For good-prognosis patients, however, drug treatment appeared to be unhelpful or even harmful.[17]

	Hospital admission rate of good-prognosis patients
Patients taking chlorpromazine	12.2%
Patients taking promazine	28.4%
Patients taking placebo	7.7%

Subsequently these researchers followed up the 129 patients who had been hospitalized to see which of them were hospitalized for a second time. The results were even more striking. Drug treatment proved effective in keeping poor-prognosis patients out of hospital longer:

	Average time before rehospitalization of poor-prognosis patients
Patients on chlorpromazine	14 months
Patients on promazine	16 months
Patients on placebo	6 months

But good-prognosis patients treated with chlorpromazine were hospitalized significantly sooner.[18]

	Average time before rehospitalization of good-prognosis patients
Patients on chlorpromazine	6 months
Patients on promazine	14 months
Patients on placebo	30 months

University of California Group

In a study at Camarillo State Hospital, California, psychologist Michael Goldstein and his associates divided a group of 54 newly hospitalized, male patients with schizophrenia into good- and poor-prognosis cases (using a scale devised by Leslie Phillips). The patients were randomly assigned to treatment with a placebo or a standard antipsychotic drug soon after admission. After three weeks of treatment the poor-prognosis patients appeared to benefit from taking active medication. The good-prognosis patients, however, did better if they were taking placebo – they improved more rapidly and were discharged sooner. This finding was particularly true for non-paranoid, good-prognosis patients.[19] The researchers uncovered a similar pattern of response when they repeated their study with a new sample of 24 males with good-prognosis schizophrenia – neuroleptic drugs failed to benefit the non-paranoid, good-prognosis patients in three weeks of treatment.[20] Unfortunately, no long-term follow-up of the patients in either of these studies was done.

Interestingly enough, this research group obtained analogous findings when they compared the effect of high versus low doses of standard antipsychotic drugs treatment on a group of 104 young people with acute schizophrenia. The good-prognosis patients – particularly males – showed a negligible rate of relapse and had fewer symptoms at the end of six months on the *lower* dose of medication.[21]

Rappaport and associates

Eighty young males with acute schizophrenia admitted to Agnews State Hospital in California were randomly assigned on admission to chlorpromazine or placebo treatment by Maurice Rappaport and his co-workers. After discharge from the hospital the patients were treated with or without active medication depending, presumably, on their clinical condition and their compliance with the psychiatrist's recommendation. Patients who did well on placebo treatment in hospital tended to be treated without medication after leaving hospital and to have had good-prognosis schizophrenia and a history of good functioning before admission. Placebo treatment failures were likely to be given active medication after discharge. At three-year follow-up the patients who took a placebo in hospital and were off medication as outpatients showed the greatest clinical improvement and the lowest levels of pathology and functional disturbance. They also had the lowest rate of rehospitalization:

Hospital/outpatient treatment	Rehospitalization rate
Placebo/no medication (N=24)	8%
Chlorpromazine/no medication (N=17)	47%
Placebo/neuroleptic (N=17)	53%
Chlorpromazine/neuroleptic (N=22)	73%

The superiority of the placebo/no medication group to the chlorpromazine/no-medication category is particularly worth noting, although part of this difference in outcome may be due to there being a greater proportion of good-prognosis patients in the former group. The authors of the study conclude: "Antipsychotic medication is not the treatment of choice, at least for certain patients, if one is interested in long-term clinical improvement."[22]

Carpenter and associates

Patients with good-prognosis schizophrenia, a record of adequate prior work and social functioning and a short history of illness were selected for a study conducted at the US National Institute of Mental Health by William Carpenter and his associates. The 49 patients were treated with or without neuroleptic medication at the discretion of their psychiatrists – the assignment to drug treatment was fairly arbitrary but not random. The two groups were equivalent in their prognostic ratings and had similar initial clinical characteristics. At one-year follow-up the patients in the drug-free treatment group demonstrated a more benign course in a number of ways:

	Drug-free	Drug-treated
Average length of hospital stay	108 days	126 days
Rehospitalization rate	35%	45%
Outpatient neuroleptic drug treatment	44%	67%

Patients receiving drug treatment in hospital were also significantly more likely to suffer a postpsychotic depression.

The research team who conducted this study

> raise the possibility that antipsychotic medication may make some schizophrenic patients more vulnerable to future relapse than would be the case in the natural course of their illness. Thus, as with tardive dyskinesia, we may have a situation where neuroleptics increase the risk of subsequent illness but must be maintained to prevent this risk from becoming manifest.[23]

Klein and Rosen

One study alone that fits the criteria of (a) immediately assigning patients to a drug-free or drug-treatment category and (b) distinguishing good-prognosis patients, fails to support the picture drawn by the research cited so far. Donald Klein and Bernard Rosen at the Hillside Hospital, New York, randomly assigned 88 inpatients with schizophrenia to chlorpromazine or placebo treatment. The researchers differentiated good- and poor-prognosis patients by means of the Premorbid Asocial Adjustment Scale. On rating the patients after six weeks of treatment the investigators found that chlorpromazine was more beneficial for the *good*-prognosis than for the poor-prognosis patients.

From the standpoint of this analysis, however, the Klein and Rosen study has two flaws. In the first place, it is not a follow-up study. It gives only the outcome of six weeks of treatment and has no bearing on whether drug-induced dopamine supersensitivity has a detrimental effect on the long-term course of schizophrenia. It therefore stands in contradiction to Goldstein's short-term studies only, and is unrelated to the findings of the research teams of Rosen and Engelhardt, Rappaport and Carpenter. Secondly, the research design itself was biased against recovery in the good-prognosis patients. The research sample was composed of patients who were referred to the drug study after they had failed to improve in milieu (drug-free) treatment and psychotherapy. This selection procedure would automatically weed out the patients who could be expected to do well in drug-free treatment.[24]

May and associates

A number of studies may be found in the literature that, while not precisely fitting the criteria established for this analysis, nevertheless yield useful information. Philip May and his colleagues, for example, in a four-year follow-up of over 200 first-admission patients with schizophrenia showed that 59–79 per cent of patients recovered in various drug-free treatments (including psychotherapy and electroconvulsive therapy) and that the successes from such treatment (presumably good-prognosis patients) did as well in the long term as patients who were initially treated with antipsychotic drugs.[25]

Schooler and associates

Nina Schooler and her co-workers made a similar finding in another immediate assignment drug study of a large sample of patients with schizophrenia conducted through the US National Institute of Mental Health. In a follow-up of the discharged patients one year after leaving hospital the researchers were surprised to find that "patients who received placebo treatment in the drug study were *less* likely to be rehospitalized than those who received any of the three active phenothiazines."[26]

Pasamanick and associates

We should recognize, however, that there is another immediate assignment study that does not discriminate good- and poor-prognosis patients – Benjamin Pasamanick's comparison of outcome of drug-treated and placebo-treated patients in home care – and that this report does *not* show a long-term benefit to placebo treatment.[27] Why should the placebo-users in Schooler's NIMH study have had a superior outcome? One possibility is that there were more good-prognosis patients admitted to that study than to Pasamanick's. The subjects in the NIMH study typically had a number of good prognostic features – the illness was at an early stage, the onset had been acute and later in life, and many of the patients were currently or previously married.[28]

The Soteria Project

Another immediate assignment study of treatment in schizophrenia is well worth examining – the Soteria Project. Under the direction of psychiatrist Loren Mosher (at the time Chief of the Center for Studies of Schizophrenia at NIMH) and social worker Alma Menn, this project set out to compare the effectiveness of a non-medical, psychosocial treatment program for people experiencing their first episode of schizophrenia with the drug-oriented treatment of a community mental health center. Acutely ill patients who had previously had no more than two weeks of inpatient psychiatric treatment were arbitrarily assigned to treatment in a short-stay inpatient unit followed by outpatient aftercare or to Soteria House, a home for up to six patients in the community staffed by non-professionals. Patients in the standard community mental health center program spent a much shorter time in their initial period of residential (hospital) care – one month compared with five-and-a-half months of residential care for Soteria patients. Whereas all the mental health center patients were initially treated with neuroleptic drugs, only eight per cent of Soteria patients received such therapy.

Follow-up, two years after admission, showed that the outcome for Soteria patients compared quite favorably with that of the people with schizophrenia treated by the community mental health center.

Two-year follow-up		
Treatment after discharge	Soteria	Mental health center
Readmitted to hospital or Soteria House	53%	67%
Taking neuroleptic drugs continuously or intermittently	34%	95%
Receiving psychiatric treatment	59%	100%
Circumstances at follow-up		
Working (full-time or part-time)	76%	79%
Living independently	58%	33%

The overall levels of psychopathology in the two groups of patients were not significantly different at follow-up.

"Our data," suggest Mosher and Menn, "indicate that antipsychotic drugs need not be used routinely with newly admitted schizophrenics if a nurturant, supportive psychosocial environment can be supplied in their stead."[29] The authors point out that their sample of patients was not composed of particularly good-prognosis cases – they selected individuals who were young and single, generally considered indicators of poor outlook. All patients, however, were at a very early stage of their illness. Patients with the fewest relapses in both treatment programs tended to have good prognostic features (better prior social competence and a later age of onset), but there is no indication that good-prognosis patients did better in drug-free care.[30]

Soteria Berne

Soteria Berne, a therapeutic household for the treatment of schizophrenia, borrows many ideas from Mosher and Menn's Soteria Project. Established by psychiatrist Luc Ciompi in a 12-room house in the middle of Berne, Switzerland, the program can accomodate up to eight patients and two nurses. Like the California-based Soteria, the household in Berne aims to manage people with schizophrenia in a small supportive environment using neuroleptic medication in low doses and only in unusual circumstances. Young people with a first episode of schizophrenia are selected fairly randomly for admission (very agitated or involuntary patients are excluded) from among cases presenting to the local emergency services. Some patients with longer-lasting illness and poor-prognosis features are also admitted.

Twenty-five people treated at Soteria Berne were compared with a matched group of 25 similar patients treated at conventional local hospitals. When the two groups were followed up after two years, conventionally treated and Soteria patients had similar levels of pathology and functioning. Soteria-treated patients, however, had used much lower doses of antipsychotic medication – one quarter as much during the acute treatment phase, half as much overall. Thus the results at Soteria Berne are very similar to those at Soteria in California.[31]

Lehtinen and associates

A recent Finnish immediate assignment study confirms the good outcomes achieved by Soteria and Soteria Berne with minimal use of medications in schizophrenia-like psychosis. In this study progress was assessed over two years for 106 patients admitted to treatment for a first episode of psychosis (excluding affective psychosis like bipolar disorder) in 1992–93 at one of six different treatment centers around Finland. All the patients were provided individual and family treatment, but at three centers the patients received only minimal doses of antipsychotic medication and nearly half received no antipsychotic medication at all over the two-year period. At the other three centers usual antipsychotic treatment approaches were used. The outcome for patients in the minimal medication group was equal to or superior to that of patients treated with usual doses of medication.[32]

Two-year follow-up

	Minimal medication	Usual medication
Took antipsychotic drugs at any time	57%	94%
Less than two weeks in hospital in two years	51%	26%
No psychotic symptoms during past year	58%	41%
Employed	33%	31%
Good social functioning	66%	55%

The authors conclude that:

> in selected cases of first-time psychosis neuroleptic treatment is not as essential as it has usually been considered if intensive psychosocial treatment measures are provided.[33]

They recommend waiting at least two weeks after admission before starting antipsychotic drug treatment in patients with a first-episode of psychosis.

The weight of evidence in these immediate assignment studies suggests that the standard antipsychotic drugs are unnecessary or harmful, in the long run, in good-prognosis schizophrenia. Taken together with the well-established fact that drug-*withdrawal* studies have consistently shown the neuroleptics to be superior to placebos in preventing psychotic relapse,[34] we now have an indication that the standard antipsychotic drugs produce a heightened risk of relapse for drug-withdrawn patients. They may do this by producing dopamine receptor supersensitivity in schizophrenia. It remains to be seen whether the novel antipsychotic drugs, which block dopamine-2 receptors for a much briefer period of time, will be less likely to produce dopamine supersensitivity and to increase the risk of relapse in drug-withdrawn patients. Whatever proves to be the case with the newer medications, we have at least one possible explanation for the failure of the standard antipsychotic drugs, over decades of use, to have a measurable impact on overall outcome in schizophrenia.

If we now look at the interactions between environmental stress and antipsychotic drug treatment in schizophrenia we may find further reasons for the poor showing of the standard antipsychotics and, in addition, useful indications as to how we can help make low-dose or drug-free treatment effective.

STRESS, SCHIZOPHRENIA AND DRUG TREATMENT

Stress, as noted in Chapter 1, may precipitate a psychotic episode in a predisposed individual.[35] The antipsychotic drugs, moreover, may be less necessary for preventing relapse in schizophrenia for people living under conditions of low social stress, and of greater utility for those in a more harsh and demanding environment. As British social psychiatrist John Wing wrote:

> Drug treatment and social treatments are not alternatives but must be used to complement each other. The better the environmental conditions, the less the need for medication: the poorer the social milieu, the greater the need (or at least the use) of drugs.[36]

A number of pieces of research support this point of view.

A series of projects conducted through the Medical Research Council Social Psychiatry Unit in London has shown that the relapse rate is higher in people with schizophrenia who return home to live with critical or over-involved relatives than in those (the majority) whose relatives are more supportive and less smothering. The relapse rate in the patients living in the more stressful households is reduced by two factors: (a) restricting the contact between patient and relatives to less than 35 hours a week and (b) using antipsychotic drugs. For patients living in the low-stress families, however, the relapse rate was found to be low regardless of whether the patients were taking medicine or not. Figure 10.2 illustrates the nine-month relapse rates for 128 people with schizophrenia (71 from low-stress homes and 57 from high-stress families) – the combined subject groups from the two studies.[37] The rate of relapse among patients living in low-stress households and taking no medication can be seen to be several times lower than the rate for those who are exposed to a high-stress environment for much of the time even when these patients are protected by medication.

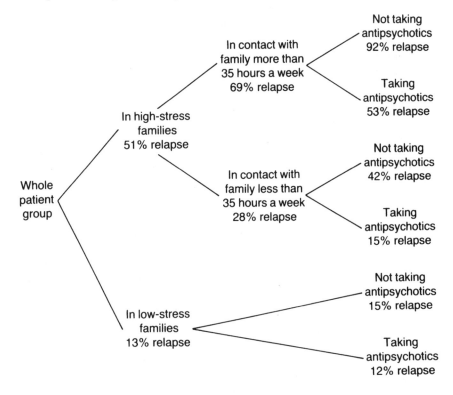

Figure 10.2   Relapse rates of schizophrenic patients in high- and low-stress families

Source: Vaughn, C. E. and Leff, J. P., "The influence of family and social factors on the course of psychiatric illness: A comparison of schizophrenic and depressed neurotic patients," *British Journal of Psychiatry*, 129: 125–37, 1976.

In a later (two-year) follow-up of one of these groups of patients, psychiatrist Julian Leff and psychologist Christine Vaughn found that drug treatment did eventually appear to be of some benefit to the patients in low-stress homes. The researchers speculated that the drugs were of value in protecting these patients against additional sources of life-event stress (e.g., job loss) to which they were exposed independent of the fact that their home environments were warm and supportive.[38] Dr Leff and Dr Vaughn had demonstrated in an earlier piece of research that relapse was unavoidably common in people with schizophrenia living in high-stress homes but that relapse in patients in low-stress homes was only likely to occur if they were subjected to additional independent stressful events.[39] One may conclude from these findings that antipsychotic drugs are less necessary for people with schizophrenia living in environments that are both supportive and also somewhat protective in warding off unpredictable stresses.

The therapeutic effect of a warm and non-critical relative has been demonstrated in two further studies carried out by the same group of researchers. Heart rate and skin conductance tests showed that people with schizophrenia had a higher level of arousal than healthy individuals, irrespective of whether the patients were living in high-stress or low-stress households. This heightened level of arousal dropped to normal in a person with schizophrenia when in the company of a non-stressful relative but continued at an elevated rate when in the company of a critical, over-involved relative. The finding held true for both patients in acute psychosis[40] and those in remission.[41] The neuroleptic drugs similarly are known to decrease the level of arousal in people with schizophrenia – a property that is thought to contribute to their antipsychotic effect. This evidence, then, also implies that antipsychotic drugs may be less necessary where the social environment is therapeutic and non-stressful.

The level of arousal in people with schizophrenia in hospital or residential treatment can be controlled by creating an environment that is optimally stimulating and supportive. In such a setting drug treatment is minimally necessary. Long-stay hospital patients withdrawn from low-dosage maintenance drugs, according to psychologist Gordon Paul's 1972 review of the research, rarely show harmful effects, and a majority of the relevant studies indicates that drug treatment is not necessary for such patients when they are in a progressive psychosocial treatment program.[42]

One such study is Gordon Paul's own report on a drug-withdrawal project involving 52 severely incapacitated, long-stay patients with schizophrenia in an Illinois state hospital. The patients were transferred to two active psychosocial treatment programs and matched groups were assigned to either continuation of their usual drugs or to placebo substitution. Staff and patients were not even aware that a drug study was in process. After four months the drug-withdrawn patients were doing equally as well as those on drugs (initially, in fact, the drug-withdrawn patients had responded *more* rapidly to the treatment program).[43] By the end of the six-year experimental program, 85 per cent of the people with schizophrenia in psychosocial treatment were still off drugs.[44] Why was drug-withdrawal supersensitivity psychosis not a problem with these patients? Perhaps because, in this instance, they were generally taking only moderate to low doses of medication before withdrawal.

Research cited earlier in this chapter – William Carpenter's study at the National Institute of Mental Health, Loren Mosher's Soteria House, Luc Ciompi's Soteria Berne and Lehtinen's Finnish study – has demonstrated that the same observation holds true for many young people with acute psychosis. Active, individualized, psychosocial treatment programs render antipsychotic drugs therapy less necessary for a substantial number of patients.

One prominent study might be seen as conflicting with the general trend of this research. The study, by Solomon Goldberg with his associates in the NIMH Collaborative Study Group, found that the relapse rate of people with schizophrenia withdrawn from antipsychotic drugs was greater than that of patients who continued the drug treatment. At the time of discharge from hospital these patients were randomly allocated to either routine outpatient care or to a more intensive program of sociotherapy – major role therapy, a combination of social casework and vocational counseling. The researchers found that, overall, the intensive sociotherapy was ineffective. This was because the therapy helped some patients and hindered others. Mildly ill patients benefited and more severely ill patients relapsed *sooner* if they were receiving intensive sociotherapy.[45] Patients taking antipsychotic drugs responded well, but those taking placebos had a *worse* community adjustment if they were in major role therapy.[46]

At first glance it appears that these results contradict the evidence for the benefits of psychosocial treatment in schizophrenia, but on closer examination this does not prove to be the case. The psychosocial treatment programs in Gordon Paul's study or on William Carpenter's research ward or at Soteria House or at Soteria Berne were comprehensive attempts to shape a total therapeutic residential environment in such a way as to maximize the psychotic patients' chances of recovery. Major role therapy, on the other hand, consisted of outpatient treatment delivered to people with schizophrenia living in any one of a number of community locations. The patients in this "intensive" therapy program were seen, on average, only twice a month.[47] The main thrust of the therapy was to urge "the patient to become more responsible and to expand his horizons."[48] The authors appropriately conclude that the major role therapy was probably too intrusive and stressful for the marginally functioning patients and that its toxic effect was similar to the influence of the critical and over-involved relatives in the British studies of the family environment of people with schizophrenia cited above.

By way of contrast, some forms of outpatient therapy that do aim to reduce the stresses in the patient's environment have proved successful. Julian

Leff and his co-workers were able to minimize the impact of critical and over-involved relatives on patients with schizophrenia through family therapy and thus to reduce the relapse rate in these patients.[49] New Zealand psychiatrist Ian Falloon in association with a team of researchers in California achieved a similar result working with the families of people with schizophrenia in their homes – family-treated patients showed fewer psychotic symptoms and fewer relapses.[50] Subsequent research has reliably shown similar benefits from programs providing family education and support in schizophrenia.[51]

We may conclude that when people with schizophrenia are in an environment that is protective but not regressive, stimulating but not stressful, and warm but not intrusive (whether it be their own family home or a residential treatment unit) many of these patients will need less antipsychotic drug treatment. On the other hand, people with schizophrenia who are exposed to significant stress (whether it be status loss, intrusive relatives, over-enthusiastic psychotherapy or hunger, cold and poverty) – will have a high relapse rate and will require substantial doses of antipsychotic drugs to achieve adequate functioning levels.

Many patients, of course, do not choose to be in a highly protective setting – they prefer independence. Life cannot be made stress-free unless one chooses to withdraw from the excitement of daily living. In practice, for most patients drug-free treatment is not feasible. In the best community treatment systems there is a place for the judicious use of antipsychotic medication. A reasonable goal for the majority of people with schizophrenia is to use moderate doses of medication that lead to a genuine improvement in quality of life without adding to their hardships.

In Western society in recent decades, nevertheless, too few people with schizophrenia have received adequate treatment or have been placed in reasonably suitable therapeutic settings. A recent US household survey of the adequacy of treatment for people with serious mental illness revealed that only 40 per cent of the seriously mentally ill had received any treatment in the prior year, and in less than 40 per cent of these cases was the treatment minimally adequate – meaning that only 15 per cent of seriously mentally ill people were getting acceptable care. People with psychotic disorders received the most inadequate care.[52] Those in institutions may fare quite poorly. A study of the mentally ill in Utah nursing homes showed that their dosage of medication progressively increased with time but that their levels of activity decreased.[53] With the advent of antipsychotic drugs and the advance of radical deinstitutionalization policies, too many have been thrust into highly stressful environments. As we saw in Chapter 8, around a third of all Americans with schizophrenia exist in settings that scarcely pretend to be therapeutic – in jail, on Skid Row, in nursing homes or boarding homes.

Here we find another explanation of the failure of the drug-treatment era in psychiatry to usher in improved outcome in schizophrenia. In the rush to transfer patients to the community – to cut institutional costs regardless of the social costs – some people have been abandoned and, for others, the antipsychotics have been used not as an *adjunct* to psychosocial treatment, as John Wing recommends, but as an *alternative* to such care. Too often the psychiatrist is called upon to wedge the person with schizophrenia into an ill-fitting slot because an appropriately therapeutic setting is not available, affordable or even considered feasible. Drug treatment becomes here an economic and political tool.

THE REVOLVING-DOOR PATIENT

The ascendancy of psychopharmacology over psychosocial treatment is epitomized by the revolving-door patient. This creation of the neuroleptic era has become a focus of public concern – the central character, for example, in a series of *New Yorker* articles and the subject of a ground-breaking court decision. Sylvia Frumkin's ten admissions to Creedmoor Hospital, New York City, by age 31, her multiple hospital admissions elsewhere, and her family's consequent suffering, all documented in the *New Yorker*,[54] represent nothing unusual. Not uncommonly, several times in one year the same patient will be medicated back to sanity in an American public hospital and discharged to an inadequate environment, placed in an unworkable setting or simply released to live on the street with the full knowledge that readmission will shortly be necessary.

Such a case was Kathy Edmiston. In a hearing concerning her circumstances in the Probate Court of Denver, Colorado, Judge Wade commented:

> On virtually innumerable occasions respondent has been certified and institutionalized for short periods of time (during which periods her condition has been stabilized by use of medication in a structured setting). She has then been placed either on out-patient status or in a nursing home. She then becomes sufficiently ill that she is picked up or delivered to the emergency room at Denver General Hospital, placed under certification, and the process begins again. Without even a minimally adequate treatment program, respondent and others like her will continue to be victims of their own inadequacies (often including their delusional systems) and will be targets for the influence and exploitation of others. For example, the behavior of this respondent in the community, which is related to the nature of her mental illness, has made her the victim of physical, sexual, and financial exploitation.[55]

The judge ruled that the next time this patient was certified the mental health agency must establish a suitable program for her treatment.

Since the Edmiston case in 1980, civil rights lawyers have won a court order requiring the City of Denver and the state of Colorado to improve services for Denver's seriously mentally ill people. As a result, services have been improved substantially by the creation of a program providing individualized care and support for the most seriously ill patients, but the problem of the revolving-door patient has by no means been eliminated.

SIDE EFFECTS

There are further reasons why we should not continue to emphasize drug treatment at the expense of environmental considerations – why we should use comprehensive psychosocial approaches to minimize the use of antipsychotic drugs. Many patients distinctly dislike taking medication. One cause of their distaste is the side effects of the drugs. Immediate reactions to the standard antipsychotic medications may include stiffness, shakiness, restlessness or acute muscle spasms. These "extrapyramidal" symptoms follow closely on the heels of the clinical benefits of the medications; positron emission tomography (PET) scans show that clinical improvement occurs when 65 per cent of dopamine-2 receptors are blocked by medication and extrapyramidal symptoms occur when 78 per cent of these receptors are occupied.[56] So, wherever possible, low doses of these medications are clearly to be preferred, and increases of dosage should be gradual. Extrapyramidal symptoms may often, but not always, be controlled by taking anti-Parkinsonian medication. Other adverse reactions to the standard antipsychotics drugs are blurred vision, oversedation, blunting of spontaneity, sexual impotence and failure of ejaculation, epileptic seizures and disorders of the eyes, liver, blood and skin. The long-term risk of developing tardive dyskinesia, a neurological consequence of using standard antipsychotic drugs, has already been mentioned.

Other possible adverse reactions to the standard antipsychotic drugs – and these are also effects that could help to explain the disappointing influence of these drugs on the long-term outlook in schizophrenia – are an increase in post-psychotic depression and an adverse effect on learning ability. A number of researchers have reported that people with schizophrenia treated with standard antipsychotic medications may become more depressed after their acute psychosis subsides, possibly as a result of their drug treatment. Some authors have observed that post-psychotic depression is associated with the slowing (akinesia) induced by the standard antipsychotic drugs.[57] In addition to frank depression, as many as 40 per cent of people with schizophrenia taking conventional antipsychotic drugs experience drug-induced dysphoria, an unpleasant subjective experience of irritability, listlessness, and lack of interest. Some researchers argue that this drug-induced dysphoria increases the likelihood that people suffering from psychosis will abuse street drugs and alcohol, in an attempt to feel better.[58] The neuroleptic drugs also diminish learning capacity in animals, normal subjects and psychiatric patients.[59] The implication of this side effect is that drug treatment may possibly reduce the capacity of people with schizophrenia to benefit from programs of social and vocational retraining and add to their employment difficulties.

The first available example of the so-called "novel," "atypical" or "second generation" antipsychotic drugs – clozapine (Clozaril) – has particularly serious side effects. Most significantly, this drug poses a one-in-a-hundred or one-in-fifty chance of causing a fatal blood disorder in which the patient's white blood cells are suddenly destroyed. To protect against this risk, patients in many developed countries may only collect the medication from the pharmacy each week if their white blood cell count is normal that week. Despite this precaution, there have been several deaths associated with the use of the drug. Interaction with other medications can cause sudden fatal respiratory depression. Recent research shows that the risk of developing diabetes is dramatically increased for people taking clozapine; the risk increases by about seven per cent each year, so that after five years 36 per cent of clozapine users have diabetes, with no sign of the mounting risk rate leveling off.[60] The risk of diabetes, strangely enough, is unrelated to the weight gain that is common with clozapine use and that averages a pound a week in the first ten weeks of treatment.[61] Not uncommonly weight gain can eventually exceed 30 or 40 pounds. Other important side effects of clozapine include epileptic seizures, elevated blood cholesterol and other fats, sedation, drooling, intestinal immobility and constipation.[62] Why is such a risky drug in use at all? – because it sometimes works well in reducing the symptoms of schizophrenia when the standard antipsychotics do not. Clozapine has a different mode of action from the standard drugs – it blocks dopamine receptors more briefly and is more effective in blocking the effects of serotonin than dopamine. If someone suffers from severe schizophrenia they may choose to assume the risks associated with this medicine in order to get relief from the illness, but clearly the use of clozapine is not to be undertaken lightly.

In the past ten years several more novel antipsychotic drugs have been introduced that share some of the same mechanisms of action of clozapine. Despite the initial optimism, and unlike clozapine, they are probably no more effective in treatment-resistant cases than the standard drugs,[63] but their side effects are different. Since many patients find them less unpleasant to take they have become very widely prescribed. Most of the novel drugs are much less likely to cause stiffness, shakiness, restlessness, akinesia, or tardive dyskinesia. Unfortunately, the longer the new drugs are used, the more apparent become their deficits. The risk of diabetes and weight gain with olanzapine (Zyprexa), for example, appears to be as severe as with clozapine.[64] For people with mental illness, many of whom smoke a lot and have chronic breathing problems, the added weight and endocrine disorder associated with the novel antipsychotics can precipitate major health problems. A survey of patients with serious mental illness in Massachusetts in 1998–99 revealed a sharply elevated death rate, with cardiac deaths in young patients reaching seven times the general population risk.[65] Another survey of seriously mentally ill people in central Massachusetts in 1999 found more than half to be over-weight or obese, over a quarter to have lung disease, over a quarter with cardiac or circulatory problems, and a fifth to suffer from endocrine disorders such as diabetes and thyroid disease.[66] Much of this increased morbidity and mortality is attributable to the introduction of the novel antipsychotic drugs. Reacting to this situation, some mental health agencies have introduced exercise and diet programs for mentally ill clients to attempt to reduce their health hazards,[67] and others have established health care clinics within the mental health programs to directly manage their mounting physical ailments.

There are good reasons, it is clear, to limit the use of the antipsychotic drugs. All patients can benefit from a user-friendly approach that minimizes the dosage of these medications.

USER-FRIENDLY MEDICATION STRATEGIES

The following strategies are designed to insure that a patient with schizo-phrenia receives the lowest dose of medication that will improve his or her illness and quality of life with the least risk of adverse effects.

When beginning treatment, *start with a low dose of medication and work up gradually*. Blood tests to estimate the serum level of the medication may be helpful. Serum levels are most useful when the patient is getting little benefit from the medication and the level is reported as being low; this lets the doctor and patient know that the poor response may be due to inadequate dosage. If the serum level is high, this suggests that the medication is just not effective for the patient. Therapeutic levels are not well established for the anti-psychotic medications, however, so they have to be interpreted with a certain amount of caution.

If an antipsychotic medication is ineffective, do not keep increasing the dosage; consider stopping or decreasing it or trying another type of anti-psychotic medication. One of the benefits of the introduction of the novel anti-psychotic drugs is that psychiatrists have become more rational in their use of antipsychotic medication. Before there was a choice of different types of medication psychiatrists rarely thought in terms of a *trial* of an antipsychotic medication; since there was only one basic type of antipsychotic available, there was a tendency to keep increasing the dosage if there was no response. Now the usual practice is to try different types of medication within the usual dosage range. If none of the antipsychotic medications work well, before turning to big doses of these drugs one should try other supplementary medi-cations, such as lithium carbonate, anticonvulsants like carbamazepine (Tegretol) or sodium valproate (Depakote), or antidepressants like fluoxetine (Prozac). It is especially important to avoid increasing the medication every time the patient has an acute increase in symptoms; there may be many reasons for increasing symptoms, one being that the medication is ineffective.

Another possibility is that the symptoms are precipitated by acute stress; in these cases, short-term use of a minor tranquilizer such as diazepam (Valium) can be very effective (see below).

Be cautious about concluding that every exacerbation of the person's condition is due to the schizophrenic illness. Sometimes the underlying problem is that the patient is experiencing severe restlessness as a side effect from the antipsychotic medications; the appropriate way to treat the resulting agitation is by reducing or changing the neuroleptic drug or by prescribing enough side-effect medicine. Sometimes the new symptoms are more psychological in nature and are a result of hysteria or dependency, in which case an increase in antipsychotic medication is not appropriate.

When a patient is in an acute psychotic episode use minor tranquilizers, not heavy doses of antipsychotic medication, to reduce agitation and other acute symptoms (see below). In general, acutely disturbed patients should only be given the dosage of antipsychotic medication that they would ordinarily need as a maintenance dose when they are doing well. In acute treatment in the hospital, however, much bigger doses of the antipsychotic medications are often given, sometimes resulting in severe side effects; the subsequent reduction in dosage when the patient has recovered from the acute episode may take much longer than necessary.

When a patient is stable, *try and establish the lowest dose of medication that keeps the worst aspects of the illness at bay without causing intolerable side effects.* This can be done by cautiously reducing the dosage every few weeks or months. Once this dosage has been established, it may be necessary to stay at that level for an extended period of time.

MINOR TRANQUILIZERS IN SCHIZOPHRENIA

People with acute schizophrenia who are overactive and excited or at risk of hurting others, attempting suicide or running away from treatment may often be helped in the short run by the use of moderate doses of the minor tranquilizers in addition to neuroleptic medication. The belief used to be widespread in psychiatry that the minor tranquilizers, including the benzodiazepine drugs, diazepam (Valium) and lorazepam (Ativan), were harmful or at best worthless in psychosis. This is not the case. These drugs are often effective in calming agitated psychotic patients – more immediately so, in fact, than the antipsychotic drugs. In some cases they even have a prompt antipsychotic action.

The effectiveness of the benzodiazepines in such cases is probably due to a reduction in the patient's level of arousal. It is also likely that the benzodiazepines exert an antipsychotic effect by their action in blocking dopamine release. They may achieve this effect by stimulating a feedback loop (in which the neurotransmitter is gamma-amino butyric acid) that damps down the release of dopamine.[68] Several reports have shown that the benzodiazepines in moderate or high doses, alone or in combination with neuroleptic drugs, are effective in controlling psychotic symptoms.[69] Somewhat fewer studies have found them to be ineffective or to produce equivocal results.[70] On balance, it appears that the benzodiazepines are sometimes effective over longer periods of time for people with schizophrenia but, without doubt, they are most useful in calming the acutely disturbed patient and in the acute treatment of the person with catatonic schizophrenia who is immobilized by a high internal level of arousal.[71]

A potential advantage of the minor tranquilizers over the standard antipsychotic drugs is that, by blocking dopamine *release* rather than dopamine *receptors*, the benzodiazepines should not lead to dopamine supersensitivity, tardive dyskinesia or prolonged withdrawal psychosis. Another advantage is that the minor tranquilizers are much more pleasant to take than the antipsychotic drugs and are generally free from serious side effects. A disadvantage is that tolerance appears to develop to the antipsychotic action of the drugs, rendering them suitable, in most cases, only for short-term use.

Many people with schizophrenia can benefit from a low-dose approach to treatment and some good-prognosis patients may be suitable for drug-free treatment or gradual withdrawal from medication early in the course of the illness. How can we tell which people do not need to be treated with antipsychotic medication long term?

PROGNOSTIC INDICATORS

Efforts to pinpoint indicators of good prognosis have revealed that people whose psychotic illness is more sudden in onset and is a response to a clear life stress, those whose psychosis developed late in life and those who have functioned well before their illness developed (including having good social relationships and getting married) are more likely to improve and recover.[72] The degree of accuracy in using these criteria to predict outcome is not high, however; at best we can correctly sort three out of four patients into good- or poor-outcome groups, but we would be wrong the other quarter of the time.[73]

One point emerges clearly from the research – the symptoms and clinical features of the psychotic episode are of little value in predicting outcome.[74] Indeed, the diagnosis of schizophrenia itself does not predict an outcome that is necessarily much worse than the prognosis in other psychoses.[75] The best indicator of future functioning, according to two pieces of research, is the patient's functioning before he or she fell ill. The measure of previous competence in any one area, furthermore, is the best predictor of functioning in that same area. Thus, a good work record predicts good vocational functioning, good social relations in the past point to good future social functioning and multiple prior hospital admissions indicate the likely extent of future hospital use.[76]

In practice it is reasonable to assume that a patient who is (a) early in the course of a schizophrenia-like illness, (b) has previously achieved a reasonable level of functioning, and (c) whose onset of illness was sudden, deserves a trial of treatment without antipsychotic drugs or gradual withdrawal from antipsychotic medication after a few weeks. Some of these patients will eventually improve and do well.

Some good-prognosis patients, however, might be diagnosed as experiencing an episode of manic-depressive illness (bipolar disorder). This affective psychosis characteristically begins later in life than schizophrenia and allows patients the opportunity to develop a higher level of social and vocational functioning. It is often difficult to distinguish between episodes of affective illness and schizophrenia, as they share many common features (see Chapter 1). A number of studies have shown that people with good-prognosis schizophrenia-like psychosis have a high incidence of manic-depressive illness among their relatives – a finding that suggests that they may themselves suffer from an affective illness.[77] A history of distinct, prior, extended episodes of pathologically elevated or depressed mood points towards a diagnosis of manic-depressive illness. Such patients can be treated with lithium carbonate or with another mood-stabilizer like carbamazepine (Tegretol) or sodium valproate (Depakote). In some instances a clear diagnosis is not possible until the passage of time has revealed a characteristic course of the illness. In such cases withdrawal from medication and a wait-and-see approach may be appropriate.

MINIMIZING MEDICATION USE

In modern times, the deliberate treatment of schizophrenia without antipsychotic drugs is seldom practiced, but the lessons learned from such approaches tell us how treatment and living environments should be structured to require minimal doses of antipsychotic medication. What must be provided is an opportunity for the acutely ill person with schizophrenia to be cared for in a non-stressful environment that maximizes the chance for a spontaneous remission or improvement to occur.

The setting

The characteristics of a therapeutic environment for people with schizophrenia have already been set down – warm, protective and enlivening without being smothering, over-stimulating or intrusive. In addition, as earlier chapters of this book have indicated, the patients should be allowed to maintain a valued social role, together with their status, dignity and a sense of belonging to the community at large. Patients must be able to stay in residential treatment long enough for their condition to improve and to be free of urgency to move on. With a week's stay in a private psychiatric hospital ward in the United States costing roughly the same as a round-the-world trip, it is clear that extended, minimal-dosage care must be provided in a low-cost, alternative community setting.

Soteria House, mentioned earlier, offers a model for such community treatment. A large house in a San Francisco Bay neighborhood, Soteria provided accommodation for six people with schizophrenia and two staff. "Recently admitted, very psychotic residents receive a great deal of special one-to-one, or two-to-two attention," wrote Loren Mosher and his associates, "and performance expectations are minimal."[78] As residents became less psychotic they participated more actively in the therapeutic community – planning and performing household tasks and working out interpersonal differences. Each pursued recreational activities of his or her own choice. When compared with the local community mental health center's inpatient ward, Soteria was found to be less orderly and controlling and the staff were more involved, supportive and spontaneous.[79]

Despite the much greater length of residential treatment for the Soteria patients (five-and-a-half months) than for the control group of patients in mental health center care (one month), the average costs of treatment at the end of the first year were almost exactly the same. One reason for this surprising finding may be the Soteria patients' more limited use of outpatient care after discharge. Another reason is that the non-professional Soteria staff were paid distinctly less than the standard salary for mental health professionals.

Somewhat similar care can be provided cost-efficiently in a community mental health system. A 15-bed, well-staffed, community-based, intensive treatment unit – essentially a low-cost, domestic-style, acute hospital ward in the community – will be described in Chapter 12. While the central purpose for an intensive treatment house of this type is to treat all types of seriously disturbed psychiatric patients in an affordable, non-coercive community setting, it can routinely be used for low-dosage treatment of people with good-prognosis psychotic disorders.

The treatment

To minimize the use of antipsychotic medication, the minor tranquilizers may be used to reduce arousal and agitation in acutely psychotic patients. Other techniques of stress reduction are equally as important. Quiet areas of the treatment facility should be available to allow patients to withdraw from an environment that may be perceived as over-stimulating. Close personal contact with staff and other residents, reassurance, and the provision of an absorbing activity may also be valuable. Dynamic, "uncovering" psychotherapy is stressful, intrusive and toxic and should be avoided. Along the same lines, expectations for the patient's functioning must be geared to his or her current capability – over-enthusiastic exhortations to become more active or sociable may lead to an increase in psychotic symptoms.

Much of the patient's treatment will involve making appropriate plans for his or her life after discharge – finding a place to live and an occupation, neither of which should be excessively stressful. Some form of supportive but independent living arrangement and supervised or sheltered employment (as described in later chapters) may be appropriate. For all but the most resilient patients a gradual transition into the new living and occupational arrangements will be required. It is useful to minimize the number of changes at any one time and to continue "drop-in" attendance at the residential treatment facility for some time after discharge.

Especially where there is a likelihood that the person with schizophrenia will return to live with his or her family, some meetings with the family members should take place. Where the home environment is accepting, and not stressful, the relatives will learn to be even more helpful if given accurate information about the patient's illness and guidance as to reasonable expectations for his or her performance. If the patient's household is found to be highly stressful, family therapy should aim to reduce the relatives' intrusiveness or hostility, and plans may be made to reduce contact between patient and family or to devise an alternate living arrangement.

Therapists' respect for the patient's individuality and strengths will help meet his or her need for status and independence. Using an unlocked community facility encourages staff to find non-coercive ways to protect the patient and others from hazards arising from psychotic thinking and behavior and poor judgment. These measures may include increased personal contact rather than restraint and distracting recreational activity instead of seclusion. Such methods maintain the patient's own reliance on self-control. Increasing levels of responsibility and involvement in the management of the household and concern for the welfare of other residents gives the patient a useful social role and a sense of personal value to others.

In short, aside from a lessened emphasis on stern paternalism and an increased emphasis on family relations, these treatment approaches attempt to recreate the principles of moral management as practiced at the York Retreat.

SUMMARY

- Antipsychotic drug treatment may have a negative long-term effect on people with a good-prognosis form of schizophrenia.
- Long-term treatment with the standard antipsychotic drugs creates dopamine receptor supersensitivity, worsening the dopamine dysregulation which is an underlying biochemical deficit of schizophrenia.

- Withdrawal of the standard antipsychotic drugs may cause a rebound of symptoms of schizophrenia to a higher level than would have been the case without treatment.
- Drug-withdrawal studies, consequently, may have given an over-optimistic impression of the benefits of the standard antipsychotic drugs in schizophrenia.
- The majority of non-withdrawal studies indicate that people with good-prognosis schizophrenia-like disorders do as well or better without anti-psychotic drugs treatment.
- Stress precipitates psychotic relapse in people with schizophrenia and drug treatment is less necessary for patients in low-stress settings.
- The revolving-door patient has been created by the use of drug treatment coupled with a neglect of the psychosocial needs of the person with a psychotic illness.
- The new generation of antipsychotic drugs has increased the range of treatment options for people with schizophrenia, but bring new side effects and health hazards.
- User-friendly medication strategies promote the use of low-doses of antipsychotic medication in schizophrenia.
- The best prognostic measures give a rather crude indication of which patients can successfully be withdrawn from antipsychotic medication or treated without drugs.
- The principles of minimal drug treatment include a non-alienating, human-scale treatment and living environment, individualized care, and family support and education.

Chapter 11

Work

"Of all the modes by which the patients may be induced to restrain themselves," wrote Samuel Tuke in his *Description of the Retreat*, "regular employment is perhaps the most generally efficacious."[1] To the moral treatment advocates, in fact, work was not merely a means to occupy and control their charges; it was a central pillar of the moral-treatment edifice. William Ellis, superintendent of the Hanwell Asylum, believed that proper employment "has frequently been the means of the patient's complete recovery."[2] In 1830, Eli Todd wrote to the family of a patient about to leave the Hartford Retreat in Connecticut: "I cannot too strenuously urge the advantage and even the necessity of his being engaged in some regular employment which shall hold out the promise of some moderate but fair compensation to his industry and prudence."[3] W.A.F. Browne, superintendent of the Montrose Royal Asylum, had this vision, in 1837, of the perfect asylum of the future:

> The house and all around appears to be a hive of industry. When you pass the lodge, it is as if you had entered the precincts of some vast emporium of manufacture: labour is divided, so that it may be easy and well performed, and so apportioned, that it may suit the tastes and powers of each labourer. You meet the gardener, the common agriculturalist, the mower, the weeder, all intent on their several occupations, and loud their merriment. . . . The curious thing is, that all are anxious to be engaged, toil incessantly, and in general without any recompense other than being kept from disagreeable thoughts and the pains of illness. They literally work in order to please themselves.[4]

Looking back upon such typically Victorian beliefs and dreams we may be excused for doubting the extent to which they were grounded upon accurate observation of the mentally ill and for wondering how far they merely reflected the prominent, middle-class work ethic of the day. Scottish philosopher Thomas Carlyle, for example, made the extravagant claim that "Work is the grand cure of all the maladies and miseries that ever beset mankind."[5] Nonetheless, we have seen evidence to support the moral-treatment advocates in their emphasis on the importance of work (Browne's fantasies aside). As previous chapters have indicated, unemployment and material factors affect the course of schizophrenia and employment may be important for recovery. Work may often be crucial for the development of self-esteem and in shaping the social role of the mentally ill person.

RESEARCH ON WORK AND SCHIZOPHRENIA

Up to this point the evidence presented in support of this position has been largely macrostatistical in scale. Such observations have included:

- increasing hospital admissions for schizophrenia during economic slumps (Chapter 2);
- the worsening outcome for schizophrenia during the Great Depression (Chapter 3);
- improved rehabilitative efforts under full-employment conditions (Chapter 4);
- high cure rates for insanity during the labor shortage of industrializing America (Chapter 5);
- better outcome for higher-class people and females with schizophrenia (Chapter 6); and
- superior outcome from schizophrenia in the Third World (Chapter 7).

At this juncture it would be valuable to change the level of magnification and to look for evidence on a smaller scale of the effect of employment and unemployment on *individuals* with schizophrenia.

For much of the postwar half-century relatively little research was conducted on work and mental illness. Until recent years there has been a general lack of interest within the psychiatric profession in vocational rehabilitation,[6] but the 1990s – years of relatively low unemployment in the US – saw an increase in interest. In the index to the two large volumes of the 1989 fifth edition of the American *Comprehensive Textbook of Psychiatry*, for example, there were only 11 references to "Work," "Working," "Vocational," etc. This number grew to 30 in the 2000 seventh edition, but it is still less than a tenth of the number of references to "Sex," "Sexual" and related items. Psychiatrists appear to have taken seriously only half of Freud's well-known dictum that the ability to love and to work are central issues in the lives of men and women.[7] The lack of interest in work has been, in large part, a response to the fact that there *is* little work available for people with schizophrenia. For people with psychotic illness not involved in an effective vocational rehabilitation program the rate of employment in recent decades in the US and Britain has rarely exceeded 15 per cent.[8] Consequently, many mental health professionals discount the possibility that their clients with schizophrenia will be able to work and they underestimate the value of vocational services.[9]

In reviewing the research, it is clear that modern vocational rehabilitation methods are successful in getting people with schizophrenia back to work. It is less clear to what extent being employed improves the symptoms and course of the illness. Before the recent era of randomized controlled studies of vocational services, several studies demonstrated that people with schizophrenia who were working fared better, but it was unclear whether employment had led to clinical improvement or whether higher functioning had made employment possible.

Psychologist Leon Cohen, for example, studied 114 people with chronic schizophrenia discharged from a Veterans Administration hospital before 1955. He found that patients who had a job to go to or a definite vocational plan at discharge and those who found employment after discharge were able to stay out of hospital longer. That work was the important element leading to the patients' success is suggested by his additional finding that the severity of the patient's psychosis at discharge was in no way related to the likelihood of rehospitalization.[10]

A British study published in 1958 reported very similar findings. Medical sociologist George Brown and his colleagues followed for a year 229 male patients (mostly diagnosed with schizophrenia) discharged from seven London-area mental hospitals. Over 40 per cent of these patients worked for six months or more and of these nearly all (97 per cent) succeeded in staying out of hospital. Another 43 per cent of the patients never worked at all, and of these fewer than half (46 per cent) succeeded in avoiding rehospitalization. Again there is a suggestion that work was more important than clinical status in determining success, for a full third of the patients who worked for most of the year were rated as moderately or severely disturbed and many more had residual symptoms.[11]

In 1963 Howard Freeman and Ozzie Simmons published *The Mental Patient Comes Home*, a comprehensive report on the fate of 649 patients with psychotic illness discharged in 1959 from nine US state hospitals and three Veterans Administration hospitals. Like the researchers before them, they found that patients who were successful in staying out of hospital were substantially more likely to have been employed than those who were rehospitalized. They also found only a moderate degree of correlation between the patient's working ability and the severity of his or her psychotic symptoms.[12]

Psychologist George Fairweather became well known in the 1960s for devising a model community program in which psychiatric patients lived together in community lodges and worked together in teams as independent businesses providing various needed services to the community. A follow-up study of patients in the lodge program showed that they realized substantial benefits when compared with a matched control group of patients who entered typical psychiatric aftercare programs. Patients in the lodge program had assured employment and those in routine aftercare, almost to the last person, were unable to find full-time work. Residents of the lodge spent five or six times as much time out of hospital as patients in the control group. Lodge patients were more satisfied with their lives in the community, but very little difference was found between the level of symptoms manifested by the two groups of patients.[13] We cannot conclude from this study that employment alone led to the patients' success, for the lodge program offered, in addition, assured accommodation and a relatively sheltered environment coupled to opportunities for autonomy, an important role within the lodge society and enhanced self-esteem.

In the early 1970s researchers painted a dismal picture of the efficacy of most work therapy programs,[14] but in recent years modern vocational programs such as supported employment have shown themselves to be more effective in helping people with serious mental illness achieve stable employment.[15] A 1995 review by psychiatrist Anthony Lehman of research studies using comparison groups indicates that vocational programs had little or no success in placing people in independent competitive employment until the late 1970s; however, as programs became more effective not only were work-related improvements noted but often clinical and social benefits as well. People involved in vocational rehabilitation were, for example, more likely to engage in activities with friends, to perform well in social and family roles, to have a driver's license, to take their antipsychotic medication regularly and to drink less alcohol. Although those enrolled in vocational programs were sometimes less likely to be readmitted to hospital, there was rarely any improvement noted in psychiatric symptoms.[16] A similar picture has emerged from more recent reviews of the supported employment research conducted by psychologist Gary Bond and colleagues – big gains in competitive employment, but rarely any improvement in hospitalization rates or symptoms.[17]

A study conducted in New Hampshire follows this general pattern. In 1995 a mental health agency decided to reduce the size of a traditional day program and emphasize competitive employment instead. Thirty-two long-term day-treatment clients volunteered to be switched to a new supported employment program. One year later the rate of competitive employment of the volunteers had increased from 13 per cent to 64 per cent, while the employment rate of a matched comparison group who were not assigned to the supported employment program scarcely changed, increasing from 16 to 19 per cent. There was no improvement in psychiatric symptoms, however, in the supported employment clients.[18]

One piece of research does suggest that work can lead to symptom reduction in schizophrenia. In the early 1990s, Morris Bell and his associates placed 150 people with schizophrenia in six-month work placements in a Veterans Affairs medical center in Connecticut and randomly assigned them to either being unpaid or paid $3.40 an hour. As expected, those who were paid worked more hours. In addition, those who were paid showed more improvement in their symptoms, particularly emotional discomfort and positive symptoms, such as hallucinations and delusions, and were less likely to be readmitted to hospital. The more the patients worked the more their symptoms were reduced.[19]

Another study that shows progressively improving course of illness for people with serious mental illness who gain employment was conducted in Boulder, Colorado. Thirty-eight people with psychotic disorders who were attending the Chinook Clubhouse, a psychosocial clubhouse modeled after Fountain House in New York (both are described in the next chapter), were matched with 38 people with similar disorders who lived in a neighboring town too far away for them to be able to attend the clubhouse. After two years, the clubhouse members had achieved higher levels of employment and a somewhat better quality of life. Most interestingly, while the costs of treatment of the unemployed people who could not attend the clubhouse increased progressively, the treatment costs for those who achieved employment through the clubhouse decreased substantially, due to a drop in both inpatient and outpatient care, indicating a progressive improvement in disability and course of illness.[20]

We may conclude that the research to date on work and individuals with schizophrenia provides only modest support for the central thesis of this book, which is based on macrostatistical data, that the availability of employment influences outcome in schizophrenia. Why is the clinical evidence for this thesis not more imposing? Perhaps because the time scale of the studies is too short – most of the research is conducted over six to twelve months, few studies are continued longer than 18 months; and perhaps because all of the research has been conducted on groups of people most of whom have been ill for substantial periods of time, for whom the symptoms and course of illness have long been established, and not on people who are in the early stages of psychosis, for whom a rapid return to a productive role might be more likely to make a difference in the long-term course of the disorder.

If we are to see work have an impact on the course of schizophrenia in the West we would need to put into place programs that routinely help provide employment for people with serious mental illness from the very earliest stages of their illness.

VOCATIONAL REHABILITATION PROGRAMS

As noted earlier, fewer than 15 per cent of the seriously mentally ill in the US are in full-time or part-time competitive employment, although 60–70 per cent of them would like to be.[21] If placed in a supported employment program, 50–60 per cent are capable of competitive employment,[22] but fewer than 25 per cent of Americans with serious mental illness receive any type of vocational assistance.[23] About half a million people with schizophrenia in the United States, we can estimate, are unemployed but potentially productive members of society. In Britain the situation is no better.[24]

It doesn't have to be this way. The employment of seriously mentally ill people in northern Italy, for example, is substantially greater. In a randomly selected group of people with schizophrenia in treatment with the public mental health service in Bologna in 1994 nearly half were employed, more than a fifth full-time.[25] In south Verona around the same time, employment of people with schizophrenia was even greater; nearly 60 per cent were employed, more than a quarter full-time.[26] Why is there such a wide variation between modern industrialized countries? The answer lies in the opportunities for work created by vocational programming and the obstacles created by disincentives in the disability pension system. Let us look first at the provision of vocational services.

In Britain and America the usual spectrum of employment opportunities for people with mental illness, from the most sheltered to the least, includes the following:

- Sheltered workshops. A widely diffused postwar model developed in northern Europe, regarded by many these days as too institutional and segregated.
- Supported employment. Transitional and continuous supported employment are American models in which jobs slots are developed for patients in competitive work settings. Training and support for patients in these jobs are provided by vocational staff known as job coaches.
- Independent employment. People with mental illness find jobs in the competitive workforce, with or without the assistance of vocational staff.

The last of these options requires no explanation; the others require some discussion.

Sheltered workshops

Sheltered workshops are no longer popular. Critics argue that people placed in these low-demand settings may fail to advance to more challenging work, even though they are capable of doing so.[27] Supporters point out that for some people with limited functioning capacity, sheltered settings may be the only feasible workplace. At the Mental Health Center of Boulder County in Colorado, for example, where both supported employment and a modernized sheltered workshop are available, a high rate of employment has been achieved. More than half of the working-age adults with psychotic illness are in paid employment, 12 per cent of the group in the sheltered workshop. It is very easy for a client to move from the sheltered workshop to supported employment, and such a move is strongly encouraged, but very few of the people employed at the sheltered workshop could hold down a job in the competitive labor market. Many of these employees work slowly and inefficiently at the most routine tasks in the workshop and require a lot of day-to-day supervision. Without the workshop most of these people would be unemployed.

To address some of the critics' concerns, it is possible to reconfigure the sheltered workshop to be more like the social firms described below, as has been done with the workshop in Boulder. In this way, employees become involved in the management of the workshop through a management council. The setting becomes more integrated by hiring mentally healthy workers – for example, a sheltered workshop can be made attractive to social service departments that are trying to find work training and evaluation options for "welfare-to-work" clients who have been unemployed for an extended period.

Sheltered workshops ordinarily obtain work from industry by bidding for contracts. The work obtained is often a series of repetitive tasks that would lead to high staff turnover under usual economic conditions if performed in-house by the private company's own employees. When business is in decline, however, such sources of work begin to dry up. Companies may cut back production, perform more work in-house, or go out of business. Competition for available contracts can become severe. Under these conditions sheltered workshops may simply go out of business themselves, they may lower their bidding rates so far that they lose money and require a bigger subsidy from the mental health service, or they may cut back operations and lay off disabled employees. In the sheltered workshop in Boulder, for example, the number of clients employed fluctuates with economic conditions between 40 and 70. In hard times the waiting list for placement may be several months long, and the lowest-functioning clients, who require a greater subsidy, may be screened out.

Supported employment

Transitional employment programs (TEP) were originally developed in the 1970s by Fountain House, the psychosocial clubhouse in New York City (see Chapter 12). Under this model, vocational staff locate jobs in businesses or agencies in the local community. A person with mental illness is trained by a job coach, and placed in one of these positions for a period of, usually, six months. At the end of that period, a new person with mental illness is placed in the job. The worker is supported on the job, to the extent necessary, by the job coach and may attend support meetings or dinner groups on a regular basis while employed. If the patient cannot work at any time, for whatever reason, the job coach will find another client to work that day or will do the job himself or herself. Consequently, the employer gets a good deal. He or she knows that the job, often a high-turnover, entry-level position, will be permanently and reliably filled and that the worker training is done by an outside service.

The principle behind transitional employment is that the person with mental illness learns basic job skills in a "transitional" position that will help the person achieve the ultimate goal – a permanent, unsupported job in the competitive marketplace. In fact, most of the research does not support the contention that those who work in TEP positions are more likely to secure independent employment[28] and, given the extreme sensitivity of people with disorders such as schizophrenia to the stresses of change, it is hard to believe that transitional employment is ideally suited to this population. In fact, one of the main reasons that programs such as Fountain House developed the transitional model of employment was that they found it difficult to locate enough jobs and provide support to all of the clients who wanted work.

More suitable for the stress-intolerant person with mental illness is the model of continuous supported employment, originally developed for people with developmental disabilities. This model is similar to the TEP approach except that the job is permanent. As the worker adjusts to the demands of the position, work supports can be gradually withdrawn and provided to another client, more recently placed in work. As a result the number of supported employment positions continues to expand over time. Supported employment offers several advantages. Employment can be designed to meet the needs of each individual client. Job-sharing can be arranged for those who, because of the disincentives in the social security system and the symptom-generating demands of full-time work, prefer to work part-time. Jobs can be sought to match the skills and preferences of individual clients, and, since positions are permanent, a career ladder is possible.

A refinement of the supported employment model is referred to as individual placement and support (IPS). Gary Bond has outlined the six principles of this approach,[29] the first of which is somewhat extreme:

- *Competitive employment is the goal.* Supporters of the IPS model contend that most people with serious mental illness can achieve competitive employment and that sheltered work settings are unnecessary. As suggested above, this is plainly not true. If it were, the success rate in placing people in competitive work through supported employment would be close to 100 per cent, not 50 per cent.
- *Rapid job search and placement.* The research suggests that preparatory work-readiness training does not increase the likelihood of eventual competitive employment and that rapid job placement is more successful.
- *Integration of vocational rehabilitation and mental health services.* Better results can be obtained, the research reveals, if vocational programs are an integrated part of a mental health agency or team, rather than provided by a separate entity.
- *Attention to the mentally ill person's preferences.* Most people with mental

illness prefer paid employment and rapid job placement to protracted unpaid training periods, and have specific preferences about the type of work, hours, location and pay. Matching the person to the job on these sorts of criteria results in higher rates of job placement and longer job tenure.

- *Continuous assessment.* Some of the most useful assessment is made *after* the person with mental illness begins working on a job, not before, as in traditional vocational rehabilitation programs.
- *Time unlimited support.* Traditional vocational services used to rate success by the number of "closures" of service that occurred 90 days after beginning competitive employment. Supported employment coaches, in contrast, recognize that the employee with mental illness may need help with employment problems for much longer periods of time.

These are the vocational models currently available in Britain and America for people with mental illness. Can we add to them?

Social firms or affirmative businesses

Social firms, also known as affirmative or consumer-employing businesses, common in parts of Europe but little known in the US, may prove to be a viable addition to the approaches described above. (The term "consumer" is used here to indicate a person who is a consumer or user of mental health services.) Worker cooperatives employing people with mental illness began in Italy in the 1970s and similar enterprises have subsequently been developed in Switzerland, Germany, Spain, Ireland, Sweden and elsewhere.[30]

In Trieste, Pordenone and Palmanova in north-eastern Italy, and in other parts of Italy, each business consortium employs a mixed workforce of mentally disabled and healthy workers in manufacturing and service enterprises. In Trieste the businesses include a hotel, a café, a restaurant, a transportation business, a building renovation company and a furniture workshop. In nearby Pordenone, the enterprises include a large cleaning business, collecting money from public telephones, making park furniture, nursing-home aides, home help for the disabled and a horticultural nursery. In Palmanova, by 1998, 11 tourist hotels had been turned into cooperatives, some of the consumer employees living in the hotels rent-free. In Rome there are 28 cooperatives, with products and services that include graphics and printing and a laundry, which employ 450 people, more than half of whom are disabled. The cooperatives in Milan and Turin are involved in gardening and catering. There are fewer cooperatives in the south of Italy, but they are to be found in such towns as Reggio Calabria and Bari.[31]

Some small and some large, the enterprises compete successfully with local businesses winning contracts by competitive bid. In Pordenone, about 90 per cent of the work contracts are made with public agencies such as hospitals, schools, the post office and the fire station. In Trieste, about 60 per cent of the contractual work is for public agencies, including the mental health service; but in other locations, such as Geneva and Dublin, all the contracts are with the community at large.

The cooperatives use varying amounts of public subsidy. In Trieste, in 1994, the subsidy, in the form of direct grants, donated space and staff time contributed by the mental health service, amounted to about 20 per cent of the total budget, and in Pordenone, to a mere one per cent. In northern Italy the businesses are organized in large consortia and employ substantial numbers of severely mentally disabled clients. In 1994, the production of the Trieste consortium totaled $5 million (£3.3 million) and, in Pordenone, $7.1 million (£4.7 million). In each consortium about half of the regular workers are mentally ill or otherwise disabled, earning a standard, full-time wage. Some mentally ill people work part-time as trainees and receive their disability pension. Unlike most US programs for people with mental illness, the cooperatives advertise widely and have high community visibility. Thus, the scale and social impact of these enterprises exceed the usual achievements of vocational programs.

Social enterprises in Germany are generally not run as worker cooperatives, but efforts have been made to create partnerships between workers and management. The main objective of these enterprises is to provide permanent full-wage work for people with psychiatric disabilities. They also employ non-disabled workers at competitive salaries. There are more than a hundred social enterprises in Germany, employing over 1,000 people. These nonprofit companies are usually specialized firms producing foods (often health foods) or technical products, or providing domestic services, such as moving, painting and repairs and offering office services and printing. Often about 30 per cent of the company's net income is derived from government subsidies in the form of wage supplements that are awarded for each disabled worker at a diminishing rate over three years. Unless new disabled workers are hired, subsidies dwindle until the company has to survive on earnings alone. With careful planning this is feasible, and only a small number of the social enterprises established in Germany have been forced to shut down.[32]

Social firms have also proven viable in Japan. In Obihiro in northern Japan, consumer-employing businesses include a vegetable farm, a coffee shop and a hotel kitchen. In Okayama mentally ill workers provide milk delivery to 250 households, operate a meals-on-wheels service and run a café.

Can mental health agencies in North America and the British Isles develop non-profit consumer-employing enterprises similar to the continental European models? There are some successful examples. Monadnock Family Services in Keene, New Hampshire, has established a consumer-owned and managed cooperative with projects that began by buying, renovating and selling houses[33] and has now moved on to building garden furniture.[34] An Asian-American mental health clinic in Washington state established a successful consumer-run espresso bar in 1995.[35] Aspen Diversified Industries, based in Colorado Springs, is a recently formed enterprise offering construction, assembly and janitorial services that contracts with Colorado mental health centers to provide rehabilitation and employment for their clients. The Americas Group of Workability International (www.americas-group.org), a federation of American affirmative businesses, lists several similar enterprises in ten states among its members. Virtually all of the vocational programming for mentally ill people in Toronto, Canada, has been converted to the social enterprise model. One such program is a consumer-run courier business, A-Way Express, which operates city-wide. The employees are people with mental illness who use the public transportation system to pick up and deliver packages all over the city, communicating with their dispatch office by walkie-talkie.[36] In Dublin, Irish Social Firms has operated a restaurant, a lunch counter, a wool shop and a retail furniture store, but one-by-one these businesses are being closed due to cost overrun. There is considerable interest in social firms in the United Kingdom. The Edinburgh Community Trust is networking with European social firms and has a second-hand clothes and dressmaking business. The Richmond Fellowship has set up a printing business in Cambridge as a consumer-employing cooperative. St James House in London is involved in catering, and picture framing and operates a café.[37] Such ventures appear possible in the economic context of North America and the British Isles, depending on the extent to which the mental health service is willing to subsidize them, but as yet they have been little developed and do not offer work to more than a few of the potential users.

How can their range be expanded? To give a competitive advantage to consumer-employing businesses, contracts with mental health agencies and other public organizations can be developed. New York State agencies, for example, are obliged by the state finance law to purchase new equipment from consumer-employing programs of the Office of Mental Health whenever possible.[38] NISH, formerly National Industries for the Severely Handicapped (www.nish.org), is a US national nonprofit agency that assists affirmative businesses in obtaining contracts to provide services to federal agencies under a congressional initiative to enhance the employment of the disabled.

At a more local level, a mental health center can shift services that are currently contracted to outside enterprises (such as courier services or secretarial help) to a consumer enterprise. Janitorial and cleaning services are often thought of in this context, but these jobs, in fact, are not popular with many mentally ill people; the work is menial and does not pay well. More clients, especially men, are interested in construction and property repair jobs such as plumbing, wiring, painting, roofing and so on. In a survey conducted at the mental health center in Boulder, Colorado, less than a quarter of the male clients expressed an interest in janitorial work; more than a third, however, were interested in property repair.[39] Consequently, in 1993, the agency started a small property repair business employing a non-disabled lead contractor and a number of part-time consumer assistants. The business took over the property maintenance that previously cost the agency $30,000 (£20,000) a year. It has since expanded and is saving the agency money. Other consumers are employed at the agency in the records office, and as research interviewers, vocational and residential staff, therapists and case managers.

Another program, a consumer-oriented pharmacy, has been started at the Mental Health Center of Boulder County with the specific intent of providing employment and other benefits to the agency's clients. An economic survey conducted in 1992 by the author and Paul Polak, a Canadian psychiatrist and Third World economic development expert, revealed that medication is one of the largest markets controlled by people with serious mental illness. (More details from this survey are presented below.) James Mandiberg, at that time director of the Mental Health Bureau for Santa Clara County, California, proposed that a profit-sharing pharmacy could create consumer employment opportunities and generate capital for other consumer-oriented activities. A feasibility study[40] led eventually to the development of such a pharmacy. Profit from the pharmacy is channeled to a $50,000 consumer-managed fund for consumer projects in the Boulder mental health center's Office of Consumer and Family Affairs. There are additional benefits to the specialty pharmacy. Consumers are employed as pharmacy technicians and couriers. Prices to customers are lower than anywhere else in the area. Customers and staff receive more education from the pharmacist on the effects of medication than they would from a retail pharmacy, and the pharmacist can monitor physician prescribing practices and provide advice to the agency's psychiatrists.

Not all social firms are as successful as the consumer-oriented pharmacy. Ultimately, consumer-operated businesses confront the same problems as sheltered workshops. The available work may be quite menial, as in the office-cleaning cooperatives in Pordenone. As economic conditions worsen, consumer-run businesses, like many small operations, are increasingly likely to fail. True self-sufficiency, moreover, is difficult to achieve, and nearly all of these enterprises rely upon some form of public subsidy. Even so, like other vocational services, they may well be cost-effective, since we must take into account the likelihood of increased treatment expenses (including hospital care) and increased social cost (such as involvement of the criminal justice system) if seriously mentally ill people are left drifting idle and unsupported.

The ideal vocational rehabilitation system will be one that provides a spectrum of opportunities, from the most sheltered to the most independent. Social firms lie between sheltered workshops and continuous supported employment in the degree to which they provide shelter and support to the employee. Consequently, they enhance the spectrum, helping to create something suitable for all those who would like to work, and making the opportunities as normalizing and as genuinely integrated into mainstream life of the community as is compatible with job tenure and job satisfaction.

AN ECONOMIC DEVELOPMENT APPROACH

An important element in improving the market advantage of a consumer-employing business is to develop enterprises that exploit the purchasing power of the consumer group. This has the additional merit of recirculating money through the community to produce an economic multiplier effect. This is equivalent to establishing local ownership of the ghetto grocery store so that outside owners do not drain capital from the neighborhood. Following this approach, the author, with Paul Polak, interviewed 50 mentally ill people living in Boulder, Colorado, to learn about their personal finances and to spot potential money-making opportunities. The consumers control a number of sizable markets, it emerges; in 1992 the average mentally ill person in Boulder consumed $2,000 (£1,300) a month in psychiatric treatment, accommodation, food, medication and other goods and services. Thus, consumer-owned enterprises that could serve the mentally ill and benefit from their spending capacity include: (1) a consumer-cooperative pharmacy, (2) treatment-related services for other clients, (3) housing cooperatives, (4) cafeterias, and (5) transportation services.[41]

The development of a successful consumer-oriented pharmacy was described above. And while medication is a large market serving people with mental illness, the consumption of psychiatric treatment is more than ten times as great. If consumers could participate in providing these services, the potential for improving their financial and work situation would be considerable. An innovative program that trains mental health consumers with long-term mental illness to work as service providers within the mental health system will be described in the next chapter.

Another large area of consumption by the mentally ill is accommodation. If consumers were cooperative property owners instead of tenants, this could be an important form of economic advancement. The possibility of developing housing cooperatives for the mentally ill will also be addressed in the next chapter.

ECONOMIC DISINCENTIVES TO WORK

The interviews with the mentally ill people in Boulder, Colorado, made it apparent that there are serious financial disincentives to work. For example, the income and benefits of mentally ill people in Boulder who work part-time add up to little more than for those who are unemployed. Part-time workers earn more than the unemployed, but receive less from Social Security, food stamps and benefits. This amounts to what economists term an "implicit tax" – and in our survey, for part-time workers, it amounted to 64 per cent of earned income. Thus, someone working part-time for minimum wage (at that time $4.25 an hour), would actually have kept, in real terms, $1.57 an hour.[42] This person's case illustrates the situation:

> Jennifer, a 28-year-old single woman with schizoaffective disorder, was receiving a Supplemental Security Income (SSI) pension of $409 (£255) a month. She took a 25-hour-a-week job as a teacher's aide for developmentally disabled children, earning $6.63 an hour. In so doing, her SSI dropped by $315 a month, she lost $17 a month in food stamps, and her rent subsidy went down by $143. Now that she was working, she could no longer stop at her parents' house and eat lunch every day, and she was often too tired to go there to eat at night: as a result, the cost of her food and meals went up by $110 a month. Overall, she found herself ahead by no more than $73 a month. The decision to continue in the job became based, therefore, not on economic gains, which were insignificant, but on the opposing factors of stress and self-esteem. Initially, because the disabled pupil to whom she was assigned was so difficult, she decided she would quit; when she was given an easier child to work with, however, she resolved to continue in the job. Without an analysis of her economic situation, her ambivalence about working would not have appeared as rational as, in fact, it was, and might have been blamed on schizophrenic apathy, deficits in functioning or just plain laziness.[43]

The situation seems to be better for full-time workers. In our sample, these subjects met an implicit tax of only 23 per cent and, after deducting the implicit tax, kept an average of $5 an hour of their earnings.[44] Many mentally ill people, however, are incapable of moving straight into full-time work.

In response to these disincentives, most mentally disabled people identify a minimum earnings level that makes work an economically sensible choice – what economists term their "reservation wage."[45] More than three-quarters of the clients we surveyed in Boulder in 1992 ruled out the option of taking a job at the official minimum wage (at that time $4.25 an hour), but over 60 per cent were willing to work for $5 an hour; 80 per cent would have worked for $6 an hour.[46] We concluded that to employ significant numbers of the mentally ill in Boulder we needed to find or create jobs that paid above the minimum wage.

In Britain, disincentives to work are worse than in America. British disabled people run the risk of losing all their benefits if they earn as little as £15 ($25) a week (or £45 ($75) of "therapeutic" earnings). A measure introduced in 1992, the Disability Work Allowance, was designed to reduce this obstacle, but another problem, the loss of housing benefits that accompany increased earnings, virtually eliminates the incentive effect of the Disability Work Allowance. (In October 1999 the Disability Work Allowance was replaced by the Disabled Persons Tax Credit, but any benefit from this change is minimal.) Since a full benefits package, including the disability pension, housing subsidy and free prescriptions, is worth about £13,000 ($22,000) a year, tax-free, and a full-time minimum-wage job yields only £9,000 ($15,000) a year of taxable income, there is little incentive for the mentally disabled to work part-time or full-time.

In Italy, work disincentives are generally less severe than in the US or Britain because (a) fewer patients qualify for a disability pension and (b) Italian patients may usually retain their disability benefits while working. (In fact, the latter point varies a good deal from area to area, as there appears to be substantial variation in the way in which the pension rules are enforced.) Work disincentives are less severe in Greece for a different reason – the disability pension is so low that working is a better option. The Greek disability pension is less than $120 (£70) a month, and a minimum-wage job brings in four times that amount.

What innovations in social policy would help increase employment for people with mental illness? Econometric labor-supply models[47] can be used to forecast the effects of disability pension policy changes on people with mental disability. Such computer models require the collection of data on work and income from a sample that is large enough to provide examples of people in each defined category of "budget constraint." To apply this method, American econometrist Susan Averett and the author[48] gathered economic information from over 200 randomly selected people with psychotic disorders in treatment with the mental health center in Boulder, Colorado.

The most prominent findings from this analysis were that unearned income was a significant disincentive to working or to increasing hours of work, and that the provision of a wage subsidy was one of the most effective ways to boost working hours. In our computer model, offering a wage subsidy of $2 (£1.35) an hour led to an increase of more than five per cent in weekly work hours. In addition, increasing the "earnings disregard" – the amount of money that a beginning worker can earn before losing money from the Supplemental Security Income (SSI) check – was beneficial. Doubling the current earnings disregard under SSI ($65) improved work hours by three per cent; increasing it to $1,000 boosted working hours by 11 per cent. By contrast, changes in SSI regulations to reduce the rate at which the pension was decreased as people increased their hours of work and their earned income (that is, reducing the implicit tax on earned income) were surprisingly ineffective in boosting work hours.

These findings suggest two possible social policy innovations: (1) increasing the amount of earned income that would be allowed before the disability pension is reduced, and (2) providing a wage subsidy.

RAISING THE EARNINGS DISREGARD

In the US, for example, the allowable earned income level could be increased from $700 a month under Social Security Disability Insurance (SSDI), and from $65 under Supplemental Security Income (SSI), to $1,000 or more a month. On July 1, 1999, the earnings disregard under SSDI was increased from $500 to $700 a month. Though this still did not bring mentally ill and other disabled people up to parity with blind people (for whom the earnings disregard has been over $1,000 a month since 1990),[49] the change, as we shall see, seems to have allowed many disabled people to increase their hours of work and income.

A recent study in Boulder County, Colorado, seized the opportunity to see what happens to the employment and income of people with serious mental illness when (a) jobs are plentiful, (b) an effective supported employment program is in place, and (c) disincentives in the disability pension system are relaxed. The author and colleagues surveyed the work and income of two different samples of more than 130 outpatients with psychotic illness, in most cases schizophrenia, at points in time three years apart, in 1997 and 2000, during which period the local unemployment rate halved from 3.9 to 2.0 per cent and the earnings disregard under SSDI increased from $500 to $700 a month. All the subjects had access to a vigorous supported employment program operated by a psychosocial clubhouse. The proportion of patients in stable employment increased dramatically from 30 per cent in 1997 to 47 per cent in 2000, indicating that more people with serious mental illness can be employed when unemployment is low and vocational services are good. Patients receiving SSDI showed a significantly greater increase in stable employment (from 35 to 47 per cent) than those receiving SSI (whose employment increased from 23 to 30 per cent). Those receiving SSDI also increased their hours of work, while SSI recipients did not. The results suggest that SSDI, with its high earnings disregard, presented fewer disincentives to employment. The rate of employment and the hours of work of SSDI recipients may well have been boosted by relaxation in the SSDI earnings limitation in 1999.[50]

Though these results are for people receiving US disability pensions, they may have broader applicability. Raising the earnings disregard in other national disability pension systems could lead more people with serious mental illness to work, improve the course of their illness and reduce treatment costs.

WAGE SUBSIDIES

We could also consider providing a wage subsidy to the most seriously disabled mentally ill people and raise earned income above the minimum wage (currently $5.15 an hour in the US). How could it be funded? Under one approach, government pension regulations could be waived to allow payments to be diverted into wage subsidies. Employers would be reimbursed the difference between the worker's rate of production and pay. The US

Department of Labor has already established a time-study process that can be used to measure this difference.[51]

Under some circumstances, it could be feasible to divert funding currently used for treatment services into wage subsidies. In the US, where much of government-funded psychiatric treatment is being converted to a capitated or managed-care funding mechanism, it might be reasonable to use treatment funds for wage subsidies. Under capitated funding, the treatment agency gets to keep any savings resulting from program innovations that reduce costs. For example, a reduction in hospital costs can be directed to community treatment. If increased employment could be shown to improve stability of illness and to reduce treatment costs, then an agency with capitated funding could choose to provide a wage subsidy for its most disabled patients.

Can treatment costs be reduced by employing patients? Psychiatric treatment costs were more than twice as high for the unemployed patients in the study conducted in Boulder by Paul Polak and the author[52] than for the part-time employed. This could be explained in a number of ways, one being that working patients do better because they are employed and need less treatment. Whatever the explanation, it is clear that the cost of outpatient treatment of the unemployed patient is so high in Boulder (around $2,500 a month) that the expense of providing a half-time wage supplement for these clients could be met by a mere ten per cent reduction in treatment costs. Such a reduction seems possible, purely because the newly employed client would be at work half the week and less available for treatment. For example, several studies have shown that the time spent in day treatment programs decreases substantially for patients who transfer to a supported employment program[53] or to other programs with a vocational component.[54] Being in a productive role, moreover, could enhance self-esteem and reduce alienation sufficiently that the course of the patient's illness would improve.

As noted above, another study conducted in Boulder by the author and his colleagues demonstrated that treatment costs declined progressively over two years in a group of patients who were enrolled as members of a rehabilitation-oriented clubhouse, while these costs remained constant in a matched group of non-clubhouse members. The treatment cost reduction for clubhouse members was restricted to those who were placed in work, suggesting that the savings may well have been a result of employment.[55] Similarly the treatment costs for clients admitted to Thresholds, the well-known psychosocial clubhouse in Chicago, which has a rehabilitation program with a strong vocational component, were less than three-quarters of the costs for those admitted to a social club with no vocational component.[56] In another study, mentally ill clients randomly selected for a program of accelerated entry into supported employment generated treatment costs that were less than three-quarters of those for similar clients placed in a gradual work entry program; the decreased costs of mental health care for the clients who were rapidly employed more than offset the increased costs of the accelerated work pro-

Sustained full employment is not feasible in modern capitalist economies, but innovations in social policy – in the design of disability pensions, job programs, wages, and health care funding – could create dramatic improvements in the quality of life and integration of people with mental illness in our society.

SUMMARY

- Modern vocational rehabilitation methods are successful in getting people with serious mental illness back to work.
- There is little evidence that working leads to an improvement in the symptoms of psychosis in the short term, but there is no evidence available on the long-term impact of work on symptoms and functioning.
- Fewer than 15 per cent of the seriously mentally ill in the US are employed, and fewer than 25 per cent receive any type of vocational assistance
- More than half of those with schizophrenia can be in paid employment when appropriate vocational services are provided.
- Supported employment is a successful vocational approach for people with serious mental illness.
- Modernized sheltered workshops are valuable for the most disabled people with mental illness.
- Social firms successfully employ large numbers of people with serious mental illness in Italy and other European countries.
- Both sheltered work and social firms become less viable as the economy declines.
- Social firms can gain a market advantage by contracting to provide services to public agencies or to the consumer group.
- A consumer-employing, consumer-oriented pharmacy for the mentally ill is a viable social enterprise.
- Mentally disabled people encounter economic disincentives to work that may be alleviated by raising the amount an individual is allowed to earn before the disability pension is reduced.
- Wage subsidies encourage the employment of people with mental illness and might pay for themselves by a reduction in treatment costs.
- Social policy innovations, such as raising the minimum wage and guaranteed jobs programs, could increase the employment and integration of people with schizophrenia.

Chapter 12

Desegregating schizophrenia

It is easy to tell horror stories, and there are plenty in this book. It is harder to come up with ways to alleviate the plight of the mentally ill in the Western world. How can we help people with schizophrenia re-enter today's society and achieve a genuine degree of social integration? In this chapter we will look at practical answers to this question.

COMMUNITY SUPPORT SYSTEMS

The treatment programs of the Mental Health Center of Boulder County, Colorado will frequently be used as examples. They illustrate what is possible given the usual level of community mental health funding[1] and a commitment to providing decent care for the most seriously ill patients. The center has been successful in keeping nearly everyone in Boulder County with serious mental illness out of inadequate living situations such as homeless shelters, nursing homes and jail and establishing them in independent domestic settings in the community. A summary of the location of mental health center clients with psychotic illness in early 2002 is given in Table 12.1. The mental health center in Boulder, like a number of others across the United States, was designated a model community support system for severely disturbed patients by the US National Institute of Mental Health in the 1970s and has continued to add new programs since then.

The services and programs that may be offered by a community support system range from individual counseling through psychosocial rehabilitation and vocational services to family support and public education. Services may be offered to patients in hospital, group homes, independent living or wherever the client can be found, whether it be in jail or a shelter for the homeless. The functions of such a system may be succinctly expressed by the following commandments. The treatment agency shall:

- adopt total responsibility for the severely disabled client's welfare, including helping the person acquire such material resources as food, shelter,

Table 12.1 Living situation of the 720 people (age 18 and over) with a psychotic disorder who were clients of the Mental Health Center of Boulder County on January 1, 2002

	Number	Per cent
Long-term hospital care	5	<1
Short-term hospital care	13	2
Hospital alternative facility	12	2
Group homes*	69	10
Foster care	1	<1
Nursing home	33**	5**
Jail	9	1
Homeless	10	1
Transitional housing	24	3
Living with family	70	10
Living independently	474	66

Figures are derived from a 42 per cent sample.
* Group homes with varying levels of staffing.
** All nursing home patients suffer from physical illness that requires nursing care, the large majority being over age 65.

clothing and medical care;
- aggressively pursue the client's interests – ensuring that other social agencies fulfill their obligations, for example, or actively searching for those who drop out of treatment;
- provide a range of supportive services that can be tailored to fit each person's needs and that will continue as long as they are needed;
- educate the person to live and work in the community; and
- offer support to family, friends and community members.[2]

Community support, then, comprises everything the old, long-stay institutions used to furnish and a host of additional services besides, which are essential for community tenure. By these means, if they are all supplied, we may virtually eliminate the revolving-door phenomenon.

Keeping the patient in the community, however, does not necessarily mean that he or she, in any real sense, is recovered. Required in addition, as the earlier chapters have argued, are efforts to raise the degraded social status of the person with schizophrenia, to offer him or her a meaningful role in life leading to a sense of worth and a reduction of alienation. Notably absent from the community support system requirements established in the 1970s were:

- place the person in a job, wherever possible;
- help the person establish real community ties; and
- work to reduce the stigma of schizophrenia.

At that time, such ideas seemed to be impossible dreams. Now, as the last chapter showed and as this one will show, they are well within reach. Seen from this perspective, treatment becomes more than just a matter of providing services to patients and their relatives – it becomes social action, political lobbying and community education directed towards the desegregation of a minority group.

ESCAPING THE GHETTO

The ghettoes of the long-term mentally ill are the inner-city boarding homes, Skid Row missions, nursing homes and jails. How do we help them break out? In Boulder County the mental health center has never placed physically healthy people with schizophrenia in nursing homes. The administrators of the center actively discouraged local nursing home operators from opening wards for chronically ill psychiatric patients, arguing that nursing homes cannot provide an adequate quality of care and environment for such patients. Federal legislation now prevents the expenditure of Medicaid funds to treat physically healthy mentally ill people in nursing homes; this statute reduced one of the worst abuses of psychiatric patients in the US.

An outreach team from the mental health center goes to the Boulder shelter for the homeless every week, and when mentally ill people are located there or living on the streets, efforts are made to provide treatment and find adequate accommodation. Another outreach team goes to the local jail with a similar mission.[3]

Harmful and degrading though it is, large numbers of people suffering from psychosis are ending up in US local jails (as described in Chapter 8). To cope with this problem it is important that mental health agencies accept that the local jail is part of their community and supply outreach services to the inmates. The object of such programs should be to arrange the transfer of all inmates suffering from an acute psychotic disorder to an appropriate treatment setting. This goal requires the development of working relationships with criminal court judges. Only in those rare instances when a judge will not release a mentally ill person because the crime is too serious, or when an inmate with a psychotic illness refuses to be transferred to a treatment setting and is too mildly disturbed for involuntary measures, should we resort to treating people with psychosis behind bars.[4]

It has, in fact, become routine in most areas of the United States for people suffering from psychosis to be treated in jail with antipsychotic drugs and to be detained for extended periods – largely because the public mental hospitals are filled to capacity and offer only brief care. Often the people with psychosis who spend most time in jail are those who have proved particularly difficult to treat in community programs. Special programs can be developed for some of these mentally ill offenders.

A JAIL DIVERSION PROGRAM

Frequently encountered in jail, for example, are people with both substance abuse problems and mental disorders such as schizophrenia and bipolar disorder. The usual office-based treatment is often not successful for such people because substance abuse interferes with treatment of the psychiatric illness and vice versa. To prevent such people cycling repeatedly through jail, the mental health center and criminal justice and correctional agencies in Boulder County, in 2000, established a collaborative community treatment program for suitable jail inmates that borrows some of the concepts of intensive community support (described below) and incorporates the following services for those who can benefit:

- collaborative treatment planning between the judge, the district attorney, the public defender, community corrections and the mental health professionals;
- daily administration of medications and monitoring of mental status;
- sobriety testing with breathalyzers and urine screens;
- case management services to help clients obtain housing, financial benefits and medical care;
- job placement and support;
- psychiatric evaluation and counseling, probation and community corrections and other services provided on the same site.

Those accepted into the program (called the PACE program) are released from jail and receive services at a neutral location not associated with the criminal justice system or the mental health center. In the first year of operation the PACE program reduced the amount of time the enrolled clients spent in jail from an average of nine days a month before enrollment to two days a month afterwards. There were also improvements in sobriety and employment and big cost savings for the criminal justice system.[5]

Besides developing special programs for repeat offenders, the task of mental health administrators and action groups is to put pressure on their legislators to maintain adequate funding for hospital care and for an array of community treatment programs such as those described below, so that jails are not used as a back-up treatment resource.

INTENSIVE RESIDENTIAL TREATMENT

Cedar House is a large house for 15 psychiatric patients in a residential and business district of the city of Boulder. It functions as both an alternative to acute care in a psychiatric hospital and as a half-way house. Like a psychiatric hospital it offers all the usual diagnostic and treatment services but, at less than half the cost of private hospital treatment, it is feasible for patients to remain in residence for quite long periods of time if necessary. Admitted with some kind of an acute psychiatric problem (most often an acute psychotic episode), a client may stay anywhere from a day to a few months; the average period is around two weeks.

Unlike a psychiatric hospital, Cedar House is non-coercive. No patients can be strapped down, locked in or medicated forcibly. Staff must encourage patients to comply voluntarily with treatment requirements and house rules. The people who cannot be managed are those who repeatedly walk away or run away and those who are violent or threatening or very agitated. Since the alternative for patients who are unable to stay at Cedar House is hospital treatment, which virtually none prefers, the large majority of residents accept the necessary restrictions. Very few patients need to be transferred to hospital. In practice, virtually all clients with psychotic depression, most of those with schizophrenia and many with acute mania can be treated at Cedar House through all phases of their illness. There is no doubt that a large number of the people treated in this residential facility would be subject to coercive measures, such as restraints or seclusion, if they were admitted to a hospital where such approaches are available and routinely used. The avoidance of coercion is the first step in maintaining the status and self-esteem of the person with psychosis. As the moral-treatment advocates recognized, to cultivate the patient's self-control is to elicit his or her collaboration in treatment.

Like the York Retreat, also, the environment is similar to that of a middle-class home, not a hospital. Residents and staff may bring their pets with them to the house. Sometimes a bird may be heard singing in one of the bedrooms, on other days a dog shares the comfortable furniture with the residents. The floors are carpeted, shelves of books are available, residents and visitors come and go fairly freely, staff and patients interact casually, eat together and are encouraged to treat one another with mutual respect. As in Tuke's establishment, the goal is to allow therapists and clients alike to retain their dignity and humanity and to foster cooperation.

In line with this emphasis, each resident is intimately involved in running the household. He or she is responsible for specific tasks that are assigned and supervised by one of the residents. These cooperative living arrangements reduce treatment costs, increase the resident's sense of belonging and can be useful training for people with problems in day-to-day functioning. A full-scale, therapeutic community style of patient government has not been established. In view of the relatively brief length of patient stay and the necessity for staff and administration to exercise close control over patients' admission and discharge (in order to make room for new acute admissions at all times) patient government is not considered workable. The ethos of the community, however, calls for residents routinely to assist in the care of others.

Residential treatment of this intensity requires a staffing pattern similar to that of a hospital. A mental health worker and a nurse are on duty at all times. At night, one of the two is awake and the other sleeps. On weekdays, two experienced therapists work with the patients. A psychiatrist is present for three hours a day, a team leader directs the program and a secretarial assistant manages the office work and the purchasing of household supplies. The treatment setting calls for staff who are tolerant and empathic and it brings out their capacity independently to find inventive solutions to difficult problems.

There is no commonly used form of psychiatric treatment (except for electro-convulsive therapy) and no diagnostic measure that cannot be provided for residents of this treatment facility. Patients with acute or chronic organic brain disorders, for example, can be evaluated using the laboratories and diagnostic equipment of local hospitals. Consulting physicians provide treatment for medical problems.

An essential step in the treatment of people entering Cedar House is the evaluation of the patient's social system. What has happened to bring the patient in for treatment at this particular time? What are his or her financial circumstances, living arrangements and work situation? Have there been recent changes? Are there family tensions? From the answers to such questions as these, a plan may be made that will hopefully diminish the chances of relapse after the patient leaves residential treatment.

In some cases the solution may be straightforward. The patient has been living on the street, sleeping in doorways on cold nights and eating out of garbage cans. Floridly psychotic at the time of admission, he (or, more rarely, she) may show few positive features of illness after a day or two of warmth and good food. This person needs help in applying for welfare entitlements, finding a place to live and, probably, a lot of supervision while settling into a new pattern of living. Another patient may relapse into acute psychosis after starting a job or losing one. He or she needs to be referred to a supported employment program for on-the-job counseling

Other situations can be more difficult to ameliorate. A patient and his or her family members may be at loggerheads, periodically inflaming the patient to psychotic outbursts, or the family members to angry rejection; yet none of the parties wishes to separate. Although the patient is calm and well while in residential treatment, careful family negotiations may be necessary before the patient can be discharged.

Most people suffering from a psychosis will benefit from some form of medication. The period of residential treatment allows the opportunity to spend time observing the patient's illness and selecting the most suitable drug (an antipsychotic may not be the best choice), monitoring and adjusting the dosage to minimize side effects and evaluating the benefits. An added advantage of the more leisurely pace of residential treatment (compared with brief hospitalization), as discussed in Chapter 10, is that it allows an opportunity to see if low doses of medication, or none at all, will be effective.[6]

The Cedar House model has been replicated in other parts of Colorado, and there are a growing number of similar domestic-style, non-alienating alternatives to hospital for acute psychiatric treatment around North America and elsewhere. Well-established examples include Venture in Vancouver, British Columbia;[7] Crossing Place in Washington, DC;[8] and the Progress Foundation in San Francisco, California.[9] A residential treatment model that is even further removed from the traditional institutional approach to acute care will be described next.

FOSTER CARE FOR THE ACUTELY ILL

As part of Southwest Denver Community Mental Health Services in Colorado, in the 1970s and 1980s, Canadian community psychiatrist Paul Polak and his team developed an innovative method of caring for the person suffering from an acute psychotic episode. They found several families in the neighborhood who were willing to take one or two acutely disturbed people into their homes. Nurses, a psychiatrist and other staff from the mental health agency worked with the foster family to provide care and treatment for the disturbed person. The patient's own family also participated. Medications were used freely and were closely monitored by the medical staff. The average length of stay was ten days.

Foster families were chosen for their warmth and acceptance. Each client was given his or her own room and was treated as a guest. When able, the patient helped with shopping, cooking and household tasks. Often he or she would become friendly with the foster family and remain in touch through telephone calls, letters or visits.

This program, which did everything possible to maintain the client's status and connection with the community, proved workable and effective. In operation for two decades, it was a viable alternative to hospital care for all but a handful of patients. A two-year study using random assignment of patients showed that the community homes were more effective in some respects than a psychiatric hospital in providing intensive treatment, one important advantage being that clients treated in the family homes felt better about themselves and their treatment.[10]

Southwest Denver Mental Health Center no longer exists as an independent agency and their system of family sponsor homes is not now in operation. A system of family crisis homes based on the Southwest Denver model, however, is currently in operation at Dane County Mental Health Center in Madison, Wisconsin. More than a dozen family homes provide care to a wide variety of people in crisis most of whom would otherwise be in hospital; about three-quarters of these clients suffer from acute psychotic illness and others are acutely suicidal. About 40 per cent of the clients are admitted from the community as an alternative to hospital care; 40 per cent are patients in transition out of the hospital; and 20 per cent are people whose clinical condition is not so severe as to require hospital care but who are having housing problems or social crises. The average length of stay is only three days.

Violence and safety are almost never a problem, in part because of careful selection of appropriate clients and in part because clients feel honored to be invited into another person's home; they try to behave with the courtesy of houseguests. These crisis homes induce the patient to exercise self-control – a key strength of human-scale domestic alternatives to hospital care.[11]

One might imagine that there are few people in the community who would open up their homes to acutely ill people in this way. When a program of this type was launched in Boulder, Colorado, however, through a combination of newspaper articles and advertising, a hundred people called showing an interest in the program in the first month, and half-a-dozen homes were selected within a few weeks.

INTENSIVE COMMUNITY SUPPORT

Providing non-alienating settings for acute treatment is an important part of the spectrum of community services. Another necessary element is preventing relapse and admission for acute treatment in the first place. A highly success-ful way of achieving this is to follow people with the most severe forms of psychotic illness so closely in the community – providing support at every step – that acute relapse is more or less eliminated. Leonard Stein, an Ameri-can community psychiatrist, Mary Ann Test, a social worker, and their col-leagues in Madison, Wisconsin, put such a program into effect in the 1970s. Their approach later came to be termed "assertive community treatment." A similar program is provided now by the mental health center in Madison, with leadership from psychiatrist, Ron Diamond. Available 24 hours a day, seven days a week, mental health staff visit patients in their own homes. They help their clients with long-standing mental illness learn to do laundry, shop-ping, cooking, grooming and budgeting. They assist them in finding work and in settling disputes with landlords. If a patient does not show up for work or treatment one day, the staff member goes to his or her home to discover the reason. Staff help patients to expand their social lives and they provide support to the patients' families. Early signs of the return of psychosis are immediately detected and lead to active treatment measures. In essence, the patient is watched and helped as closely as he or she would be on many hospital wards, but the treatment is provided instead in the patient's own neighborhood. This type of daily practical help and advocacy has come to be termed "case management."

When these measures fail, the patient may be admitted briefly to hospital; such a move is rarely necessary, however. In a study of the course of illness in patients referred for admission to hospital with a severe psychiatric problem, it was found that nearly all of those randomly assigned to the Stein and Test intensive case management program in Madison could be treated without hospital care; of the patients assigned to standard outpatient care, on the other hand, nearly all were initially treated in hospital. At the end of a year the rate of readmission to hospital was six per cent for clients of the intensive community treatment team, in contrast to 58 per cent for patients in routine outpatient care. Mobile and intensive community treatment had put a stop to the revolving door.

The clients in this program reaped other benefits. Compared with the patients in standard community care, they had fewer symptoms, greater self-esteem and were more satisfied with their lives after one year of treatment. They were more likely to be living independently and had spent less time in jail.[12] This was accomplished, furthermore, with no increase in social cost to the patient's family or the community; there was no increased burden of social disruption or suicidal gestures.[13]

A program at the Mental Health Center of Boulder County, based on the Madison model, provides similar services and achieves equivalent results. In Boulder, the 20 per cent of the agency's clients who are suffering from psychosis and who have the greatest likelihood of relapse are assigned to an intensive case management team. Caseloads are small; each therapist is responsible for only 12 to 15 clients. The services they receive, when necessary, include:

- daily, flexible, unscheduled contact,
- twice daily medication administration,
- daily monitoring of funds (the therapist may be payee for the client's disability pension),
- supervised and subsidized housing,
- assistance with acquiring entitlements, housing and health care,
- advocating for clients with social agencies and the criminal justice system,
- ensuring that clients get adequate medical care for physical health problems.

Because medication can be administered daily, few clients assigned to this team receive long-acting intramuscular (depot) antipsychotic drugs. Patients appreciate this fact; almost none choose intramuscular medication, even though coming in daily for oral medication is a chore – a telling comment on the dislike that clients have for the increased side effects associated with the past misuse of depot medications. Patients with bipolar disorder show the greatest improvement after assignment to the team, presumably because their lithium carbonate or other mood-stabilizing medication is carefully monitored. Clients whose mental illness is complicated by drug and alcohol abuse also do better on this team; in part this is because their money is often disbursed in modest daily amounts – too little to allow the recipient to get too drunk or high. Their illness, consequently, is less severe, their rent is paid regularly and they are no longer at risk of being admitted to hospital acutely psychotic, hungry and homeless halfway through the month. Before they were assigned to this intensive treatment team in 1984, 28 per cent of the initial sample of severely disturbed clients were revolving-door patients with several hospital admissions a year; six years later less than five per cent were in this frequent-admission category. With treatment, most of the group developed a stable course of illness. Only four per cent of the cohort had originally been free of hospital admissions over a two-year period; six years after assignment to intensive treatment nearly 60 per cent were this stable.

The effectiveness of assertive community treatment has been demonstrated in many studies conducted in different countries including the US, Sweden and Australia.[14] Curiously, some major British studies have not found the approach to be effective.[15] One reason for the disappointing results found by the British studies may be the researchers' failure to adhere to one of the important principles of assertive community treatment – the approach is to be reserved for those people with psychosis, about 20 per cent of the whole group, who are at high risk of relapse. These people may be poorly compliant with treatment, or continue to have quite severe psychotic symptoms despite treatment, or they may abuse drugs and alcohol heavily, or have difficulty taking care of their daily affairs and basic needs. If less severely ill people are enrolled in assertive community treatment, as occurred in the British studies, many of them will get worse due to the harmful effect of excessive restrictions.

If the treatment is this restrictive, we have to ask ourselves if the more severely ill who do relapse less when enrolled in assertive community treatment are better off in the community, under these kind of controls, than they would be in hospital. One study attempts to answer this question. In Britain, in the early 1990s, more psychiatric hospital beds were available than in the US. There were ten times as many beds *per capita* in Manchester, England, at that time, as in Boulder, Colorado.[16] Consequently, most of the very disturbed patients who would have been enrolled in assertive community treatment in Boulder would have been in hospital in Manchester. In a comparison of Boulder clients in intensive community treatment with patients in long-term care in the psychiatric ward of a general hospital in Manchester, it was found that psychopathology was greater in the Boulder outpatient sample but their quality of life scores were better.[17] Patients maintained outside hospital with intensive services continue to be quite disturbed, it appears, but they enjoy life more. The reason is fairly clear – few people, well or ill, like to live in an institution. If they can get the same services outside of hospital, they are more content.

DO WE NEED PSYCHIATRIC HOSPITALS?

In the 1960s politicians and mental health professionals alike were heralding the death of the psychiatric hospital – but it is still with us. Does it serve a useful purpose? Even using the assertive community treatment programs described above, there remains a handful of patients who cannot be adequately cared for outside a hospital. A few patients, for example, consistently refuse any type of treatment and will always walk away from an open-door establishment; a few become violent at times and, if they fail to improve with treatment, represent a danger to the public. Some people with psychosis routinely make their illnesses worse by the constant abuse of hallucinogenic drugs, by heavy drinking or by sniffing glue and volatile solvents.

Attempts to treat such people in the community are more likely to fail. These mentally ill people will be found in jail, held for minor offenses; they will be committed by the criminal courts to forensic psychiatric hospitals for more serious offenses; or they will end up living on the streets, leading degrading lives and becoming physically debilitated. Eventually many will suffer brain damage as a result of substance abuse, and some will die prematurely. The effort to help such patients, nevertheless, will have put an immense strain on the community support system. Many hours of work will have been put into makeshift treatment plans that have little hope of success.

The number of patients that cannot be treated in the community is extremely small, however. On any day in the past decade in Boulder County, around five patients with psychosis are likely to be in long-term, public hospital care, placed there by the mental health center. Another 15 mental health center patients with psychosis are likely to be receiving medium- or short-term hospital treatment (lasting from a few days to three months) in a general hospital psychiatric ward or in a public psychiatric hospital, before returning to community care.[18] These patients are drawn from a county population of 275,000 people and a caseload of over 4,500 mental health center clients, over 700 of whom suffer from psychosis. The number of patients in long-term, non-forensic hospital care emerges as less than one per cent of all the patients with functional psychosis in treatment at the mental health center.

It is important to identify these few clients and arrange for them to receive hospital care as the humane course of treatment. This may be easier said than done. Long-term hospital care in the United States is virtually a thing of the past. State budget cuts have so reduced hospital capacity that hospital staff feel obliged to discharge any patient who loses his or her symptoms of acute psychosis regardless of what the patient's trajectory is likely to be after release. Community mental health administrators must first fight to see a bare sufficiency of hospital beds funded; and then they must stand firm against the pressure to discharge from the hospital patients who cannot be properly treated once they leave.

If community support services were provided on a truly comprehensive basis, we would only need small hospitals but they would serve a highly specialized function. Based on the experience in Boulder and elsewhere, only one or two hospital beds for adults (aged 18–65) would be needed for each 10,000 of the general population. (Mental health staff working with the population of large cities might arrive at a higher estimate for the number of required hospital beds. States or countries with a mental illness statute that does not permit involuntary outpatient treatment would also need more hospital beds.) Some inpatients, however, would be resistant or unresponsive to treatment and locked doors would be necessary. For the tiny handful of long-term inpatients hopes for improvement would depend upon their being provided with work therapy, a range of recreational activities, skilled, humane care in small attractive units and access to a pleasant, open-air environment. In other words, they would be as unlike nursing homes as it is possible for such places to be.

AN ALTERNATIVE TO LONG-TERM HOSPITAL CARE

One reason that the number of patients in Boulder County in long-term hospital care is so low is because an open-door domestic alternative to hospital has been established for some of these very difficult-to-treat people. Friendship House is a long-term intensive-treatment household for six very disturbed young and middle-aged adults. Each of these people has been ill for well over a decade with a brittle psychosis that has shown relatively little benefit from psychiatric medication. Many have significant problems with substance abuse in addition to their mental illness. Most are somewhat uncooperative with treatment and so volatile and lacking in social skills that they have been unable to live outside of an inpatient setting for more than a few weeks or months since the illness began, even when surrounded by an elaborate array of community supports. These residents represent a new generation of the severely ill who have become chronically institutionalized in an era when few indigent people in the US get to stay in a hospital for any time at all.

The household is a cooperative venture between the Mental Health Center of Boulder County and the Naropa Institute, a Buddhist university with an East-West psychology training program. It is a cost-effective application of the principles embodied in contemplative therapy – an approach that emphasizes patience and compassion[19] – to the rehabilitation of the very ill. Within the household, each resident is provided with his or her own team comprised of a part-time therapist (paid) and some part-time psychology interns (unpaid). The remaining staff include two resident house-parents and a program director. All of these staff work with the residents to create a therapeutic community and learning environment in which compassion, respect and openness are core values. The program has been successful in bringing equilibrium to the lives of people who had not known stability since they became ill, and in encouraging people who had been in involuntary treatment for years to accept voluntary treatment. What makes this program work are the same things that make Cedar House work. It is small and domestic. It is so much more pleasant than being in hospital that people will draw upon all their resources of self-control in order to stay there – the essence of moral treatment.

SUPERVISED APARTMENTS

Like one's job, a powerful indicator of status is one's living environment. The unemployed person with schizophrenia, unless living with his or her family, is likely to occupy seedy, low-rent rooms, a boarding house or a homeless shelter. Many, having fallen ill early in life, have little experience of independent living. Some have poor judgment and lack the capacity to manage a household. For such people, supervised and subsidized housing is a necessity.

Many mental health agencies have demonstrated that cooperative apartments (or group homes, as they are often called) work well for people with long-term mental illness who are leaving mental hospital after several years of residence.[20] The same approach has been shown to be viable also for young adults with psychosis who have not spent years in mental hospitals. For those who are more volatile, disruptive and subject to relapse a more intensive level of supervision may be required. Group homes with varying levels of supervision are common in Europe and the US.[21] In the Boulder supervised living program, staff members hold house meetings for the residents at least once weekly in their apartments and provide individual outpatient counseling in addition. Help with household management often includes sorting out problems with "crashers" – initially welcome guests who end up exploiting the residents or stealing from them. The advantage of such group living is that it offers a substitute family to clients who may have difficulties in setting up a stable family of their own or in living with their parents. Achieving amiable domestic relations, however, may require the residential staff to arbitrate disputes.

For many people with schizophrenia, living alone is the best arrangement – the stresses of cooperative living may provoke relapse; others find loneliness to be a major problem. Supervised living situations in Boulder range in size from apartment buildings with one- or two-person apartments and a staff member present for a few hours a day to six-person households with round-the-clock staff. At some of the living situations people with mental illness are hired to provide supervision. The larger, better-staffed living situations can accommodate clients who have more limited capacity for independent living. By supplying increasing amounts of staff support on the premises it is possible to develop a range of community living arrangements for clients with progressively lower levels of functioning.

In high-rent Boulder, some form of rent subsidy is necessary for clients who must often exist on limited Social Security income. Such financial assistance is available through the federal Department of Housing and Urban Development, either as direct rent subsidies or as grants to mental health agencies to build or buy new accommodation. In some instances, the center operates as a tenant, subleasing the house or apartment to the residents.

RESIDENTIAL SETTINGS BASED ON MUTUAL SUPPORT

Some residential settings provide security and support for the residents by developing a strong sense of community and employing the tenants in staff positions. An interesting cooperative housing project of this type, Columbia University Community Services, operates five apartment buildings on the Upper West Side of Manhattan for mentally ill and mentally healthy poor people. In this project, a private non-profit housing corporation owns the buildings (obtained cheaply from the city of New York), the mental health agency at Columbia University provides treatment and practical assistance (case management) to all tenants, and a board composed of residents, mental health staff and representatives of the landlord screens potential tenants and manages the day-to day operations of the building. Some tenants are given paid jobs on the 24-hour-a-day "tenant patrol" which provides security and assistance to the residents.[22]

Another residential program in California – the clustered apartment project of Santa Clara County Mental Health Center – was designed to build community strength among clients living independently in apartments in the same neighborhood. These were to be communities of mentally ill people based on mutual support and interdependence – assertively non-clinical in style. Staff were encouraged to abandon traditional roles and to become, instead, community organizers. It was hoped that these strengthened communities would develop ways to support their members so that hospital admission for acute psychiatric distress became less necessary. As the project took shape, each of the communities developed different strengths. In one program, all of the staff were drawn from among the consumer group. In another, the program developed a strong sense of community around its Latino identity. In a third, community members provided respite care in a crisis apartment to members who were acutely disturbed. The programs varied in the extent to which they met the needs of new or established members but they were all successful in building a sense of empowerment among the residents.[23]

LONG-TERM FOSTER CARE

Many patients who have not yet developed the ability to live independently may do well in long-term foster care. Dr Polak's short-term foster care program was established to treat acutely ill patients. In other mental health programs, however, a client moves in to live with a foster family when his or her condition is stable and may stay as long as he or she wishes. Fort Logan Mental Health Center in Denver, Colorado, has successfully operated such a system of family care for several decades, their clients often graduating to independent living. Similar schemes have been established in Salisbury and in Hampshire, England,[24] and in Boulder, Colorado. The historically famous origin of this model is the village of Gheel in Belgium that has been boarding out people with mental illness since the fourteenth century.[25]

SMALL IS BEAUTIFUL

There is an important common quality to each of the model treatment programs discussed so far – the setting is small. This factor can have a powerful influence upon the patient's social role and sense of worth. Where there are relatively few members of a group the contribution of each is seen as correspondingly more important. Students in small high schools, for example, have been found to have a better-developed sense of responsibility and usefulness than students of large schools. In the small schools each student is more likely to be relied upon to contribute to sporting events, the band, dramatic productions and similar activities. Studies have shown that people in small settings such as these are more active and that they tackle more varied, difficult and useful tasks. In consequence, they feel challenged, valued and better satisfied with themselves.[26]

A patient living in a small community setting, therefore, where he or she is called upon to contribute to the operation of the household, will be more valued for any special abilities and will develop greater self-esteem and practical skills. More than this, he or she will be better accepted and socially integrated. As in the Third World village, where there is no labor surplus, it is necessary to accept those who are available to do the job. Where there are more people than are strictly required, the research of psychologist Roger Barker reveals, deviance and individual differences are not tolerated nearly as well.[27] This is one reason why boarding homes and nursing homes containing scores or hundreds of patients have such a pernicious influence on the course of schizophrenia.

COOPERATIVELY-OWNED HOUSING

If mentally ill people were to become property owners instead of tenants, this would be a form of social and economic advancement. Housing cooperatives provide a mechanism for poor people to own their accommodation and offer a number of advantages besides. They not only provide long-term affordable housing, they also create a better quality of life for residents, particularly those with special needs, by developing a strong feeling of community. They build leadership skills among members of the cooperative through the financial, maintenance and managerial tasks required for the operation of the housing. Housing cooperatives can be hard to establish, however, as both mortgage lenders and potential residents may be put off by the cooperative governance structure.[28]

There are a number of reasons why cooperative housing is more affordable. Each member owns a share of the cooperative corporation and then leases his or her own housing unit from the corporation. Since members are "leasers," therefore, they qualify for rent subsidies, including federal Section 8 certificates. Nevertheless, they retain ownership rights, including the ability to profit from resale of the share. Since departing members could sell their shares at an escalated current market value, a mechanism is required to ensure permanent affordability; this is achieved through a "limited equity" formula. Under this arrangement, the cooperative buys back shares, when the owner departs, at a predetermined rate of appreciation. Another financial advantage is that the ongoing cost of operating a cooperative tends to be lower than that of rental apartments because of resident involvement in management and the absence of a profit line in the budget.[29]

The basic financing method for establishing a cooperative is a blanket mortgage, based on the value of the building, for which the cooperative corporation is liable. Members pay an initial membership price and a monthly assessment. Members can obtain cooperative share loans, backed by the individual's cooperative share, to allow them to meet the membership price. For example, poor families joining the Hillrise Mutual Housing Association in Lancaster, Pennsylvania, are required to pay a membership price of $1,500, but most pay $300 in cash and finance the rest through a share loan. Low-income housing cooperatives in the US may obtain subsidies through local government low-interest loans and grants, homeownership assistance programs and property tax forgiveness.[30]

In fact, there are relatively few successful examples of cooperative home-ownership for the mentally ill because of a variety of problems. The mentally ill tend to be a fairly mobile group with little capital or monthly income. If hospitalized for a prolonged period, the person may lose benefits and be unable to pay the monthly assessment. Recipients of Supplemental Security Income (SSI), furthermore, cannot accumulate capital to purchase housing without adversely affecting their eligibility for benefits.

One novel attempt to develop a housing cooperative for the mentally ill achieved only limited success. The Mental Health Law Project in New York filed a class-action suit on behalf of a large number of mentally ill clients whose Social Security benefits had been suspended during the Reagan administration.[31] The suit was successful and the clients were due to receive large, retroactive payments. Ironically, this could have led to their funds being discontinued again, as their assets would have exceeded the maximum allowable under social security regulations. To avoid this outcome, the Mental Health Law Project established a housing trust to receive the clients' retroactive payments. The project was only partially successful, however, because, by the time the necessary waiver of regulations had been obtained from the Social Security Administration allowing the clients to invest their assets in future housing, most of the clients had spent their awards. The number of remaining participants was too small to leverage private development funds to create low-cost housing. The trust, however, continues to be suitable vehicle for those who need to shelter retroactive SSI payments and want to invest them in housing.[32]

A small-scale attempt to create a housing association in which mentally ill people participate in a limited equity housing agreement, the Newell Street Cooperative in Pittsfield, Massachusetts, also ended in failure. The project obtained a waiver that allowed state rent subsidies (like HUD Section 8 subsidies) to be applied to the purchase of a four-apartment building; when the rent subsidy program was trimmed, however, the cooperative collapsed. During the one-year period that the cooperative was in operation significant improvements were noted in the participants' management skills, self-esteem and sense of mastery.[33]

Despite difficulties and failures, however, housing cooperatives for the mentally ill are a viable concept. Some chapters of the National Alliance for the Mentally Ill (a US organization of relatives and friends of mentally ill people), including the Greater Chicago branch, have established non-profit housing trusts. The residents of these housing projects are usually mentally ill relatives of the investors; if one of the residents moves, the investor may dispose of his/her share to another family or claim a tax deduction. A trust of this type can establish small homes or large apartment complexes and can contract with a local mental health agency to provide appropriate services on premises. The settings may include disabled and non-disabled residents. The National Alliance for the Mentally Ill has proposed a low-cost revolving loan fund that, by building a large reservoir of capital, could access favorable loan rates. Although plans of this type do not necessarily place ownership of the property in the hands of the mentally ill people themselves, they are a valuable source of stable and affordable housing.[34]

PSYCHOTHERAPY

Serious questions have been raised as to the efficacy of psychotherapy in general and its value in schizophrenia in particular. The research suggests that insight-oriented, uncovering psychotherapy has little or no application in psychosis and that environmental considerations and various types of drug treatment are usually of more immediate relevance. None of the treatment approaches discussed so far would be possible, however, without some of the basic ingredients of psychotherapy. The person with schizophrenia and his or her therapist must be able to form a relationship of mutual trust and to work through disagreements that arise between them in the course of treatment. The therapist should also be able to help the patient resolve conflicts with other people that may surface. The patient should feel free to discuss concerns about his or her life, illness and treatment. Where denial is preventing the patient from recognizing problems, the therapist must be able to approach the issues sensitively; and where resistance holds the patient back from a useful course of action, the therapist must attempt to uncover the reasons. In other words, while social considerations and drug therapy are important, they must be humanized if the person with schizophrenia is to re-enter society.

The frustration of failure inherent in working in an inadequate system of care can lead staff to feel a degree of contempt for their clients. Such an attitude can be expressed in jokes that attribute negative characteristics to their psychotic patients or as more subtle forms of denigration. Sociologist David Rosenhan, for example, revealed that hospital staff often fail to respond to a patient's question, passing by as if the inquirer were not present.[35] Therapy that hopes to increase the schizophrenic person's sense of worth must begin with respect; and professionals with the greatest authority within a treatment agency are under the heaviest obligation to demonstrate respect for the clientele on all occasions. In a similar vein, therapy should aspire to identify and emphasize the patient's special strengths and individuality and not merely aim to control pathology.

An important element in avoiding frustration in therapy for the patient, relatives and therapist alike is to set suitable expectations. Like the moral-treatment pioneers, we should look for a certain level of self-control and performance from the person with psychosis, but goals must be achievable. The client should not be encouraged to apply for work that is beyond his or her current capacity; the family should be warned that the ambitions for their relative may need to be restricted in some spheres; and the therapist should not see the patient's occasional relapse as a failure.

While the patient may be given the hope that one day medication will be unnecessary, such an option should not be seen as an end in itself. The individual's goals should be to do well and to feel good – the medication is a tool towards that end. The patient, however, may identify the medicine with the illness and see it as a stigmatizing and controlling force (which it often is, of course). To get around this problem one may do a number of things – help the person identify certain goals and the extent to which medication can assist in reaching them; discuss his or her reaction to the illness, to the medication, to control and to stigma as separate but related issues; and delegate to the patient authority over his or her own medications at the earliest workable opportunity so that he or she can set the dosage to achieve the desired benefit.

The person with schizophrenia does not respond well to ambiguity in therapy or to a neutral and distant therapist. Communication should be straightforward, expectations clear-cut and the therapist should not hesitate to act as a role model for the patient. Psychotic experiences may be discussed frankly, not to uncover dynamic origins, but to alleviate the person's fears and perplexity about them and to identify stresses that provoke their appearance. The emphasis in therapy, though, needs to be on problems in daily living – work, personal and family relationships, finances and accommodation – and a major goal of treatment should be the reduction of stress in these areas.

Paradoxically, the therapist for people with psychosis will find that he or she is encouraging many clients that they can overcome their disability and accomplish more, while he or she must persuade the others that they suffer from an illness and should accept restrictions and limit their horizons. As argued in Chapter 8, this phenomenon is exacerbated by the stigma of mental illness. To consider oneself both mentally ill and capable creates cognitive dissonance; people tend either to accept the label of mental illness and adopt the associated stereotype of incompetence or they reject the notion that they are ill or disabled. The solution is to proceed slowly, to avoid pushing the person who accepts the diagnosis to do too much too soon and to avoid vigorously attacking the denial of the person who rejects the illness label.

Herein lies one of the potential advantages of group therapy for people with psychosis. Cognitive-dissonance research demonstrates that people are more likely to change their attitudes if they can be encouraged to express in public an opinion different from their usual belief. By bringing together in a therapy group people with psychosis who variously accept or reject the illness label and who have a variety of levels of functioning, one may hope that the less competent patients will accept the possibility of becoming more capable and that those who deny their illness will change their opinion. A group focus on practical accomplishments and the development of social skills is indicated. A review of the research on the effectiveness of group psychotherapy for outpatients with psychosis has suggested, in fact, that such treatment is particularly valuable in boosting both the clients' levels of social functioning and their morale.[36]

COGNITIVE-BEHAVIORAL THERAPY FOR PSYCHOTIC SYMPTOMS

Despite the long-held belief that it is a pointless exercise to try and dissuade people from tenacious delusional beliefs, recent research reveals that talking to people about their psychotic symptoms, and about their personal meaning, can lead to an improvement in symptoms. It emerges that the gentle challenge of the evidence used by people with psychotic disorders to support their delusions – presenting alternative viewpoints, reality-testing and enhancing coping strategies – can be helpful.

In a study conducted by British psychologist Nicholas Tarrier and his colleagues,[37] people with schizophrenia who continued to experience positive symptoms of psychosis, despite optimal drug treatment, improved when they received a cognitive-behavioral treatment called "coping strategy enhancement." In this approach, patients were helped to identify coping strategies that could be used to reduce both the cues and the reactions to symptoms like hallucinations or delusions. For one person, for example, being alone or bored may be a cue to an increase in hallucinations; he or she can be taught to adopt strategies to reduce isolation or boredom. Others can learn to reduce auditory hallucinations by humming, conversing with others, or even reasoning with the voices and telling them to go away and come back later. Similarly, a person might be taught to test the reality of delusional beliefs against the therapist's interpretation of events and, for example, return to a church social group about which he or she had harbored paranoid fears. After six months, the people who received this type of coping strategy treatment had less intense delusions and anxiety, compared to those who received a less specific form of cognitive therapy called "problem solving training." However, people who received problem solving therapy also improved to a degree, so, in a later study, the researchers combined both of these cognitive approaches with a third, called "relapse prevention," in an attempt to maximize benefits. One year after the end of the treatment, patients receiving this cognitive-behavioral therapy were experiencing significantly lower levels of positive symptoms than a control group of patients receiving routine care.[38]

Another randomized study of cognitive-behavioral therapy for people with persistent symptoms of schizophrenia, conducted at three centers in East Anglia and London, UK, achieved a 25 per cent reduction in total psychopathology, primarily in hallucinations and delusions.[39] In this study, about half of those with persistent symptoms appeared to show benefit from cognitive therapy, primarily those with persistent delusions who initially accepted, to a degree at least, that they might be mistaken in their beliefs.[40] Benefits were sustained over a long period and the treatment led to a reduced need for services in the following months.[41] A study conducted in London demonstrated that cognitive-behavioral therapy provided as group therapy is as effective as individual treatment in teaching coping strategies to people with persistent psychotic symptoms and giving them control over their hallucinations.[42]

Cognitive therapy, it appears, is also effective for patients in an episode of acute psychosis, speeding up the resolution of positive symptoms. Patients in inpatient treatment for acute psychotic illness, in Birmingham, England, were provided with individual and group cognitive therapy during the hospital stay. The individual treatment gently challenged and tested key delusional beliefs. In the group therapy, group members offered alternative explanations for the irrational beliefs of others, challenged negative beliefs about psychotic illness, and bolstered one another's attempts to integrate the concept of illness into their lives and to develop new coping strategies. Other cognitive procedures were family sessions to enlist family support in the patient's attempts to manage his or her symptoms, and an activity program aimed at improving interpersonal and self-care skills. Positive symptoms decreased faster and dropped to a lower level of severity in patients who received cognitive therapy than in a control group receiving non-specific therapist support and structured activities.[43] The evidence is getting stronger that the treatment of schizophrenia should include cognitive-behavioral therapy and efforts to enhance the self-esteem and coping strategies of the person with the illness.

FAMILY THERAPY

Although family therapy can be as effective in the treatment of schizophrenia as the antipsychotic drugs, it is often neglected. It must be made clear that family therapy, here, does not mean efforts to uncover the root cause of the psychosis in family dynamics. As indicated in Chapter 1, there is little evidence to suggest that family pathology contributes to the *development* of schizophrenia. The successful family therapy programs, rather, have concentrated on the influence of the family environment on the *course* of the condition, and have relied heavily upon practical support and education as the essential ingredients.

In Chapter 10, the research conducted by Julian Leff and his associates in London on the family environment of people with schizophrenia was reviewed in some detail. These researchers have shown that people with schizophrenia who return to a home in which their relatives are critical and over-involved have a higher relapse rate than those who return to a low-stress home. The greater the proportion of time the patient spends with high-stress relatives, the greater the risk of relapse. Since this early British research was conducted, dozens of similar studies have been carried out in several countries around the world, nearly all of them confirming the original findings. If the results of these studies are pooled so that hundreds of cases are included we see that the overall rate of relapse in the critical and over-involved families is more than twice the rate in the families without these features – 50 per cent *versus* 23 per cent at the end of a year.[44]

Studies of family therapy for people with high-relapse schizophrenia (who are taking medication), using random assignment of cases to therapy or to a control group, show a marked degree of benefit for family treatment. In the control groups relapse rates are as high as might be expected for high-risk cases who are taking medication – usually around 50 per cent over the course of nine months. Patients receiving family therapy, however, experience relapse rates of under ten per cent.[45] If we look back to Figure 10.2, we may see that antipsychotic drugs reduce the rate of relapse for people with schizophrenia spending large amounts of time in high-stress households from a virtual certainty to a 50–50 chance. Now we see that family intervention can change the stress pattern of such a household and almost eliminate the remaining risk (at least over a nine-month period).

What are the elements of effective family therapy? In most studies the family intervention is rather similar. In a study conducted by Julian Leff, for example, the family treatment comprised (a) a series of sessions of education about mental illness, (b) participation in a relatives' group and (c) individual family therapy conducted in the patient's home. The relatives' group, which was the central component of the program, offered support for the relatives, who often felt isolated and lonely; practical strategizing for those who were having trouble coping with difficult behavior; and role-playing to assist in the development of new attitudes.[46]

In his latest work, Dr Leff has been broadening the availability of family interventions for people with schizophrenia, by training community nurses and family members in Britain to provide the therapy to families. An organization called Carer Education and Support (CESP), in cooperation with the National Schizophrenia Fellowship in Britain, has been training relatives of people with mental illness to provide education and support to the families of people with schizophrenia.[47] This approach is also proving successful in Boulder, Colorado, where members of the local chapter of the National Alliance for the Mentally Ill and mental health staff run support and education groups.

Many families of mentally ill people feel that 'therapy' implies pathology and, hence, blame, so non-stigmatizing approaches must be used. Education for the mentally ill and their relatives, for example, can be provided as an evening class. Such courses have been run annually at the Mental Health Center of Boulder County for over 20 years, sponsored by local organizations of the mentally ill and their relatives. An outline of the topics for one series of classes is set out in Table 12.2. Such a course can be run at low cost, for the speakers may be drawn from among the agency consumers and staff and community professionals. For the teacher, the class is an agreeable experience; rarely does one encounter students so hungry for knowledge and so interested in the subject matter.

Table 12.2 Facts about Mental Illness: A course for people with mental illness, their family members and friends

Class*	Topic
I	*Living with Mental Illness* People who have suffered episodes of serious mental illness describe the experience.
2	*Schizophrenia: Its Features, Causes, Outcome and Treatment* Why do people develop schizophrenia? Who recovers and why? The latest research. The range of treatment options.
3	*Bipolar Disorder: Its Features, Causes, Outcome and Treatment* How does the illness progress, with and without treatment? Effective treatment.
4	*Disorders of Childhood and Adolescence* Attention deficit disorder, bipolar disorder and other disorders of childhood and adolescence. Features and treatment.
5	*Obsessive-Compulsive Disorder* People with OCD and mental health professionals discuss the features of the condition and its treatment.
6	*Coping with Mental Illness* People who suffer from mental illness and their family members talk about mastering the symptoms, handling crises and gaining independence.

* Each class runs for 90 minutes.

For the students, the class is more than an educational program. On each occasion the course has been run, the participants have gained support from the informal sharing of experiences – the recognition that they are not alone, that other people have found strategies for the problems with which they have been struggling in isolation.

CONSUMER GROUPS

Many observers would argue that one of the most important developments in psychiatry in the past 30 years has been the growth of organizations of relatives of people with serious mental illness. In the US the National Alliance for the Mentally Ill has lobbied for improvements in services for people with mental illness, influencing decisions to direct public mental health funding to the most seriously disturbed and to focus research efforts on schizophrenia. Media reports of the mentally ill have changed in response to a drive by the Alliance to reduce stigma and to establish a new openness about psychiatric illness. In Britain the National Schizophrenia Fellowship, established a few years earlier than its American counterpart, has been similarly active in providing emotional support for its members, lobbying for needed services, fostering public education and sponsoring research. Its publications have covered such topics as inadequate services, mental health law and the importance of work for the mentally disabled.[48] In Australia, SANE has mounted a strong countrywide anti-stigma campaign and is closely involved in the shaping of mental health policy.

There has also been growth in the organization of *direct* or *primary* consumers of mental health services in recent decades. The consumer (or service-user) movement, while gaining prominence in many parts of the world, is somewhat fragmented. A listing of some of the important service-user organizations in Britain illustrates both the growing strength and the lack of cohesion of the movement – MIND, Survivors Speak Out, Making Space, Turning Point, the Zito Trust, the Self Harm Network, the All Wales User Network, the Scottish User Network, the All Ireland User Network, the Campaign Against Psychiatric Oppression, Voices, the British Network for Alternatives to Psychiatry, Good Practices in Mental Health, the Afro-Caribbean Mental Health Association, and so on.

In the US, there is a similar proliferation of consumer groups. Two prominent organizations, the National Mental Health Consumer Association and the National Alliance of Mental Patients vie for membership, sponsor national conferences, send speakers to professional meetings, combat stigma through media presentations and lobby for political objectives. Many groups make effective use of the internet. The Support Coalition (www.mindfreedom.org) operates a listserve called Dendron. The National Association for Rights Protection and Advocacy (NARPA) is another web establishing itself (www.connix.com/~narpa). Recovery, Inc. is a well-developed organization with local chapters across the country, and the National Empowerment Center (www.power2u.org) is another prominent organization. Other consumer organization websites include the National Mental Health Consumer Self-Help Clearinghouse at www.mhselfhelp.org and People Who Net at www.peoplewho.net.

Lacking unified national leadership, some of the strongest US consumer group activity is at a local level. California, Ohio and New York have particularly active consumer groups. Consumers are appointed to the governing boards of many mental health centers, and state regulations in California require that the boards of residential facilities include consumer members. In half of the states in the US, consumers have been appointed to paid positions in the state mental health administrative offices.[49]

Fundamental philosophical disagreements over such issues as involuntary treatment and the reality of mental illness increase the tendency for splintering among consumer groups. Group leadership by people with schizophrenia is also held back by the fact that most people who develop this disorder do so before they are old enough to have had any experience of how organizations operate. The fragmentation of the primary consumer movement, however, has not prevented it from changing the face of mental health service delivery.

CONSUMER INVOLVEMENT IN SERVICE PROVISION

In recent years, in the USA and elsewhere, consumers of mental health services have become increasingly involved in running their own programs or
providing treatment services. Consumer organizations have set up drop-in
centers, support groups, speaker's bureaus, housing cooperatives, telephone
hot-lines and a variety of other services.

A consumer action group in Denver has opened its own psychiatric clinic.
The Capitol Hill Action and Recreation Group (CHARG), is a coalition of
consumers and professionals that has established a consumer-run drop-in
center and a full-scale psychiatric clinic for the treatment of severely ill
people. The clinic is directly accountable to an elected consumer board and to
a second board comprised of professionals and other interested people. All
matters of clinic policy require the consent of the consumer board. CHARG
also provides consumer advocates for patients at the local state hospital, in
boarding homes and in other locations. The advocates visit the hospital
wards, attend treatment-planning meetings and accompany clients to court
hearings; among other services, they help clients find apartments, apply for
public assistance, appeal adverse Social Security rulings and contest
involuntary treatment certifications.[50]

An innovative program in Denver, Colorado, at the Regional Assessment
and Training Center (RATC), has trained mental health consumers with
long-term mental illness to work as aides to case managers within the state
mental health system, as residential counselors and as vocational rehabilitation staff.[51] Trainees with well-controlled major mental illness receive 21
credit hours of college education during six weeks of classroom training
and a 14-week field placement. Classroom courses include mathematics,
writing, interviewing techniques, case management skills, crisis intervention
and professional ethics. Following the supervised internship in a community mental health program, trainees earn a certificate from the local
community college and are guaranteed employment with a community
mental health program. As case manager aides, the program graduates help
mentally ill clients with budgeting, applying for welfare entitlements and
finding housing, and they counsel their clients on treatment, work and
other issues. By 2002, after 16 years of the program's operation, well over a
hundred consumer mental health workers had been placed in employment
throughout the service system, providing models for patients and staff alike
of successful recovery from mental illness. Two-thirds of the trainees continue to be successfully employed in the mental health system two years
after graduation from the training program. Building on the initial success,
RATC now trains consumers for other mental health staff positions, such
as residential care workers and job coaches for clients in supported
employment.

This program has been replicated in other states of the union. In Houston,

Texas, a similar program has trained and placed over 50 consumer case managers, and other replication projects have been established in Washington state, Utah and Oregon.[52] The consumer aides are paid a standard wage but are still relatively cheap; they perform tasks (for example, apartment hunting) that professionals are happy to see others take on and they achieve some things that professionals cannot. In particular, they serve as role models for clients who are struggling to manage their lives better and they effectively reduce the antagonism that many clients show towards treatment. The consumer staff also raise the staff and patient level of optimism about outcome from illness.

It does not require a special program for a mental health agency to involve consumers in delivering treatment. At the Mental Health Center of Boulder County, in Colorado, people with serious mental illness are part of the governing board, several advisory boards and the board of the agency's fund-raising foundation. The center's vocational workshop is being converted into a business enterprise in which the consumer workers have input into and authority over such issues as working conditions, career ladders, fringe benefits and budgetary changes. Throughout the agency, consumers are employed as case managers, residential counselors, rehabilitation staff, records department and office workers, consumer organizers, research interviewers and in a variety of positions in consumer-employing enterprises set up by the agency, such as a property repair business and a consumer-oriented pharmacy (see Chapter 11). Other mental health agencies have also found the position of peer research interviewer to be one which can be successfully filled by a consumer even when he or she suffers from persistent psychotic symptoms.[53] Increasingly, the experience of having coped with a serious mental illness comes to be seen as a hiring advantage, similar to being bilingual. At the Mental Health Center of Boulder County most of the entry-level staff position announcements are posted in the lobby of the agency's offices and clients are encouraged to apply.

THE DEATH OF DAY CARE

Developments in consumer-run programs and community treatment and rehabilitation programs have made traditional day care more or less obsolete. Day care programs are in essence a transfer of the institutional setting to the community. Writing of British practice, psychiatrist Mounir Ekdawi concludes,

> Severely disabled people attending a day unit have often led dependent, institutional lives for many years; nevertheless, it often seems that their past hospital experience was, if anything, richer and more socially stimulating.[54]

For many patients, day care offers close observation, daily medication monitoring and a welcome release from an otherwise aimless existence. These advantages, however, can be achieved, with much greater empowerment and rehabilitative potential, through a combination of intensive outpatient treatment (described above) and a Fountain House style of clubhouse with consumer involvement.

Organizations such as Fountain House, in New York City, and Thresholds, in Chicago, have gained international prominence for establishing a model in which people with mental illness are involved in running a program that meets many of their recreational, social and vocational needs. In these programs, clients are called "members" and work with staff in running the operations of the clubhouse – putting out the daily newsletter, working in the food service, staffing the reception desk or serving in the clubhouse thrift shop (second-hand clothes store). The clubhouse is open in the evenings, on weekends and on holidays, providing a refuge for people who may live in cramped, cheerless housing and sometimes cannot fit in well in other social settings. Psychiatric treatment is definitely not part of the program. Instead the emphasis is on developing work skills and job opportunities for the members.[55]

For example, at the Chinook Clubhouse in Boulder, which is modeled on Fountain House, staff operate a supported employment program, locating jobs for the members in local businesses and training and supporting them as they settle into the new work (see Chapter 11). In preparation for this, the members join clubhouse work groups like those at Fountain House. The program is not for everyone, however; lower-functioning clients are scared off by the emphasis on work and higher-functioning clients are not keen to mingle with other mentally ill people. A substantial number, nevertheless, take part in the program and report a distinct improvement in their quality of life.[56]

Clubhouses with even more consumer involvement have sprung into being. Spiritmenders Community Center in San Francisco's inner city was established by the San Francisco Network of Mental Health Clients. The program is democratically run and is funded and maintained solely by mental health service consumers. It offers a number of activities, a safe place to drop in and socialize (important in the inner city), and education for its members and the general public. It aims to empower its members through peer counseling, advocacy and by fostering self-advocacy. Members clearly do not see the center as being part of the traditional mental health system. As one of the organizers frames their goal: "efforts are made to prevent those situations that force individuals to receive involuntary services and/or other mental health services."[57]

As discussed in Chapter 8, the existential neurosis is a problem that stands in the way of recovery from schizophrenia for people living in the community. To combat this obstacle we can use ingredients of the therapeutic community approach that helped us tackle the institutional syndrome in the postwar decades of the twentieth century – the normalizing effect of small, domestic treatment settings coupled with patient participation in their own treatment and control over their environment. How these ingredients may be added to community care has been discussed in this chapter.

EARLY INTERVENTION IN SCHIZOPHRENIA

Many researchers have expressed the optimistic view that early intervention in schizophrenia will lead to a milder course of illness.[58] This optimism is based on the repeated observation that the duration of untreated psychosis is associated with worse outcome – with an increased risk of relapse,[59] psychosocial decline,[60] prolonged morbidity,[61] increased treatment costs,[62] a worse course of illness,[63] and increased duration of the acute episode.[64] Unfortunately, however, this research is no better than the statistics used by the madhouse proprietors of early nineteenth-century Britain and America (cited in Chapter 5) to show that patients brought in to treatment within the first few weeks of illness were much more likely to recover than those who were admitted after the illness had been present for months or years. Like the madhouse proprietors, present-day early-intervention advocates suggest that delayed treatment has a direct effect in prolonging psychosis. Some have even suggested that untreated psychosis may be toxic to brain function.[65] But the association between prolonged psychosis and poor outcome may not be causative at all. We know from data presented earlier in this book that about half of the first episodes of schizophrenia-like conditions in the Developed World progress to remission.[66] Samples of patients with a long duration of illness will exclude such good-prognosis cases, but patients who progress rapidly to remission will be included in samples with a short duration of psychosis. Early detection samples, therefore, are biased to include more good-prognosis cases.

If the association between duration of untreated psychosis and poor outcome is primarily due to the fact that psychoses of recent onset are more likely to result in remission of symptoms, then we should find that those studies that demonstrate an association between duration of illness and outcome are those that include cases of recent onset. In fact, this is the case. Virtually all the studies showing a positive association use samples with a duration of illness of less than six months;[67] those that exclude such cases do not show an association between duration of untreated psychosis and outcome.[68]

No one, of course, is in favor of late intervention in schizophrenia and there are many reasons to intervene early in psychotic disorders. Doing so is likely to decrease the social disruption for the patient and his or her family, reduce damage to self-respect, family ties and friendships, and help the patient maintain his or her employment, studies and accommodation. On the other hand we have to be careful not to leap in too early and diagnose someone with a long-lasting condition when, in fact, they may only have a psychotic disorder of brief duration. A number of studies have demonstrated that the outcome of early psychosis can be good for many people even if they are not treated with medication.[69] To mistakenly label and treat the person with a brief psychosis as having a long-term disorder may lock him or her into a career as a psychiatric patient unnecessarily.

Comprehensive, or even adequate, treatment services for people with a first episode of psychosis are not universally available, and a focus on early intervention concentrates attention on optimal treatment and increases prospects for improving treatment services more broadly. The positivistic approach of the early-intervention advocates raises optimism in general for the treatment of schizophrenia, increases community awareness and assists in stigma reduction. Even though the theoretical basis for early intervention is weak and it carries the risk of over-treatment of some cases, it has a positive side effect on community attitudes to schizophrenia. There are other ways, however, with which we may tackle the enormous problem of the stigma of schizophrenia.

FIGHTING STIGMA

Although the mentally ill have been in the community for half a century, we have scarcely begun to educate the public about the nature of major mental illness. Community mental health professionals in parts of Italy have taken this challenge far more seriously and have succeeded to a greater extent. Leading up to 1978, when Italy enacted its mental health reform law, daily newspaper articles, radio broadcasts, television interviews, discussions and books involved the general public, politicians and union officials in a debate that was genuinely theirs, not just an issue for psychiatrists.[70] In Trieste, the emptying of the mental hospital in the 1970s was celebrated with a city-wide parade and other festive occasions; the old mental hospital was thrown open to the public for film festivals, repertory theater and art exhibitions;[71] businesses employing the mentally ill are very prominent in the public eye, advertised by brilliantly designed brochures filled with graphic art. These initiatives, writes sociologist Michael Donelly,

> mobilized a wide sympathy and interest among the people of Trieste, and probably displaced at least some of the fears which the breaking down of the asylum walls would otherwise have occasioned.[72]

Can we be as effective as the Italian reformers in tackling stigma?

Neighborhood campaigns

Surveys of public attitudes reveal negative attitudes but also a reservoir of goodwill toward the mentally ill. When neighbors of a new group home for people with mental illness in south London were surveyed, two-thirds expressed a willingness to help the new facility and showed interest in learning more about mental illness.[73] Organizers found that this goodwill could be mobilized by a focused education campaign that encouraged neighbors to initiate social contact with mentally ill residents.[74] During the campaign, informational packets (videotapes and written materials) were distributed, and social events and informal discussion sessions were organized. The campaign decreased fearful and rejecting attitudes and increased contacts between group-home residents and their new neighbors. Thirteen per cent of the neighbors made friends with patients or invited them into their homes, whereas no neighbors did so in an area that was not exposed to the educational program.[75] Campaigns that increase contact with patients can be expected to improve attitudes, since personal knowledge of someone with mental illness is associated with greater tolerance.[76]

Such projects suggest that neighborhood action campaigns are feasible and effective. Can broader social campaigns achieve a similar impact? One approach is to tackle the mass media that shape the public perception of mental illness.

Media-watch groups

Through advocacy groups, we can educate people who work in the news and entertainment media. At a national level such groups can lobby the entertainment media to include positive characters with schizophrenia with the goal of educating the public and changing attitudes toward the illness. Pure entertainment soap operas, for example, can be adapted to incorporate characters with a social message. In the US, a group calling itself the "Soap Summit" analyzes the content of soap operas (looking at such topics as teenage sexual behavior), lobbies script-writers to change the content of their programs to create positive social messages, and measures the impact of their lobbying on soap-opera content. A character with schizophrenia was introduced into the most widely watched program in Britain, "EastEnders" in the 1990s. The National Schizophrenia Fellowship reported that this story-line attracted unprecedented attention and did more to reduce stigma than any number of worthy media appeals. The program humanized the illness and exploded the myths that schizophrenia means someone has a split personality and or that it is likely to make someone violent.[77] In Australia, a character with schizophrenia was inserted into the TV soap opera "Home and Away" in response to lobbying by a consumer group.

Local and national advocacy groups can also lobby the news and entertainment media to exclude negative portrayals of people with schizophrenia. Such groups are known as "stigma-busters" or "media-watch" groups. The stigma-busting approach calls upon members to be alert to stigmatizing messages in any medium and to respond appropriately. The National Stigma Clearinghouse, begun in 1990 by the New York State Alliance for the Mentally Ill, is an example of such a program. The Clearinghouse collects examples of negative portrayals of people with mental illness from across the United States, from television, advertising, films and the print media. Members of the organization write or phone the responsible journalists, editors or others in the media, explaining why the published material is offensive and stigmatizing, and providing more accurate information about mental illness. The group also encourages local organizations to take local action and distributes a monthly newsletter summarizing recent negative media portrayals and the actions taken to inform people at the responsible media source. In this way the group educates other advocates about what kinds of media portrayals to look for and how to correct them.[78]

An example of a successful stigma-busting intervention was the response coordinated by the National Stigma Clearinghouse to the advance publicity for the November 1992 issue of Superman comic reporting that the issue would reveal how Superman was to be killed by "an escapee from an interplanetary insane asylum."[79] The Clearinghouse and other advocacy groups lobbied D.C. Comics, explaining that depicting the killer of the superhero as mentally ill would further add to the stereotype of mentally ill people as evil and violent. When the death issue hit the news-stands the killer was no longer described as an escaped mental patient or a "cosmic lunatic," nor depicted wearing remnants of a strait-jacket.[80]

The National Alliance for the Mentally Ill, in the US, achieved similar success with a coordinated national response to the TV series "Wonderland." In the initial episode of this 1999 TV series, set in a New York psychiatric hospital, mentally ill people were seen committing numerous violent acts, such as stabbing a pregnant psychiatrist with a syringe. Following a NAMI appeal disseminated by e-mail to advocacy groups across the nation, a mass mailing by concerned citizens to the network, the producers and the commercial sponsors led to the show being pulled from the air after two episodes, despite the fact that 13 shows had already been filmed.

A local media-watch group does not need to be large or complex. One or two people can be designated as coordinators. They will establish links, perhaps by e-mail, to a broader group of interested advocacy group members who will immediately report instances of stigmatizing news reporting or entertainment content, whether they be local or national in scope. The coordinators will discuss the issue and devise an appropriate response. They may forward items of national scope to a national stigma-busters group or respond directly to a local newspaper or business.

Stigma-busting groups have to tread a narrow line between educating the media about inaccurate, stigmatizing messages, on the one hand, and, on the other, coming across as intolerant nitpickers. The stigma-busters' response should not be so mild that editors and producers harbor the misconception that their media content is accurate and harmless, nor so fierce that they generate fears of censorship by a vociferous minority group. All groups struggling with stereotypic images, be they based on race, gender or disability status, have to cope with these issues of communication style and strategy. Involving a journalist or other communication professional in the media-watch program can help the group achieve the right balance.

An approach of gradual escalation has shown itself to be effective. Begin with a polite request, perhaps including a suggestion that the stigmatizing reference must have been inadvertent. A positive response should be rewarded with a letter of thanks from the media-watch group. Often those guilty of such an offense are appropriately concerned and may later become supporters of the stigma-watch group. If the offender is unresponsive, increasing pressure can be brought to bear in gradual increments, escalating to a consumer boycott of, say, an offending business, if an appropriate response is not forthcoming.[81]

Social marketing

Modern communications technology gives us more ways to tackle stigma. Since the unsuccessful anti-stigma campaigns of the postwar period (see Chapter 8), public education methods and techniques for health promotion have improved dramatically. Such "social marketing" campaigns, as they are known in the communication field, have been used successfully around the world in reducing infant mortality, AIDS prevention, family planning, improving nutrition, smoking cessation and a variety of other causes.[82] Carefully designed campaigns can have substantial effects on behavior.[83] Effectiveness is increased by "audience segmentation" – partitioning a mass audience into sub-audiences that are relatively homogeneous and devising promotional strategies and messages that are more relevant and acceptable to those target groups.[84]

In developing such campaigns, it is important to conduct a needs assessment that gathers information about cultural beliefs, myths and misapprehensions, and the media through which people would want to learn about the topic. The needs assessment method may incorporate focus groups, telephone surveys and information from opinion leaders. A pre-testing mechanism is then established that allows the promotional strategy to be continuously refined.[85] Initially, specific objectives, audiences, messages and media are selected, and an action plan is drawn up. The messages and materials are pre-tested with the intended target group and revised. The plan is implemented and, with continuous monitoring of impact, a new campaign plan is developed and constantly refined.

Health promotion campaigns aim to heighten awareness and to provide information; the former is possible without the latter, but not the reverse. Awareness campaigns need to be supported by an infrastructure that can link people to sources of information and support – for example, a telephone number to call and trained people to respond to the caller. Ideally, the infrastructure should be a central organization with a local network.

A national anti-stigma campaign

Building on these advances in communication technology, the Defeat Depression Campaign was conducted in Britain between 1991 and 1996 with the goals of reducing the stigma associated with depression, educating the public about the disorder and its treatment, encouraging people to seek treatment early and improving professional treatment expertise. Campaign media directed at the general public included newspaper and magazine articles, television and radio interviews, acknowledgement by celebrities of their own episodes of depression, press conferences, books, leaflets in multiple languages, audio cassettes and a self-help video. A program to educate general practitioners, which included conferences, consensus statements, practice guidelines and training videotapes, was also launched.[86]

The results of the campaign were positive. Knowledge about and attitudes towards depression and its treatment were tested before, during and after the campaign and showed progressive improvement of around five to ten per cent. At all stages of testing, counseling was regarded positively; antidepressants were viewed with suspicion, as being addictive and ineffective, but attitudes towards them improved substantially during the campaign. By the end, members of the general public regarded people suffering from depression as being more worthy of understanding and support, and were more likely to acknowledge the experience of depression in themselves and in close friends. They saw depression as more like other medical disorders and were increasingly positive about general practitioners' capacity to treat the disorder.[87]

Setting up a local anti-stigma program

The World Psychiatric Association (WPA) Programme to Reduce Stigma and Discrimination Because of Schizophrenia, which was launched in the late 1990s, has established a simple process for setting up anti-stigma projects in local communities worldwide.[88] Using social-marketing principles, the steps in creating a local program include:

- setting up a local action committee;
- conducting a local survey of sources of stigma and types of discrimination;
- selecting target groups;

- choosing messages and media for these target groups;
- trying out interventions and testing their impact;
- broadening the scale of intervention; and
- establishing some permanent changes.

The composition of the local action committee is important to the success of a local anti-stigma campaign. People from relevant advocacy groups can be included, along with representatives of potential target groups, such as police and judges, health professionals, high-school students, school teachers or school board members, and journalists. Consumers and family members are especially valuable group members. Members of the action committee have to be willing to devote a fair amount of effort and time to the campaign as most of the work is voluntary. It is useful to include on the action committee one or two prominent citizens with local name recognition. When requesting a meeting with, say, the editorial board of the local newspaper, the presence of someone of prominence increases the impact of the event. A media or public relations professional can also be a valuable committee member. A group of 10 to 20 action committee members is practicable; if the group is large it is possible to split into smaller task groups to develop the action plans for the different target groups.

After conducting a survey of local consumers, family members and other concerned figures, the action committee must select a manageable number of target groups – three is a good number. It is not advisable to target the entire general population – to do so would be expensive and unlikely to have a measurable impact. For each target group the action committee needs to develop realistic goals and objectives. For example, for a group such as high-school students the goals might be to increase awareness about the stigma of mental illness, to increase knowledge and understanding about schizophrenia, and to reduce stigmatizing attitudes. Measurable objectives for high-school students might include:

- make presentations about stigma and schizophrenia to 10 per cent of the high-school students in the district; and
- achieve an improvement in knowledge of 20 per cent and a reduction of social distance (measured by a simple attitudes scale) of 10 per cent among students who hear the presentation.

Based on goals and objectives like these, the action committee should establish some key messages and choose the media that will be used to put them across. In the case of the teenage target group the messages might be, for example:

- Mental illness does not equal violence.
- No one is to blame for mental illness.

- Watch your language. (Don't use objectionable terms, like "nutcase," when referring to someone with mental illness.)

The media to be used in reaching high-school students could include a consumer speakers' bureau, a teachers' guide, the website of the WPA campaign (www.openthedoors.com), an art competition for students to produce anti-stigma materials, posters in the schools and advertisements inside city buses commonly used by teenagers.

In fact, many sites in the WPA global anti-stigma campaign, including Boulder, Colorado, Calgary, Alberta, various sites in Egypt, and several centers in Germany, Austria and England, opted to target high-school students. They proved to be a popular target for a number of reasons: they are the next generation of people with mental illness and those who will stigmatize them; they are easily accessible to an educational campaign; and mental illness is not usually included in the high-school curriculum. The high-school interventions were found to be effective. Pre- and post-testing revealed lasting improvements in knowledge and attitudes at many of these sites.[89]

A local anti-stigma campaign cannot run forever, but some more permanent structures and partnerships can be developed. Examples from the WPA project sites include:

- a change in the high-school health curriculum to include mental illness;
- the creation of a local media-watch group;
- a change in institutional or health service policy, such as establishing emergency-room procedures for the proper evaluation and treatment of people with mental illness; and
- the formation of a consumer speakers' bureau.

A consumer speakers' bureau can be highly effective in addressing school classes, police, organizations of businesspeople and so on. A study from Innsbruck in Austria demonstrated that when mental health professionals addressed high-school students they had no measurable effect on attitudes towards the mentally ill, but when a psychiatrist and consumer spoke to a similar group of students they produced a measurable improvement.[90] Commonly a speakers' bureau will comprise some people who have experienced mental illness, a family member of a mentally ill person and a mental health professional.

People with mental illness can react to the stress of public speaking by experiencing an increase in symptoms shortly after the event. To minimize the likelihood of this reaction it is important to select consumers with good stress-tolerance and, where necessary, gradually introduce them to the speaking experience. In the successful consumer speakers' bureau run by the Partnership Program of the Schizophrenia Society in Calgary, Alberta, potential new speakers initially observe others making a presentation, in later sessions they may speak briefly and eventually they find themselves able to participate fully without stress. Speakers are debriefed after each presentation to see if they found the experience stressful. A fairly large number of speakers are trained so that the demand on any one person is not too great. The coordinator of the Calgary Partnership Program, Fay Herrick, handles many day-to-day issues such as maintaining a diary of engagements, selecting and contacting speakers, debriefing them after each engagement, and asking the host of the event to provide an assessment, but, importantly, she also nurtures a sense of community in the group through regular meetings and celebratory events. Consumers appearing as public speakers demonstrate the reality of recovery. They may educate the listeners about the experience of the psychotic state and problems of stigma and discrimination, but their presence also evinces feelings of compassion and an understanding that mental illness is a human problem that can affect anyone.

A stigma-reducing campaign need not be expensive. A three-year campaign in Boulder cost around $6,000 (£4,000) and was able to have an impact on several different target groups. All the police, probation officers and judges in the county received several hours of education. High-school students were reached through a variety of media including an annual anti-stigma art competition, city bus ads and slides shown in cinemas before the main feature. The editorial boards of the local newspapers were involved in discussions about the fair coverage of mental illness in the news media, and journalists were provided with a list of consumers who were willing to be contacted for human interest when covering mental health issues. The most expensive intervention was the use of cinema slides – $3,000 (£2,000) for a run of three months in ten cinemas – but exit interviews indicated that 16 per cent of people leaving the cinema could remember one of the three messages displayed, adding up to over 10,000 patrons who took away a message over the course of three months.[91]

Similar local campaigns are feasible in any locality, and a manual on how to conduct one is available from Professor Norman Sartorius at the World Psychiatric Association Programme to Reduce Stigma and Discrimination Because of Schizophrenia, Hôpitaux Universitaires de Genève, Département de psychiatrie, Belle-Idée, Bâtiment Salève, 2 chemin du Petit-Bel-Air, 1225 Chêne-Bourg, Geneva, Switzerland.

CONCLUSION

We have far to go before the person with schizophrenia is welcome in Western society and before he or she can view himself or herself as an equal and useful member of society. Until that time schizophrenia is likely to continue to be a malignant condition.

We have the knowledge, nevertheless, to render the illness benign. We would need to:

- treat the acute phase of the illness in small, domestic, non-coercive settings that reflect the humane principles of moral treatment;
- ensure adequate psychological and clinical support in the community, including a full range of independent and supervised, non-institutional accommodation;
- give recognition and support for the care offered by the family of the person with schizophrenia, and provide family education and counseling;
- provide a variety of work opportunities for the mentally disabled – work that is neither too demeaning nor too stressful;
- establish economic incentives to work by increasing the earnings disregard in disability pension schemes or by providing wage subsidies for the severely handicapped;
- encourage economic and social advancement through consumer-cooperative businesses, housing and services;
- fight for the rights of people with schizophrenia and their families to participate as fully integrated members of society, through local action and coordinated efforts to counter the misrepresentations generated by the news and entertainment media;
- use the antipsychotic drugs as a supplement to these measures, not as a substitute for them.

Parts of this plan would be expensive but it may cost little more than our current, vast expenditure on the treatment and support of people with schizophrenia and on the associated disruption, crime and imprisonment that result from inadequate care. Our society is inherently unequal, however, and to provide such a quality of life for the person with schizophrenia is difficult because such a large proportion of the population – including armies of unemployed, homeless and incarcerated people – would be left in worse circumstances. To render schizophrenia benign we may, in essence, have to restructure our provisions for all of the poor.

Notes

INTRODUCTION

1 Harris, M., *Cultural Materialism: The Struggle for a Science of Culture*, New York: Random House, 1979. See also the preface to Marx, K., *A Contribution to the Critique of Political Economy*, New York: International Publishers, 1970; first published 1859.

1 WHAT IS SCHIZOPHRENIA?

1 Lee, R.B., "!Kung bushman subsistence: An input–output analysis," in A.P. Vayda (ed.), *Environment and Cultural Behavior: Ecological Studies in Cultural Anthropology*, Garden City, New York: Natural History Press, 1969, pp. 47–9.
2 This is a broad definition of political economy as is commonly used in anthropology. It is drawn from Harris, M., *Culture, Man, and Nature*, New York: Thomas Y. Crowell, 1971, p. 145. Similarly broad definitions may be found in Lange, O., *Political Economy*, vol. 1, New York: Macmillan, 1959 ("Political economy is concerned with the social laws of production and distribution"); and in Marshall, A., *Principles of Economics*, 8th edn. London: Macmillan, 1920, p.1 ("Economics is a study of mankind in the ordinary business of life: it examines that part of individual and social action which is most closely connected with the attainment and with the use of material requisites of wellbeing").
3 Szasz, T.S., *The Myth of Mental Illness: Foundations of a Theory of Personal Conduct*, revised edn, New York: Harper & Row, 1974.
4 American Psychiatric Association, *Diagnostic and Statistical Manual of Mental Disorders*, 4th edn (DSM-IV), Washington, DC, 1994.
5 Kraepelin, E., *Dementia Praecox and Paraphrenia*, Edinburgh: Livingstone, 1919, pp. 38–43.
6 Leff, J., *Psychiatry Around the Globe: A Transcultural View*, New York: Marcel Dekker, 1981, ch. 5.
7 Bleuler, E., *Dementia Praecox, or the Group of Schizophrenias*, translated by J. Zinkin, New York: International Universities Press, 1950. The German language edition first appeared in 1911.
8 Ibid., pp. 246–7.
9 Ibid., p. 248.
10 Ibid., pp. 258–9.
11 Ibid., p. 471.
12 Ibid., p. 475.
13 Ibid., p. 476.

14 Ibid., p. 471.
15 Ibid., p. 472.
16 Ibid., p. 480.
17 Ibid., p. 478.
18 Ibid., p. 479.
19 Langfeldt, G., "The prognosis in schizophrenia and the factors influencing the course of the disease," *Acta Psychiatrica et Neurologica Scandinavica*, supplement 13, 1937.
20 Leff, *Psychiatry Around the Globe*, pp. 37–40; Wing, J.K., *Reasoning About Madness*, New York: Oxford University Press, 1978.
21 Cooper, J.E., Kendell, J.E., Gurland, B.J. et al., *Psychiatric Diagnosis in New York and London*, Maudsley Monograph Number 20, London: Oxford University Press, 1972.
22 World Health Organization, *The International Pilot Study of Schizophrenia*, vol. 1, Geneva, 1973.
23 Cade, J.F.J., "Lithium salts in the treatment of psychotic excitement," *Medical Journal of Australia*, 36: 349 et seq., 1949.
24 Schou, M., Juel-Nielsen, N., Stromgren, E. and Voldby, H., "The treatment of manic psychoses by the administration of lithium salts," *Journal of Neurology, Neurosurgery and Psychiatry*, 17: 250 et seq., 1954.
25 Fieve, R.R., "Lithium therapy," in H.I. Kaplan, A.M. Freedman and B.J. Sadock (eds), *Comprehensive Textbook of Psychiatry-III*, vol. 3l, Baltimore: Williams & Wilkins, 1980, pp. 2348–52. The reference is to p. 2348.
26 American Psychiatric Association, *Diagnostic and Statistical Manual of Mental Disorders*, 3rd edn (DSM-III), Washington, DC, 1980, pp. 181–203.
27 Taylor, M.A. and Abrams, R., "The prevalence of schizophrenia: A reassessment using modern diagnostic criteria," *American Journal of Psychiatry*, 135: 945–8, 1978; Helzer, J., "Prevalence studies in schizophrenia," presented at the World Psychiatric Association Regional Meeting, New York, October 30–November 3, 1981; Endicott, J., Nee, J., Fleiss, J. et al., "Diagnostic criteria for schizophrenia; Reliabilities and agreement between systems" *Archives of General Psychiatry*, 39: 884–9, 1982; Jablensky, A., Sartorius, N., Ernberg, G. et al., "Schizophrenia: Manifestions, incidence and course in different cultures: A World Health Organization ten-country study," *Psychological Medicine*, supplement 20; Warner, R. and de Girolamo, G., *Epidemiology of Mental Health and Psychosocial Problems: Epidemiology of Schizophrenia*, Geneva: World Health Organization, 1993.
28 Ciompi, L., "Catamnestic long-term study on the course of life and aging of schizophrenics," *Schizophrenia Bulletin*, 6: 606–18, 1980.
29 Jablensky et al., "Schizophrenia: Manifestations, incidence and course."
30 Kiev, A., *Transcultural Psychiatry*, New York: Free Press, 1972, p. 45.
31 Strauss, J.S. and Carpenter, W.T., *Schizophrenia*, New York: Plenum, 1981, ch. 2.
32 Gottesman, I.I., *Schizophrenia Genesis: The Origins of Madness*, New York: W.H. Freeman, 1991, pp. 94–7.
33 Heston, L.L., "Psychiatric disorders in foster-home-reared children of schizophrenic mothers," *British Journal of Psychiatry*, 112: 819–25, 1966; Kety, S.S., Rosenthal, D., Wender, O.H. and Shulsinger, F., "The types and prevalence of mental illness in the biological and adoptive families of adopted schizophrenics," in D. Rosenthal and S.S. Kety (eds), *The Transmission of Schizophrenia*, Oxford: Pergamon, 1968, pp. 345 et seq.; Kety, S.S., Rosenthal, D., Wender, P.H. et al., "Mental illness in the biological and adoptive families of adopted individuals who have become schizophrenic," in R.R. Fieve, D. Rosenthal and H. Brill (eds),

Genetic Research in Psychiatry, Baltimore: Johns Hopkins University Press, 1975, pp. 147 et seq.

34 Gottesman, *Schizophrenia Genesis*, p. 103.

35 Twin studies of the inheritance of schizophrenia are summarized in Gottesman, *Schizophrenia Genesis*, pp. 105–32.

36 Kallman, F.J., "The genetic theory of schizophrenia: An analysis of 691 schizophrenic twin index families," *American Journal of Psychiatry*, 103: 309–22, 1946.

37 Kringlen, E., "An epidemiological-clinical twin study of schizophrenia," in Rosenthal and Kety (eds), *The Transmission of Schizophrenia*, pp. 49 et seq.

38 Straub, R.E., MacLean, C.J., O'Neill F.A. et al., "Support for possible schizophrenia vulnerability locus in region 5q22–31 in Irish families," *Molecular Psychiatry*, 2: 148–55, 1997; Schwab, S.G., Eckstein, G.N., Hallmayer, J. et al., "Evidence suggestive of a locus on chromosome 5q31 contributing to susceptibility of schizophrenia in German and Israeli families by multipoint affected sib-pair linkage analysis," *Molecular Psychiatry*, 2: 156–60, 1997; Wang, S., Sun, C., Walczak, C.A., et al., "Evidence for a susceptibility locus for schizophrenia on chromosome 6pter-p22," *Nature Genetics*, 10: 41–6, 1995; Freedman, R., Coon, H., Myles-Worsley, M. et al., "Linkage of a neurophysiological deficit in schizophrenia to a chromosome 15 locus," *Proceedings of the National Academy of Sciences of the USA*, 94: 587–92, 1997.

39 Meltzer, H.Y. and Stahl, S.M., "The dopamine hypothesis of schizophrenia: A review," *Schizophrenia Bulletin*, 2: 19–76, 1976; Haracz, J.L., "The dopamine hypothesis: An overview of studies with schizophrenic patients," *Schizophrenia Bulletin*, 8: 438–69, 1982.

40 Reynolds, G.P., "Beyond the dopamine hypothesis: The neurochemical pathology of schizophrenia," *British Journal of Psychiatry*, 155: 305–16, 1989; Wyatt, R.J., Alexander, R.C., Egan, M.F. and Kirch, D.G., "Schizophrenia: Just the facts. What do we know, how well do we know it?" *Schizophrenia Research*, 1: 3–18, 1988.

41 Hirsch, S.R. and Weinberger, D.R. (eds) *Schizophrenia*, Oxford: Blackwell Science, 1995; Seeman, P., "Dopamine receptors: Clinical correlates," in F.E. Bloom and D.J. Kupfer (eds) *Psychopharmacology: The Fourth Generation of Progress*, New York: Ravens Press, 1995.

42 Averback, P. "Lesions of the nucleus ansa peduncularis in neuropsychiatric disease," *Archives of Neurology*, 38: 230–5, 1981; Stevens, J.R., "Neuropathology of schizophrenia," *Archives of General Psychiatry*, 39: 1131–9, 1982; Weinberger and Kleinman, "Observations on the brain in schizophrenia," pp. 52–5.

43 Weinberger, D.R., DeLisi, L.E., Perman, G.P. et al., "Computer tomography in schizophreniform disorder and other acute psychiatric disorders," *Archives of General Psychiatry*, 39: 778–83, 1982; Van Horn, J.D. and McManus, I.C. "Ventricular enlargement in schizophrenia: A meta-analysis of studies of the ventricle:brain ratio (VBR)," *British Journal of Psychiatry*, 160: 687–97, 1992; Weinberger and Kleinman, "Observations on the brain in schizophrenia," pp. 43–8; Wyatt et al., "Schizophrenia: Just the facts," p. 12.

44 Weinberger, D.R. and Kleinman, J.E., "Observations on the brain in schizophrenia," in A.J. Frances and R.E. Hales (eds), *Psychiatry Update: American Psychiatric Association Annual Review: Volume 5*, Washington, DC: American Psychiatric Press, 1986, pp. 42–67.

45 Vita, A., Dieci, M., Giobbio, M. et al., "Time course of cerebral ventricular enlargement in schizophrenia supports the hypothesis of its neurodevelopmental nature," *Schizophrenia Research*, 23: 25–30, 1997; Weinberger et al., "Computer tomography in schizophreniform disorder," p.782.

46 Weinberger and Kleinman, "Observations on the brain in schizophrenia," p. 46–7.
47 Weinberger et al., "Computed tomography in schizophreniform disorder," p. 782.
48 McNeil, T.F., "Perinatal influences in the development of schizophrenia," in H. Helmchen and F.A. Henn (eds) *Biological Perspectives of Schizophrenia*, New York: John Wiley, 1987, pp. 125–38.
49 Reveley, A.M., Reveley, M.A., Clifford, C.A. et al., "Cerebral ventricular size in twins discordant for schizophrenia," *Lancet*, 1: 540–1, 1982; Suddath, R.L., Christison, G., Torrey, E.F. et al., "Quantitative magnetic resonance imaging in twin pairs discordant for schizophrenia," *Schizophrenia Research*, 2: 129, 1989.
50 Turetsky, B., Cowell, P.E., Gur, R.C. et al., "Frontal and temporal lobe brain volumes in schizophrenia: Relationship to symptoms and clinical subtype," *Archives of General Psychiatry*, 52: 1061–70, 1995; Weinberger and Kleinman, "Observations on the brain in schizophrenia," p. 47.
51 Bradbury, T.N. and Miller, G.A., "Season of birth in schizophrenia: a review of evidence, methodology and etiology," *Psychology Bulletin*, 98: 569–94, 1985.
52 Eaton, W.W., Day, R. and Kramer, M., "The use of epidemiology for risk factor research in schizophrenia: An overview and methodologic critique," in M.T. Tsuang and J.L. Simpson (eds), *Handbook of Schizophrenia, Volume 3: Nosology, Epidemiology and Genetics*, Amsterdam: Elsevier Science Publishers, 1988.
53 Warner and de Girolamo, *Epidemiology of Schizophrenia*.
54 Beiser, M. and Iacono, W.G., "An update on the epidemiology of schizophrenia," *Canadian Journal of Psychiatry*, 35: 657–68, 1990.
55 Watson, C.G., Kucala, T., Tilleskjor, C. and Jacobs, L., "Schizophrenic birth seasonality in relation to the incidence of infectious diseases and temperature extremes," *Archives of General Psychiatry*, 41: 85–90, 1984; Torrey, E.F., Rawlings, R. and Waldman, I.N., "Schizophrenic births and viral disease in two states," *Schizophrenia Research*, 1: 73–7, 1988; Mednick, S.A., Parnas, J. and Schulsinger, F., "The Copenhagen high-risk project, 1962–1986," *Schizophrenia Bulletin*, 13: 485–95, 1987; O'Callaghan, E., Sham, P., Takei, N. et al., "Schizophrenia after prenatal exposure to 1957 A2 influenza epidemic," *Lancet*, 337: 1248–50; Barr, C.E., Mednick, S.A. and Munk-Jørgensen, P., "Exposure to influenza epidemics during gestation and adult schizophrenia: A 40-year study," *Archives of General Psychiatry*, 47: 869–74, 1990.
56 Kendell, R.E. and Kemp, I.W., "Maternal influenza in the etiology of schizophrenia," *Archives of General Psychiatry*, 46: 878–82, 1989; Bowler, A.E. and Torrey, E.F., "Influenza and schizophrenia: Helsinki and Edinburgh," *Archives of General Psychiatry*, 47: 876–7, 1990.
57 Sham, P.C., O'Callaghan, E., Takei, N. et al., "Schizophrenia following pre-natal exposure to influenza epidemics between 1939 and 1960," *British Journal of Psychiatry*, 160: 461–6, 1992.
58 Sacchetti, E., Calzeroni, A., Vita, A. et al., "The brain damage hypothesis of the seasonality of births in schizophrenia and major affective disorders: Evidence from computerized tomography," *British Journal of Psychiatry*, 160: 390–7, 1992.
59 Joseph, M.H., Frith, C.D. and Waddington, J.L., "Dopaminergic mechanisms and cognitive deficit in schizophrenia: A neurobiological model," *Psychopharmacology*, 63: 273–80, 1979; Strauss and Carpenter, *Schizophrenia*, ch. 7; Freedman, R., Waldo, M., Bickford-Wimer, P. and Nagamoto, H., "Elementary neuronal dysfunctions in schizophrenia," *Schizophrenia Research*, 4: 233–43, 1991.
60 Freedman et al., "Elementary neuronal dysfunctions in schizophrenia," pp. 233–6.
61 Ibid., pp. 238–9.
62 Adler, L.E., Hoffer, L.J., Griffiths, J. et al., "Normalization by nicotine of deficient auditory sensory gating in the relatives of schizophrenics," *Biological Psychiatry*,

32: 607–16, 1992; Freedman et al., "Linkage of a neurophysiological deficit in schizophrenia to a chromosome 15 locus."

63 Franzen, G. and Ingvar, D.H., "Abnormal distribution of cerebral activity in chronic schizophrenia," *Journal of Psychiatric Research*, 12: 199–214, 1983; Weinberger and Kleinman, "Observations on the brain in schizophrenia," pp. 48–52; Steinberg, J.L., Devous, M.D., Paulman, R.G. et al., "Regional cerebral blood flow in first break and chronic schizophrenic patients and normal controls," *Schizophrenia Research*, 17: 229–40, 1995; Sabri, O., Erkwoh, R., Schreckenberger, M. et al., "Regional blood flow and negative/positive symptoms in 24 drug-naïve schizophrenics," *Journal of Nuclear Medicine*, 38: 181–8, 1997.

64 Weinberger and Kleinman, "Observations on the brain in schizophrenia," p. 52.

65 Lawrence, D.H., *Apocalypse and the Writings on Revelation*, Cambridge: Cambridge University Press, 1980, p. 149. *Apocalypse* was first published in 1931.

66 Cooper, D., *The Death of the Family*, New York: Vintage Books, 1971.

67 Fromm-Reichmann, F., "Notes on the development of treatment of schizophrenia by psychoanalytic psychotherapy," *Psychiatry*, 11: 263–73, 1948.

68 Lidz, T., Fleck, S. and Cornelison, A., *Schizophrenia and the Family*, New York: International Universities Press, 1965.

69 Bateson, G., Jackson, D. and Haley, J., "Towards a theory of schizophrenia," *Behavioral Science*, 1: 251–64, 1956.

70 Laing, R.D. and Esterton, A., *Sanity, Madness and the Family: Families of Schizophrenics*, Baltimore: Penguin Books, 1970.

71 Wynne, L.C. and Singer, M., "Thought disorder and family relations," *Archives of General Psychiatry*, 9: 199–206, 1963.

72 Hirsch, S. and Leff, J., *Abnormality in Parents of Schizophrenics*, London: Oxford University Press, 1975.

73 Woodward, J. and Goldstein, M., "Communication deviance in the families of schizophrenics: A comment on the misuse of analysis of covariance," *Science*, 197: 1096–7, 1977.

74 Tienari, P., Lahti, I., Sorri, A. et al., "The Finnish adoptive family study of schizophrenia: Possible joint effects of genetic vulnerability and family environment," *British Journal of Psychiatry*, 155: supplement 5, 29–32, 1989.

75 Brown, G.W., Birley, J.L.T. and Wing, J.K., "Influence of family life on the course of schizophrenic disorders: A replication," *British Journal of Psychiatry*, 121: 241–58, 1972; Vaughn, C.E. and Leff, J.P., "The influence of family and social factors on the course of psychiatric illness: A comparison of schizophrenic and depressed neurotic patients," *British Journal of Psychiatry*, 129: 125–37, 1976; Parker, G. and Hadzi-Pavlovic, D., "Expressed emotion as a predictor of schizophrenic relapse: An analysis of aggregated data," *Psychological Medicine*, 20: 961–5, 1990; Kavanagh, D.J., "Recent developments in expressed emotion and schizophrenia," *British Journal of Psychiatry*, 160: 601–20, 1992.

76 Tarrier, N., Vaughn, C.E., Lader, M.H., and Leff, J.P., "Bodily reaction to people and events in schizophrenics," *Archives of General Psychiatry*, 36: 311–15, 1979; Sturgeon, D., Kuipers, L., Berkowitz, R. et al., "Psychophysiological responses of schizophrenic patients to high and low expressed emotion relatives," *British Journal of Psychiatry*, 138: 40–5, 1981.

77 Warner, R. and Atkinson, M., "The relationship between schizophrenic patients' perceptions of their parents and the course of their illness," *British Journal of Psychiatry*, 153: 344–53, 1988.

78 Brown et al., "Influence of family life on the course of schizophrenic disorders;" Vaughn and Leff, "The influence of family and social factors on the course of psychiatric illness;" Leff, J. and Vaughn, C., "The role of maintenance therapy

and relatives' expressed emotion in relapse in schizophrenia," *British Journal of Psychiatry*, 139: 102–4, 1981.

79 Warner, R., Miklowitz, D. and Sachs-Ericsson, N., "Expressed emotion, patient attributes and outcome in psychosis," presented at Royal College of Psychiatrists Spring Quarterly Meeting, Leicester, April 16–17, 1991.

80 Cheek, F.E., "Family interaction patterns and convalescent adjustment of the schizophrenic," *Archives of General Psychiatry*, 13: 138–47, 1965; Angermeyer, M.C., " 'Normal deviance': Changing norms under abnormal circumstances," presented at the Seventh World Congress of Psychiatry, Vienna, July 11–16, 1983.

81 Wig, N.N., Menon, D.K. and Bedi, H., "Coping with schizophrenic patients in developing countries," presented at the Seventh World Congress of Psychiatry, Vienna, July 11–16, 1983.

82 Brown, G.W. and Birley, J.L.T., "Crises and life changes and the onset of schizophrenia," *Journal of Health and Social Behavior*, 9: 203–14, 1968.

83 Jacobs, S. and Myers, J., "Recent life events and acute schizophrenic psychosis: A controlled study," *Journal of Nervous and Mental Disease*, 162: 75–87, 1976; Ventura, J., Nuechterlein, K.H., Lukoff, D. et al., "A prospective study of stressful life events and schizophrenic relapse," *Journal of Abnormal Psychology*, 98: 407–11, 1989.

84 Day, R., Nielsen, J.A., Korten, G. et al., "Stressful life events preceding the acute onset of schizophrenia: A cross-national study from the world health organization," *Culture, Medicine and Psychiatry*, 11: 123–205, 1987.

85 Norman, M.G. and Malla, A.K., "Stressful life events and schizophrenia. I: A review of the research," *British Journal of Psychiatry*, 162: 161–6, 1989; Beck, J. and Worthen, K., "Precipitating stress, crisis theory, and hospitalization in schizophrenia and depression," *Archives of General Psychiatry*, 26: 123–9, 1972.

86 Ventura J., Nuechterlein, K.H., Hardesty, J.P. and Gitlin M., "Life events and schizophrenic relapse after withdrawal of medication," *British Journal of Psychiatry*, 161: 615–20, 1992.

87 Dohrenwend, B. and Egri, G., "Recent stressful life events and episodes of schizophrenia," *Schizophrenia Bulletin*, 7: 12–23, 1981; Andrews, G. and Tennant, C., "Life event stress and psychiatric illness," *Psychological Medicine*, 8: 545–9, 1978.

2 HEALTH, ILLNESS AND THE ECONOMY

1 Thompson, E.P., *The Making of the English Working Class*, New York: Vintage, 1966, pp. 330–1.

2 Ibid., p. 325.

3 Doyal, L., *The Political Economy of Health*, Boston: South End Press, 1981.

4 Antonovsky, A., "Social class, life expectancy and overall mortality," in E.G. Jaco (ed.), *Patients, Physicians and Illness: A Sourcebook in Behavioral Science and Health*, 2nd edn, New York: Free Press, 1972, pp. 5–30; Lerner, M., "Social differences in physical health," in J. Kosa, A. Antonovsky and I.K. Zola (eds), *Poverty and Health: A Sociological Analysis*, Cambridge, Massachusetts: Harvard University Press, 1969, pp. 69–167.

5 Comstock, G.W., "Fatal arteriosclerotic heart disease, water hardness at home and socioeconomic characteristics," *American Journal of Epidemiology*, 94: 1–8, 1971; Kitagawa, F.M. and Hauser, P.M., *Differential Mortality in the United States: A Study in Socioeconomic Epidemiology*, Cambridge, Massachusetts: Harvard University Press, 1973, pp. 11–33, 78–9; Weinblatt, E., Ruberman, W., Goldberg, J.D. et al., "Relation of education to sudden death after myocardial infarction," *New England Journal of Medicine*, 299: 60–5, 1978; Lown, B., Desilva, R.A, Reich, P.

and Murawski, B.J., "Psychophysiological factors in sudden cardiac death," *American Journal of Psychiatry*, 137: 1325–35, 1980.

6 National Center for Health Statistics, *Health, United States, 2002, with Chartbook on Trends in the Health of Americans*, Hyattsville, Maryland, 2002; National Center for Health Statistics, *Health, United States, 1998, with Socioeconomic Status and Health Chartbook*, Hyattsville, Maryland, 1998.

7 Doyal, *Political Economy of Health*, p.65.

8 *Health, United States, 2002; Health, United States, 1998*.

9 McDonough, J.R., Garrison, G.E. and Hames, C.G., "Blood pressure and hypertensive disease among negroes and whites in Evans County, Georgia" in J. Stamler, R. Stamler and T.N. Pullman (eds), *The Epidemiology of Hypertension*, New York: Grune & Stratton, 1967; Dawber, T.R., Kannel, S.B., Kagan, A. et al., "Environmental factors in hypertension," in Stamler, Stamler and Pullman, *Epidemiology of Hypertension*; Borhani, N.O. and Borkman, T.S., *Alameda County Blood Pressure Study*, Berkeley: California State Department of Public Health, 1968; Shekelle, R.B., Ostfeld, A.M. and Paul, O., "Social status and incidence of coronary heart disease," *Journal of Chronic Disability*, 22: 381–94, 1969; Syme, S.L., Oakes, T.W., Friedman, G.D. et al., "Social class and differences in blood pressure," *American Journal of Public Health*, 64: 619–20, 1974; Hypertension Detection and Follow-up Program Cooperative Group, "Race, education and prevalence of hypertension," *American Journal of Epidemiology*, 106: 352–61, 1977.

10 Schwab, J.J. and Traven, N.D., "Factors related to the incidence of psychosomatic illness," *Psychosomatics*, 20: 307–15, 1979.

11 Eyer, J. and Sterling, P., "Stress-related mortality and social organization," *Review of Radical Political Economics*, 9: 1–44, 1977.

12 Coates, D., Moyer, S. and Wellman, B., "The Yorklea Study of urban mental health: Symptoms, problems and life events," *Canadian Journal of Public Health*, 60: 471–81, 1969.

13 Myers, J.K., Lindenthal, J.J. and Pepper, M.P., "Social class, life events and psychiatric symptoms: A longitudinal study," in B.S. Dohrenwend and B.P. Dohrenwend (eds), *Stressful Life Events: Their Nature and Effects*, New York: Wiley, 1974; Dohrenwend, B.S., "Social status and stressful life events," *Journal of Personal and Social Psychology*, 28: 225–35, 1973.

14 Pearlin, L.I. and Radabaugh, D.W., "Economic strains and coping functions of alcohol," *American Journal of Sociology*, 82: 652–63, 1976.

15 Wilkinson, R.G., Kawachi, I. and Kennedy, B.P., "Mortality, the social environment, crime and violence," in M. Bartley, D. Blane and G.D. Smith (eds), *The Sociology of Health Inequalities*, Oxford: Blackwell, 1998, pp. 19–37; Kawachi, I., "Income inequality and health," in L.F. Berkman and I. Kawachi (eds), *Social Epidemiology*, New York: Oxford University Press, 2000, pp. 76–94.

16 Kaplan, G.A., Pamuk, E., Lynch, J.W. et al., "Income inequality and mortality in the United States: Analysis of mortality and potential pathways," *British Medical Journal*, 312: 999–1003, 1996.

17 Ben-Shlomo, Y., White, I.R. and Marmot, M., "Does the variation in the socioeconomic characteristics of an area affect mortality?" *British Medical Journal*, 312: 1013–14, 1996.

18 Wilkinson, "Mortality, the social environment, crime and violence, p.19; Kawachi, I., 'Income inequality and health,' p. 86.

19 Wilkinson, "Mortality, the social environment, crime and violence," pp. 21–2.

20 Faris, R.E.L. and Dunham, H.W., *Mental Disorders in Urban Areas: An Ecological Study of Schizophrenia and Other Psychoses*, Chicago: University of Chicago Press, 1939.

21 Schroeder, C.W., "Mental disorders in cities," *American Journal of Sociology*, 48: 40–8, 1942.
22 Gerard, D.L. and Houston, L.G., "Family setting and the social ecology of schizophrenia," *Psychiatric Quarterly*, 27: 90–101, 1953.
23 Gardner, E.A. and Babigian, H.M., "A longitudinal comparison of psychiatric service to selected socioeconomic areas of Monroe County, New York," *American Journal of Orthopsychiatry*, 36: 818–28, 1966.
24 Klee, G.D., Spiro E., Bahn, A.K. and Gorwitz, K., "An ecological analysis of diagnosed mental illness in Baltimore," in R.R. Monroe, G.D. Klee and E.B. Brody (eds), *Psychiatric Epidemiology and Mental Health Planning*, Washington, DC: American Psychiatric Association, 1967, pp. 107–48.
25 Sundby, P. and Nyjus, P., "Major and minor psychiatric disorders in males in Oslo: An epidemiological study," *Acta Psychiatrica Scandinavica*, 39: 519–47, 1963.
26 Hare, E.H., "Mental illness and social conditions in Bristol," *Journal of Mental Science*, 102: 349–57, 1956.
27 Clark, R.E., "Psychoses, income and occupational prestige," *American Journal of Sociology*, 54: 433–40, 1949.
28 Hollingshead, A.B. and Redlich, F.C., *Social Class and Mental Illness*, New York: Wiley, 1958.
29 Srole, L., Langner, R.S., Michael, S.T. et al, *Mental Health in the Metropolis: The Midtown Manhattan Study*, (2 vols), New York: McGraw-Hill, 1962.
30 Leighton, D.C., Harding, J.S., Macklin, D.B. et al., *The Character of Danger: Psychiatric Symptoms in Selected Communities*, New York: Basic Books, 1963, pp. 279–94.
31 Ödegard, Ö., "The incidence of psychoses in various occupations," *International Journal of Social Psychiatry*, 2: 85–104, 1956.
32 Stein, L., " 'Social class' gradient in schizophrenia," *British Journal of Preventive and Social Medicine*, 11: 181–95, 1957.
33 Eaton, W.W., "Epidemiology of schizophrenia," *Epidemiologic Reviews*, 7: 105–26, 1985.
34 Goldberg, E.M. and Morrison, S.L., "Schizophrenia and social class," *British Journal of Psychiatry*, 109: 785–802, 1963.
35 Turner, R.J. and Wagenfeld, M.O., "Occupational mobility and schizophrenia: An assessment of the social causation and social selection hypotheses," *American Sociological Review*, 32: 104–13, 1967.
36 Turner and Wagenfeld, "Occupational mobility and schizophrenia."
37 Kohn, "Social class and schizophrenia: A critical review and a reformulation," *Schizophrenia Bulletin*, 7: 60–79, 1973, p. 62.
38 Bloom, B.L. "An ecological analysis of psychiatric hospitalizations," *Multivariate Behavioral Research*, 3: 423–64, 1968.
39 Goodman, A.B., Siegel, C., Craig, T.J. and Shang, P.L., "The relationship between socioeconomic class and prevalence of schizophrenia, alcoholism, and affective disorders treated by inpatient care in a suburban area," *American Journal of Psychiatry*, 140: 166–70, 1983.
40 Leighton, D.C., Hagnell, O., Leighton, A.H. et al., "Psychiatric disorder in a Swedish and a Canadian community: An exploratory study," *Social Science and Medicine*, 5: 189–209, 1971.
41 Brown, G.W., Davidson, S., Harris, T. et al., "Psychiatric disorder in London and North Uist," *Social Science and Medicine*, 11: 367–77, 1977; Rutter, M., Yule, B., Quinton, D. et al., "Attainment and adjustment in two geographical areas: III. Some factors accounting for area differences," *British Journal of Psychiatry*, 126: 520–9, 1975.

42 Nielsen, J. and Nielsen, J.A., "A census study of mental illness in Samsö," *Psychological Medicine*, 7: 491–503, 1977.

43 Ray, I., "Statistics of insanity in Massachusetts," *North American Review*, 82: 79–81, 1856.

44 White, W.A., "The geographical distribution of insanity in the United States," *Journal of Nervous and Mental Disease*, 30: 257–79, 1903, p. 276.

45 Pollock, H.M. and Noland, W.J., "Mental disease in cities, villages and rural districts of New York State, 1915–1920," *State Hospital Quarterly*, 7: 38–65, 1921; Malzberg, B., "The prevalence of mental diseases in the urban and rural populations of New York State," *Psychiatric Quarterly*, 9: 35–87, 1935.

46 Frumkin, R.M., "Comparative rates of mental illnesses for urban and rural populations in Ohio," *Rural Sociology*, 19: 70–2, 1954; Jaco, E.G., *The Social Epidemiology of Mental Disorders: A Psychiatric Study of Texas*, New York: Russell Sage Foundation, 1960; Eaton, W.W., "Residence, social class and schizophrenia," *Journal of Health and Social Behavior*, 15: 289–99, 1974.

47 Torrey, E.F. and Bowler, A., "Geographical distribution of insanity in America: Evidence for an urban factor," *Schizophrenia Bulletin*, 16: 591–604, 1990.

48 Lewis, G., David, A., Andreasson, S. et al., "Schizophrenia and city life," *Lancet*, 340: 137–40, 1992; Takei, N., Sham, P.C., O'Callaghan, E. et al., "Schizophrenia: increased risk associated with winter and city birth – a case control study in 12 regions within England and Wales," *Journal of Epidemiology and Community Health*, 49: 106–7, 1995.

49 Mortensen, P.B., Pedersen, C.B., Westergaard, T. et al., "Effects of family history and place and season of birth on the risk of schizophrenia," *New England Journal of Medicine*, 340: 603–8, 1999.

50 Mandel, E., *Long Waves of Capitalist Development: The Marxist Interpretation*, Cambridge: Cambridge University Press, 1980; Saul, S.B., *The Myth of the Great Depression, 1873–1896*, London: Macmillan, 1969; Church, R.A., *The Great Victorian Boom, 1850–1873*, London: Macmillan, 1975.

51 Willcox, W.G., "A study in vital statistics," *Political Science Quarterly*, 8 (1), 1893.

52 Hooker, R.H., "On the correlation of the marriage rate with foreign trade," *Journal of the Royal Statistical Society*, 64: 485, 1901.

53 Ogburn, W.F. and Thomas, D.S., "The influence of the business cycle on certain social conditions," *Journal of the American Statistical Association*, 18: 324–40, 1922.

54 Thomas, D.S., *Social Aspects of the Business Cycle*, New York: Gordon & Breach, 1968. First published by Knopf in 1927.

55 Catalano, R. and Dooley, C.D., "Economic predictors of depressed mood and stressful life events in a metropolitan community," *Journal of Health and Social Behavior*, 18: 292–307, 1977; Dooley, D. and Catalano, R., "Economic, life, and disorder changes: Time-series analyses," *American Journal of Community Psychology*, 7: 381–96, 1979.

56 Dooley and Catalano, op. cit., p. 393.

57 Dooley, D., Catalano, R., Jackson, R. and Brownell, A., "Economic, life, and symptom changes in a nonmetropolitan community," *Journal of Health and Social Behavior*, 22: 144–54, 1981.

58 Ibid.

59 Gore, S., "The effect of social support in moderating the health consequences of unemployment," *Journal of Health and Social Behavior*, 19: 157–65, 1978.

60 Brenner, M.H., *Estimating the Social Costs of National Economic Policy: Implications for Mental and Physical Health, and Criminal Aggression*, prepared for the Joint Economic Committee of the Congress of the United States, Washington, DC: US Government Printing Office, 1976.

61 Ibid., p. 41.

62 Ibid., p. 39.

63 Kasl, S.V., "Mortality and the business cycle: Some questions about research strategies when utilizing macro-social and ecological data," *American Journal of Public Health*, 69: 784–8, 1979, p. 786.

64 Mandel, E., *Marxist Economic Theory*, vol.1, translated by B. Pearcel, New York: Monthly Review Press, 1968, ch. 11.

65 Samuelson, P.A., *Economics*, 11th edn, New York: McGraw-Hill, 1980, ch. 14.

66 Eyer and Sterling, "Stress-related mortality;" Eyer, J., "Prosperity as a cause of death," *International Journal of Health Services*, 7: 125–50, 1977; Eyer, J., "Does unemployment cause the death rate peak in each business cycle? A multifactor model of death rate change," *International Journal of Health Services*, 7: 625–62, 1977.

67 Eyer and Sterling, "Stress-related mortality."

68 Bunn, A.R., "Ischaemic heart disease mortality and the business cycle in Australia," *American Journal of Public Health*, 69: 772–81, 1979.

69 Brenner, M.H., "Fetal, infant, and maternal mortality during periods of economic instability," *International Journal of Health Services*, 3: 145–59, 1973.

70 Hewitt, M., *Wives and Mothers in Victorian Industry*, Westport, Connecticut: Greenwood Press, 1958, pp. 115–16.

71 Ibid., chs. 2,3,8,9,10.

72 Thomas, *Social Aspects of the Business Cycle*, footnote on p. 111.

73 Kinnersly, P., *The Hazards of Work: How to Fight Them*, London: Pluto Press, 1973, cited in Doyal, *Political Economy of Health*, p. 67.

74 *Health, United States, 1998*.

75 Doyal, *Political Economy of Health*, p. 74.

76 Lown et al., "Sudden cardiac death;" Rahe, R.H., Bennett, L., Rorio, M. et al., "Subjects' recent life changes and coronary heart disease in Finland," *American Journal of Psychiatry*, 130: 1222–6, 1973.

77 Rabkin, S.W., Mathewson, F.A.L. and Tate, R.B., "Chronobiology of cardiac sudden death in men," *Journal of the American Medical Association*, 244: 1357–8, 1980, p. 1358.

78 Rogot, E., Fabsitz, R. and Feinleib, M., "Daily variation in USA mortality," *American Journal of Epidemiology*, 103: 198–211, 1976.

79 Russek, H.I. and Zohman, B.L., "Relative significance of heredity, diet and occupational stress in coronary heart disease of young adults," *American Journal of Medical Science*, 235: 266–77, 1958.

80 Liljefors, I. and Rahe, R.H., "An identical twin study of psychosocial factors in coronary heart disease in Sweden," *Psychosomatic Medicine*, 32: 523 et seq., 1970; Theorell, T. and Rahe, R.H., "Behavior and life satisfaction characteristics of Swedish subjects with myocardial infarction," *Journal of Chronic Disability*, 25: 139 et seq., 1972; Floderus, B., "Psycho-social factors in relation to coronary heart disease and associated risk factors," *Nordisk Hygienisk Tidskrift*, Supplement 6, 1974.

81 Friedman, M., Rosenman, R.H. and Carroll, V., "Changes in the serum cholesterol and blood clotting time in men subjected to cyclic variation of occupational stress," *Circulation*, 17: 852–61, 1958.

82 Theorell, T., "Life events before and after the onset of a premature myocardial infarction," in Dohrenwend and Dohrenwend, *Stressful Life Events*, pp. 101–17.

83 Theorell, T., Lind, E. and Floderus, B., "The relationship of disturbing life-changes and emotions to the early development of myocardial infarction and other serious illnesses," *International Journal of Epidemiology*, 4: 281–93, 1975.

84 Haynes, S.G., Feinleib, M., Levine, S. et al., "The relationship of psychosocial factors to coronary heart disease in the Framingham Study: II. Prevalence of coronary heart disease," *American Journal of Epidemiology*, 107: 384–402, 1978.

85 Senate Bill 3916 (1972) sought

> to provide for research for solutions to the problems of alienation among American workers in all occupations and industries and technical assistance to those companies, unions, State and local governments seeking to find ways to deal with the problem.

Quoted in Rubin, L.B., *Worlds of Pain: Life in the Working Class Family*, New York: Basic Books, 1976, footnote on p. 233.

86 Marx, K., *The Economic and Philosophic Manuscripts of 1844*, New York: International Publishers, 1964; Novack, G., "The problem of alienation" in E. Mandel and G. Novack (eds), *The Marxist Theory of Alienation*, New York: Pathfinder Press, 1973, pp. 53–94; Ollman, B., *Alienation: Marx's Conception of Man in Capitalist Society*, Cambridge: Cambridge University Press, 1971.

87 Garson, B., *All the Livelong Day: The Meaning and Demeaning of Routine Work*, New York: Penguin, 1977, p. 95.

88 Ibid., p. 88.

89 Ibid., p. 204.

90 Terkel, S., *Working*, New York: Avon, 1975, p. 2.

91 Ibid., p. 3.

92 Rubin, *Worlds of Pain*, p. 169.

93 Ibid., p. 183.

94 Jahoda, M. and Rush, H., *Work, Employment and Unemployment*, University of Sussex Science Policy Research Unit Occasional Paper, no. 12, Brighton: University of Sussex, 1980, pp. 15–16.

95 Kornhauser, A., *Mental Health of the Industrial Worker: A Detroit Study*, New York: Wiley, 1965, p. 270.

96 Jahoda and Rush, *Work, Employment and Unemployment*, pp. 16–17.

97 Kornhauser, *Mental Health of the Industrial Worker*, pp. 260–2.

98 Kohn, M.L. and Schooler, C., "Occupational experience and psychological functioning: An assessment of reciprocal effects," *American Sociological Review*, 38: 97–118, 1973.

99 Dalgard, O.S., "Occupational experience and mental health, with special reference to closeness of supervision," *Psychiatry and Social Science*, 1: 29–42, 1981.

100 Kasl, S.V., "Changes in mental health status associated with job loss and retirement," in Barrett, Rose and Klerman, *Stress and Mental Disorder*, pp. 179–200. The reference is to pp. 182–3.

101 Ibid.; Kasl, S.V. and Cobb, S., "Blood pressure changes in men undergoing job loss: A preliminary report," *Psychosomatic Medicine*, 22: 19–38, 1970.

102 Liem, R. and Rayman, P., "Health and social costs of unemployment: Research and policy considerations," *American Psychologist*, 37: 1116–23, 1982.

103 Little, C., "Technical-professional unemployment: Middle-class adaptability to personal crisis," *Sociological Quarterly*, 17: 262–74, 1976.

104 Eisenberg, P. and Lazarsfeld, P.F., "The psychological effects of unemployment," *Psychological Bulletin*, 35: 358–90, 1938.

105 Liem and Rayman, "Health and social costs of unemployment," p. 1120.

106 Strangle, W.G., "Job loss: A psychological study of worker reactions to a plant closing in a company town in Southern Appalachia," Doctoral dissertation,

School of Industrial and Labor Relations, Cornell University, Ithaca, New York, 1977.

107 Warr, P., "Studies of psychological wellbeing," presented at the British Psychological Society Symposium on Unemployment, London, 1980.

108 Parnes, H.S. and King, R., "Middle-aged job loser," *Industrial Gerontology*, 4: 77–95, 1977.

109 Lahelma, E., "Unemployment and mental wellbeing: Elaboration of the relationship," *International Journal of Health Services*, 22: 261–74, 1992.

110 Studnicka, M., Studnicka-Benke, A., Wögerbauer, G. et al., "Psychological Health, self-reported physical health and health service use: Risk differential observed after one year of unemployment," *Social Psychiatry and Psychiatric Epidemiology*, 26: 86–91, 1991.

111 Hendry, L.B., Shucksmith, J. and Love, J.G., *Lifechances: Developing Adolescent Lifestyles*, London: Routledge, 1991.

112 Warr, P., Jackson, P. and Banks, M., "Unemployment and mental health: Some British studies," *Journal of Social Issues*, 44: 47–68, 1988.

113 Kessler, R.C., Turner, J.B. and House, J.S., "Effects of unemployment on health in a community survey: Main, modifying, and mediating effects," *Journal of Social Issues*, 44: 69–85, 1988.

114 Brenner, S.-E. and Starrin, B., "Unemployment and health in Sweden: Public Issues and private troubles," *Journal of Social Issues*, 44: 125–40, 1988.

115 Theorell, Lind and Flodérus, "Disturbing life changes."

116 Coates, Moyer and Wellman, "The Yorklea Study."

117 Eyer and Sterling, "Stress-related mortality." Brenner, *Social Costs of National Economic Policy*; Henry, A.F. and Short, J.F., *Suicide and Homicide*, Glencoe, Illinois: Free Press, 1954; Vigderhous, G. and Fishman, G., "The impact of unemployment and familial integration on changing suicide rates in the U.S.A., 1920–1969," *Social Psychiatry*, 13: 239–48, 1978; Hamermesh, D.S. and Soss, N.M., "An economic theory of suicide," *Journal of Political Economy*, 82: 83–98, 1974; Ahlburg, D.A. and Shapiro, M.O., "The darker side of unemployment," *Hospital and Community Psychiatry*, 34: 389, 1983.

118 Vigderhous and Fishman, "Impact of unemployment;" Ahlburg and Shapiro, "The darker side of unemployment."

119 Dooley, D., Catalano, R., Rook, K. and Serxner, S., "Economic stress and suicide: Multilevel analyses. Part I: Aggregate time-series analyses of economic stress and suicide," *Suicide and Life-Threatening Behavior*, 19: 321–36, 1989.

120 Pierce, A., "The economic cycle and the social suicide rate," *American Sociological Review*, 32: 457–62, 1967.

121 Personal communication from J.P. Marshall to D. Dooley and R. Catalano, cited in Dooley, D., and Catalano, R., "Economic change as a cause of behavioral disorder," *Psychological Bulletin*, 87: 450–68, 1980, p. 455; Yang, B. "The economy and suicide: A time-series study of the USA," *American Journal of Economics and Sociology*, 51: 87–99, 1992.

122 Durkheim, E., *Suicide*, Glencoe, Illinois: Free Press, 1951, p. 243.

123 Hamermesh and Soss, "An economic theory of suicide."

124 Powell, E., "Occupation, status and suicide: Towards a redefinition of anomie," *American Social Review*, 22: 131–9, 1958.

125 Resnik, N.L.P. and Dizmang, L.H., "Observations on suicidal behavior among American Indians," *American Journal of Psychiatry*, 127: 58–63, 1971.

126 Dublin, L.I., *Suicide: A Sociological and Statistical Study*, "New York: Ronald Press, 1963, ch. 8; Hamermesh and Soss, "An economic theory of suicide"; *Health, United States, 1998*.

127 Yap, R.M., "Aging and mental health in Hong Kong," in R.H. Williams (ed.), *Processes of Aging: Social and Psychological Perspectives*, vol. 2, New York: Atherton, 1963, pp. 176–91.

128 Lendrum, F.C., "A thousand cases of attempted suicide," *American Journal of Psychiatry*, 13: 479–500, 1933; Sainsbury, P., *Suicide in London: An Ecological Study*, London: Chapman & Hall, 1955; Morris, J.B., Kovacs, M., Beck, A. and Wolffe, S., "Notes towards an epidemiology of urban suicide," *Comprehensive Psychiatry*, 15: 537–47, 1974; Sanborn, D.E., Sanborn, C.J. and Cimbolic, P., "Occupation and suicide," *Diseases of the Nervous System*, 35: 7–12, 1974; Shepherd, D.M. and Barraclough, B.M., "Work and suicide: An empirical investigation," *British Journal of Psychiatry*, 136: 469–78, 1980.

129 Olsen, J. and Lajer, M. "Violent death and unemployment in two trade unions in Denmark," *Social Psychiatry*, 14: 139–45, 1979.

130 Breed, W., "Occupational mobility and suicide among white males," *American Sociological Review*, 28: 179–88, 1963; Portersfield, A.L. and Gibbs, J.P., "Occupational prestige and social mobility of suicides in New Zealand," *American Journal of Sociology*, 66: 147–52, 1960; Sanborn, Sanborn and Cimbolic, "Occupation and suicide;" Shepherd and Barraclough, "Work and suicide."

131 Platt, S., "Unemployment and suicidal behaviour: A review of the literature," *Social Science and Medicine*, 19: 93–115, 1984.

132 Tuckman, J. and Labell, M., "Study of suicide in Philadelphia," *Public Health Reports*, 73: 547–53, 1958; Shepherd and Barraclough, "Work and suicide;" Fruensgaard, K., Bejaminsen, S., Joensen, S. and Helstrup, K., Psychosocial characteristics of a group of unemployed patients consecutively admitted to a psychiatric emergency department," *Social Psychiatry*, 18: 137–44, 1983.

133 Rogot, Fabsitz and Feinleib, "Daily variation in USA mortality;" Baldamus, W., *The Structure of Sociological Inference*, New York: Barnes & Noble, 1976, p. 94. Curiously, Baldamus presented the data on the daily frequency of suicide declining from Monday to Sunday as an example of a phenomenon that defies explanation. This, he argued, is because of "the difficulty of visualizing a characteristic quality inherent in each day of the week." His experience of the work week was clearly different from that of the average working person.

134 Brenner, M.H., *Mental Illness and the Economy*, Cambridge, Massachusetts: Harvard University Press, 1973.

135 Pollock, H.M., "The Depression and mental disease in New York State," *American Journal of Psychiatry*, 91: 736–71, 1935; Mowrer, E.R., "A study of personal disorganization," *American Sociological Review*, 4: 475–87, 1939; Dayton, N.A., *New Facts on Mental Disorders: Study of 89,190 Cases*, Springfield, Illinois: Charles C. Thomas, 1940; Dunham, H.W., *Sociological Theory and Mental Disorder*, Detroit, Michigan: Wayne State University Press, 1959; Pugh, T.F. and MacMahon, B., *Epidemiologic Findings in the United States Mental Hospital Data*, Boston: Little, Brown, 1962.

136 Brenner, *Mental Illness and the Economy*, p. 45.

137 Marshall, J.R. and Funch, D.P., "Mental illness and the economy: A critique and partial replication," *Journal of Health and Social Behavior*, 20: 282–9, 1979.

138 Dear, M., Clark, G. and Clark, S., "Economic cycles and mental health care policy: An examination of the macro-context for social service planning," *Social Science and Medicine*, 136: 43–53, 1979.

139 Ahr, P.R., Gorodezky, M.J. and Cho, D.W., "Measuring the relationship of public psychiatric admissions to rising unemployment," *Hospital and Community Psychiatry*, 32: 398–401, 1981.

140 Parker, J.J., "Community mental health center admissions and the business cycle:

A longitudinal study," Doctoral dissertation, Department of Sociology, University of Colorado, Boulder, 1979.

141 Brenner, *Mental Illness and the Economy*, ch. 9.

142 Ahr, Gorodezky and Cho, "Public psychiatric admissions;" Draughon, M., "Relationship between economic decline and mental hospital admissions continues to be significant," *Psychological Reports*, 36: 882, 1975.

3 RECOVERY FROM SCHIZOPHRENIA

1 Strecker, H.P., "Insulin treatment of schizophrenia," *Journal of Mental Science*, 84: 146–55, 1938; Freyhan, F.A., "Course and outcome of schizophrenia," *American Journal of Psychiatry*, 112: 161–7, 1955; Leiberman, D.M., Hoenig, J. and Auerback, I., "The effect of insulin coma and E.C.T. on the three year prognosis of schizophrenia," *Journal of Neurology, Neurosurgery and Psychiatry*, 20: 108–13, 1957; Ödegard, Ö., "Changes in the prognosis of functional psychoses since the days of Kraepelin," *British Journal of Psychiatry*, 113: 813–22, 1967.

2 Kelly, D.H.W. and Sargant, W., "Present treatment of schizophrenia: A controlled follow-up study," *British Medical Journal*, 2: 147–50, 1965; Holmboe, R., Noreik, K. and Astrup, C., "Follow-up of functional psychoses at two Norwegian mental hospitals," *Acta Psychiatrica Scandinavica*, 44: 298–310, 1968; Gross, G. and Huber, G., "Zur Prognose der Schizophrenien," *Psychiatrica Clinica* (Basel), 6: 1–16, 1973; Cottman, S.B. and Mezey, A.G. "Community care and the prognosis of schizophrenia," *Acta Psychiatrica Scandinavica*, 53: 95–104, 1976; Bland, R.C., Parker, J.H. and Orn, H., "Prognosis in schizophrenia; Prognostic predictors and outcome," *Archives of General Psychiatry*, 35: 72–7, 1978.

3 Lehmann, H.E., "Schizophrenia: Clinical features," in H.I. Kaplan, A.M. Freedman and B.J. Sadock (eds), *Comprehensive Textbook of Psychiatry-III*, Baltimore: Williams & Wilkins, 1980, p. 1187.

4 Hegarty, J.D., Baldessarini, R.J., Tohen, M. et al., "One hundred years of schizophrenia: A meta-analysis of the outcome literature," *American Journal of Psychiatry*, 151: 1409–16, 1994.

5 Horwitz, W.A. and Kleinman, C., "Survey of cases discharged from the Psychiatric Institute and Hospital," *Psychiatric Quarterly*, 10: 72–85, 1936; Henisz, J., "A follow-up study of schizophrenic patients," *Comprehensive Psychiatry*, 7: 524–8, 1966; Bockoven, J.S. and Solomon, H.C., "Comparison of two five-year follow-up studies: 1947 to 1952 and 1967 to 1972," *American Journal of Psychiatry*, 132: 796–801, 1975; Harrow, M., Grinker, R.R., Silverstein, M.L. and Holzman, P., "Is modern-day schizophrenic outcome still negative?" *American Journal of Psychiatry*, 135: 1156–62, 1978.

6 Stephens, J.H., "Long-term prognosis and follow-up in schizophrenia," *Schizophrenia Bulletin*, 4: 25–47, 1978.

7 Bleuler, M., "A 23-year longitudinal study of 208 schizophrenics and impressions in regard to the nature of schizophrenia," in D. Rosenthal, and S.S. Kety (eds), *The Transmission of Schizophrenia*, Oxford: Pergamon, 1968, p. 3.

8 Ibid., p. 5.

9 Ibid., p. 6.

10 The studies included in Table 3.1 are listed in the general bibliography.

11 Kirchhof, T., *Geschichte der Psychiatrie*, Leipzig: Franz Deuticke, 1912.

12 Source of unemployment statistics: US, 1881–9, Ever, J. and Sterling, P., "Stress-related mortality and social organization," *Review of Radical Political Economics*, 9: 1–44, 1977; 1890–1970, US Bureau of the Census, *Historical Statistics of the*

United States: Colonial Times to 1970: Part I, Washington, DC: 1975; 1970–1985, US Bureau of the Census, *Statistical Abstract of the United States: 1990*, Washington, DC: 1990; UK, 1881–7, Mitchell, B.R. and Deane, P., *Abstract of British Historical Statistics*, Cambridge: Cambridge University Press, 1962; 1888–1970, Mitchell, B.R., *European Historical Statistics, 1750–1970*, New York: Columbia University Press, 1978; 1970–1985, Organisation for Economic Cooperation and Development, *Labour Force Statistics*, Paris: 1992.

13 Hegarty, "One hundred years of schizophrenia."

14 Lehmann, "Schizophrenia: Clinical features," p. 1178.

15 American Psychiatric Association, *Diagnostic and Statistical Manual of Mental Disorder*, 3rd edn, (DSM-III), Washington, DC, 1980.

4 DEINSTITUTIONALIZATION

1 Davis, J.M., "Organic therapies," in H.I. Kaplan, A.M. Freedman and B.J. Sadock (eds), *Comprehensive Textbook of Psychiatry-III*, Baltimore: Williams & Wilkins, 1981, pp. 2257–89. The quotation is on p. 2257.

2 Ödegard, Ö., "Pattern of discharge from Norwegian psychiatric hospitals before and after the introduction of the psychotropic drugs," *American Journal of Psychiatry*, 120: 772–8, 1964.

3 Norton, A., "Mental hospital ins and outs: A survey of patients admitted to a mental hospital in the past 30 years," *British Medical Journal*, i: 528–36, 1961.

4 Shepherd, M., Goodman, N. and Watt, D.C., "The application of hospital statistics in the evaluation of pharmacotherapy in a psychiatric population," *Comprehensive Psychiatry*, 2: 11–19, 1961.

5 Lewis, A., untitled paper, in R.B. Bradley, P. Deniker and C. Radouco-Thomas (eds) *Neuropsychopharmacology*, vol. 1, Amsterdam: Elsevier, 1959, pp. 207–12, cited in Scull, A., *Decarceration: Community Treatment and the Deviant — A Radical View*, Englewood Cliffs, New Jersey: Prentice-Hall, 1977, p. 82.

6 Pugh, T.F. and MacMahon, B., *Epidemiologic Findings in United States Mental Hospital Data*, Boston: Little, Brown, 1962.

7 Chittick, R.A., Brooks, G.W. and Deane, W.N., *Vermont Project for the Rehabilitation of Chronic Schizophrenic Patients: Progress Report*, Vermont State Hospital, 1959, cited in Scull, *Decarceration*, p. 82.

8 Epstein, L.J., Morgan, R.D. and Reynolds, L., "An approach to the effect of ataraxic drugs on hospital release rates," *American Journal of Psychiatry*, 119: 36–45, 1962.

9 Linn, E.L., "Drug therapy, milieu change, and release from a mental hospital," *Archives of Neurology and Psychiatry*, 81: 785–94, 1959.

10 Brill, H. and Patton, R.E., "Analysis of population reduction in New York State mental hospitals during the first four years of large-scale therapy with psychotropic drugs," *American Journal of Psychiatry*, 116: 495–509, 1959, p. 495.

11 Scull, *Decarceration*, p. 83.

12 Davis, "Organic therapies," p. 2257.

13 Freudenberg, R.K., Bennet, D.H. and May, A.R., "The relative importance of physical and community methods in the treatment of schizophrenia," in *International Congress of Psychiatry, Zurich, 1957*, Fussli, 1959, pp. 157–78. The quotation is on p. 159.

14 All of the information in this paragraph is from Clark, D.H., *Social Therapy in Psychiatry*, Baltimore: Penguin, 1974, pp. 22–5; and Langsley, D.G., "Community psychiatry," in Kaplan, Freedman and Sadock *Comprehensive Textbook of Psychiatry*, pp. 2836–53. The reference is to pp. 2839–40.

15 Jones, M., *Social Psychiatry in Practice*, Baltimore: Penguin, 1968, p. 17; Clark, *Social Therapy in Psychiatry*, p. 29.

16 Clark, *Social Therapy in Psychiatry*, pp. 25–6.

17 Ödegard, "Pattern of discharge," p. 776.

18 Rathod, N.H., "Tranquillizers and patients' environment," *Lancet*, i: 611–13. 1958.

19 The statistics in this paragraph are from Scull, *Decarceration*, p. 149.

20 Bassuk, E.L. and Gerson, S., "Deinstitutionalization and mental health services," *Scientific American*, 238(2): 46–53, February 1978, p. 50.

21 These examples are from Langsley, "Community psychiatry," p. 2847; and Lamb, H.R. and Goertzel, V., "The demise of the state hospital: A premature obituary?" *Archives of General Psychiatry*, 26: 489–95, 1972.

22 Lehman, A.F., Ward, N.C. and Linn, L.S., "Chronic mental patients: The quality of life issue," *American Journal of* Psychiatry, 139: 1271–6, 1982.

23 Lamb, H.R., "The new asylums in the community," *Archives of General Psychiatry*, 36: 129–34, 1979.

24 Van Putten, T. and Spar, J.E., "The board and care home: Does it deserve a bad press?" *Hospital and Community Psychiatry*, 30: 461–4, 1979, pp. 461–2.

25 Bassuk and Gerson, "Deinstitutionalization," p. 49.

26 Morgan, C.H., "Service delivery models." Prepared for the Special National Workshop on Mental Health Services in Local Jails, Baltimore, Maryland, September 27–9, 1978; Gibbs, J.J., "Psychological and behavioral pathology in jails: A review of the literature," presented at the Special National Workshop on Mental Health Services in Local Jails, 1978; Olds, E., *A Study of the Homeless, Sick and Alcoholic Persons in the Baltimore City Jail*, Baltimore: Baltimore Council of Social Agencies, 1956; Arthur Bolton Associates, Report to the California State Legislature, October 1976; Swank, G.E. and Winer, D., "Occurrence of psychiatric disorder in a county jail population," *American Journal of Psychiatry*, 133: 1331–6, 1976; unidentified author, "Mental ill inmates untreated, says GAO," *Psychiatric News*, February 6, 1981, p. 1; Torrey, E.F., Stieber, J., Ezekiel, J. et al., *Criminalizing the Seriously Mentally Ill: The Abuse of Jails as Mental Hospitals*, Washington, DC: Public Citizens Health Research Group, 1992, p. iv.

27 Roth, L.H. and Ervin, F.R., "Psychiatric care of federal prisoners," *American Journal of Psychiatry*, 128: 424–30, 1971.

28 Rollin, H., "From patients into vagrants," *New Society*, January 15, 1970, pp. 90–3.

29 Tidmarsh, D. and Wood, S., "Psychiatric aspects of destitution: A study of the Camberwell Reception Centre," in J.K. Wing and A.M. Haily (eds), *Evaluating a Community Psychiatric Service: The Camberwell Register 1964–1971*, London: Oxford University Press, 1972, pp. 327–40.

30 Rollin, "From patients into vagrants," p. 92; National Schizophrenia Fellowship, *Home Sweet Nothing: The Plight of Sufferers from Chronic Schizophrenia*, Surbiton: 1971; Coid, J., "How many psychiatric patients in prison?" *British Journal of Psychiatry*, 145: 78–86, 1984; Gunn, J., Maden, A. and Swinton, M., "Treatment needs of prisoners with psychiatric disorders," *British Medical Journal*, 303: 338–41, 1991.

31 Morris, B., "Recent developments in the care, treatment, and rehabilitation of the chronic mentally ill in Britain," *Hospital and Community Psychiatry*, 34: 159–63, 1983.

32 Korer, J., *Not the Same as You: The Social Situation of 190 Schizophrenics Living in the Community*, Dalston, London: Psychiatric Rehabilitation Association, 1978;

Ebringer, L. and Christie-Brown, J.R.W., "Social deprivation amongst short stay psychiatric patients," *British Journal of Psychiatry*, 136: 46–52, 1980.

33 Hencke, D., "Squalor in mental homes kept secret," *Guardian*, July 20, 1983, p. 1; Hencke, D., "Hospital report reveals faults," *Guardian*, July 22, 1983, p. 3.

34 Leff, J., "Why is care in the community perceived as a failure?" *British Journal of Psychiatry*, 179: 381–3, 2001.

35 Rose, N., "Historical changes in mental health practice," in G. Thornicroft and G. Szmukler (eds) *Textbook of Community Psychiatry*, Oxford: Oxford University Press, 2001, pp. 13–27.

36 Adams, C.E., Pantelis, C., Duke, P.J. and Barnes, T.R.E., "Psychopathology, social and cognitive functioning in a hostel of homeless women," *British Journal of Psychiatry*, 168: 82–6, 1996.

37 Marshall, E.J. and Reed, J.L., "Psychiatric morbidity in homeless women," *British Journal of Psychiatry*, 160: 761–8, 1992.

38 Timms, P.W. and Fry, A.H., "Homelessness and mental illness," *Health Trends*, 21: 70–1, 1989.

39 Marshall, M., "Collected and neglected: Are Oxford hostels filling up with disabled patients?" *British Medical Journal*, 229: 706–9, 1989.

40 Craig, T. and Timms, P.W., "Out of the wards and onto the streets? Deinstitutionalization and homelessness in Britain," *Journal of Mental Health*, 1: 265–75, 1992; Hamid, W.A., Wykes, T. and Stansfeld, S., "The social disablement of men in hostels for homeless people. II. A comparison with patients from long-stay wards," *British Journal of Psychiatry*, 166: 809–12, 1995.

41 Leff, J., "The downside of reprovision," in J. Leff (ed.), *Care in the Community: Illusion or Reality?* Chichester: John Wiley & Sons, 1997, pp. 167–74. The reference is to p.171.

42 Medical Campaign Project, *A Paper Outlining Good Practice on Discharge of Single Homeless People with Particular Reference to Mental Health Units*, London: Policy Studies Institute, 1990.

43 Quirk, A. and Lelliott, P., "What do we know about life on acute psychiatric wards in the UK? A review of the research evidence," *Social Science and Medicine*, 53: 1565–74, 2001.

44 Craig and Timms, "Out of the wards and onto the streets?" p. 265.

45 McCulloch, A., Muijen, M. and Harper, H., "New developments in mental health policy in the United Kingdom," *International Journal of Law and Psychiatry*, 23: 261–76, 2000.

46 Trieman, N., "Patients who are too difficult to manage in the community," in J. Leff (ed.), *Care in the Community*, pp. 175–87. The reference is to p. 183.

47 Coid, J., "How many psychiatric patients in prison?" *British Medical Journal*, 145: 78–86, 1984.

48 Gunn, J., Maden, A. and Swinton, M., "Treatment needs of prisoners with psychiatric disorders," *British Medical Journal*, 303: 338–41, 1991.

49 Trieman, "Too difficult to manage in the community," p. 184.

50 Singleton, N., Meltzer, H., Gatward, R. et al., *Psychiatric Morbidity among Prisoners in England and Wales*, London: Office for National Statistics, 1998.

51 Coid, J.W., "Mentally abnormal prisoners on remand: I – Rejected or accepted by the NHS?" *British Medical Journal*, 296: 1779–82, 1988.

52 Trieman, "Too difficult to manage in the community," p. 184.

53 Levy, C.J., "For mentally ill, death and misery," *New York Times*, April 28, 2002, pp. 1 & 34–35; Levy, C.J., "Here life is squalor and chaos," *New York Times*, April 29, 2002, pp. A1 & A26-A27; Levy, C.J., "Voiceless, defenseless and a source of cash," *New York Times*, April 30, 2002, pp. A1 & A28-A29; Levy, C.J., "Inquiries

start on conditions in homes for the mentally ill," *New York Times*, May 1, 2002, pp. A1 & C18.

54 Ditton, P.M., *Mental Health and Treatment of Inmates and Probationers*, Washington, DC: Bureau of Justice Special Report, July 1999; Guy, E., Platt., Zwerling, I. and Bullock, S., "Mental health status of prisoners in an urban jail," *Criminal Justice and Behavior*, 12: 29–53, 1985; Steadman, H., Fabisiak, S., Dvoskin, J. and Holohean, E., "A survey of mental disability among prison inmates," *Hospital and Community Psychiatry*, 38: 1086–90, 1989; Teplin, L.A., "The prevalence of severe mental disorders among male urban jail detainees: Comparison with the Epidemiologic Catchment Area Program," *American Journal of Public Health*, 80: 663–9, 1990.

55 Mandiberg, J.M., *Strategic Technology Transfer in the Human Services: A Case Study of the Mental Health Clubhouse Movement and the International Diffusion of the Clubhouse Model*, unpublished doctoral dissertation, University of Michigan, Ann Arbor.

56 Allness, D.J. and Knoedler, W.H., *The PACT Model of Community-Based Treatment for Persons with Severe and Persistent Mental Illnesses: A Manual for PACT Start-Up*, Arlington, Virginia: National Alliance for the Mentally Ill, 1998.

57 Bond., G.R., Drake, R.E., Mueser, K.T. and Becker, D.R., "An update on supported employment for people with severe mental illness," *Psychiatric Services*, 48: 335–46, 1997; Drake, R.E., McHugo, G.J., Bebout, R.R. et al., "A randomized clinical trial of supported employment for inner-city patients with severe mental disorders," *Archives of General Psychiatry*, 56: 627–33, 1999; Warner, R., "The employment and income of people with psychotic disorders in a tight labor market," unpublished manuscript.

58 Scull, *Decarceration*, p. 152.

59 Fraser, D., *The Evolution of the British Welfare State: A History of Social Policy Since the Industrial Revolution*, New York: Harper & Row, 1973, pp. 212–16; Leiby, J., *A History of Social Welfare and Social Work in the United States*, New York: Columbia University Press, 1978, p. 289.

60 Ödegard, Ö., "Changes in the prognosis of functional psychoses since the days of Kraepelin," *British Journal of Psychiatry*, 113: 813–22, 1967, p. 819.

61 Foucault, M., *Madness and Civilization: A History of Insanity in the Age of Reason*, New York: Vintage Books, 1965, p. 49.

62 Parry-Jones, W.L., *The Trade in Lunacy: A Study of Private Madhouses in England in the Eighteenth and Nineteenth Centuries*, London: Routledge & Kegan Paul, 1972, p. 72.

63 All the material in this paragraph is taken from Sinfield, A., *What Unemployment Means*, Oxford: Martin Robertson, 1981, pp. 130–1.

64 Clark, *Social Therapy in Psychiatry*, p. 23.

65 Ödegard, "Prognosis of functional psychoses," p. 819.

66 Pugh and MacMahon, *Epidemiologic Findings*.

67 Camberwell group prevalence study, 1965, cited in Torrey, E.F., *Schizophrenia and Civilization*, New York: Jason Aronson, 1980, p. 89.

68 McGowan, J.F. and Porter, T.L., *An Introduction to the Vocational Rehabilitation Process*, Washington, DC: US Department of Health, Education and Welfare, Vocational Rehabilitation Administration, 1967.

69 Tizard, J. and O'Connor, N., "The employment of high-grade mental defectives. I," *American Journal of Mental Deficiency*, 54: 563–76, 1950.

70 Field, M.G. and Aronson, J., "The institutional framework of Soviet psychiatry," *Journal of Nervous and Mental Disease*, 138: 305–22, 1964; Field, M.G. and Aronson, J., "Soviet community mental health services and work therapy: A report of

two visits," *Community Mental Health Journal*, 1: 81–90, 1965; Hein, G., "Social psychiatric treatment of schizophrenia in the Soviet Union," *International Journal of Psychiatry*, 6: 346–62, 1968; Gorman M., "Soviet psychiatry and the Russian citizen," *International Journal of Psychiatry*, 8: 841–57, 1969.

71 Warner, "Employment and income in a tight labor market."
72 Maxwell Jones, personal communication.
73 Maddison, A., *Economic Growth in the West*, New York: Twentieth Century Fund, 1964, p. 220.
74 de Plato, G. and Minguzzi, G.F., "A short history of psychiatric renewal in Italy," *Psychiatry and Social Science*, 1: 71–7, 1981.
75 Donnelly, M. *The Politics of Mental Health in Italy*, London: Routledge, 1992.
76 For a fuller discussion of this analysis see Warner, R., "Mental hospital and prison use: An international comparison," *Mental Health Administration*, 10: 239–58, 1983.
77 World Health Organization, *World Health Statistics Annual 1977*, vol. III, Geneva: 1977; Maxwell Jones and Loren Mosher, personal communications.
78 Field and Aronson, "Institutional framework of Soviet psychiatry;" Field and Aronson, "Soviet community mental health;" Hein, "Soviet psychiatric treatment;" Gorman, "Soviet psychiatry;" Wing, J.R., *Reasoning About Madness*, New York: Oxford University Press, 1978.

5 MADNESS AND THE INDUSTRIAL REVOLUTION

1 Charles-Gaspard de la Rive, a Swiss doctor. Quoted in Foucault, M., *Madness and Civilization: A History of Insanity in the Age of Reason*, New York: Vintage Books, 1973, p. 242. Also quoted in Jones, K., *A History of the Mental Health Services*, London: Routledge & Kegan Paul, 1972, p. 47. According to Foucault the passage appeared in a letter to the editors of the *Bibliothèque britannique*; according to Jones it was written in the visitors' book of the Retreat. One assumes both are correct, and that Dr de la Rive used the same material twice.
2 Daniel Hack Tuke stated that the name Retreat was suggested by his grandmother, William Tuke's daughter-in-law, to convey the idea of a haven. Quoted by Jones, *History of Mental Health Services*, p. 47.
3 These details of moral treatment at the York Retreat are drawn from the following sources: Mora, G., "Historical and theoretical trends in psychiatry," in H.I. Kaplan, A.M. Freedman and B.J. Sadock (eds), *Comprehensive Textbook of Psychiatry-III*, Baltimore: Williams & Wilkins, 1980, pp. 4–98. The reference is to pp. 55–7; Jones, *History of Mental Health Services*, pp. 45–54; Foucault, *Madness and Civilization*, pp. 241–55.
4 Thurnam, J., *Observations and Essays on the Statistics of Insanity*, London: Simpkin, Marshall, 1845, reprint edition New York: Arno Press, 1976. Quoted in Jones, *History of Mental Health Services*, p. 66.
5 Both passages are from Godfrey Higgins' letter to the *York Herald*, 10 January 1814. Quoted in Jones, *History of Mental Health Services*, p. 70.
6 Both quotations are from Dickens, C. and Wills, W.H., "A curious dance around a curious tree," in H. Stone (ed.), *Charles Dickens' Uncollected Writings from Household Words 1850–1859*, Bloomington: Indiana University Press, 1968, pp. 381–91. The passages quoted are on pp. 382–3.
7 Parry-Jones, W.L., *The Trade in Lunacy: A Study of Private Madhouses in England in the Eighteenth and Nineteenth Centuries*, London: Routledge & Kegan Paul, 1972, p. 289.
8 Scull, A., "Moral treatment reconsidered: Some sociological comments on an

episode in the history of British psychiatry," in A. Scull (ed.), *Madhouses, Mad-doctors, and Madmen: The Social History of Psychiatry in the Victorian Era*, Philadelphia: University of Pennsylvania Press, 1981, pp. 105–18. This reference is on p. 107.

9 Foucault, *Madness and Civilization*, p. 68.

10 Ibid., pp. 74–5.

11 Ibid., pp. 68–78; Scull, "Moral treatment reconsidered," pp. 106–10.

12 Dr de la Rive's remarks are translated from the original French which was quoted in Jones, *History of Mental Health Services*, p. 49.

13 *Regolamento dei Regi Spedali di Santa Maria Nuova de Bonifazio.* Hospital regulations prepared under the supervision of Vincenzo Chiarugi in 1789. Quoted in Mora, "Historical and theoretical trends," p. 42.

14 Daquin, J., *La Philosophie de la folie*, Chambéry, 1791, cited in Mora, "Historical and theoretical trends," p. 57.

15 Mora, "Historical and theoretical trends," p. 54.

16 Jones, *History of Mental Health Services*, p. 44.

17 Ferriar, J., *Medical Histories and Reflections* (3 vols), London: Cadell & Davies, vol. 2, pp. 111–12. Quoted in Scull, "Moral treatment reconsidered," p. 106.

18 Mora, "Historical and theoretical trends," pp. 58–9.

19 Ibid., p. 54.

20 Hobsbawm, E.J., *The Age of Revolution 1789–1848*, New York: New American Library, 1962, p. 37.

21 Ibid., p. xv.

22 Ibid., p. 46.

23 Ibid., p. 38.

24 Ibid., pp. 40, 103.

25 Ibid., pp. 72, 77.

26 Tuma, E.H., *European Economic History: Tenth Century to the Present*, Palo Alto, California: Pacific Books, 1979, p. 202.

27 Hobsbawm, *Age of Revolution*, p. 79.

28 Inglis, B., *Poverty and the Industrial Revolution*, London: Panther Books, 1972, p. 78; Piven, F.F. and Cloward, R.A., *Regulating the Poor: The Functions of Public Welfare*, New York: Vintage Books, 1972, p. 21.

29 Ashton, T.S., *The Industrial Revolution 1760–1830*, Oxford: Oxford University Press, 1968, p. 46.

30 Ibid., p. 46.

31 Hobsbawm, *Age of Revolution*, pp. 93, 212.

32 Maidstone Poor Law authorities. Quoted in Jones, *History of Mental Health Services*, p. 18.

33 Jones, *History of Mental Health Services*, p. 18.

34 Ibid., pp. 10–12.

35 Parry-Jones, *Trade in Lunacy*, p. 30.

36 Scull, A., *Museums of Madness: The Social Organization of Insanity in Nineteenth-Century England*, London: Allen Lane (New York: St Martin's Press), 1979, p. 39.

37 Ibid., pp. 27–34, 247; Jones, *History of Mental Health Services*, pp. 88–9.

38 Foucault, *Madness and Civilization*, p. 232.

39 Ibid., pp. 234–40.

40 Parry-Jones, *Trade in Lunacy*, p. 204.

41 Scull, *Museums of Madness*, pp. 71–3; Scull, "Moral treatment reconsidered," pp. 112–15.

42 It had been difficult enough to maintain mentally disabled relatives at home before the Industrial Revolution, as revealed by a cottager's petition of 1681 in the

Lancashire Quarter Sessions Records, quoted in Allderidge, P., "Hospitals, madhouses and asylums: Cycles in the care of the insane," *British Journal of Psychiatry*, 134: 321–34, 1979, p. 327.

43 Best, G., *Mid-Victorian Britain 1851–70*, Bungay, Suffolk: Fontana, 1979, p. 161.

44 Scull, *Museums of Madness*, pp. 224, 244.

45 Jones, *History of Mental Health Services*, pp. 48, 123.

46 Ibid., pp. 93–6.

47 Thurnam, *Statistics of Insanity*, pp. 138–9.

48 Walton, J., "The treatment of pauper lunatics in Victorian England: The case of Lancaster Asylum, 1816–1870," in Scull, *Madhouses, Mad-doctors, and Madmen*, pp. 166–97. This reference is on p. 168. Jones, *History of Mental Health Services*, pp. 114–21.

49 Walton, "Pauper lunatics in Victorian England," p. 180.

50 Ibid., pp. 186–91; Scull, *Museums of Madness*, pp. 214–18.

51 Parry-Jones, *Trade in Lunacy*, p. 290.

52 Ibid., p. 288.

53 Ibid., p. 177.

54 Ibid., p. 175.

55 Ibid., pp. 175, 185.

56 Ibid., pp. 154, 185–6.

57 Thurnam, *Statistics of Insanity*, p. 36.

58 Ibid., calculated from Table 12.

59 Tuke, D.H., *Chapters in the History of the Insane in the British Isles*, London: Kegan Paul, Trench, 1882, p. 491.

60 Walton, "Pauper lunatics in Victorian England," p. 182.

61 For a discussion of the standard of living debate see: Taylor, A.J. (ed.), *The Standard of Living in Britain in the Industrial Revolution*, London: Methuen, 1975.

62 Harrison, J.F.C., *Early Victorian Britain 1832–51*, Bungay, Suffolk: Fontana, 1979, p. 34; Hobsbawm, E.J., *Labouring Men: Studies in the History of Labour*, London: Weidenfeld & Nicolson, 1968, pp. 72–82.

63 Mayhew, H., *London Labour and the London Poor II*, p. 338. Quoted in E.P. Thompson, *The Making of the English Working Class*, New York: Vintage Books, 1966, p. 250.

64 Hobsbawm, E.J., *Industry and Empire*, Harmondsworth, Middlesex: Penguin, 1969, p. 161.

65 Church, R.A., *The Great Victorian Boom 1850–1873*, London: Macmillan, 1975, pp. 72–3.

66 Piven and Cloward, *Regulating the Poor*, pp. 32–8.

67 Flinn, M.W., *British Population Growth 1700–1850*, London: Macmillan, 1970, p. 57; Kemmerer, D.L. and Hunter, M.H., *Economic History of the United States*, Totowa, New Jersey: Littlefield, Adams, 1967, pp. 61, 65; Boorstin, D.J., *The Americans: Volume II: The National Experience*, Harmondsworth, Middlesex: Penguin, p. 46.

68 Boorstin, *The National Experience*, p. 51.

69 Hunt, E.H., *British Labour History 1815–1914*, London: Weidenfeld & Nicolson, 1981, p. 108; Tucker, R.S., "Real wages of artisans in London, 1729–1935," in Taylor, *Standard of Living in the Industrial Revolution*, p. 33.

70 Rothman, D.J., *The Discovery of the Asylum: Social Order and Disorder in the New Republic*, Boston: Little Brown, 1971, p. 158.

71 Ibid., p. 160.

72 Ibid., pp. 160, 205.

73 Garraty, J.A., *Unemployment in History: Economic Thought and Public Policy*, New York: Harper, 1979, p. 109.

74 This material on the corporate asylums is drawn from Scull, A., "The Discovery of the Asylum revisited: Lunacy reform in the new American republic," in Scull, *Madhouses, Mad-doctors and Madmen*, pp. 144–65; and Rothman, *Discovery of the Asylum*, pp. 130–54.

75 For example, see Caplan, R.B., *Psychiatry and the Community in Nineteenth-Century America*, New York: Basic Books, 1969, p. 4.

76 Mora, "Historical and theoretical trends," p. 62.

77 Rothman, *Discovery of the Asylum*, p. 277.

78 Ibid., p. 151.

79 Dain, N., *Disordered Minds: The First Century of Eastern State Hospital in Williamsburg*, Virginia 1766–1866, Williamsburg, Virginia: Colonial Williamsburg Foundation, 1971, pp. 66, 107.

80 The Boston Prison Discipline Society report. Quoted in Dain, *Disordered Minds*, p. 62.

81 Dain, *Disordered Minds*, pp. 43, 127.

82 Grob, G.N., *Mental Institutions in America: Social Policy to 1875*, New York: Free Press, 1973, p. 392.

83 Rothman, *Discovery of the Asylum*, pp. 144–51; Dain, N., *Concepts of Insanity in the United States, 1789–1865*, New Brunswick, New Jersey: Rutgers University Press, p. 128.

84 Bockoven, J.S., "Moral treatment in American Psychiatry," *Journal of Nervous and Mental Disease*, 124: 167–94, 292–321, 1956, p. 181.

85 Thurnam, *Statistics of Insanity*, Table 16.

86 Rothman, *Discovery of the Asylum*, p. 149.

87 Dickens, D., *American Notes for General Circulation*, Harmondsworth, Middlesex: Penguin, 1972, p. 97.

88 Ibid., p. 122.

89 Ibid., p. 140.

90 Dickens and Wills, "A curious dance," pp. 386–91.

91 Dickens, *American Notes*, p. 141.

92 Rothman, *Discovery of the Asylum*, p. 283.

93 Ibid., pp. 144–6.

94 Caplan, *Psychiatry and the Community*, p. 43.

95 Ibid., pp. 37–8; Grob, *Mental Institutions in America*, p. 179.

96 Hall, B., *Travels in North America in the Years 1827 and 1828*, Edinburgh: Cadell, 1829. Quoted in Bromberg, W., *From Shaman to Psychotherapist: A History of the Treatment of Mental Illness*, Chicago: Henry Regnery, 1975, p. 124; and cited in Caplan, *Psychiatry and the Community*, p. 90; and in Tourney, G., "A history of therapeutic fashions in psychiatry, 1800–1966," *American Journal of Psychiatry*, 124: 784–96, 1967. According to Scull in "Discovery of the Asylum Revisited," p. 164, E.S. Abdy made similar remarks in his *Journal of a Residence and Tour in the United States of North America*, London: Murray, 1835.

97 Bromberg, *Shaman to Psychotherapist*, p. 125.

98 Quoted in Bromberg, *Shaman to Psychotherapist*, p. 125.

99 Deutsch, A., *The Mentally Ill in America*, New York: Columbia University Press, 1949, ch. 11.

100 See Caplan, *Psychiatry and the Community*, pp. 90–1 for a detailed list of the flaws in the recovery statistics.

101 Bromberg, *Shaman to Psychotherapist*, p. 124; Parry-Jones, *Trade in Lunacy*, pp. 202–5.

102 Thurnam, *Statistics of Insanity*, p. 57.

103 Ibid., Table 6.

104 Pliny Earle published his views on the curability of insanity as an article in 1876, and later in book form: *The Curability of Insanity: A Series of Studies*, Philadelphia: Lippincott, 1887. See Rothman, *Discovery of the Asylum*, p. 268; Caplan, *Psychiatry and the Community*, p. 93; Bromberg, *Shaman to Psychotherapist*, p. 126.

105 Bockoven, J.S., *Moral Treatment in Community Mental Health*, New York: Springer, 1972, ch. 5.

106 Rothman, *Discovery of the Asylum*, p. 357.

107 Bockoven, *Moral Treatment*, p. 67.

108 An exception would be Grob, *Mental Institutions in America*, pp. 184–5. After reviewing Dr Park's follow-up study of Dr Woodward's patients. Grob concludes that it indicates "a record that compares quite favorably with mid-twentieth century discharge rates from mental hospitals."

109 Ray, I., *American Journal of Insanity*, 16: 1–2, 1861–2. Quoted in Caplan, *Psychiatry and the Community*, pp. 73–4.

110 Rothman, *Discovery of the Asylum*, p. 266.

111 Ibid., p. 281; Scull, "Discovery of the Asylum revisited," pp. 157–9.

112 Scull, "Discovery of the Asylum revisited," p. 159.

113 Mora, "Historical and theoretical trends," p. 73.

114 "The German asylum tradition issued more from the prison than the monastery, and this is, according to Kirchhof, the reason for their tremendous use of coercive measures." Ellenburger, H.F., "Psychiatry from ancient to modern times," in S. Arieti (ed.) *American Handbook of Psychiatry*, vol. I, New York: Basic Books, 1974, pp. 3–27. This reference is on p. 22.

6 LABOR, POVERTY AND SCHIZOPHRENIA

1 Brenner, M.H., *Mental Illness and the Economy*, Cambridge, Massachusetts: Harvard University Press, 1973, p. 207.

2 Scull, A.T., *Decarceration: Community Treatment and the Deviant – A Radical View*, Englewood Cliffs, New Jersey: Prentice-Hall, 1977, p. 157; Sharfstein, S.S. and Nafziger, J.C., "Community care: Costs and benefits for a chronic patient," *Hospital and Community Psychiatry*, 27: 170–3, 1976; Murphy, J.G. and Datel, W.E., "A cost-benefit analysis of community versus institutional living," *Hospital and Community Psychiatry*, 27: 165–70, 1976.

3 All quotations in this paragraph are drawn from Marsden, D. and Duff, E., *Workless: Some Unemployed Men and Their Families*, Baltimore: Penguin, 1975, pp. 191–202.

4 Eisenberg, P. and Lazarsfeld, P.F., "The psychological effects of unemployment," *Psychological Bulletin*, 35: 358–90, 1938; The Pilgrim Trust, *Men Without Work*, New York: Greenwood Press, 1968, p. 143 et seq.

5 Bemporad, J.R. and Pinsker, H., "Schizophrenia: The manifest symptomatology," in S. Arieti and E.B. Brody (eds), *American Handbook of Psychiatry*, vol. III, New York: Basic Books, 1974, pp. 525–50. The quotation is on p. 540.

6 Marsden and Duff, *Workless*, p. 211.

7 Israeli, N., "Distress in the outlook of Lancashire and Scottish unemployed," *Journal of Applied Psychology*, 19: 67–9, 1935.

8 Ibid., p. 67.

9 Brenner, *Mental Illness and the Economy*, pp. 38, 56, 169.

10 Brown, G.W., Birley, J.L.T. and Wing, J.K., "Influence of family life on the

course of schizophrenic disorders: A replication," *British Journal of Psychiatry*, 121: 241–58, 1972; Vaughn, C.E. and Leff, J.P., "The influence of family and social factors on the course of psychiatric illness," *British Journal of Psychiatry*, 129: 125–37, 1976.

11 Leff, J., "Preventing relapse in schizophrenia," presented at the World Psychiatric Association Regional Meeting, New York City, October 30–November 3, 1981.

12 Brown, G.W., Bone, M., Dalison, B. et al., *Schizophrenia and Social Care*, London: Oxford University Press, 1966.

13 Wing, J.K. and Brown, G.W., *Institutionalism and Schizophrenia*, London: Cambridge University Press, 1970.

14 Huessy, H.R., "Discussion," *Schizophrenia Bulletin*, 7: 178–80, 1981.

15 Brown, G.W. and Birley, J.L.T., "Crises and life changes and the onset of schizophrenia," *Journal of Health and Social Behavior*, 9: 203–14, 1968.

16 Engels, F., *The Condition of the Working Class in England*, London: Granada, 1969, p. 117. First published in Leipzig in 1845.

17 Marx, K., *Capital*, vol. I, New York: International Publishers, 1967; reproduction of the English edition of 1887, p. 632.

18 Ibid., p. 643.

19 Ibid., pp. 743–4.

20 Ibid., p. 644.

21 Braverman, H., *Labor and Monopoly Capital: The Degradation of Work in the Twentieth Century*, New York: Monthly Review Press, 1974, pp. 386–401.

22 Anderson, C.H., *The Political Economy of Class*, Englewood Cliffs, New Jersey: Prentice-Hall, 1974, p. 149.

23 Silk, L., "Stocks jump as jobs slump: So what's next?," *New York Times*, October 10, 1982, p. E1; Pear, R., "Ranks of US poor reach 35.7 million, the most since '64," *New York Times*, September 4, 1992, pp. A1 & A10; Bovee, T., "More American workers holding low-paying jobs," Associated Press report in *Boulder Daily Camera*, May 12, 1992, p. 5A.

24 Mora, G., "Historical and theoretical trends in psychiatry," in H.I. Kaplan, A.M. Freedman and B.J. Sadock (eds), *Comprehensive Textbook of Psychiatry-III*, Baltimore: Williams & Wilkins, 1980, pp. 4–98. The material in this paragraph is from pp. 73–91.

25 Scull, A.T., *Museums of Madness: The Social Organization of Insanity in Nineteenth Century England*, London: Allen Lane (New York: St Martin's Press), 1979, pp. 196–9.

26 Clark, D.H., *Social Therapy in Psychiatry*, Baltimore: Penguin, 1974, p. 23.

27 Mora, "Historical and theoretical trends," pp. 80, 90.

28 Among those making an ideological switch in tune with the economy was psychiatrist Werner Mendel, nationally recognized in the 1970s for his advocacy of community treatment of schizophrenia. Appearing for the City and County of Denver, the defendants in the case, Dr Mendel modified his earlier views and testified that community care and vocational rehabilitation for people with schizophrenia just do not work. In his deposition of May 7, 1983, for the Probate Court (case number 81-MH–270) and the District Court (civil action number 81-CV–6961) of the City and County of Denver, he claimed that it would be just as well for people with schizophrenia if the whole mental health profession disappeared overnight. His pessimistic appraisal grew largely out of his own research and experience with a program treating patients with psychosis in Los Angeles through a period of increasing unemployment and declining mental health funds.

29 For positive evaluations of the efficacy of psychosocial treatment and community support systems see Mosher, L.R. and Keith, S.J., "Psychosocial treatment:

Individual, group, family, and community support approaches," *Schizophrenia Bulletin*, 6: 11–41, 1980; Stein, L.I. and Test, M.A., "Alternative to mental hospital treatment: I. Conceptual model, treatment program, and clinical evaluation," *Archives of General Psychiatry*, 37: 392–7, 1980; Weisbrod, B.A., Test, M.A. and Stein, L.I., "Alternative to mental hospital treatment: II. Economic benefit-cost analysis," *Archives of General Psychiatry*, 37: 400–5l, 1980; Test, M.A. and Stein, L.I., "Alternative to mental hospital treatment: III. Social cost," *Archives of General Psychiatry*, 37: 409–12, 1980; Pasamanick, G., Scarpitti, F. and Dinitz, S., *Schizophrenics in the Community: An Experimental Study in the Prevention of Hospitalization*, New York: Appleton-Century-Crofts, 1967; Mosher, L.R., Menn, A.Z. and Methews, S., "Soteria: Evaluation of a home-based treatment for schizophrenia," *American Journal of Orthopsychiatry*, 45: 455–69, 1975; Polak, P.R. and Kirby, M.W., "A model to replace psychiatric hospitals," *Journal of Nervous and Mental Disease*, 162: 13–22, 1976.

30 Aronson, E., *The Social Animal*, 2nd edn, San Francisco: W.H. Freeman, 1976, pp. 186–9.

31 Clark, *Social Therapy in Psychiatry*, ch. 2.

32 Carstairs, G.M., "Advances in psychological medicine," *Practitioner*, Symposium on Advances in Treatment, 187: 495–504, 1961. Quoted in Jones, K., *A History of the Mental Health Services*, London: Routledge & Kegan Paul, 1972, p. 292.

33 Star, S., "The public's idea of mental illness," presented at National Association for Mental Health meeting, Chicago, Illinois, November 1955; Cumming, E. and Cumming, J., *Closed Ranks: An Experiment in Mental Health Education*, Cambridge, Massachusetts: Harvard University Press, 1957; Nunally, J.C., *Popular Conceptions of Mental Health*, New York: Holt, Rinehart & Winston, 1961.

34 Lemkau, P.V. and Crocetti, G.M., "An urban population's opinion and knowledge about mental illness," *American Journal of Psychiatry*, 118: 692–700, 1962; Meyer. J.K., "Attitudes towards mental illness in a Maryland community," *Public Health Reports*, 79: 769–72, 1964.

35 D'Arcy, C. and Brockman, J., "Changing public recognition of psychiatric symptoms? Blackfoot revisited," *Journal of Health and Social Behavior*, 17: 302–10, 1976; Olmsted, D.W. and Durham, K., "Stability of mental health attitudes: A semantic differential study," *Journal of Health and Social Behavior*, 17: 35–44, 1976.

36 See Chapter 10 of Warner, R. *The Environment of Schizophrenia: Innovations in Practice, Policy and Communications*, London: Brunner-Routledge, 2000.

37 Jones, *History of Mental Health Services*, p. 291.

38 Ibid., pp. 283, 289–91, 304.

39 Dickens, D., *American Notes for General Circulation*, Harmondsworth, Middlesex: Penguin, 1972, first published 1842, p. 100.

40 Clark, *Social Therapy in Psychiatry*, p. 21.

41 Brenner, *Mental Illness and the Economy*, pp. 170–2.

42 Thurnam, J., *Observations and Essays on the Statistics of Insanity*, London: Simpkin, Marshall, 1845; reprint edn, New York, Arno Press, 1976, p. 27.

43 Ödegard, Ö., "Statistical study of factors influencing discharge from psychiatric hospitals," *Journal of Mental Science*, 106: 1124–33, 1960.

44 Salokangas, R.K.R. "Prognostic implications of the sex of schizophrenic patients," *British Journal of Psychiatry*, 142: 145–51, 1983.

45 Beck, J.C., "Social influences on the prognosis of schizophrenia," *Schizophrenia Bulletin*, 4: 86–101, 1978.

46 World Health Organization, *Schizophrenia: An International Follow-up Study*, Chichester: Wiley, 1979, pp. 162, 273, 278, 286; Jablensky, A., Sartorius, N.,

Ernberg, M. et al., "Schizophrenia: Manifestations, incidence and course in different cultures: A World Health Organization ten-country study," *Psychological Medicine*, supplement 20, 1992, tables 4.16 & 4.17.

47 Brenner, *Mental Illness and the Economy*, p. 170.

48 Seeman, M. and Lang, M. "The role of estrogens in schizophrenia gender differences," *Schizophrenia Bulletin*, 16: 185–94, 1990; Szymanski, S., Lieberman, J.A., Alvir, J.M. et al., "Gender differences in onset of illness, treatment response, course, and biological indexes in first-episode schizophrenic patients," *American Journal of Psychiatry*, 152: 698–703, 1995; Stevens, J.R., "Schizophrenia: Reproductive hormones and the brain," *American Journal of Psychiatry*, 159: 713–9, 2002.

49 Henry, A.F. and Short, J.F., *Suicide and Homicide*, Glencoe, Illinois: Free Press, 1954.

50 Brenner, *Mental Illness and the Economy*, p. 53.

51 Cooper, B., "Social class and prognosis in schizophrenia: Parts I and II, *Journal of Preventive and Social Medicine*, 15: 17–30, 31–41, 1961.

52 Ibid., p. 36.

53 Brooke, E.M., "Report on the Second International Congress for Psychiatry, Zurich," vol. III, 1957, p. 52. Cited in Cooper, "Social class and prognosis in schizophrenia," p. 19.

54 Hollingshead, A.B. and Redlich, F.C., *Social Class and Mental Illness*, New York: Wiley, 1958.

55 Myers, J.K. and Bean, L.L., *A Decade Later: A Follow-up of Social Class and Mental Illness*, New York: Wiley, 1968.

56 Astrachan, B.M., Brauer, L., Harrow, M. et al., "Symptomatic outcome in schizophrenia," *Archives of General Psychiatry*, 31: 155–60, 1974.

57 World Health Organization, *Schizophrenia*, p. 288.

58 Wing, J.K., Denham, J. and Munro, A.B., "Duration of stay of patients suffering from schizophrenia," *British Journal of Preventive and Social Medicine*, 13: 145–8, 1959; Carstairs, G.M., Tonge, W.L., O'Connor, N. et al., *British Journal of Preventive and Social Medicine*, 9: 187 et seq., 1955, cited in Cooper, "Social class and prognosis in schizophrenia," p. 19.

59 Ödegard, "Discharge from psychiatric hospital," pp. 1127–9.

60 Astrachan et al, "Symptomatic outcome from schizophrenia," pp. 159–60.

61 Ciompi, L., "Catamnestic long-term study on the course of life and aging of schizophrenics," *Schizophrenia Bulletin*, 6: 606–18, 1980.

62 Mitchell, B.R., *European Historical Statistics 1750–1970*, abridged edn, New York: Columbia University Press, 1978.

63 Ciompi, "Life and aging of schizophrenics," p. 615.

64 Ellman, M., *Socialist Planning*, Cambridge: Cambridge University Press, 1979, p. 257.

65 Ibid., p. 161.

66 Barker, D., "Moscow mayor has his say on jobless," *Guardian*, July 11, 1983.

67 Wing, J.K., *Reasoning About Madness*, Oxford: Oxford University Press, 1978; Field, M.G. and Aronson, J., "Soviet community mental health services and work therapy: A report of two visits," *Community Mental Health Journal*, 1: 81–90, 1965; Hein, G., "Social psychiatric treatment of schizophrenia in the Soviet Union," *International Journal of Psychiatry*, 6: 346–62, 1968.

68 World Health Organization, *Schizophrenia*, p. 160.

7 SCHIZOPHRENIA IN THE THIRD WORLD

1 Norquist, G.S., Regier, D.A. and Rupp, A., "Estimates of the cost of treating people with schizophrenia: Contributions of data from epidemiological surveys," in M. Moscarelli, A. Rupp and N. Sartorius (eds), *Handbook of Mental Health Economics and Health Policy: Volume I: Schizophrenia*, Chichester: John Wiley & Sons, 1996, pp. 96–101.

2 Collomb, H., "Bouffées délirantes en psychiatrie Africaine," *Transcultural Psychiatric Research*, 3: 29–34, 1966, p. 29.

3 Schwartz, R., "Beschreibung einer ambulanten psychiatrischen Patientenpopulation in der Grossen-Kabylie (Nordalgerien): Epidemiologische und Klinische Aspekte," *Social Psychiatry* (West Germany), 12: 207–18, 1977.

4 Smartt, C.G.F., "Mental maladjustment in the East African," *Journal of Mental Science*, 102: 441–66, 1956.

5 Opler, M.K., "The social and cultural nature of mental illness and its treatment," in S. Lesse, (ed.), *An Evaluation of the Results of the Psychotherapies*, Springfield, Illinois: C.C. Thomas, 1968, pp. 280–91.

6 Tewfik, G.I., "Psychoses in Africa," in *Mental Disorders and Mental Health in Africa South of the Sahara*, CCTA/CSA-WFMH-WHO meeting of specialist on mental health, Bukavu, London: 1958.

7 Field, M.J., *Search for Security: An Ethno-psychiatric Study of Rural Ghana*, Chicago: Northwestern University Press, 1962.

8 Fortes, M. and Mayer, D.Y., "Psychosis and social change among the Tallensi of northern Ghana," in S.H. Foulkes and G.S. Prince (eds) *Psychiatry in a Changing Society*, London: Tavistock, 1969, pp. 33–73.

9 Berne, E., "Some oriental mental hospitals," *American Journal of Psychiatry*, 106: 376–83, 1949; Seligman, C.G., "Temperament, conflict and psychosis in a stone-age population," *British Journal of Medical Psychology*, 9: 187–202, 1929; Jilek, W.G. and Jilek-Aall, L., "Transient psychoses in Africans," *Psychiatrica Clinica* (Basel), 3: 337–64, 1970.

10 Murphy, H.B.M., "Cultural factors in the genesis of schizophrenia," in D. Rosenthal and S.S. Kety (eds), *The Transmission of Schizophrenia*, Oxford: Pergamon, 1968, p. 138.

11 American Psychiatric Association, *Diagnostic and Statistical Manual of Mental Disorders (DSM-IV)*, Washington, DC: 1994.

12 Wintrob, R.M., "Malaria and the acute psychotic episode," *Journal of Nervous and Mental Disease*, 156: 306–17, 1973.

13 Rin, H. and Lin, T., "Mental illness among Formosan aborigines as compared with the Chinese in Taiwan," *Journal of Mental Science*, 108: 134–46, 1962.

14 De Wet, J.S. Du T., "Evaluation of a common method of convulsion therapy in Bantu schizophrenics," *Journal of Mental Science*, 103: 739–57, 1957, p. 745.

15 Laubscher, B.J.F., *Sex, Custom and Psychopathology: A Study of South African Pagan Natives*, London: Routledge & Kegan Paul, 1937; Simons, H.J., "Mental disease in Africans: Racial determinism," *Journal of Mental Science*, 104: 371–88, 1958.

16 Westermeyer, J., "Psychosis in a peasant society: Social outcomes," *American Journal of Psychiatry*, 137: 1390–4, 1980, p. 393.

17 Ibid.

18 Westermeyer, J. and Wintrob, R., " 'Folk' criteria for diagnosis of mental illness in rural Laos: On being insane in sane places," *American Journal of Psychiatry*, 136: 755–61, 1979, p. 755.

19 Westermeyer, J., "Dr Westermeyer replies," *American Journal of Psychiatry*, 138: 699, 1981.

20 Brown, G.W., Bone, M., Dalison, B. and Wing, J.K., *Schizophrenia and Social Care*, London: Oxford University Press, 1966.

21 Kulhara, P. and Wig, N.N., "The chronicity of schizophrenia in North West India: Results of a follow-up study," *British Journal of Psychiatry*, 132: 186–90, 1978.

22 Ran, M., Xiang, M., Huang, M. and Shan, Y. "Natural course of schizophrenia," *British Journal of Psychiatry*, 178: 154–8, 2001.

23 Sethi, B.B., Dube, K.C., John, J. et al., "Factors associated with the course and outcome of schizophrenia. Part II: Results of one year follow-up," *Indian Journal of Social Psychiatry*, 3, 53–80, 1987.

24 Srinivasan, T.N., Rajkumar, S. and Padmavathi, R., "Initiating care for untreated schizophrenic patients and results of one year follow-up," *International Journal of Social Psychiatry*, 47: 73–80, 2001.

25 Murphy, H.B.M. and Raman, A.C., "The chronicity of schizophrenia in indigenous tropical peoples," *British Journal of Psychiatry*, 118: 489–97, 1971.

26 Waxler, N.E., "Is outcome for schizophrenia better in nonindustrial societies? The case of Sri Lanka," *Journal of Nervous and Mental Disease*, 167: 144–58, 1979.

27 Lo, W.H. and Lo, T., "A ten-year follow-up study of Chinese schizophrenics in Hong Kong," *British Journal of Psychiatry*, 131: 63–6, 1977.

28 Tsoi, W.F., Kok, L.P. and Chew, S.K., "A five-year follow-up study of schizophrenia in Singapore," *Singapore Medical Journal*, 26: 171–7, 1985; Tsoi, W.F. and Wong, K.E., "A 15-year follow-up study of Chinese schizophrenic patients," *Acta Psychiatrica Scandinavica*, 84: 217–20, 1991.

29 Verghese, A., John, J.K., Rajkumar, S. et al., "Factors associated with the course and outcome of schizophrenia in India: Results of a two-year multicentre follow-up study," *British Journal of Psychiatry*, 154: 499–503, 1989.

30 Thara, R., Henrietta, M., Joseph, A. et al., "Ten-year course of schizophrenia – the Madras longitudinal study," *Acta Psychiatrica Scandinavica*, 90: 329–36, 1994.

31 Makanjuola, R.O.A. and Adedapo, S.A., "The DSM-III concepts of schizophrenic disorder and schizophreniform disorder: A clinical and prognostic evaluation," *British Journal of Psychiatry*, 151: 611–18, 1987.

32 Kurihara, T., Kato, M., Reverger, R. and Yagi, G., "Outcome of schizophrenia in a non-industrialized society: Comparative study between Bali and Tokyo," *Acta Psychiatrica Scandinavica*, 101: 148–52, 2000.

33 World Health Organization, *Schizophrenia: An International Follow-up Study*, Chichester, England: Wiley, 1979.

34 Jablensky, A., Sartorius, N., Ernberg, G. et al., "Schizophrenia: Manifestations, incidence and course in different cultures: A World Health Organization ten-country study," *Psychological Medicine*, supplement 20, 1992.

35 Hopper, K., and Wanderling, J., "Revisiting the developed versus developing country distinction in course and outcome in schizophrenia: Results from ISoS, the WHO collaborative follow-up project," *Schizophrenia Bulletin*, 26: 835–46, 2000.

36 Harris, M., *Culture, Man and Nature: An Introduction to General Anthropology*, New York: Thomas Y. Crowell, 1971, p. 480.

37 Lambo, T., "The importance of cultural factors in psychiatric treatment," in I. Al-Issa and W. Dennis (eds), *Cross-Cultural Studies of Behavior*, New York: Holt, Rinehart & Winston, 1970, pp. 548–52.

38 World Health Organization, *Schizophrenia*, p. 104.

39 Ran, "Natural course of schizophrenia."

40 Wing, J.K., "The social context of schizophrenia," *American Journal of Psychiatry*, 135: 1333–9, 1978.

41 World Health Organization, *Schizophrenia*, p. 104.

42 Sahlins, M., *Stone Age Economics*, Chicago: Aldine-Atherton, 1972, pp. 63–4; Neff, W.S., *World and Human Behavior*, Chicago: Aldine, 1968; Sharp, L., "People without politics," in V.F. Ray (ed.), *Systems of Political Control and Bureaucracy in Human Societies*, Seattle: University of Washington Press, 1958, p. 6.

43 Lee, R.E., *The !Kung San: Men, Women and Work in a Foraging Society*, New York: Cambridge University Press, 1979.

44 Richards, A.I., *Land, Labour and Diet in Northern Rhodesia*, London: Oxford University Press, 1961, appendix E; Guillard J., "Essai de mesure de l'activité d'un paysan Africain: Le Toupouri," *L'Agronomie Tropicale*, 13: 415–28, 1958. Both works are cited in Sahlins, *Stone Age Economics*, pp. 62–4.

45 Eyer, J. and Sterling, P., "Stress-related mortality and social organization," *The Review of Radical Political Economics*, 9: 1–44, 1977, p. 15.

46 Fei, H. and Chang, C., *Earthbound China: A Study of Rural Economy in Yunnan*, Chicago: University of Chicago Press, 1945, pp. 30–4, 145; Eyer and Sterling, "Stress-related mortality," p. 15.

47 Sahlins, *Stone Age Economics*, ch. 2.

48 Chayanov, A.V., *The Theory of Peasant Economy*, Homewood, Illinois: Richard D. Irwin, 1966, p. 77, cited in Sahlins, *Stone Age Economics*, p. 89.

49 Richards, *Land, Labour and Diet*, p. 402; Douglas, M., "Lele economy as compared with the Bushong," in G. Dalton and P. Bohannen (eds), *Markets in Africa*, Evanston, Illinois: Northwestern University Press, 1962, p. 231, cited in Sahlins, *Stone Age Economics*, pp. 52–4.

50 Linn, J.F., *Cities in the Developing World: Policies for Their Equitable and Efficient Growth*, New York: World Bank/Oxford University Press, 1983, pp. 36–42; Squire, L., *Employment Policy in Developing Countries*, New York: World Bank/Oxford University Press, 1981, pp. 66–75, 83–90.

51 World Health Organization, *Schizophrenia*, ch. 10.

52 Doyal, L., *The Political Economy of Health*, Boston: South End Press, 1981, pp. 112–13; Fortes and Mayer, "Psychosis among the Tallensi."

53 World Health Organization, *Schizophrenia*, pp. 271, 283.

54 Squire, *Employment Policy in Developing Countries*, p. 71.

55 World Health Organization, *Schizophrenia*, p. 283.

56 Ibid., pp. 287–8.

57 McGoodwin, J.R., "No matter how we asked them, they convinced us that they suffer," *Human Organization*, 37: 378–83, 1978.

58 Paul, B.D., "Mental disorder and self-regulating processes in culture: A Guatemalan illustration," in R. Hunt (ed.), *Personalities and Cultures: Readings in Psychological Anthropology*, Garden City, New York: Natural History Press, 1967.

59 Gelfand, M., "Psychiatric disorders as recognized by the Shona," in A. Kiev (ed.), *Magic, Faith and Healing*, New York: Free Press, 1964, pp. 156–73.

60 Collomb, "Bouffées délirantes en psychiatrie Africaine," p. 30.

61 Rogler, L.H. and Hollingshead, A.B., *Trapped: Families and Schizophrenia*, New York: Wiley, 1965, p. 254.

62 Erinosho, O.A. and Ayonrinde, A., "Educational background and attitude to mental illness among the Yoruba in Nigeria," *Human Relations*, 34: 1–12, 1981.

63 D'Arcy, C. and Brockman, J., "Changing public recognition of psychiatric symptoms? Blackfoot revisited," *Journal of Health and Social Behavior*, 17: 302–10, 1976.

64 Ibid.

65 Binitie, A.O., "Attitude of educated Nigerians to psychiatric illness," *Acta Psychiatrica Scandinavica*, 46: 391–8, 1970.

66 Colson, A.C. "The perception of abnormality in a Malay village," in N.N. Wagner and E. Tan (eds), *Psychological Problems and Treatment in Malaysia*, Kuala Lumpar: University of Malaya Press, 1971.

67 Leff, J., *Psychiatry Around the Globe: A Transcultural View*, New York: Marcel Dekker, 1981, p. 19.

68 Westermeyer and Wintrob, " 'Folk' diagnosis in rural Laos;" Westermeyer, J. and Kroll, J., "Violence and mental illness in a peasant society: Characteristics of violent behaviors and 'folk' use of restraints," *British Journal of Psychiatry*, 133: 529–41, 1978.

69 Edgerton, R.B., "Conceptions of psychosis in four East African societies," *American Anthropologist*, 68: 408–25, 1966.

70 Edgerton, R.B., *The Individual in Cultural Adaptation*, Berkeley: University of California Press, 1971, p. 188.

71 Edgerton, "Psychosis in four East African societies."

72 Ibid., p. 417.

73 Makanjuola, "The DSM-III concepts of schizophrenic disorder."

74 Mojtabai, R., Varma, V.K., Malhotra, S., et al., "Mortality and long-term course in schizophrenia with a poor 2-year course," *British Journal of Psychiatry*, 178: 71–5, 2001.

75 Rin and Lin, "Mental illness among Formosan aborigines."

76 Waxler, N.E., "Is mental illness cured in traditional societies? A theoretical analysis," *Culture, Medicine and Psychiatry*, 1: 233–53, 1977, p. 242.

77 World Health Organization, *Schizophrenia*, p. 105.

78 Levy, J.E., Neutra, R. and Parker, D., "Life careers of Navajo epileptics and convulsive hysterics," *Social Science and Medicine*, 13: 53–66, 1979.

79 Sontag, S., *Illness as Metaphor*, New York: Vintage Books, 1979.

80 Eliade, M., *Shamanism: Archaic Techniques of Ecstasy*, Princeton: Princeton University Press/Bollingen Paperback, 1972; Black Elk, *The Sacred Pipe*, Baltimore: Penguin, 1971.

81 Rogler and Hollingshead, *Trapped: Families and Schizophrenia*, p. 254.

82 Ozturk, O.M., "Folk treatment of mental illness in Turkey," in Kiev, *Magic, Faith and Healing*, p. 349.

83 Benedict, R., *Patterns of Culture*, Boston: Houghton-Mifflin, 1934, pp. 267–8.

84 Ackernecht, E.H., "Psychopathology, primitive, medicine and primitive culture," *Bulletin of the History of Medicine*, 14: 30–67, 1943; Silverman, J., "Shamans and acute schizophrenia," *American Anthropologist*, 69: 21–31, 1967.

85 Torrey, E.F., *The Mind Game: Witchdoctors and Psychiatrists*, New York: Emerson Hall, 1972; Torrey, E.F., *Schizophrenia and Civilization*, New York: Jason Aronson, 1980.

86 Silverman, "Shamans and acute schizophrenia," p. 29.

87 Linton, R., *Culture and Mental Disorders*, Springfield, Illinois: Charles C. Thomas, 1956.

88 Mischel, W., and Mischel, F., "Psychological aspects of spirit possession," *American Anthropologist*, 60: 249–60, 1958.

89 Prince, R., "Indigenous Yoruba psychiatry," in Kiev, *Magic, Faith and Healing*, pp. 84–120.

90 Messing, S.D., "Group therapy and social status in the Zar cult of Ethiopia," in J. Middleton (ed.), *Magic, Witchcraft and Curing*, Garden City, New York: Natural History Press, 1967, pp. 285–93.

91 Fox, J.R., "Witchcraft and clanship in Cochiti therapy," in Middleton, *Magic, Witchcraft and Curing*, pp. 255–84.
92 Dawson, J., "Urbanization and mental health in a West African community," in Kiev, *Magic, Faith and Healing*, pp. 305–42.
93 Benedict, *Patterns of Culture*, p. 72.
94 Kaplan, B. and Johnson, D., "The social meaning of Navajo psychopathology and psychotherapy," in Kiev, *Magic, Faith and Healing*, pp. 203–29; Leighton, A.H. and Leighton, D.C., "Elements of psychotherapy in Navaho religion," *Psychiatry*, 4: 515–23, 1941.
95 Waxler, "Is mental illness cured in traditional societies?, p. 241.
96 World Health Organization, *Schizophrenia*, p. 288; Jablensky et al., "Schizophrenia: Manifestations, incidence and course in different cultures," Table 4.17.
97 Hare, E.H., "Mental illness and social conditions in Bristol," *Journal of Mental Science*, 103: 349–57, 1956; Stein, L., " 'Social class' gradient in schizophrenia," *British Journal of Preventive and Social Medicine*, 11: 181–95, 1957; Cooper, B., "Social class and prognosis in schizophrenia: Part I," *British Journal of Preventive and Social Medicine*, 15: 17–30, 1961; Jaco, E.G., "The social isolation hypothesis and schizophrenia," *American Sociological Review*, 19: 567–77, 1954.
98 Levi-Strauss, C., *Structural Anthropology*, Harmondsworth, Middlesex: Penguin, 1972, p. 180.
99 Warner, W.L., *A Black Civilization*, New York: Harper, 1937, pp. 241–2.
100 Beiser, M. and Collomb, H., "Mastering change: Epidemiological and case studies in Senegal, West Africa," *American Journal of Psychiatry*, 138: 455–9, 1981.
101 Thara, R. and Rajkumar, S., "Gender differences in schizophrenia: Results of a follow-up study from India," *Schizophrenia Research*, 7: 65–70, 1992.
102 Srinivasan, "Initiating care for untreated schizophrenia patients."
103 Thara, "Gender differences in schizophrenia."
104 El-Islam, M.F., "A better outlook for schizophrenics living in extended families," *British Journal of Psychiatry*, 135: 343–7, 1979.
105 Wig, N.N., Menon, D.K. and Bedi, H., "Coping with schizophrenic patients in developing countries: A study of expressed emotions in the relatives," presented at the Seventh World Congress of Psychiatry, Vienna, July 11–16, 1983; Leff, *Psychiatry Around the Globe*, p. 157.

8 THE PERSON WITH SCHIZOPHRENIA IN WESTERN SOCIETY

1 Kraft, S. and Shulins, N., "Cardboard is home for box people," Associated Press release in the *Boulder Daily Camera*, January 17, 1982, p. 5.
2 Hopper, K., Baxter, E. and Cox, S., "Not making it crazy: The young homeless patients in New York City," *New Directions for Mental Health Services*, no. 14: 33–42, 1982.
3 US Department of Health and Human Services, *Toward a National Plan for the Chronically Mentally Ill*, Report to the Secretary by the Steering Committee on the Chronically Mentally Ill, Washington, DC: Department of Health and Human Services Publication Number (ADM) 81–1077, 1981, part 2, p. 11.
4 Reich, R. and Siegel, L., "The emergence of the Bowery as a psychiatric dumping ground," *Psychiatric Quarterly*, 50: 191–201, 1978; Reich, R. and Siegel, L., "The chronically mentally ill shuffle to oblivion," *Psychiatric Annals*, 3: 35–55, 1973.
5 Spitzer, R.L., Cohen, G., Miller, D.J. and Endicott, J., "The psychiatric status of 100 men on Skid Row," *International Journal of Social Psychiatry*, 15: 230–4, 1969.

6 Baxter, E., and Hopper, K., "The new mendicancy: Homeless in New York City," *American Journal of Orthopsychiatry*, 52: 393–408, 1982, p. 398.

7 Ibid., pp. 398–400.

8 Hopper, Baxter and Cox, "Not making it crazy," p. 34.

9 Priest, R.G., "A USA–UK comparison," *Proceedings of the Royal Society of Medicine*, 63: 441–5, 1970.

10 Bogue, D.J., *Skid Row in American Cities*, Chicago: Community and Family Study Center, University of Chicago, 1963, p. 208.

11 Farr, R., unpublished manuscript, 1983.

12 Torrey, E.F., "The real twilight zone," *Washington Post*, August 26, 1983.

13 Bassuk, E.L., Rubin, L. and Lauriat, A., "Is homelessness a mental health problem?", *American Journal of Psychiatry*, 141: 1546–50, 1984.

14 Morse, G. and Calsyn, R., "Mentally disturbed homeless people in St. Louis: Needy, willing, but underserved," *Journal of Mental Health*, 14: 74–94, 1986.

15 Colorado Bar Association, Report concerning the implementation of the Colorado Act for the Care and Treatment of the Mentally Ill, submitted to the Board of Governors of the Colorado Bar Association by the Disability Law Committee on July 31, 1981, p. 22.

16 Spitzer, "The psychiatric status of 100 men on Skid Row;" Priest, "A USA-UK comparison;" Baxter, "The new mendicancy;" Arce, A.A., Tadlock, M., Vergare, M.J. and Shapiro, S.H., "A psychiatric profile of street people admitted to an emergency shelter," *Hospital and Community Psychiatry*, 34: 812–17, 1983; Bassuk, "Is homelessness a mental health problem?;" Fischer, P.J., Shapiro, S., Breakey, W.R. et al., "Mental health and social characteristics of the homeless: A survey of mission users," *American Journal of Public Health*, 76: 519–24, 1986; Sacks, J.M., Phillips, J. and Cappelletty, G., "Characteristics of the homeless population in Fresno County," *Community Mental Health Journal*, 23: 114–19, 1987; Gelberg, L., Linn, L.S. and Leake, B.D., "Mental health, alcohol and drug use, and criminal history among homeless adults," *American Journal of Psychiatry*, 145: 191–6, 1988; Koegel, P., Burnam, A. and Farr, R.K., "The prevalence of specific psychiatric disorders among homeless individuals in the inner city of Los Angeles," *Archives of General Psychiatry*, 45: 1085–92, 1988; Vernez, G., Burnam, M.A., McGlynn, E.A. et al., *Review of California's program for the homeless mentally disabled*, Santa Monica, California: Rand Corporation, 1988; Susser, E., Struening, E.L. and Conover, S., "Psychiatric problems in homeless men: Lifetime psychosis, substance use, and current distress in new arrivals at New York City shelters," *Archives of General Psychiatry*, 46: 845–50; Morse, "Mentally disturbed homeless people in St. Louis;" Breakey, W.R., Fischer, P.J., Kramer, M. et al., "Health and mental health problems of homeless men and women in Baltimore," *Journal of the American Medical Association*, 262: 1352–7, 1989; Toro, P.A. and Wall, D.D., "Research on homeless persons: Diagnostic comparisons and practice implications," *Professional Psychology: Research and Practice*, 22: 479–88, 1991; North, C.S. and Smith, E.M., "A systematic study of mental health services utilization by homeless men and women," *Social Psychiatry and Psychiatric Epidemiology*, 28: 77–83, 1992; Leda, C., Rosenheck, R. and Gallup, P., "Mental illness among homeless female veterans," *Hospital and Community Psychiatry*, 43: 1026–8, 1992; Culhane, D.P., Avery, J.M. and Hadley, T.R., "Prevalence of treated behavioral disorders among adult shelter users: A longitudinal study," *American Journal of Orthopsychiatry*, 68: 63–72, 1998; Haugland, G., Siegel, C., Hopper, K. and Alexander, M.J., "Mental illness among homeless individuals in a suburban county," *Psychiatric Services*, 48: 504–9, 1997; Reich, "The emergence of the Bowery as a psychiatric dumping ground;" Lodge Patch, I., "Homeless men in

London. I. Demographic findings in a lodging house sample," *British Journal of Psychiatry*, 118: 313–17, 1971; Tidmarsh, D. and Wood, S., Psychiatric aspects of destitution: A study of the Camberwell reception centre, in Wing J.K. and Hailey, A.M., (eds.) *Evaluating a Community Psychiatry Service: The Camberwell Register, 1964–1971*, Oxford: Oxford University Press, 1972; Marshall, M.," Collected and neglected: Are Oxford hostels for the homeless filling up with disabled psychiatric patients?" *British Medical Journal*, 299: 706–9, 1989; Weller, M., Tobiansky, R.I., Hollander, D. and Ibrahimi, S., "Psychosis and destitution at Christmas 1985–88," *Lancet*, ii: 1509–11, 1989; Timms, P.W. and Fry, A.H., "Homelessness and mental illness," *Health Trends*, 21: 70–1, 1989; Stark, C., Scott, J., Hill, M. et al., *A Survey of the "Long-Stay" Users of DSS Resettlement Units: A Research Report*, London: Department of Social Security, 1989; Sclare, P.D., "Psychiatric disorder among the homeless in Aberdeen," *Scottish Medical Journal*, 42: 173–7, 1997; Hamid, W.A., Wykes, T. and Stansfeld, S., "The social disablement of men in hostels for homeless people. II. A comparison with patients from long-stay wards," *British Journal of Psychiatry*, 166: 809–12, 1995; Geddes, J.R., Newton, J.R., Bailey, S. et al., "Prevalence of psychiatric disorder, cognitive impairment and functional disability among homeless people resident in hostels," *Health Bulletin*, 54: 276–9, 1996; Marshall, E.J. and Reed, J.L., "Psychiatric morbidity in homeless women," *British Journal of Psychiatry*, 160: 761–8, 1992; Adams, C.E., Pantelis, C., Duke, P.J. and Barnes, T.R.E., "Psychopathology, social and cognitive functioning in a hostel for homeless women," *British Journal of Psychiatry*, 168: 82–6, 1996.

17 Koegel, P. et al., "The Causes of Homelessness," in *Homelessness in America*, Washington, DC: Oryx Press, 1996.

18 Federal Task Force for the Homeless and Severe Mental Illness, *Outcasts on Main Street: A Report of the Federal Task Force on Homelessness and Severe Mental Illness*, Washington, DC: Interagency Council on the Homeless, 1992.

19 National Coalition for the Homeless, *Fact Sheet Number 5*, Washington, DC, 1999.

20 Kaufman, T.L., *Out of Reach: Rental Housing At What Cost?* Washington, DC: National Low Income Housing Coalition, 1997.

21 Tidmarsh, "Psychiatric aspects of destitution."

22 Lodge Patch, I., "Homeless men in London."

23 Priest, R.G., "The Edinburgh homeless: A psychiatric survey," *American Journal of Psychotherapy*, 25: 191–213, 1971.

24 Lim, M.H., "A psychiatric emergency clinic: A study of attendances over six months," *British Journal of Psychiatry*, 143: 460–1, 1983.

25 Medical Campaign Project, *A Paper Outlining Good Practice on Discharge of Single Homeless People with Particular Reference to Mental Health Units*, London: Policy Studies Institute, 1990.

26 Sclare, "Psychiatric disorder among the homeless in Aberdeen;" Hamid, "The social disablement of men in hostels for homeless people;" Geddes, "Prevalence of psychiatric disorder among homeless people."

27 Adams, "Psychopathology, social and cognitive functioning in a hostel for homeless women."

28 Bolton, A., *A Study of the Need for and Availability of Mental Health Services for Mentally Disordered Jail Inmates and Juveniles in Detention Facilities*, Boston: Arthur Bolton Associates, 1976; Swank, G.E. and Winer, D., "Occurrence of psychiatric disorder in a county jail population," *American Journal of Psychiatry*, 133: 1331–3, 1976; Schuckit, M.A., Herrman, G. and Schuckit, J.J., "The importance of psychiatric illness in newly arrested prisoners," *Journal of Nervous and*

Mental Disease, 165: 118–25, 1977; Krefft, K.M. and Brittain, T.H., "A prisoner assessment survey: Screenings of a municipal prison population," *International Journal of Law and Psychiatry*, 6: 113–24, 1983; Teplin, L.A., "The prevalence of severe mental disorder among male urban jail detainees: Comparison with the Epidemiologic Catchment Area Program," *American Journal of Public Health*, 80: 663–9, 1990; Guy, E., Platt, J.J., Zwerling, I. and Bullock, S., "Mental health status of prisoners in an urban jail," *Criminal Justice and Behavior*, 12: 29–53, 1985; Chiles, J.A., Von Cleve, E., Jemelka, R.P. and Trupin, E.W., "Substance abuse and psychiatric disorder in prison inmates," *Hospital and Community Psychiatry*, 41: 1132–4, 1990; Teplin, L.A., Abram, K.M. and McClelland, G.M., "Prevalence of psychiatric disorders among incarcerated women. I. Pretrial jail detainees," *Archives of General Psychiatry*, 53: 505–12, 1996; Powell, T.A., Holt, J.C. and Fondacaro, K.M., "The prevalence of mental illness among inmates in a rural state," *Law and Human Behavior*, 21: 427–38, 1997; Gibbens, T.C.N., *Aspects of After-care. Annual Report*, London: Royal London Prisoners' Aid Society, 1996, pp. 8–11; Blugrass, R., *A Psychiatric Study of Scottish Convicted Prisoners*, MD thesis, University of St Andrews, Scotland, 1996; Gunn, J., Robertson, G., Dell, S. and Way, C., *Psychiatric Aspects of Imprisonment*, London: Academic Press, 1978; Faulk, M., "A psychiatric study of men serving a sentence in Winchester Prison," *Medicine, Science and the Law*, 16: 244–51, 1976; Gunn, J., Maden, A. and Swinton, M., "Treatment needs of prisoners with psychiatric disorders," *British Medical Journal*, 303: 338–41, 1991; Maden, T., Swinton, M. and Gunn, J., "Psychiatric disorder in women serving a prison sentence," *British Journal of Psychiatry*, 164: 44–54, 1994; Watt, F., Tomison, A. and Torpy, D., "The prevalence of psychiatric disorder in a male remand population: a pilot study," *Journal of Forensic Psychiatry*, 4: 75–83, 1993; Brooke, D., Taylor, C., Gunn, J. and Maden, A., "Point prevalence of mental disorder in unconvicted male prisoners in England and Wales," *British Medical Journal*, 313: 1524–7, 1996; Birmingham, L., Mason, D. and Grubin, D., "Prevalence of mental disorder in remand prisoners: Consecutive case study," *British Medical Journal*, 313: 1521–4, 1996; Singleton, N., Meltzer, H., Gatward, R. et al., *Psychiatric Morbidity among Prisoners in England and Wales*, London: Office of National Statistics, 1998.

29 Gibbens, *Aspects of After-care*; Blugrass, *A Forensic Psychiatry Service at HM Prison, Perth*; Gunn, *Psychiatric Aspects of Imprisonment*; Faulk, "A psychiatric study of men serving a sentence in Winchester Prison;" Gunn, "Treatment needs of prisoners with psychiatric disorders;" Maden, "Psychiatric disorder in women serving a prison sentence;" Watt, "The prevalence of psychiatric disorder in a male remand population."

30 Brooke, "Point prevalence of mental disorder in unconvicted male prisoners in England and Wales;" Birmingham, "Prevalence of mental disorder in remand prisoners."

31 Singleton, *Psychiatric Morbidity among Prisoners in England and Wales.*

32 Ditton, P.M., *Bureau of Justice Statistics Special Report: Mental Health and Treatment of Inmates and Probationers*, Washington, DC: US Department of Justice, July 1999, pp. 12.

33 Warner, R., "Psychotics in jail," presented at the Mental Health Center of Boulder County Symposium on Controversial Issues in Community Care, Boulder, Colorado, March 27, 1981.

34 Torrey *Criminalizing the Seriously Mentally Ill*, pp. 1–3.

35 Ibid., p. 4.

36 Cherry, A.L., "On jailing the mentally ill," *Health and Social Work*, 3: 189–92, 1978.

37 Roth, L.H. and Ervin, F.R., "Psychiatric care of federal prisoners," *American Journal of Psychiatry*, 128: 424–30, 1971; Kaufman, E., "The violation of psychiatric standards of care in prisons," *American Journal of Psychiatry*, 137: 566–70, 1980.

38 James, J.F., Gregory, D., Jones, R.K. and Rundell, O.H., "Psychiatric morbidity in prisons," *Hospital and Community Psychiatry*, 31: 674–7, 1980.

39 Unpublished data from the Division of Community Psychiatry, University of Washington, 1988, cited in Jemelka, R., Trupin, E. and Chiles, J.A. "The mentally ill in prisons: A review," *Hospital and Community Psychiatry*, 40: 481–5, 1989.

40 Neighbors, H.W., "The prevalence of mental disorder in Michigan prisons," *DIS Newsletter*, Department of Psychiatry, University of Washington, St. Louis, 7: 8–11, 1987.

41 Steadman, H.J., Fabisiak, S., Dvoskin, J. and Holohean, E.J., "A survey of mental disability among prison inmates," *Hospital and Community Psychiatry*, 38: 1086–90, 1987.

42 Jemelka, R. et al., "The mentally ill in prisons."

43 Keith, S.J., Regier, D.A. and Rae, D.S., "Schizophrenic disorders," in L.N. Robins and D.A. Regier (eds.), *Psychiatric Disorders in America: The Epidemiologic Catchment Area Study*, New York: Maxwell Macmillan International, 1991, pp. 33–52. The reference is to p. 37.

44 Stelovich, S., "From the hospital to the prison: A step forward in deinstitutionalization?" *Hospital and Community Psychiatry*, 31: 674–7, 1980.

45 US Census Bureau, *Statistical Abstract of the United States: 2001: The National Data Book*, 121st edition, Washington, DC: US Department of Commerce, Economics and Statistics Administration, 2001, p. 200; Morrissey, J.P., Thakur, N., Steadman, H.J. and Preisser, J., "The impact of managed care on the use of jails, mental services, and Medicaid: A population-based perspective," unpublished manuscript, September, 2002.

46 Morrissey, "The impact of managed care on the use of jails."

47 Goldstrom, I., Henderson, M., Male, A. and Manderscheid, R.W., "Jail mental health services: A national survey," in R.W. Manderscheid and M.A. Sonnenschein (eds.), *Mental Health, United States, 1998*, Washington, DC: Department of Health and Human Services, Center for Mental Health Services, pp. 176–87.

48 Joseph Morrissey, personal communication, 2003; Ditton, *Mental Health and Treatment of Inmates*.

49 Ditton, *Mental Health and Treatment of Inmates*.

50 Velde, R.W., associate administrator of the Law Enforcement Assistance Administration of the US Department of Justice, writing in *The Correctional Trainer*, Newsletter for Illinois Correctional Staff Training, Fall 1979, p. 109.

51 Goldfarb, *Jails: The Ultimate Ghetto*, Garden City, New York: Anchor Press, 1975, p. 89 Kaufman, "Violation of psychiatric standards."

52 Waldron, R.J. and Pospichal, T.J., "The relationship between unemployment rates and prison incarceration rates," NCJRS microfiche, 1980; Jankovic, I., "Labor market and imprisonment," *Crime and Social Justice*, 8: 17–31, 1977; Carlson, K., Evans, P. and Flanagan, J., *American Prisons and Jails: Volume II: Population Trends and Projections*, Washington, DC: US Department of Justice, National Institute of Justice, 1980; Greenberg, D.G., "The dynamics of oscillatory punishment processes," *Journal of Criminal Law and Criminology*, 68: 643–51, 1977; Brenner, M.H., *Estimating the Social Costs of National Economic Policy: Implications for Mental and Physical Health and Criminal Aggression*, Washington, DC: US Government Printing Office, 1976; Nagel J.H., "Crime and incarceration: A

reanalysis," NCJRS microfiche, 1977; Nagel, W.G., "A statement on behalf of a moratorium on prison construction," proceedings of the 106th Annual Congress of the American Correctional Association, Denver, August 1976, pp. 79–87.

53 Warner, R., "The effect of the labor market on mental hospital and prison use: An international comparison," *Administration in Mental Health*, 10: 239–58, 1983.

54 US DHHS, *Toward a National Plan*, part 2, p. 20.

55 A study of the chronically mentally ill in Los Angeles board and care homes found two-thirds to be suffering from schizophrenia: see Lehman, A.F., Ward, A.C. and Linn, L.S., "Chronic mental patients: The quality of life issue," *American Journal of Psychiatry*, 139: 1271–6, 1982.

56 US Congress, *Board and Care Homes in America: A National Tragedy: A Report by the Chairman of the Subcommittee on Health and Aging of the Select Committee on Aging*, Washington, DC: House of Representatives, March 1986, Committee Publication number 101–711.

57 Ibid.

58 Levy, C.J., "For mentally ill, death and misery," *New York Times*, April 28, 2002, pp. 1 & 34–6; Levy, C.J., "Here, life is squalor and chaos," *New York Times*, April 29, 2002, pp. A1 & A26–7; Levy, C.J., "Voiceless, defenseless and a source of cash," *New York Times*, April 30, 2002, pp. A1 & A28–9; Levy, C.J., "Inquiries start on conditions in homes for the mentally ill," *New York Times*, May 1, 2002, pp. A1 & C18.

59 US Department of Health and Human Services, *Toward a National Plan*, Part 2, p. 19. Minkoff, K., "A map of the chronic mental patient," in J.A. Talbott (ed.), *The Chronic Mental Patient*, Washington, DC: American Psychiatric Association, 1978, pp. 18–19.

60 Colorado General Assembly, *The Placement and Utilization of Mental Health Services by Medicaid Clients in Nursing Homes and Alternative Care Facilities: Report to the Joint Budget Committee*, Denver: 2001, p. 16.

61 Levy, C.J., "Mentally ill and locked away in nursing homes in New York," *New York Times*, October 6, 2002, pp. 1 & 29. The reference is to p. 29.

62 Ibid., p. 29.

63 Keith et al., "Schizophrenic disorders," p. 37.

64 US Census Bureau, *Statistical Abstract of the United States: 2001*, p. 117.

65 The number of Americans with schizophrenia is calculated from a one-year prevalence estimate of 6.3 per 1,000 of the United States population over age 18 in the 2000 US Census. The prevalence estimate is the average of one-year and point prevalence figures for Europe and North America in Warner, R. and de Girolamo, G., *Epidemiology of Mental Disorders and Psychosocial Problems: Schizophrenia*, Geneva: World Health Organization, 1995. This estimate is similar to the figure derived by the US National Comorbidity Study, but less than the rate derived by the Epidemiologic Catchment Area Study that, as Warner and de Girolamo have shown, was inflated for technical reasons. *Lifetime* prevalence estimates will yield a higher number of people with schizophrenia, but here we are concerned with *active* cases of schizophrenia and the lower point or one-year prevalence rate is more appropriate.

66 Binder, R.L., "The use of seclusion on an inpatient crisis intervention unit," *Hospital and Community Psychiatry*, 30: 266–9, 1979.

67 Wadeson, J. and Carpenter, W.T., "The impact of the seclusion room experience," *Journal of Nervous and Mental Disease*, 163: 318–28, 1976.

68 Telintelo, S., Kuhlman, T.L. and Winget, C., "A study of the use of restraint in a psychiatric emergency room," *Hospital and Community Psychiatry*, 34: 164–5, 1983.

69 Sologg, P.H., "Behavioral precipitants of restraint in the modern milieu," *Comprehensive Psychiatry*, 19: 179–84, 1978, p. 182.

70 Mattson, M.R. and Sacks, M.H., "Seclusion: Uses and complications," *American Journal of Psychiatry*, 135: 1210–13, 1978, p. 1211.

71 Colorado Bar Association Report, pp. 9–107. Subsequently, conditions at the two Colorado State Hospitals have substantially improved.

72 "In Your Community," radio program in the series "Breakdown," produced at Seven Oaks Productions, Boulder, Colorado, by R. Warner and K. Kindle.

73 Anonymous, "On being diagnosed schizophrenic," *Schizophrenia Bulletin*, 3: 4, 1977.

74 Star, S., "The public's idea about mental illness," presented at the National Association for Mental Health meeting, Chicago, Illinois, November 1955.

75 Cumming, E. and Cumming, J., *Closed Ranks: An Experiment in Mental Health Education*, Cambridge: Harvard University Press, 1957.

76 Nunally, J.C., *Popular Conceptions of Mental Health: Their Development and Change*, New York: Holt, Rinehart and Winston, 1961, p. 46.

77 Ibid., p. 51.

78 Ibid., p. 233.

79 Lemkau, P.V. and Crocetti, G.M., "An urban population's opinions and knowledge about mental illness," *American Journal of Psychiatry*, 118: 692–700, 1962; Meyer, J.K., "Attitudes toward mental illness in a Maryland community," *Public Health Reports*, 79: 769–72, 1964; Bentz, W.K., Edgerton, J.W. and Kherlopian, M., "Perceptions of mental illness among people in a rural area," *Mental Hygiene*, 53: 459–65, 1969; Crocetti, G., Spiro, J.R. and Siassi, I., "Are the ranks closed? Attitudinal social distance and mental illness," *American Journal of Psychiatry*, 127: 1121–7, 1971.

80 Cockerham, W.C., *Sociology of Mental Disorder*, Englewood Cliffs, New Jersey: Prentice-Hall, 1981, pp. 295–9.

81 Olmsted, D.W. and Durham, K., "Stability of mental health attitudes: A semantic differential study," *Journal of Health and Social Behavior*, 17: 35–44, 1976.

82 D'Arcy, C. and Brockman, J., "Changing public recognition of psychiatric symptoms? Blackfoot revisited," *Journal of Health and Social Behavior*, 17: 302–10, 1976.

83 Hall, P., Brockington, I.F., Levings, J. et al., "A comparison of responses to the mentally ill in two communities," *British Journal of Psychiatry*, 162: 99–108, 1993.

84 Sayce, L., "Stigma, discrimination and social exclusion: What's in a word?" *Journal of Mental Health*, 7: 331–43, 1998.

85 O'Grady, T.J., "Public attitudes to mental illness," *British Journal of Psychiatry*, 168: 652, 1996.

86 Borenstein, A.B., "Public attitudes towards persons with mental illness," *Health Affairs*, Fall issue, 186–96, 1992.

87 Weiner, B., Perry, R.P. and Magnusson, J., "An attributional analysis of reactions to stigmas," *Journal of Personality and Social Psychology*, 55: 738–48, 1988.

88 Page, S., "Effects of the mental illness label in attempts to obtain accommodation," *Canadian Journal of Behavioural Science*, 9, 85–90, 1977.

89 Miller, D. and Dawson, W.H., "Effects of stigma on re-employment of ex-mental patients," *Mental Hygiene*, 49: 281–7, 1965.

90 Aviram, U. and Segal, S.P., "Exclusion of the mentally ill: Reflection of an old problem in a new context," *Archives of General Psychiatry*, 29: 126–31, 1973.

91 Boydall, K.M., Trainor, J.M. and Pierri, A.M., "The effect of group homes for the mentally ill on residential property values," *Hospital and Community Psychiatry*, 40: 957–8, 1989.

92 Robert Wood Johnson Foundation, *Public Attitudes Toward People with Chronic Mental Illness*, The Robert Wood Johnson Foundation Program on Chronic Mental Illness, New Jersey, 1990.

93 Repper, J., Sayce, L., Strong, S. et al., *Tall Stories from the Backyard: A Survey of "Nimby" Opposition to Community Mental Health Facilities, Experienced by Key Service Providers in England and Wales*, London: Mind, 1997.

94 Read, J. and Baker, S., *Not Just Sticks and Stones: A Survey of the Stigma, Taboos and Discrimination Experienced by People with Mental Health Problems*. London: Mind, 1996.

95 Alisky, J.M. and Iczkowski, K.A., "Barriers to housing for deinstitutionalized psychiatric patients," *Hospital and Community Psychiatry*, 41: 93–5, 1990.

96 Farina, A. and Felner, R.D., "Employment interviewer reactions to former mental patients," *Journal of Abnormal Psychology*, 82: 268–72, 1973.

97 Parashos, J., *Athenians' views on mental and physical illness*, Athens: Lundbeck Hellas, 1998.

98 Tringo, J.L., "The hierarchy of preference towards disability groups," *Journal of Special Education*, 4: 295–306, 1970.

99 Lamy, R.E., "Social consequences of mental illness," *Journal of Consulting Psychology*, 30: 450–5, 1966.

100 Lamb, H.R., "Roots of neglect of the long-term mentally ill," *Psychiatry*, 42: 201–7, 1979.

101 Munoz, R.A. and Morrison, J.R., "650 private psychiatric patients," *Journal of Clinical Psychiatry*, 40: 114–16, 1979.

102 Page, S., "Social responsiveness toward mental patients: The general public and others," *Canadian Journal of Psychiatry*, 25: 242–6, 1980.

103 Scheper-Hughes, N., *Saints, Scholars and Schizophrenics: Mental Illness in Rural Ireland*, Berkeley: University of California Press, 1979, p. 89.

104 Giovannoni, J.M. and Ullman, L.P., "Conceptions of mental health held by psychiatric patients," *Journal of Clinical Psychology*, 19: 398–400, 1963; Manis, M., Houts, P.S. and Blake, J.B., "Beliefs about mental illness as a function of psychiatric status and psychiatric hospitalization," *Journal of Abnormal and Social Psychology*, 67: 226–33, 1963; Crumpton, E., Weinstein, A.D., Acker, C.W. and Annis, A.P., "How patients and normals see the mental patient," *Journal of Clinical Psychology*, 23: 46–9, 1967.

105 Bentinck, C., "Opinions about mental illness held by patients and relatives," *Family Process*, 6: 193–207, 1967; Swanson, R.M. and Spitzer, S.P., "Stigma and the psychiatric patient career," *Journal of Health and Social Behavior*, 11: 44–51, 1970.

106 Scheff, T.J., *Being Mentally Ill: A Sociological Theory*, Chicago: Aldine, 1966.

107 Phillips, D.L., "Public identification and acceptance of the mentally ill," *American Journal of Public Health*, 56: 755–63, 1966.

108 Rosenhan, D.L., "On being sane in insane places," *Science*, 179: 250–8, 1973.

109 Gove, W.R., "Labelling and mental illness," in W.R. Gove (ed.), *The Labelling of Deviance: Evaluating a Perspective*, New York: Halsted, 1975.

110 Link, B.G., Cullen, F.T., Frank, J. et al., "The social rejection of former mental patients: Understanding why labels matter," *American Journal of Sociology*, 92: 1461–1500, 1987.

111 Penn, D.L., Guynan, K., Daily, T. et al., "Dispelling the stigma of schizophrenia: What sort of information is best?" *Schizophrenia Bulletin*, 20: 567–78, 1994.

112 Strauss, J.S. and Carpenter, W.T., *Schizophrenia*, New York: Plenum, 1981, p. 128.

113 Festinger, L., *A Theory of Cognitive Dissonance*, Stanford, California: Stanford

University Press, 1957; Festinger, L. and Carlsmith, J.M., "Cognitive consequences of forced compliance," *Journal of Abnormal and Social Psychology*, 58: 203–10, 1959.

114 Van Putten, J., Crumpton, E. and Yale, C., "Drug refusal in schizophrenia and the wish to be crazy," *Archives of General Psychiatry*, 33: 1443–6, 1976.

115 Lamb, H.R. and Goertzel, V., "Discharged mental patients – Are they really in the community?" *Archives of General Psychiatry*, 24: 29–34, 1971; Wing, J.K., "The social context of schizophrenia," *American Journal of Psychiatry*, 135: 1333–9, 1978.

116 Doherty, E.G., "Labeling effects in psychiatric hospitalization: A study of diverging patterns of inpatient self-labeling processes," *Archives of General Psychiatry*, 32: 562–8, 1975.

117 Warner, R., Taylor, D., Powers, M. and Hyman, J. "Acceptance of the mental illness label by psychotic patients: Effects on functioning," *American Journal of Orthopsychiatry*, 59: 398–409, 1989.

118 Pattison, E.M., DeFrancisco, D., Wood, P. et al., "A psychosocial kinship model for family therapy," *American Journal of Psychiatry*, 132: 1246–51, 1975; Cohen, C.I. and Sokolovsky, J., "Schizophrenia and social networks: Ex-patients in the inner city," *Schizophrenia Bulletin*, 4: 546–60, 1978; Pattison, E.M. and Pattison, M.L., "Analysis of a schizophrenic psychosocial network," *Schizophrenia Bulletin*, 7: 135–43, 1981; Lipton, F.R., Cohen, C.I., Fischer, E. and Katz, S.E., "Schizophrenia: A network crisis," *Schizophrenia Bulletin*, 7: 144–51, 1981; Minkoff, "Map of the chronic mental patient," p. 25.

119 Lipton et al., "A network crisis."

120 Westermeyer, J. and Pattison, E.M., "Social networks and mental illness in a peasant society," *Schizophrenia Bulletin*, 7: 125–34, 1981.

121 Cohen and Sokolovsky, "Schizophrenia and social networks."

122 Yarrow, M., Clausen, J. and Robbins, P., "The social meaning of mental illness," *Journal of Social Issues*, 11: 33–48, 1955.

123 Kreisman, D.E. and Joy, V.D., "Family response to the mental illness of a relative: A review of the literature," *Schizophrenia Bulletin*, issue 10: 34–57, 1974.

124 Hatfield, A., "Psychosocial costs of schizophrenia to the family," *Social Work*, 23: 355–9, 1978, p. 358.

125 Creer, C., "Living with schizophrenia," *Social Work Today*, 6: 2–7, 1975.

126 Grinspoon, L., Courtney, P.H. and Bergen, H.M., "The usefulness of a structured parents' group in rehabilitation," in M. Greenblatt, D.J. Levinson and G.L. Klerman (eds), *Mental Patients in Transition: Steps in Hospital–Community Rehabilitation*, Springfield, Illinois: Charles C. Thomas, 1961, p. 245.

127 Maddox, S., "Profiles: Tom Hansen," *Boulder Monthly*, January 1979, p. 19.

128 Thompson, E.H. and Doll, W., "The burden of families coping with the mentally ill: An invisible crisis," *Family Relations*, 31: 379–88, 1982.

129 Phelan, J.C., Bromet, E.J. and Link, B.G., "Psychiatric illness and family stigma," *Schizophrenia Bulletin*, 24, 115–26, 1988.

130 Brown, G.W., Birley, J.L.T. and Wing, J.K., "Influence of family life on the course of schizophrenic disorders: A replication," *British Journal of Psychiatry*, 121: 241–58, 1972; Vaughn, C.E. and Leff, J.P., "The influence of family and social factors on the course of psychiatric illness," *British Journal of Psychiatry*, 129: 125–37, 1976.

131 Marx, K., *The Economic and Philosophic Manuscripts of 1844*, New York: International Publishers, 1964; Novack, G., "The problem of alienation," in E. Mandel and G. Novack, *The Marxist Theory of Alienation*, New York: Pathfinder

Press, 1973, pp. 53–94; Ollman, B., *Alienation: Marx's Conception of Man in Capitalist Society*, Cambridge: Cambridge University Press, 1971.

132 Robinson, J.P. and Shaver, P.R., *Measures of Social Psychological Attitudes*, Ann Arbor, Michigan: Institute for Social Research, 1969, p. 249.

133 Fromkin, K.R. "Gender differences among chronic schizophrenics in the perceived helpfulness of community-based treatment programs," unpublished doctoral dissertation, Department of Psychology, University of Colorado, 1985.

134 Robinson and Shaver, *Measures of Social Psychological Attitudes*, p. 271.

135 Safer, D.J., "Substance abuse by young adult chronic patients," *Hospital and Community Psychiatry*, 38: 853–8, 1985; Atkinson, R.M., "Importance of alcohol and drug abuse in psychiatric emergencies," *California Medicine*, 118: 1–4, 1973.

136 Warner, R., Taylor, D., Wright, J. et al., "Substance use among the mentally ill: Prevalence, reasons for use and effects on illness," *American Journal of Orthopsychiatry*, 64: 465–76, 1994.

137 Henry, J., *Culture Against Man*, New York: Random House, 1964.

138 Berreman, G.D., "Structure and function of caste systems," in G. DeVos and H. Wagatsuma (eds), *Japan's Invisible Race: Caste in Culture and Personality*, Berkeley, California: University of California Press, 1972, pp. 277–307. The reference is to p. 288.

139 Harris, M., *Culture, Man, and Nature*, New York: Thomas Y. Crowell, 1971, ch. 18.

9 THE INCIDENCE OF SCHIZOPHRENIA

1 Barker, D.J.P., "Rise and fall of Western diseases," *Nature*, 338: 371–2, 1989.

2 Barker, D.J.P. and Phillips, D.I.W., *Lancet*, ii: 567–70, 1984, cited in Barker, "Rise and fall of Western diseases."

3 Kraepelin, E., *Dementia Praecox and Paraphrenia*, Edinburgh: Livingstone, 1927, p. 1145.

4 Warner, R. and de Girolamo, G., *Epidemiology of Mental Health and Psychosocial Problems: Schizophrenia*, Geneva: World Health Organization, 1995, Chapter 3.

5 Ibid.

6 Torrey, E.F., *Schizophrenia and Civilization*, New York: Jason Aronson, 1980.

7 Jeste, D.V., Carman, R., Lohr, J.B. and Wyatt, R.J. "Did schizophrenia exist before the eighteenth century?" *Comprehensive Psychiatry*, 26: 493–503, 1985; Ellard, J. "Did schizophrenia exist before the eighteenth century?" *Australia and New Zealand Journal of Psychiatry*, 21: 306–14, 1987.

8 Jeste, "Schizophrenia before the eighteenth century."

9 Ellard, "Schizophrenia before the eighteenth century."

10 Hare, E., "Was insanity on the increase?" *British Journal of Psychiatry*, 142: 439–5, 1983.

11 Scull, A., *Museums of Madness: The Social Organization of Insanity in Nineteenth-Century England*, London: Allen Lane, 1979, p. 225.

12 Tuke, D.H., "Increase in insanity in Ireland," *Journal of Mental Science*," 40: 549–58, 1894.

13 Hare, "Was insanity on the increase?"

14 Hare, E., "Schizophrenia as a recent disease," *British Journal of Psychiatry*, 153: 521–31, 1988.

15 Jablensky, A., "Epidemiology of schizophrenia: A European perspective," *Schizophrenia Bulletin*, 12: 52–73, 1986.

16 Bamrah, J.S., Freeman, H.L. and Goldberg, D.P., "Epidemiology in Salford, 1974–84: Changes in an urban community over ten years," *British Journal of Psychiatry*, 159: 802–10, 1991; Castle, D., Wessely, S., Der, G. and Murray, R.M., "The incidence of operationally defined schizophrenia in Camberwell, 1965–84," *British Journal of Psychiatry*, 159: 790–4, 1991; de Alarcon, J., Seagroatt, V. and Goldacre, M., "Trends in schizophrenia (letter)," *Lancet*, 335: 852–3, 1990; Der, G., Gupta, S. and Murray, R.M., "Is schizophrenia disappearing?" *Lancet*, 335: 513–16, 1990; Dickson, W.E. and Kendell, R.E., "Does maintenance lithium therapy prevent recurrences of mania under ordinary clinical conditions?" *Psychological Medicine*, 16: 521–30, 1986; Eagles, J.M., Hunter, D. and McCance, C., "Decline in the diagnosis of schizophrenia among first contacts with psychiatric services in north-east Scotland, 1969–1984," *British Journal of Psychiatry*, 152: 793–8, 1988; Eagles, J.M. and Whalley, L.J., "Decline in the diagnosis of schizophrenia among first admissions to Scottish mental hospitals from 1969–78," *British Journal of Psychiatry*, 146: 151–4, 1985; Folnegović, Z., Folnegović-Šmalc, V. and Kulčar, Ž., "The incidence of schizophrenia in Croatia," *British Journal of Psychiatry*, 156: 363–5, 1990; Häfner, H. and an der Heiden, W., "The Mannheim case register: The long-stay population," in G.H.M.M. ten Horn, R. Giel, W.H. Gulbinat and J.H. Henderson (eds), *Psychiatric Case Registers in Public Health*, Amsterdam: Elsevier, 1986, pp. 28–38; Harrison, G., Cooper, J.E. and Gancarczyk, R., "Changes in the administrative incidence of schizophrenia," *British Journal of Psychiatry*, 159: 811–16, 1991; Joyce, P.R., "Changing trends in first admissions and readmissions for mania and schizophrenia in New Zealand," *Australian and New Zealand Journal of Psychiatry*, 21: 82–6, 1987; Munk-Jørgensen, P., "Decreasing first-admission rates of schizophrenia among males in Denmark from 1970 to 1984," *Acta Psychiatrica Scandinavica*, 73: 645–50, 1986; Munk-Jørgensen, P. and Jørgensen, P., "Decreasing rates of first-admission diagnoses of schizophrenia among females in Denmark from 1970 to 1984," *Acta Psychiatrica Scandinavica*, 74: 379–83, 1986; Munk-Jørgensen, P. and Mortensen, P.B., "Incidence and other aspects of the epidemiology of schizophrenia in Denmark, 1971–1987," *Journal of Psychiatry*, 161: 489–95, 1992; Parker, G., O'Donnell, M. and Walter, S., "Changes in the diagnoses of the functional psychoses associated with the introduction of lithium," *British Journal of Psychiatry*, 146: 377–82, 1985; D'Arcy, C., Rawson, N.S.B., Lydick, E. and Epstein, R., "The epidemiology of treated schizophrenia, Saskatchewan, 1976–1990," poster presentation, World Psychiatric Association, Section of Epidemiology and Community Psychiatry, conference on "Changing the Course and Outcome of Mental Disorder," Groningen, the Netherlands: September 1–3, 1993; Oldehinkel, A.J. and Giel, R., "Time trends in the care-based incidence of schizophrenia," *British Journal of Psychiatry*, 167: 777–82, 1995; Takei, N., Lewis, G., Sham, P.C., and Murray, R.M., "Age-period-cohort analysis of the incidence of schizophrenia in Scotland," *Psychological Medicine*, 26: 963–73, 1996; Brewin, J., Cantwell, R., Dalkin, T. et al., "Incidence of schizophrenia in Nottingham: A comparison of two cohorts, 1978–80 and 1992–94," *British Journal of Psychiatry*, 171: 140–4, 1997; Suvisaari, J.M., Haukka, J.K., Tanskanen, A.J. and Lönnqvist, J.K., "Decline in the incidence of schizophrenia in Finnish cohorts born from 1954 to 1965," *Archives of General Psychiatry*, 56: 733–40, 1999; Allardyce, J., Morrison, G., van Os, J. et al., "Schizophrenia is not disappearing in south-west Scotland," British Journal of Psychiatry, 177: 38–41, 2000.
17 Strömgren, E., "Changes in the incidence of schizophrenia," *British Journal of Psychiatry*, 150: 1–7, 1967; Crow, T.J., "Trends in schizophrenia" (letter), *Lancet*, 335: 851, 1990.

18 Parker et al., "Changes in the diagnoses of the functional psychoses."
19 Dickson and Kendell, "Does maintenance lithium therapy prevent recurrences of mania?;" Eagles et al., "Decline in the diagnosis of schizophrenia."
20 Kendell, R.E., Malcolm, D.E. and Adams, W., "The problem of detecting changes in the incidence of schizophrenia," *British Journal of Psychiatry*, 162: 212–18, 1993.
21 Crow, "Trends in schizophrenia;" Munk-Jørgensen and Mortensen, "Incidence and other aspects of the epidemiology of schizophrenia in Denmark."
22 Graham, P.M., "Trends in schizophrenia" (letter), *Lancet*, 335: 1214, 1990; de Alarcon, J. et al., "Trends in schizophrenia."
23 Cooper, J.E., Goodhead, D., Craig, T. et al., "The incidence of schizophrenia in Nottingham," *British Journal of Psychiatry*, 151: 619–26, 1987.
24 Gottesman, I.I., *Schizophrenia Genesis: The Origins of Madness*, New York: W.W. Freeman, 1991, p. 102.
25 Barker, "Rise and fall of Western diseases."
26 Gupta, S. and Murray, R.M., "The changing incidence of schizophrenia: Fact or artefact?" *Directions in Psychiatry*, 11: 1–8, 1991.
27 Rose, A.M., "The prevalence of mental disorders in Italy," *International Journal of Social Psychiatry*, 10: 87–100, 1964.
28 Rao, S., "Caste and mental disorders in Bihar," *American Journal of Psychiatry*, 122: 1045–55, 1966.
29 Nandi, D.N., Mukherjee, S.P., Boral, G.C. et al., "Socio-economic status and mental morbidity in certain tribes and castes in India: A cross-cultural study," *British Journal of Psychiatry*, 136: 73–85, 1980.
30 Dube and Kumar, "Epidemiological study of schizophrenia."
31 Elnagar, M.N., Maitra, P. and Rao, M.N., "Mental health in an Indian rural community," *British Journal of Psychiatry*, 118: 499–503, 1971.
32 Lin, "Incidence of mental disorder in Chinese," pp. 326–7; Lin, Rin, Yeh et al., "Mental disorders in Taiwan," pp. 82–7.
33 McNeil, T.F., "Perinatal influences in the development of schizophrenia," In H. Helmchen and F.A. Henn (eds), *Biological Perspectives of Schizophrenia*, New York: John Wiley, 1987, pp. 125–38.
34 Goodman, R., "Are complications of pregnancy and birth causes of schizophrenia?" *Developmental Medicine and Child Neurology*, 30: 391–5, 1988; Günther-Genta, F., Bovet, P. and Hohlfeld, P., "Obstetric complications and schizophrenia: A case-control study," *British Journal of Psychiatry*, 164: 165–70, 1994; Geddes, J.R. and Lawrie, S.M., "Obstetric complications and schizophrenia," *British Journal of Schizophrenia*, 167: 786–93, 1995; Geddes, J.R., Verdoux, H., Takei, N. et al., "Schizophrenia and complications of pregnancy and labour: An individual patient data meta-analysis," *Schizophrenia Bulletin*, 25: 413–23, 1999; Jones, P.B., Rantakallio, P., Hartikainen, A-L. et al., "Schizophrenia as a long-term outcome of pregnancy, delivery, and perinatal complications: A 28-year follow-up of the 1996 north Finland general population birth cohort," *American Journal of Psychiatry*, 155: 355–64, 1998; Dalman, C., Allebeck, P., Cullberg, J. et al., "Obstetric complications and the risk of schizophrenia," *Archives of General Psychiatry*, 56: 234–40, 1999; Hultman, C.M., Sparen, P., Takei, N. et al., "Prenatal and perinatal risk factors for schizophrenia, affective psychosis, and reactive psychosis of early onset: Case control study," *British Medical Journal*, 318: 421–6, 1999; Byrne, M., Browne, R., Mulryan, N. et al., "Labour and delivery complications and schizophrenia: Case-control study using contemporaneous labour ward records," *British Journal of Psychiatry*, 176: 531–6, 2000; Cannon, T.D., Rosso, I.M., Hollister, J.M. et al., "A prospective cohort study of genetic and perinatal influences in the etiology of schizophrenia," *Schizophrenia Bulletin*, 26: 351–66,

2000; Kendell, R.E., McInneny, K., Juszczak, E. et al., "Obstetric complications and schizophrenia: Two case-control studies based on structured obstetric records," *British Journal of Psychiatry*, 176: 516–22, 2000.

35 Wilcox, J.A. and Nasrallah, H.A., "Perinatal insult as a risk factor in paranoid and and non-paranoid schizophrenia," *Psychopathology*, 20: 285–7, 1987; Schwarzkopf, S.B., Nasrallah, H.A., Olson, S.C. et al., "Perinatal complications and genetic loading in schizophrenia; Preliminary findings," *Psychiatry Research*, 27: 233–9, 1989.

36 Cannon, T.D., Mednick, S.A. and Parnas, J., "Genetic and perinatal determinants of structural brain deficits in schizophrenia," *Archives of General Psychiatry*, 46: 883–9, 1989; Fish, B., Marcus, J., Hans, J.L. et al., "Infants at risk for schizophrenia: Sequelae of a genetic neurointegrative defect," *Archives of General Psychiatry*, 49: 221–35, 1992.

37 McNeil, "Perinatal influences in the development of schizophrenia;" Geddes and Lawrie, "Obstetric complications and schizophrenia."

38 Geddes and Lawrie, "Obstetric complications and schizophrenia."

39 North, A.F. and MacDonald, H.M., "Why are neonatal mortality rates lower in small black infants of similar birth weights?" *Journal of Pediatrics*, 90: 809–10, 1977.

40 Cannon et al., "Genetic and perinatal determinants."

41 Lane, E. and Albee, G.W., "Comparitive birthweights of schizophrenics and their siblings," *Journal of Psychiatry*, 64: 227–31, 1966; Stabenau, J.R. and Pollin W., "Early characteristics of MZ twins discordant for schizophrenia," *Archives of General Psychiatry*, 17: 723–34, 1967.

42 Gupta and Murray, "The changing incidence of schizophrenia."

43 Eagles, J.M., "Is schizophrenia disappearing?" *British Journal of Psychiatry*, 158: 834–5, 1991.

44 Arieti, S., *The Interpretation of Schizophrenia*, New York: Basic Books, 1974, p. 494; Leff, J., *Psychiatry Around the Globe: A Transcultural View*, Second edition, London: Gaskell, 1988, p. 163.

45 US Department of Health, Education and Welfare, *Vital Statistics of the United States*, Washington, DC: US Government Printing Office, 1923; Malzberg, B., "A statistical study of mental diseases among natives of foreign white parentage in New York State," *Psychiatric Quarterly*, 10: 127–42, 1936; Malzberg, B., *Social and Biological Aspects of Mental Disease*, Utica, New York: State Hospital Press, 1940; Malzberg, B., "Are immigrants psychologically disturbed?" in S.C. Plog and R.B. Edgerton (eds), *Changing Perspectives in Mental Illness*, New York: Holt, Rinehart & Winston, 1969, pp. 395–421.

46 Eitinger, L., "The incidence of mental disease among refugees in Norway," *Journal of Mental Science*, 105: 326–38, 1959.

47 Hemsi, L.K., "Psychiatric morbidity of West Indian immigrants," *Social Psychiatry*, 2: 95–100, 1967.

48 Bagley, C., "The social aetiology of schizophrenia in immigrants groups," *International Journal of Social Psychiatry*, 17: 292–304, 1971; Giggs, J., "High rates of schizophrenia among immigrants in Nottingham," *Nursing Times*, 69: 1210–12, 1973; Rwegellera, G.G.C., "Psychiatric morbidity among West Africans and West Indians living in London," *Psychological Medicine*, 7: 317–29, 1977; Carpenter, I. and Brockington, I.F., "A study of mental illness in Asians, West Indians, and Africans living in Manchester," *British Journal of Psychiatry*, 137: 201–5, 1980; Bebbington, P.E., Hurry, J, and Tennant, C., "Psychiatric disorders in selected immigrant groups in Camberwell," *Social Psychiatry*, 16: 43–51, 1981; Dean, G., Walsh, D., Downing, H. and Shelley, E., "First admissions of native born and

immigrants to psychiatric hospitals in South East England, 1976," *British Journal of Psychiatry*, 139: 506–12, 1981; Harrison, G., Owens, D., Holton, T. et al., "A prospective study of severe mental disorder in Afro-Caribbean patients," *Psychological Medicine*, 18: 643–57, 1988.

49 Cochrane, R., "Mental illness in immigrants to England and Wales: An analysis of mental hospital admissions, 1971," *Social Psychiatry*, 12: 25–35, 1977; Cochrane, R. and Bal, S.S., "Migration and schizophrenia: An examination of five hypotheses," *Social Psychiatry*, 22: 181–91, 1987; Glover, G.R., The pattern of psychiatric admissions of Caribbean-born immigrants in London," *Social Psychiatry and Psychiatric Epidemiology*, 24: 49–56, 1989.

50 Cade, J.F.J. and Krupinski, J., "Incidence of psychiatric disorders in Victoria in relation to country of birth," *Medical Journal of Australia*, 49: 400–4, 1962.

51 Halevi, H.S., "Frequency of mental illness among Jews in Israel," *International Journal of Social Psychiatry*, 9: 268–82, 1963.

52 Cochrane, "Mental illness in immigrants to England and Wales."

53 Malzberg, "Are immigrants psychologically disturbed?" pp. 416–17.

54 Bland, R.C. and Orn, H., "Schizophrenia: Sociocultural factors," *Canadian Journal of Psychiatry*, 26: 186–8, 1981.

55 Bagley, C. and Binitie, A., "Alcoholism and schizophrenia in Irishmen in London," *British Journal of Addiction*, 65: 3–7, 1970; Clare, A.W., "Alcoholism and schizophrenia in Irishmen in London: A reassessment," *British Journal of Addiction*, 69: 207–12, 1974.

56 Arieti, *The Interpretation of Schizophrenia*, pp. 499–501.

57 Ödegard, Ö., "Emigration and insanity," *Acta Psychiatrica et Neurologica Scandinavica*, supplement 4, 1932.

58 Royes, K., "The incidence and features of psychoses in a Caribbean community," *Proceedings of the 3rd World Congress of Psychiatry*, 2: 1121–5, 1962; Burke, A.W., "First admissions and planning in Jamaica," *Social Psychiatry*, 9: 39–45, 1974; Hickling, F.W. and Rodgers-Johnson, P., "The incidence of first-contact schizophrenia in Jamaica," *British Journal of Psychiatry*, 167: 193–6, 1995; Bhugra, D., Hilwig, M., Hossein, B. et al., "First-contact incidence rates of schizophrenia in Trinidad and one-year follow-up," *British Journal of Psychiatry*, 169: 587–92, 1996; Mahy, G.E., Mallett, R., Leff, J. and Bhugra, D., "First-contact rate of schizophrenia on Barbados," *British Journal of Psychiatry*, 175: 28–33, 1999.

59 Clare, "Alcoholism and schizophrenia in Irishmen;" Walsh, D., O'Hare, A., Blake, B. et al., "The treated prevalence of mental illness in the Republic of Ireland – The three county register study," *Psychological Medicine*, 10: 465–70, 1980.

60 Adelstein, A.M. and Marmot, M.G., "The health of migrants in England and Wales: Causes of death," in J.K. Cruickshank, and D.G. Beevers (eds), *Ethnic Factors in Health and Disease*, Kent, England: Wright, 1989.

61 Lumb, K.M., Congdon, P.G. and Lealman, G.T., "A comparative review of Asian and British born maternity patients in Bradford, 1974–8," *Journal of Epidemiology and Community Health*, 35: 106–9, 1981.

62 Terry, P.B., Condie, R.G., Bissenden, J.G. and Keridge, D.F., "Ethnic differences in incidence of very low birthweight and neonatal deaths among normally formed infants," *Archives of Disease of Childhood*, 62: 709–11, 1987; Griffiths, R., White, M. and Stonehouse, M., "Ethnic differences in birth statistics from central Birmingham," *British Medical Journal*, 298: 94–5, 1989.

63 Tuck, S.M., Cardozo, L.D., Studd, J.W.W. et al., "Obstetric characteristics in different social groups," *British Journal of Obstetrics and Gynaecology*, 90: 892–7, 1983.

64 World Health Organization, "Deliveries and complications of pregnancy, childbirth and the puerperium," *World Health Statistics Report*, 21: 468–71, 1968.

65 Terry, P.B., Condie, R.G. and Settatree, R.S., "Analysis of ethnic differences in perinatal statistics," *British Medical Journal*, 281: 1307–8, 1980.

66 Terry et al., "Incidence of very low birthweight and neonatal deaths;" Griffiths et al., "Ethnic differences in birth statistics."

67 Harrison et al., "Severe mental disorder in Afro-Caribbean patients."

68 McGovern, D. and Cope, R.V., "First psychiatric admission rate of first and second generation Afro-Caribbeans," *Social Psychiatry*, 22: 139–49, 1987.

69 Wessely, S., Castle, D., Der, G. and Murray, R., "Schizophrenia and Afro-Caribbeans; A case-control study," *British Journal of Psychiatry*, 159: 795–801, 1991.

70 Thomas, C.S., Stone, K., Osborn, M. et al., "Psychiatric morbidity and compulsory admissions among UK-born Europeans, Afro-Caribbeans, and Asians in Central Manchester," *British Journal of Psychiatry*, 163: 91–9, 1993.

71 Sugarman, P.A. and Craufurd, D., "Schizophrenia in the Afro-Caribbean community," *British Journal of Psychiatry*, 164: 474–80, 1994.

72 Hutchinson, G., Takei, N., Fahy, T.A. et al., "Morbid risk of schizophrenia in first-degree relatives of white and African-Caribbean patients with psychosis," *British Journal of Psychiatry*, 169: 776–80, 1996.

73 Hutchinson, G., Takei, N., Bhugra, D. et al., "Increased rate of psychosis among African-Caribbeans in Britain is not due to an excess of pregnancy and birth complications," *British Journal of Psychiatry*, 171: 145–7, 1997.

74 Harrison, "Searching for the causes of schizophrenia;" Eagles, J.M., "The relationship between schizophrenia and immigration: Are there alternatives to psychosocial hypotheses? *British Journal of Psychiatry*, 159: 783–9, 1991.

75 Wing, J.K., "Schizophrenic psychoses: Causal factors and risks," in P. Williams, G. Wilkinson and K. Rawnsley (eds), *The Scope of Epidemiological Psychiatry*, London: Routledge & Kegan Paul, 1989, pp. 225–39.

76 Harrison, "Searching for the causes of schizophrenia."

77 Warner and de Girolamo, *Epidemiology of Schizophrenia*, section 3.2.2.

78 Jablensky, A., Sartorius, N., Ernberg, G. et al., "Schizophrenia: Manifestations, incidence and course in different cultures: A World Health Organization ten-country study," *Psychological Medicine*, supplement 20, 1992.

79 ni Nuallain, M., O'Hare, A. and Walsh, W., "Incidence of schizophrenia in Ireland," *Psychological Medicine*, 17: 943–8, 1987.

80 Häfner, H. and Gattaz, W.F., "Is schizophrenia disappearing?" *European Archives of Psychiatry and Clinical Neuroscience*, 240: 374–6, 1991.

81 "Relationships between aging and schizophrenia now being studied," *Clinical Psychiatry News*, September, 1982, pp. 1, 24; Strauss, J.S. and Carpenter, W.T., *Schizophrenia*, New York: Plenum, 1981, p. 73.

82 US Bureau of the Census, *Historical Statistics of the United States: Colonial Times to 1970*, Washington, DC: 1975, Series D 29–41, p. 131 and Series D 87–101, p. 135.

83 US Bureau of the Census, *Social Indicators 1976*, Washington, DC: 1977, Table 8/5, pp. 372–3.

84 Seeman, M.V. and Lang, M., "The role of estrogens in schizophrenia gender differences," *Schizophrenia Bulletin*, 16: 185–94, 1990; Szymanski, S., Lieberman, J.A., Alvir, J.M. et al., "Gender differences in onset of illness, treatment response, course, and biologic indexes in first-episode schizophrenic patients," *American Journal of Psychiatry*, 152: 698–703, 1995.

85 Gottesman, *Schizophrenia Genesis*.

86 Bennedsen, B.E., Mortensen, P.B., Olesen, A.V. and Henriksen, T.B., "Preterm birth and intra-uterine growth retardation among children of women with schizophrenia," *British Journal of Psychiatry*, 175: 239–45, 1999; Sacker, A., Done, D.J. and Crow, T.J., "Obstetric complications in children born to parents with schizophrenia: A meta-analysis of case-control studies," *Psychological Medicine*, 26: 279–87, 1996.

87 Kelly, R.H., Danielsen, B.H., Golding, J.M. et al., "Adequacy of prenatal care among women with psychiatric diagnoses giving birth in California in 1994 and 1995," *Psychiatric Services*, 50: 1584–90, 1999.

88 Miller, W.H.J., Bloom, J.D. and Resnick, M.P., "Prenatal care for pregnant chronic mentally ill patients," *Hospital and Community Psychiatry*, 43: 942–3, 1992.

89 Sacker, "Obstetric complications in children born to parents with schizophrenia."

90 Marcelis, M., van Os, J., Sham, P. et al., "Obstetric complications and familial morbid risk of psychiatric disorders," *American Journal of Medical Genetics*, 81: 29–36, 1998.

91 Burr, W.A., Falek, A., Strauss, L.T. et al., "Fertility in psychiatric outpatients," *Hospital and Community Psychiatry*, 30: 527–31, 1979; Gottesman, *Schizophrenia Genesis*.

92 Kelly, "Adequacy of prenatal care among women with psychiatric diagnoses."

93 Racine, A., Joyce, T. and Anderson, R., "The association between prenatal care and birth weight among women exposed to cocaine in New York City," *Journal of the American Medical Association*, 270: 1581–6, 1993.

94 MacGregor, S.N., Keith, L.G., Bachicha, J.A. et al., "Cocaine abuse during pregnancy: Correlation between prenatal care and perinatal outcome," *American Journal of Obstetrics and Gynecology*, 74: 882–5, 1989.

95 Zuckerman, B., Frank, D.A., Hingson, R. et al., "Effects of maternal marijuana and cocaine use on fetal growth," *New England Journal of Medicine*, 320: 762–8, 1989.

96 Geddes and Lawrie, "Obstetric complications and schizophrenia;" Geddes, "Schizophrenia and complications of pregnancy and labor."

97 Gottesman, *Schizophrenia Genesis*.

98 Hu, T.-W., Hargreaves, W.A. and Shumway, M., "Estimating costs of schizophrenia and its treatment," in M. Moscarelli, A. Rupp, and N. Sartorius (eds), *Handbook of Mental Health Economics and Health Policy: Volume 1: Schizophrenia*, New York: John Wiley, pp. 359–71, 1996.

99 Gottesman, *Schizophrenia Genesis*.

100 Goode, E., "Doctors try a bold move against schizophrenia," *New York Times*, pp. D1 & D6, December 7, 1999.

101 Lieberman, J.A., "Importance of early diagnosis and treatment of schizophrenia," *NARSAD Research Newsletter*, 11: 4–6, 1999.

102 Jablensky, A., "Prevalence and incidence of schizophrenia spectrum disorders: Implications for prevention," *Australian and New Zealand Journal of Psychiatry*, 34 (supplement): S26–34, 2000.

103 Klosterkötter, J., Hellmich, M., Steinmeyer, E.M. and Schultze-Lutter, F., "Diagnosing schizophrenia in the initial prodromal phase," *Archives of General Psychiatry*, 58: 158–64, 2001.

104 Warner, R., "The prevention of schizophrenia: What interventions are safe and effective?" *Schizophrenia Bulletin*, 27: 551–62, 2001.

105 Phillips, L.J., Yung, A.R. and McGorry, P.D., "Identification of young people at risk of psychosis: Validation of Personal Assessment and Crisis Evaluation clinic intake criteria," *Australian and New Zealand Journal of Psychiatry*, 34 (supplement): S164–9, 2000; McGorry, P.D. and Edwards, J.E., "Response to

'The prevention of schizophrenia: What interventions are safe and effective?' " *Schizophrenia Bulletin*, 28: 177–80, 2002.

106 Carr, V., Halpin, S., Lau, N. et al., "A risk factor screening and assessment protocol for schizophrenia and related psychosis," *Australian and New Zealand Journal of Psychiatry*, 34 (supplement): S170–80, 2000.

107 McGorry, P.D. and Jackson, H.J., *The Recognition and Management of Early Psychosis*, Cambridge: Cambridge University Press, 1999.

108 Goode, "Doctors try a bold move against schizophrenia."

109 Falloon, I., "Early intervention for first episodes of schizophrenia: A preliminary exploration," *Psychiatry*, 55: 4–15, 1992.

110 McGorry, P.D., "The nature of schizophrenia: Signposts to prevention," *Australian and New Zealand Journal of Psychiatry*, 34 (supplement): S14–21, 2000.

10 ANTIPSYCHOTIC DRUGS: USE, ABUSE AND NON-USE

1 Davis, J.M., "Antipsychotic drugs," in H.I. Kaplan, A.M. Freedman and B.J. Sadock (eds), *Comprehensive Textbook in Psychiatry – III*, Baltimore: Williams & Wilkins, 1981, p. 2257.

2 Gardos, G. and Cole, J.O., "Maintenance antipsychotic therapy: Is the cure worse than the disease?" *American Journal of Psychiatry*, 133: 32–6, 1976.

3 Kane, J.M., Honigfeld, G., Singer, J., Meltzer, H.Y. and the Clozaril Collaborative Group, "Clozapine for the treatment-resistant schizophrenic," *Archives of General Psychiatry*, 45: 789–96, 1988; Fleischhacker, W.W., "Clozapine: A comparison with other novel antipsychotics," *Journal of Clinical Psychiatry*, 60 (supplement 12): 30–4, 1999; Sartorius, N., Fleischhacker, W.W., Gjerris, A. et al., "The usefulness of the second-generation antipsychotic medications," *Current Opinion in Psychiatry*, 15 (supplement 1): S7–16, 2002.

4 Kapur, S. and Seeman, P. "Does fast dissociation from the dopamine D_2 receptor explain the action of atypical antipsychotics? A new hypothesis," *American Journal of Psychiatry*, 158: 360–9, 2001.

5 Kinon, B.J. and Lieberman, J.A., "Mechanisms of action of atypical antipsychotic drugs: A critical analysis," *Psychopharmacology*, 124: 2–34, 1996; Sartorius, "The usefulness of the second-generation antipsychotic medications."

6 For reviews of research on the dopamine hypothesis of schizophrenia see Meltzer, H.Y. and Stahl, S.M., "The dopamine hypothesis of schizophrenia: A review," *Schizophrenia Bulletin*, 2: 19–76, 1976; Haracz, J.L., "The dopamine hypothesis: An overview of studies with schizophrenic patients," *Schizophrenia Bulletin*, 8: 438–69, 1982; Andreasen, N.C., Carson, R., Diksic, M. et al., "Workshop on schizophrenia, PET, and dopamine D_2 receptors in the human neostratum," *Schizophrenia Bulletin*, 14: 471–84, 1988; Kapur, S. and Remington, G., "Dopamine D_2 receptors and their role in atypical antipsychotic action: Still necessary and may even be sufficient," *Biological Psychiatry*, 50: 873–83, 2001. For a discussion of the dopamine theory of schizophrenia and the novel antipsychotic medications see Kapur, S. and Seeman, P., "Does fast dissociation from the dopamine D_2 receptor explain the action of atypical antipsychotics? A new hypothesis," *American Journal of Psychiatry*, 158: 360–9, 2001.

7 Kapur, S., Zipursky, R., Jones, C. et al. "Relationship between dopamine D_2 occupancy, clinical response, and side effects: A double-blind PET study of first-episode schizophrenia," *American Journal of Psychiatry*, 157: 514–20, 2000.

8 Smythies, J.R. and Adey, W.T., *The Neurological Foundation of Psychiatry*, New York: Academic Press, 1966, pp. 150–7.

9 Melamud, N., "Psychiatric disorder with intracranial disorders of the limbic sys-
   tem," *Archives of Neurology* (Chicago), 17: 113–24, 1967; Horowitz, M.J. and
   Adams, J.E., "Hallucinations on brain stimulation: Evidence for revision of the
   Penfield hypothesis," in W. Keup (ed.), *Origins and Mechanisms of Hallucinations*,
   New York: Plenum Publishing, 1970, pp. 13–22; Torrey, E.F. and Peterson, M.R.,
   'Schizophrenia and the limbic system,' *Lancet*, 2: 942–6, 1974.
10 Abi-Dargham, A., Gil, R., Krystal, J. et al., "Increased striatal dopamine trans-
    mission in schizophrenia: Confirmation in a second cohort," *American Journal of
    Psychiatry*, 155: 761–7, 1998; Kapur, S., "Psychosis as a state of aberrant salience:
    A framework linking biology, phenomenology, and pharmacology in schizo-
    phrenia," *American Journal of Psychiatry*, 160: 13–23, 2003; Wong, D.F., Wagner,
    H.N., Tune, L.E. et al., "Positron emission tomography reveals elevated D_2
    dopamine receptors in drug-naïve schizophrenics," *Science*, 234: 1558–63, 1986;
    Farde, L., Wiesel, F.-A., Stone-Enlander, S. et al., "D_2 dopamine receptors in
    neuroleptic-naïve schizophrenic patients: A positron emission tomography study
    with [^{11}C]raclopride," Archives of General Psychiatry, 47: 213–19, 1990.
11 Kapur, "Does fast dissociation explain the action of atypical antipsychotics?;"
    Kapur, "Relationship between dopamine D_2 and side effects."
12 Judd, L.L., Goldstein, M.J., Rodnick, E.H. and Jackson, N.L.P., "Phenothiazine
    effects in good premorbid schizophrenics divided into paranoid non-paranoid
    status," *Archives of General Psychiatry*, 29: 207–11, 1973.
13 Rosen B., Engelhardt, D.M., Freedman, N et al., "The hospital proneness scale as
    a predictor of response to phenothiazine treatment. II: Delay of psychiatric hospi-
    talization," *Journal of Nervous and Mental Disease*, 152: 405–11, 1971.
14 Bowers, M.B., "Central dopamine turnover in schizophrenic syndromes," *Archives
    of General Psychiatry*, 31: 50–4, 1974.
15 Burt, D.R., Creese, I. and Snyder, S.H., "Antischizophrenic drugs: Chronic treat-
    ment elevates dopamine receptor binding in brain," *Science*, 196: 326–8, 1977;
    Muller, P. and Seeman, P., "Brain neurotransmitter receptors after long-term
    haloperidol: Dopamine, acetylcholine, serotonin, α-noradrenergic and naloxone
    receptors," *Life Sciences*, 21: 1751–8, 1977; Abi-Dargham, "Increased striatal
    dopamine transmission in schizophrenia;" Kapur, "Relationship between dopa-
    mine D_2 and side effects;" Kapur, "Does fast dissociation explain the action of
    atypical antipsychotics?"
16 Farde, "D_2 dopamine receptors in neuroleptic-naïve schizophrenic patients;"
    Kapur, "Dopamine D_2 receptors and their role in atypical antipsychotic action;"
    Kapur, "Relationship between dopamine D_2 and side effects."
17 Rosen, B., Engelhardt, D.M., Freedman, N. et al., "The hospitalization proneness
    scale as a predictor of response to phenothiazine treatment. I: Prevention of
    psychiatric hospitalization," *Journal of Nervous and Mental Disease*, 146: 476–80,
    1968.
18 Rosen B., Engelhardt, D.M., Freedman, N. et al., "The hospital proneness scale as
    a predictor of response to phenothiazine treatment. II: Delay of psychiatric hospi-
    talization," *Journal of Nervous and Mental Disease*, 152: 405–11, 1971.
19 Goldstein, M.J., "Premorbid adjustment, paranoid status, and patterns of
    response to phenothiazine in acute schizophrenia," *Schizophrenia Bulletin*, 3: 24–
    37, 1970; Evans, J.R., Rodnick, E.H., Goldstein, M.J. and Judd, L.L., "Premorbid
    adjustment, phenothiazine treatment, and remission in acute schizophrenics,"
    Archives of General Psychiatry, 27: 486–90, 1972.
20 Judd, L.L., Goldstein, M.J., Rodnick, E.H. and Jackson, N.L.P., "Phenothiazine
    effects in good premorbid schizophrenics divided into paranoid non-paranoid
    status," *Archives of General Psychiatry*, 29: 207–11, 1973.

21 Goldstein, M.J., Rodnick, E.H., Evans, J.R. et al., "Drug and family therapy in the aftercare of acute schizophrenics," *Archives of General Psychiatry*, 35: 1169–77, 1978.

22 Rappaport, M., Hopkins, H.K., Hall, K. et al. "Are there schizophrenics for whom drugs may be unnecessary or contraindicated?" *International Pharmacopsychiatry*, 13: 100–11, 1978, p. 107.

23 Carpenter, W.T., McGlashan, T.H. and Strauss, J.S., "The treatment of acute schizophrenia without drugs: An investigation of some current assumptions," *American Journal of Psychiatry*, 134: 14–20, 1977, p. 19.

24 Klein, D.G. and Rosen, B., "Premorbid asocial adjustment and response to phenothiazine treatment among schizophrenic inpatients," *Archives of General Psychiatry*, 29: 480–5, 1973.

25 May, P.R.A., Tuma, A.H. and Dixon, W.J., "Schizophrenia – A follow-up study of results of treatment. I: Design and other problems," *Archives of General Psychiatry*, 33: 474–8, 1976; May, P.R.A., Tuma, A.H. and Dixon, W.J., "Schizophrenia: A follow-up study of the results of five forms of treatment," *Archives of General Psychiatry*, 38: 776–84, 1981.

26 Schooler, N.R., Goldberg, S.C., Boothe, H. and Cole, J.O., "One year after discharge: Community adjustment of schizophrenic patients," *American Journal of Psychiatry*, 123: 986–95, 1967.

27 Pasamanick, B., Scarpetti, F., and Dinitz, S., *Schizophrenics in the Community: An Experimental Study of the Prevention of Rehospitalization*," New York: Appleton-Century-Crofts, 1967.

28 National Institute of Mental Health Psychopharmacology Service Center Collaborative Study Group, "Phenothiazine treatment in acute schizophrenia," *Archives of General Psychiatry*, 10: 246–61, 1964.

29 Mosher, L.R. and Menn, A.Z., "Community residential treatment for schizophrenia: Two-year follow-up," *Hospital and Community Psychiatry*, 29: 715–23, 1978, p. 722.

30 Matthews, S.M., Roper, M.T., Mosher, L.R. and Menn, A.Z., "A non-neuroleptic treatment for schizophrenia: Analysis of the two-year postdischarge risk of relapse," *Schizophrenia Bulletin*, 5: 322–33, 1979.

31 Ciompi, L., Dauwalder, H.-P., Maier, C. et al., "The Pilot Project 'Soteria Berne:' Clinical Experiences and Results," *British Journal of Psychiatry*, 161, supplement 18: 145–53, 1992; Ciompi, L., Dauwalder, H.-P., Aebi, E. et al., "A new approach to acute schizophrenia: Further results of the pilot project 'Soteria Berne,' " lecture given at the tenth International Symposium on the Psychotherapy of Schizophrenia, Stockholm, Sweden, August 11–15, 1991.

32 Lehtinen, V., Aaltonen, J., Koffert, T. et al., "Two-year outcome in first-episode psychosis treated according to an integrated model. Is immediate neuroleptisation always needed?" *European Psychiatry*, 15: 312–20, 2000.

33 Ibid., p. 319.

34 Davis, J., "Overview: Maintenance therapy in psychiatry. 1: Schizophrenia," *American Journal of Psychiatry*, 132: 1237–45, 1975.

35 Brown, G.W. and Birley, J.L.T., "Crises and life changes and the onset of schizophrenia," *Journal of Health and Social Behavior*, 9: 203–14, 1968; Birley, J.L.T. and Brown, G.W., "Crises and life changes preceding the onset or relapse of acute schizophrenia: Clinical aspects," *British Journal of Psychiatry*, 116: 327–33, 1970; Strahilevitz, M., "Possible interaction of environmental and biological factors in the etiology of schizophrenia," *Canadian Psychiatric Association Journal*, 19: 207–17, 1974; Jacobs, S.C. and Myers, J., "Recent life events and acute schizophrenic psychosis: A controlled study," *Journal of Nervous and Mental Disease*, 162:

75–87, 1976; Leff, J.P. and Vaughn, C.E., "The interaction of life events and relatives' expressed emotion in schizophrenia and depressive neurosis," *British Journal of Psychiatry*, 136: 146–53, 1980; Dohrenwend, B.P. and Egri, G., "Recent stressful life events and episodes of schizophrenia," *Schizophrenia Bulletin*, 7: 12–23, 1981; Spring, B., "Stress and schizophrenia: Some definitional issues," *Schizophrenia Bulletin*, 7: 24–33, 1981.

36 Wing, J.K., "The social context of schizophrenia," *American Journal of Psychiatry*, 135: 1333–9, 1978, p. 1335.

37 Brown, G.W., Birley, J.L.T. and Wing, J.K., "Influence of family life on the course of schizophrenic disorders: A replication," *British Journal of Psychiatry*, 121: 241–58, 1972; Vaughn, C.E. and Leff, J.P., "The influence of family and social factors on the course of psychiatric illness: A comparison of schizophrenic and depressed neurotic patients," *British Journal of Psychiatry*, 129: 125–37, 1976.

38 Leff, J.P. and Vaughn, C.E., "The role of maintenance therapy and relatives' expressed emotion in relapse of schizophrenia: A two-year follow-up," *British Journal of Psychiatry*, 139: 40–5, 1981.

39 Leff and Vaughn, "Interaction of life events and expressed emotion."

40 Sturgeon, D., Kuipers, L., Berkowitz, R. et al., "Psychophysiological responses of schizophrenic patients to high and low expressed emotion relatives," *British Journal of Psychiatry*, 138: 40–5, 1981.

41 Tarrier, N., Vaughn, C.E., Lader, M.H. and Leff, J.P., "Bodily reaction to people and events in schizophrenics," *Archives of General Psychiatry*, 36: 311–5, 1979.

42 Paul, G.L., Tobias, L.L. and Holly, B.L., "Maintenance psychotropic drugs in the presence of active treatment programs: A 'triple-blind' withdrawal study with long-term mental patients," *Archives of General Psychiatry*, 27: 106–15, 1972.

43 Ibid.

44 Paul, G.L. and Lentz, R.J., *Psychosocial Treatment of Chronic Mental Patients: Milieu versus Social Learning Programs*, Cambridge: Harvard University Press, 1977.

45 Goldberg, S.C., Schooler, N.R., Hogarty, G.E. and Roper, M., "Prediction of relapse in schizophrenic outpatients treated by drug and sociotherapy," *Archives of General Psychiatry*, 34: 171–84, 1977.

46 Hogarty, G.E., Goldberg, S.C., Schooler, N.R. and the Collaborative Study Group, "Drug and sociotherapy in the aftercare of schizophrenic patients. III: Adjustment of nonrelapsed patients," *Archives of General Psychiatry*, 31: 609–18, 1974.

47 Hogarty, G.E., Goldberg, S.C., Schooler, N.R. et al., "Drug and sociotherapy in the aftercare of schizophrenic patients. II: Two-year relapse rates," *Archives of General Psychiatry*, 31: 603–8, 1974.

48 Goldberg et al., "Prediction of relapse," p. 171.

49 Leff, J.P., "Preventing relapse in schizophrenia," presented at the World Psychiatric Association Regional Meeting, New York, October 30–November 3, 1981; Berkowitz, R., Kuipers, L., Eberlein-Fries, R. and Leff, J.P., "Lowering expressed emotion in relatives of schizophrenics," *New Direction in Mental Health Services*, 12: 27–48, 1981.

50 Falloon, I.R.H., Boyd, J.L., McGill, C.W. et al., "Family management in the prevention of exacerbations of schizophrenia: A controlled study," *New England Journal of Medicine*, 306: 1437–40, 1982.

51 McFarlane, W.R. (ed.) *Family Therapy in Schizophrenia*, New York; Guilford Press, 1983; Leff, J. and Vaughn, C., *Expressed Emotion in Families*, New York: Guildford Press, 1985; Leff, J., "Working with families of schizophrenic patients; Effects on clinical and social outcomes," in M. Moscarelli, A. Rupp, and

N. Sartorius (eds), *Handbook of Mental Health Economics: Volume 1. Schizophrenia*, New York: Wiley, pp. 261–70, 1996.

52 Wang, P.S., Demier, O. and Kessler, R.C., "Adequacy of treatment for serious mental illness in the United States," *American Journal of Public Health*, 92: 92–8, 2002.

53 Schmidt, L.J., Reinhardt, A.M., Kane, R.L. and Olsen, D.M., "The mentally ill in nursing homes: New back wards in the community," *Archives of General Psychiatry*, 34: 687–91, 1977.

54 Sheehan, S., "A reporter at large," *New Yorker*, May 25, June 1, June 8, June 15, 1981.

55 *In the interest of Edmiston*, Civil Action 80 MH 378, Denver Probate Court, December 17, 1980.

56 Kapur, "Relationship between dopamine D_2 and side effects."

57 Quitkin, F., Rifkin, A. and Klein, D.F., "Very high dosage versus standard dosage fluphenazine in schizophrenia," *Archives of General Psychiatry*, 32: 1276–81, 1975; McGlashan, T.H. and Carpenter, W.T., "Postpsychotic depression in schizophrenia," *Archives of General Psychiatry*, 33: 231–9, 1976; Van Putten T. and May, P.R.A., " 'Akinetic depression' in schizophrenia," *Archives of General Psychiatry*, 35: 1101–7, 1978; Hogarty, G.E., Schooler, N.R., Ulrich, R. et al., "Fluphenazine and social therapy in the aftercare of schizophrenic patients: Relapse analyses of a two-year controlled study of fluphenazine decanoate and fluphenazine hydrochloride," *Archives of General Psychiatry*, 36: 1283–94, 1979; Goldstein et al., "Drug and family therapy."

58 Voruganti, L.N.P., Heslegrave, R.J. and Awad, A,G., "Neuroleptic dysphoria may be the missing link between schizophrenia and substance abuse," *Journal of Nervous and Mental Disease*, 185: 463–5, 1997; Warner, R., Taylor, D., Wright, J. et al., "Substance use among the mentally ill: Prevalence, reasons for use and effects on illness," *American Journal of Orthopsychiatry*, 64: 465–76, 1994.

59 Hartlage, L.C., "Effects of chlorpromazine on learning," *Psychological Bulletin*, 64: 235–45, 1965; Bruening, S.E., Davis, V.J., Matson, J.L. and Ferguson, D.G., "Effects of thioridazine and withdrawal dyskinesias on workshop performance of mentally retarded young adults," *American Journal of Psychiatry*, 139: 1447–54, 1982.

60 Henderson, D.C., Cagliero, E., Gray, C. et al., "Clozapine, diabetes mellitus, weight gain, and lipid abnormalities: A five-year naturalistic study," *American Journal of Psychiatry*, 157: 975–81, 2000.

61 Blackburn, G.L., "Weight gain and antipsychotic medication," *Journal of Clinical Psychiatry*, 61 (supplement 8): 36–41, 2000.

62 *Physicians' Desk Reference*, 47th Edition, Montvale, New Jersey: Medical Economics Data, 1993, pp. 2093–7; Henderson, "Clozapine, diabetes mellitus, weight gain, and lipid abnormalities."

63 Chakos, M., Lieberman, J., Hoffman, E. et al., "Effectiveness of second-generation antipsychotics in treatment-resistant schizophrenia: A review and meta-analysis of randomized trials," *American Journal of Psychiatry*, 158: 518–26, 2001; Geddes, J., Freemantle, N., Harrison, P. and Bebbington, P. "Atypical antipsychotics in the treatment of schizophrenia: Systematic overview and meta regression analysis," *British Medical Journal*, 321: 1371–2000, 2000.

64 Newcomer, J.W., Haupt, D.W., Fucetola, R. et al., "Abnormalities in glucose regulation during antipsychotic treatment of schizophrenia," *Archives of General Psychiatry*, 59: 337–45, 2002.

65 Commonwealth of Massachusetts Executive Office of Health and Human Services Department of Mental Health, *Mortality Report 1998–1999*, Boston, Massachusetts, 2001.

66 Department of Mental Health Central Massachusetts Area Office, *Morbidity Study: Medical Illnesses of Central Massachusetts Area DMH Residential Clients*, Worcester, Massachusetts, 2001.

67 Bradley, K., Nguyen, M. and Pelletier, J.R., "Genesis Wellness Project," presented at the second meeting of the Research Advisory Committee for the Program for Clubhouse Research, University of Massachusetts Medical School, Worcester, Massachusetts, June 22, 2002.

68 Taylor, D.P., Riblet, L.A., Stanton, H.C. et al., "Dopamine and anti-anxiety activity," *Pharmacology, Biochemistry and Behavior*, vol. 17, supplement 1, pp. 25–35, 1982; Haefely, W.E., "Behavioral and neuropharmacological aspects of drugs used in anxiety and related states," in M.A. Lipton, A. DiMascio and K.F. Killam (eds), *Psychopharmacology: A Generation of Progress*, New York: Raven Press, 1978; Nestoros, J.N., "Benzodiazepines in schizophrenia: A need for a reassessment," *International Pharmacopsychiatry*, 15: 171–9, 1980; Bunney, G.S. and Aghajanian, G.K., "The effect of antipsychotic drugs on the firing of dopaminergic neurons: A reappraisal," in G. Sedvall, G. Uvnäs and Y. Zotterman, *Antipsychotic Drugs: Pharmacodynamics and Pharmacokinetics*, New York: Pergamon, 1976.

69 Feldman, P.E., "An analysis of the efficacy of diazepam," *Journal of Neuropsychiatry*, 3, supplement 1: S62–7, 1962; Pignatoro, F.P., "Experience with chemotherapy in refractory psychiatric disorders," *Current Therapeutic Research*, 4: 389–98, 1962; Maculans, G.A., "Comparison of diazepam, chlorprothixene and chlorpromazine in chronic schizophrenic patients," *Diseases of the Nervous System*, 25: 164–8, 1964; Kramer, J.C., "Treatment of chronic hallucinations with diazepam and phenothiazines," *Diseases of the Nervous System*, 28: 593–4, 1967; Irvine, B.M. and Schaecter, F., "'Valium' in the treatment of schizophrenia," *Medical Journal of Australia*, i: 1387, 1969; Trabucchi, M. and Ba., G., "Are benzodiazepines an antipsychotic agent," *Southern Medical Journal*, 72: 636, 1979; Ansari, J.M.A., "Lorazepam in the control of acute psychotic symptoms and its comparison with flupenthixol," in E. Usdin, H. Eckert and I.S. Forrest (eds), *Phenothiazines and Structurally Related Drugs*, New York: Elsevier/North-Holland, 1980; Beckman, H. and Haas, S., "High-dose diazepam in schizophrenia," *Psychopharmacology*, 71: 70–82, 1980; Lingjaerde, O., "Effect of the benzodiazepine derivative estazolam in patients with auditory hallucinations: A multicentre double-blind cross-over study," *Acta Psychiatrica Scandinavica*, 65: 339–54, 1982; "Diazepam shown to reduce many schizophrenic symptoms," *Psychiatric News*, August 20, 1982; Haas, S., Emrich, H.M. and Beckmann, H., "Analgesic and euphoric effects of high-dose diazepam in schizophrenia," *Neuropsychobiology*, 8: 123–8, 1982. Several similar studies are listed in the review article – Nestoros, "Benzodiazepines in schizophrenia," – which draws the conclusion that benzodiazepines have generally positive effects in schizophrenia.

70 The following studies yield equivocal results: Hollister, L.E., Bennett, J.L., Kimbell, I. et al., "Diazepam in newly admitted schizophrenics," *Diseases of the Nervous System*, 24: 746–50, 1963; Kellner, R., Wilson, R.M., Muldawer, M.D. and Pathak, D., "Anxiety in schizophrenia: The responses to chlordiazepoxide in an intensive design study," *Archives of General Psychiatry*, 32: 1246–54, 1975; Jimerson, D.C., Van Kammen, D.P., Post, R.M. et al., "Diazepam in schizophrenia: A preliminary double-blind trial," *American Journal of Psychiatry*, 139: 489–91, 1982. Clearly negative results are reported in: Lehmann, H.E. and Ban, T.A., "Notes from the log-book of a psychopharmacological research unit II," *Canadian Psychiatric Association Journal*, 9: 111–13, 1964; Weizman, A., Weizman, S., Tyano, S. et al., "The biphasic effect of gradually increased doses of diazepam on prolactin secretion in acute schizophrenic patients," *Israeli Annals of Psychiatry*,

17: 233–40, 1979; Ruskin, P., Averbukh, I., Belmaker, R.H. and Dasberg, H., "Benzodiazepines in chronic schizophrenia," *Biological Psychiatry*, 14: 557–8, 1979; Karson, C.N., Weinberger, D.R., Bidelow, L. and Wyatt, R.J., "Clonazepam treatment of chronic schizophrenia: Negative results in a double-blind, placebo-controlled trial," *American Journal of Psychiatry*, 139: 1627–8, 1982. For a generally negative review of the value of the benzodiazepines in schizophrenia, see Greenblatt, D.J. and Shader, R.I., *Benzodiazepines in Clinical Practice*, New York: Raven Press, 1974, ch. 4.

71 Beckman and Haas, "High-dose diazepam in schizophrenia;" Feldman, "The efficacy of diazepam;" Maculan, "Diazepam in chronic schizophrenic patients;" and "Diazepam shown to reduce many schizophrenic symptoms," *Psychiatric News*, August 20, 1982.

72 Phillips, L., "Case history data and prognosis in schizophrenia," *Journal of Nervous and Mental Disease*, 117: 515–25, 1953; Stephens, J.H., Astrup, C. and Mangrum, J.C., "Prognostic factors in recovered and deteriorated schizophrenics," *American Journal of Psychiatry*, 122: 1116–21, 1966; Marder, S.R., van Kammen, D.P., Docherty, J.P. et al., "Predicting drug-free improvement in schizophrenic psychosis," *Archives of General Psychiatry*, 36: 1080–5, 1979.

73 Bromet, E., Harrow, M. and Kasl, S., "Premorbid functioning and outcome in schizophrenics and nonschizophrenics," *Archives of General Psychiatry*, 30: 203–7, 1974; Strauss, J.S. and Carpenter, W.T., "The prognosis of schizophrenia: Rationale for a multidimensional concept," *Schizophrenia Bulletin*, 4: 56–77, 1978; Bland, R.C., Parker, J.H. and Orn, H., "Prognosis in schizophrenia: Prognostic predictors and outcome," *Archives of General Psychiatry*, 35: 72–7, 1978.

74 Harrow, M., Bromet, E. and Quinlan, D., "Predictors of post-hospital adjustment in schizophrenia: Thought disorders and schizophrenic diagnosis," *Journal of Nervous and Mental Disease*," 158: 25–32, 1974; Strauss, J.S. and Carpenter, W.T., "Characteristic symptoms and outcome in schizophrenia," *Archives of General Psychiatry*, 30: 429–34, 1974; Carpenter, W.T., Barko, J.J., Strauss, J.S. and Hawk, A.B., "Signs and symptoms as predictors of outcome: A report from the International Pilot Study of Schizophrenia," *American Journal of Psychiatry*, 135: 940–5, 1978.

75 Strauss, J.S. and Carpenter, W.T., "The prediction of outcome in schizophrenia. I: Characteristics of outcome," *Archives of General Psychiatry*, 27: 739–46, 1972; Hawk, A.B., Carpenter, W.T. and Strauss, J.S., "Diagnostic criteria and five-year outcome in schizophrenia: A report from the International Pilot Study of Schizophrenia," *Archives of General Psychiatry*, 32: 343–7, 1975.

76 Strauss, J.S. and Carpenter, W.T., "The prediction of outcome in schizophrenia. II: Relationships between predictor and outcome variables: A report from the WHO International Pilot Study of Schizophrenia," *Archives of General Psychiatry*, 31: 37–42, 1974; Strauss, J.S. and Carpenter, W.T., "Prediction of outcome in schizophrenia. III: Five-year outcome and its predictors," *Archives of General Psychiatry*, 34: 159–63, 1977; Mintz, J., O'Brien, C.P. and Luborsky, L., "Predicting the outcome of psychotherapy for schizophrenics: Relative contributions of patient, therapist, and treatment characteristics," *Archives of General Psychiatry*, 33: 1183–6, 1976.

77 Kant, O., "The incidence of psychoses and other mental abnormalities in the families of recovered and deteriorated schizophrenic patients," *Psychiatric Quarterly*, 16: 176–86, 1942; Vaillant, G.E., "Prospective prediction of schizophrenic remission," *Archives of General Psychiatry*, 11: 509–18, 1964; Welner, J. and Strömgen, E., "Clinical and genetic studies on benign schizophreniform psychoses based on a follow-up," *Acta Psychiatrica Scandinavica*, 33: 377–99, 1958; McCabe,

M.S., Fowler, R.C., Cadoret, R.J. and Winokur, G.,"Familial differences in schizophrenia with good and poor prognosis," *Psychological Medicine*, 1: 326–32, 1971; Fowler, R.D., McCabe, M.S., Cadoret, R.J. and Winokur, G., "The validity of good prognosis schizophrenia," *Archives of General Psychiatry*, 26: 182–5, 1972; Taylor, M.A. and Abrams, R., "Manic-depressive illness and good prognosis schizophrenia," *American Journal of Psychiatry*, 132: 741–2, 1975; Hirschowitz, J., Casper, R., Garver, D.L. and Chang, S., "Lithium response in good prognosis schizophrenia," *American Journal of Psychiatry*, 137: 916–20, 1980.

78 Mosher, L.R., Menn, A. and Matthews, S.M., "Soteria: Evaluation of a home-based treatment for schizophrenia," *American Journal of Orthopsychiatry*, 45: 455–67, 1975, p. 458.

79 Ibid., pp. 460–1.

11 WORK

1 Tuke, S., *Description of the Retreat*, London: Dawson, 1964, facsimile of 1813 edn. Quoted in Scull, A.T., *Museums of Madness: The Social Organization of Insanity in Nineteenth-Century England*, London: Allen Lane (New York: St Martin's Press), 1979, p. 69.

2 Ellis, W.C., *A Treatise on the Nature, Symptoms, Causes, and Treatment of Insanity*, London: Samuel Holdsworth, 1838, p. 197.

3 Todd, E., unpublished letter in the Institute of Living archives, Hartford, Connecticut, 1830. Quoted in Braceland, F.J., "Rehabilitation," in S. Arieti (ed.), *American Handbook of Psychiatry*, 2nd edn, vol. 5, New York: Basic Books, 1975, pp. 683–700. The quotation is on p. 684.

4 Browne, W.A.F., *What Asylums Were, Are, and Ought to Be: Being the Substance of Five Lectures Delivered before the Managers of the Montrose Royal Lunatic Asylum*, Edinburgh: Black, 1837, pp. 229–31. Quoted in Scull, *Museums of Madness*, pp. 105–6.

5 Carlyle, T., Inaugural address at Edinburgh University, 1866, in M. Strauss (ed.), *Familiar Medical Quotations*, Boston: Little, Brown, 1968.

6 Becker, D.R. and Drake, R.E., "Individual placement and support: A community mental health center approach to vocational rehabilitation," *Community Mental Health Journal*, 30: 193–206, 1994.

7 Freud, S., *Civilization and Its Discontents*, in J. Strachey (ed.), *Standard Edition of the Complete Psychological Works of Sigmund Freud*, vol. 21, London: Hogarth Press, 1953–1966. First published in 1930.

8 Marshak, L.E., Bostick, D. and Turton, L.J., "Closure outcomes for clients with psychiatric disabilities served by the vocational disability system," *Rehabilitation Counseling Bulletin*, 33: 247–50, 1990; Anthony, W.A. and Blanch, A., "Supported employment for persons who are psychiatrically disabled: A historical and conceptual perspective," *Psychosocial Rehabilitation Journal*, 11: 5–23, 1987; Jacobs, H.E., Kardashian, S., Kreinbring, S. et al., "A skills-oriented model for facilitating employment among psychiatrically disabled persons," *Rehabilitation Counseling Bulletin*, 28: 87–96, 1984; Anthony, W.A. and Liberman, R.P., "The practice of psychiatric rehabilitation: Historical, conceptual and research base," *Schizophrenia Bulletin*, 12: 542–99, 1986; Connors, K.A., Graham, R.S. and Pulso, R., "Playing store: Where is the vocational in psychiatric rehabilitation?" *Psychosocial Rehabilitation Journal*, 10: 21–33, 1987; Bailey, E.L., Ricketts, S.K., Becker, D.R. et al., "Do long-term day treatment clients benefit from supported employment?" *Psychiatric Rehabilitation Journal*, 22: 24–9, 1998; Consumer Health Sciences, *The Schizophrenia Patient Project: Brief Summary of Results –*

September 1997, Princeton, New Jersey: Consumer Health Sciences, 1997; Glazer, W.M., "Formulary decisions and health economics," *Journal of Clinical Psychiatry*, 59, supplement 19: 23–9, 1998; Chandler, D., Meisel, J., Hu, T.-W. et al., "A capitated model for a cross-section of severely mentally ill clients: Employment outcomes," *Community Mental Health Journal*, 33: 501–16, 1997; Office of National Statistics, *Labour Force Survey*, London: Office of National Statistics, 1995.

 9 Bond, G.R., "Implementing supported employment as an evidence-based practice," *Psychiatric Services*, 52: 313–22, 2001.

10 Cohen, L., "Vocational planning and mental illness," *Personnel and Guidance Journal*, 34: 28–32, 1955.

11 Brown, G.W., Carstairs, G.M. and Topping, G., "Post-hospital adjustment of chronic mental patients," *Lancet*, ii: 685–9, 1958.

12 Freeman, H.E. and Simmons, O.G., *The Mental Patient Comes Home*, New York: Wiley, 1963, ch. 4.

13 Fairweather, G.W., Sanders, D.H., Maynard, H. et al., *Community Life for the Mentally Ill*, Chicago: Aldine, 1969.

14 Anthony, W.A., Buell, G.W., Sharatt, S. and Althoff, M.D.,"The efficacy of psychiatric rehabilitation," *Psychological Bulletin*, 78: 447–56, 1972.

15 Bond, G.R., Drake, R.E., Mueser, K.T. and Becker, D.R., "An update on supported employment for people with severe mental illness," *Psychiatric Services*, 48: 335–46, 1997; Bailey, "Do long-term day treatment clients benefit from supported employment?"; Lysaker, P. and Bell, M., "Work performance over time for people with schizophrenia," *Psychosocial Rehabilitation Journal*, 18: 141–5, 1995.

16 Lehman, A.F., "Vocational rehabilitation in schizophrenia," *Schizophrenia Bulletin*, 21: 645–56, 1995.

17 Bond et al., "An update on supported employment;" Bond, "Implementing supported employment."

18 Bailey et al., "Do long-term day treatment clients benefit from supported employment?"

19 Bell, M.D., Lysacker, P.H. and Milstein, R.M., "Clinical benefits of paid work activity in schizophrenia," *Schizophrenia Bulletin*, 22: 51–67, 1996.

20 Warner, R., Huxley, P. and Berg, T., "An evaluation of the impact of clubhouse membership on quality of life and treatment utilization," *International Journal of Social Psychiatry*, 45: 310–21, 1999.

21 Bond, "Implementing supported employment."

22 Bond, G.R. "Critical ingredients of supported employment," American Psychiatric Association Institute on Psychiatric Services, New Orleans, November 2, 1999.

23 Bond, "Implementing supported employment."

24 Wansbrough, N. and Cooper, O., *Open Employment after Mental Illness*, London: Tavistock, 1980, p. 38; Office of National Statistics, *Labour Force Survey*.

25 Warner, R., de Girolamo, G., Belelli, G. et al., "The quality of life of people with schizophrenia in Boulder, Colorado, and Bologna, Italy," *Schizophrenia Bulletin*, 24: 559–68, 1998.

26 Warner, R. and Ruggieri, M., "The quality of life of people with schizophrenia in Boulder, Colorado, and Verona, Italy." Unpublished manuscript, Mental Health Center of Boulder County, Boulder, Colorado, 1997.

27 Lehman, "Vocational rehabilitation in schizophrenia;" Bond et al., "An update on supported employment."

28 Lehman, "Vocational rehabilitation in schizophrenia."

29 Bond, G.R., "Principles of individual placement and support," *Psychiatric Rehabilitation Journal*, 22: 11–23, 1998.

30 Information about Italian, Irish, Canadian and Swiss cooperatives reported throughout this chapter was gathered by the author during a series of visits in the 1990s. Further information is available on the Pordenone cooperatives in Conte, S. and Comis S.,"Social enterprise in Italy" presented at the Third Congress of the World Association for Psychosocial Rehabilitation, October 13–16, 1991; and on the Trieste cooperatives in Dell'Acqua, P. and Dezza, M.G.C., "The end of the mental hospital: A review of the psychiatric experience in Trieste," *Acta Psychiatrica Scandinavica*, supplement 316: 45–69, 1985; De Leonardis, O., Mauri, D. and Rotelli, F. "Deinstitutionalization, another way: The Italian mental health reform," *Health Promotion*, 1: 151–64, 1986; Warner, R. and Polak, P., "The economic advancement of the mentally ill in the community: Economic opportunities," *Community Mental Health Journal*, 31: 381–96, 1995. See also the website www.cefec.org

31 Warner, "The economic advancement of the mentally ill;" www.cefec.org, August 2002.

32 Stastny, P., Gelman, R. and Mayo, H.,"The European experience with social firms in the rehabilitation of persons with psychiatric disabilities," unpublished report of a study visit to Germany and Austria, May, 1992; www.cefec.org; www.faf-gmbh.de

33 Boyles, P. "Mentally ill gain a foothold in working world," *Boston Sunday Globe*, June 5, 1988.

34 Silvestri, F., personal communication, 1997.

35 Kakutani, K., "New Life Espresso: Report on a business run by people with psychiatric disabilities," *Psychiatric Rehabilitation Journal*, 22: 111–15, 1998.

36 Creegan, S., "An investigation of vocational programmes in North America," *British Journal of Occupational Therapy*, 58: 9–13, 1995.

37 www.cefec.org

38 Surles, R.C., Morrison, B.J., Sheets, J.L. et al., *Buy OMH Directory of Products and Services*, New York State Office of Mental Health Bureau of Psychiatric Rehabilitation Services, Albany, NY, 1992.

39 Warner, R., and Polak, P., "An economic development approach to the mentally ill in the community," concept paper written under contract to the National Institute of Mental Health, Rockville, Maryland, January 16, 1993, p. 24.

40 Polak, P., Warner, R. and Mosher, L.R.,"Final report: Feasibility study on the development of a consumer-oriented system of pharmacies for the seriously mentally ill," prepared for the Robert Wood Johnson Foundation, Princeton, New Jersey, January 15, 1992.

41 Warner and Polak, "An economic development approach."

42 Ibid., p. 12.

43 Ibid., p. 12.

44 Ibid., p. 13.

45 Berndt, E.R., *The Practice of Econometrics: Classic and Contemporary*, Reading, Massachussetts: Addison-Wesley, 1990, Chapter 11, pp. 593–651.

46 Warner and Polak,"An economic development approach," p. 13.

47 Burtless, G. and Hausman, J., "The effects of taxation on labor supply: Evaluating the Gary Income Maintenance Experiment," *Journal of Political Economy*, 86: 1103–30, 1978; Moffit, R., "The econometrics of kinked budget constraints," *Journal of Economic Perspectives*, 4: 119–39, 1990.

48 Averett, S., Warner, R., Little, J. and Huxley, P., "Labor supply, disability benefits and mental illness," *Eastern Economic Journal*, 25: 279–88, 1999.

49 Arnold, R., "Employment and disability," *Psychiatric Services*, 49: 1361, 1998.

50 Warner, R., Marine, S., Evans, S. and Huxley, P., "The employment and income of people with schizophrenia and other psychotic disorders in a tight labor market," unpublished manuscript.

51 Roberts, J.D. and Ward, I.M., *Commensurate Wage Determination for Service Contracts*, Columbus, Ohio: Ohio Industries for the Handicapped, 1987.

52 Polak, P. and Warner, R., "The economic life of seriously mentally people in the community," *Psychiatric Services*, 47: 270–4, 1996.

53 Bailey et al., "Do long-term day treatment clients benefit from supported employment?"

54 Kirszner, M.L., McKay, C.D. and Tippett, M.L., "Homeless and mental health replication of the PACT model in Delaware," Proceedings of the Second Annual Conference on State Mental Health Agency Services Research, NASMHPD Research Institute, Alexandria, Virginia, pp. 68–82, 1991; McFarlane, W.R., Stastny, P. and Beakins, S. "Family aided assertive community treatment: A comprehensive rehabilitation and intensive case management approach for persons with schizophrenic disorders," *New Directions in Mental Health Services*, 53; 43–54, 1992; Meisel, J., McGowan, M., Patotzka, D. and Madison, K., *Evaluation of AB 3777 client and cost outcomes: July 1990 through March 1992*. Sacramento, California: California Department of Mental Health, 1993.

55 Warner, R. et al., "The impact of clubhouse membership on quality of life and treatment utilization."

56 Bond, G.R., "An economic analysis of psychosocial rehabilitation," *Hospital and Community Psychiatry*, 35: 356–62, 1984.

57 Bond, G.R., Dietzen, L.L., Vogler, K. et al., "Toward a framework for evaluating costs and benefits of psychiatric rehabilitation: Three case examples," *Journal of Vocational Rehabilitation*, 5: 75–88, 1995.

58 Drake, R.E., Becker, D.R., Biesanz, J.C. et al., "Partial hospitalization versus supported employment: I. Vocational outcomes," *Community Mental Health Journal*, 30: 519–32, 1994; Rogers, E.S., Sciarappa, K., MacDonald-Wilson, K. and Danley, K., "A benefit-cost analysis of a supported employment model for persons with psychiatric disabilities," *Evaluation and Program Planning*, 18: 105–15, 1995.

59 Ellwood, D., *Poor Support*, New York: Basic Books, 1988.

60 Kaus, M., "The work ethic state," *New Republic*, July 7, 1986, pp. 22–33.

12 DESEGREGATING SCHIZOPHRENIA

1 The Mental Health Center of Boulder County is a comprehensive community mental health center that offers a full range of psychiatric services to the 275,000 residents of the mixed urban and rural region of Boulder County and Broomfield County, Colorado. Clients' fees are on a sliding scale and services for the indigent are free. In the year ending June 2002 the center saw more than 7,000 clients; over 4,600 cases were active at any one time and over 720 of these were suffering from a functional psychosis. Of the clients, 37 per cent were children and adolescents, 58 per cent were adults between the ages of 18 and 64, and five per cent were age 65 or older. Nearly 30 per cent of the clients belonged to an ethnic minority, primarily Hispanic-American.

The center employs approximately 450 part-time and full-time staff (300 full-time equivalent employees). Around two-thirds of the full-time equivalent employees provide clinical services and one-third have administrative and clerical duties.

The center's budget for 2001–2 was $22.5 million (£15 million). The sources of revenue were as follows:

Federal government	$7.0 million
State government	$6.8 million
Local government (cities and counties)	$4.3 million
Fees and health insurance	$0.8 million
Other sources	$3.5 million

Most of the federal and state government revenue came in the form of per capita payments for recipients of governmental Medicaid health insurance.

2 Turner, J.C. and Tenhoor, W.J., "The NIMH community support program: Pilot approach to a needed social reform," *Schizophrenia Bulletin*, 4: 319–48, 1978.

3 Warner, R., "Jail services and community care for the mentally ill in Boulder County, Colorado," in H.J. Steadman, D.W. McCarty and J.P. Morrisey (eds), *The Mentally Ill in Jail: Planning for Essential Services*, New York: Guilford Press, 1989, pp. 198–213.

4 Ibid.

5 For a description of the PACE program and the client outcomes after the first year of operation go to the web page of the Mental Health Center of Boulder County, www.mhcbc.org, and click on "research."

6 Warner, R. and Wollesen, C., "Cedar House: A non-coercive hospital alternative in Boulder, Colorado," in R. Warner (ed.), *Alternatives to the Hospital for Acute Psychiatric Treatment*, Washington, DC: American Psychiatric Press, 1995, pp. 3–17.

7 Sladen-Dew, N., Young, A.-M., Parfitt, H. and Hamilton, R., "Venture: The Vancouver experience," in Warner, *Alternatives to the Hospital for Acute Psychiatric Treatment*, pp. 21–36.

8 Bourgeois, P. "Crossing Place, Washington, D.C.," in Warner, *Alternatives to the Hospital for Acute Psychiatric Treatment*, pp. 37–56.

9 Fields, S.L., "Progress Foundation, San Francisco," in Warner, *Alternatives to the Hospital for Acute Psychiatric Treatment*, pp. 57–73.

10 Polak, P.R., Kirby, M.W. and Deitchman, W.S., "Treating acutely ill psychotic patients in private homes," in Warner, *Alternatives to the Hospital for Acute Psychiatric Treatment*, pp. 213–23; Brook, B.D., Cortes, M., March, R. and Sundberg-Stirling, M., "Community families: An alternative to psychiatric hospital intensive care," *Hospital and Community Psychiatry*, 27: 195–7, 1976.

11 Bennett, R., "The crisis home program of Dane County," in Warner, *Alternatives to the Hospital for Acute Psychiatric Treatment*, pp. 227–36.

12 Stein, L.I. and Test, M.A., "Alternative to mental hospital treatment: I. Conceptual model, treatment program, and clinical evaluation," *Archives of General Psychiatry*, 37: 392–7, 1980.

13 Test, M.A. and Stein, L.I., "Alternative to mental hospital treatment: III. Social cost," *Archives of General Psychiatry*, 37: 409–12, 1980.

14 Rosen, A. and Teeson, M., "Does case management work? The evidence and the abuse of evidence-based medicine," *Australian and New Zealand Journal of Psychiatry*, 35: 731–46, 2001.

15 Burns, T., Creed, F., Fahy, T. et al., "Intensive versus standard case management for severe psychotic illness trial UK 700 Group," *Lancet*, 353: 2185–9, 1999; Thornicroft, G., Strathdee, G., Phelan, M. et al., "Rationale and design, Prism Psychosis Study," *British Journal of Psychiatry*, 173: 363–70, 1998.

16 Warner, R. and Huxley, P., "Psychopathology and quality of life among mentally ill patients in the community: British and US samples compared," *British Journal of Psychiatry*, 163: 505–9.

17 Ibid.

18 To this number we should add about 20 patients with psychosis who have been placed in the forensic unit of the state hospital by the Boulder County criminal courts. Other people with psychosis from Boulder County receive inpatient and outpatient care in the private sector. It is not possible to say how many of these patients would be in hospital treatment if they were under the care of the mental health center. One may safely assume, however, that virtually none of the people in treatment for psychosis with the private sector is a candidate for long-term hospital care – such patients rapidly pass the point of being able to pay for private hospital treatment, the limited provisions of their health insurance having been exhausted.

19 Podvoll, E.M., *The Seduction of Madness: Revolutionary Insights into the World of Psychosis and a Compassionate Approach to Recovery at Home*, New York: Harper Collins Publishers, 1990.

20 Sandall, H., Hawley, T.T. and Gordon, G.C., "The St. Louis community homes program: Graduated support for long-term care," *American Journal of Psychiatry*, 132: 617–22, 1975; Shepherd, G. and Murray, A., "Residential care," in G. Thornicroft and G. Szmukler (eds), *Textbook of Community Psychiatry*, Oxford: Oxford University Press, 2001, pp. 309–20.

21 Morris, B., "Residential units," in J.K. Wing and B. Morris (eds), *Handbook of Psychiatric Rehabilitation Practice*, Oxford: Oxford University Press, 1981, pp. 99–121. The reference is to p. 109; Shepherd and Murray, "Residential care."

22 Personal communication, Ellen Baxter and Ezra Susser; Warner, R., "Creative Programming," in S. Ramon (ed.), *Beyond Community Care*, Basingstoke, Hampshire: Macmillan, 1991, pp. 114–35.

23 Mandiberg, J., "Can interdependendent mutual support function as an alternative to hospitalization? The Santa Clara County Clustered Apartment Project," in Warner, *Alternatives to the Hospital for Acute Psychiatric Treatment*, pp. 193–210.

24 Morris "Residential units," p. 106.

25 Bromberg, W., *From Shaman to Psychotherapist: A History of the Treatment of Mental Ilness*, Chicago: Henry Regnery, 1975, p. 128.

26 Barker, R.G., *Ecological Psychology: Concepts and Methods for Studying the Environment of Human Behavior*, Stanford: Stanford University Press, 1968, ch. 7.

27 Ibid.

28 Davis, M. and Thompson, B., *Cooperative Housing: A Development Primer*, Washington, DC: National Cooperative Business Association, 1992.

29 Ibid.

30 Ibid.

31 City of New York v. Bowen.

32 Leonard Rubenstein, personal communication.

33 Kathy Burns, personal communication.

34 Laurie Flynn, personal communication.

35 Rosenhan, D.L., "On being sane in insane places," *Science*, 179: 250–8, 1973.

36 Mosher, L.R. and Keith, S.J., "Research on the psychosocial treatment of schizophrenia: A summary report," *American Journal of Psychiatry*, 136: 623–31, 1979.

37 Tarrier, N., Beckett, R., Harwood, S. et al. "A trial of two cognitive-behavioural methods of treating drug-resistant residual psychotic symptoms in schizophrenic patients: I. Outcome," *British Journal of Psychiatry*, 162: 524–32, 1993.

38 Tarrier, N., Wittowski, A., Kinney, C. et al., "Durability of the effects of cognitive-behavioural therapy in the treatment of chronic schizophrenia: 12-month follow-up," *British Journal of Psychiatry*, 174: 500–4, 1999.

39 Kuipers, E., Garety, P., Fowler, D. et al.. "London–East Anglia randomized

controlled trial of cognitive-behavioral therapy for psychosis. I: Effects of the treatment phase," *British Journal of Psychiatry*, 171: 319–27, 1997.

40 Garety, P., Fowler, D., Kuipers, E. et al., "London–East Anglia randomized controlled trial of cognitive-behavioral therapy for psychosis. II: Predictors of outcome," *British Journal of Psychiatry*, 173, 420–6, 1998.

41 Kuipers, E., Fowler, D., Garety, P. et al., "London–East Anglia randomized controlled trial of cognitive-behaviour therapy for psychosis. II: Follow-up and economic evaluation at 18 months," *British Journal of Psychiatry*, 173: 61–8, 1998.

42 Wykes, T., Parr, A-M. and Landau, S., "Group treatment of auditory hallucinations: Exploratory study of effectiveness," *British Journal of Psychiatry*, 175: 180–5, 1999.

43 Drury, V., Birchwood, M., Cochrane, R. et al., "Cognitive therapy and recovery from acute psychosis: A controlled trial: I. Impact on psychotic symptoms," *British Journal of Psychiatry*, 169: 593–601, 1996; Drury, V., Birchwood, M., Cochrane, R. et al., "Cognitive therapy and recovery from acute psychosis: A controlled trial: II. Impact on recovery time," *British Journal of Psychiatry*, 169: 602–7, 1996.

44 Kavanagh, D.J., "Recent developments in expressed emotion and schizophrenia," *British Journal of Psychiatry*, 160: 601–20, 1992.

45 Goldstein, M.J., Rodnick, E.H., Evans, J.R. et al., "Drug and family therapy in the aftercare treatment of acute schizophrenia," *Archives of General Psychiatry*, 35: 169–77, 1978; Leff, J.P., Kuipers, L., Berkowitz, R. et al., "A controlled trial of intervention in the families of schizophrenic patients," *British Journal of Psychiatry*, 141: 121–34, 1982; Falloon, I.R.H., Boyd, J.L., McGill, C.W. et al., "Family management in the prevention of exacerbations of schizophrenia," *New England Journal of Medicine*, 306: 1437–40, 1982; Hogarty, G.E., Anderson, C.M., Reiss, D.J. et al., "Family psychoeducation, social skills training, and maintenance chemotherapy in the aftercare treatment of schizophrenia: I. One-year effects of a controlled study of relapse and expressed emotion," *Archives of General Psychiatry*, 43: 633–42, 1986.

46 Leff et al., "A controlled trial of intervention in the families of schizophrenic patients."

47 Personal communication, Julian Leff.

48 Pyke-Lees, P., "The National Schizophrenia Fellowship," in Wing and Morris, *Handbook of Psychiatric Rehabilitation*, pp. 126–9.

49 Geller, J.L., Brown, J.-M., Fisher, W.H. et al., "A national survey of 'consumer empowerment' at the state level," *Psychiatric Services*, 49: 498–503, 1998.

50 Jones, L., "*A Matter of Community II*," Denver, Colorado: Capitol Hill Action and Recreation Group.

51 Sherman, P.S. and Porter, R., "Mental health consumers as case management aides," *Hospital and Community Psychiatry*, 42: 494–8, 1991.

52 Warner, R. and Polak, P., "An economic development approach to the mentally ill in the community," Washington, DC: NIMH Community Support Program document, 1993.

53 Lecomte, T., Wilde, J.B. and Wallace, C.J. "Mental health consumers as peer interviewers," *Psychiatric Services*, 50: 693–5, 1999.

54 Ekdawi, M.K., "The role of day units in rehabilitation," in Wing and Morris, *Handbook of Psychiatric Rehabilitation*, pp. 95–8. The quotation is from p. 98.

55 Beard, J.H., Propst, R. and Malamud, T.J., "The Fountain House model of psychiatric rehabilitation," *Psychosocial Rehabilitation Journal*, 5: 47–53, 1982.

56 Warner, R., Huxley, P. and Berg, T., "An evaluation of the impact of clubhouse

membership on quality of life and treatment utilization," *International Journal of Social Psychiatry*, 45: 310–20, 1999.

57 Hasher, R., "Spiritmenders: A client-operated community center," presented at American Psychiatric Association annual meeting, San Francisco, May 6–11, 1989.

58 McGorry, P.D. and Jackson, H.J., *The Recognition and Management of Early Psychosis*, Cambridge University Press, Cambridge, 1999; McGlashan, T.H., Miller, T.J. and Woods, S.W., "Pre-onset detection and intervention researching schizophrenia psychoses: Current estimates of benefit and risk," *Schizophrenia Bulletin*, 27: 563–70, 2001.

59 Crow, T.J., MacMillan, J.F., Johnson, A.L., and Johnstone, E.C., "A randomized controlled trial of prophylactic neuroleptic treatment," *British Journal of Psychiatry*, 148: 120–7, 1986.

60 Jones, P.B., Bebbington, P., Foerster, A. et al., "Premorbid social underachievement in schizophrenia: Results of the Camberwell Collaborative Psychosis Study," *British Journal of Psychiatry*, 162: 65–71, 1993.

61 Wyatt, R.J., Green, M.F. and Tuma, A.H., "Long-term morbidity associated with delayed treatment of first admission schizophrenic patients," *Psychological Medicine*, 27: 261–8, 1997.

62 Moscarelli, M., Capri, S. and Neri, L., "Cost evaluation of chronic schizophrenic patients during the first three years after the first contact," *Schizophrenia Bulletin*, 17: 421–6, 1991.

63 Haas, G.L., Garrett, L.S. and Sweeney, J.A., "Delay to first antipsychotic medication in schizophrenia: Impact on symptomatology and clinical course of illness," *Journal of Psychiatric Research*, 32: 151–9, 1998; Helgason, L., "Twenty years' follow-up of first psychiatric presentation for schizophrenia: What could have been prevented?" *Acta Psychiatrica Scandinavica*, 81: 231–5, 1990.

64 Loebel, A.D., Lieberman, J.A., Alvir, J.M.J. et al., "Duration of psychosis and outcome in first-episode schizophrenia," *American Journal of Psychiatry*, 149: 1183–8, 1992; McGorry, P.D., Edwards, J., Mihalopoulos, C. et al., "EPPIC: An evolving system of early detection and optimal management," *Schizophrenia Bulletin*, 22: 305–26, 1996.

65 Wyatt et al., "Long-term morbidity associated with delayed treatment."

66 Ciompi, L., "Catamnestic long-term study on the course of life and aging of schizophrenics," *Schizophrenia Bulletin*, 6: 606–18, 1980; World Health Organization, *Schizophrenia: An International Follow-up Study*, Chichester, England: Wiley, 1979; Shepherd, M., Watt, D., Falloon, I. and Smeeton, M., "The natural history of schizophrenia: A five-year follow-up in a representative sample of schizophrenics," *Psychological Medicine*, Monograph supplement 15, 1989.

67 Johnstone, E.C., Crow, T.J., Johnson, A.L. and Macmillan, J.F., "The Northwick Park study of first episodes of schizophrenia: I. Presentation of the illness and problems relating to admission," *British Journal of Psychiatry*, 148: 115–20, 1986; Makanjuola, R.O.A. and Adedapo, S.A., "The DSM-III concepts of schizophrenic disorder and schizophreniform disorder: A clinical and prognostic evaluation," *British Journal of Psychiatry*, 151: 611–18, 1987; Tsoi, W.F. and Wong, K.E., "A 15-year follow-up study of Chinese schizophrenic patients," *Acta Psychiatrica Scandinavica*, 84: 217–20; Helgason, "Twenty years' follow-up of first psychiatric presentation for schizophrenia;" Moscarelli et al., "Cost evaluation of chronic schizophrenic patients;" Loebel et al., "Duration of psychosis and outcome in first-episode schizophrenia;" Waddington, J.L., Youssef, H.A. and Kinsella, A., "Sequential cross-sectional and 10-year prospective study of severe

negative symptoms in relation to duration of initially untreated psychosis in chronic schizophrenia," *Psychological Medicine*, 25: 849–57, 1995; McGorry et al., "EPPIC: An evolving system of early detection and optimal management;" Scully, P.J., Coakley, G., Kinsella, A., and Waddington, J.L., "Psychopathology, executive (frontal) and general cognitive impairment in relation to duration of initially untreated versus subsequently treated psychosis in chronic schizophrenia," *Psychological Medicine*, 27: 1303–10, 1997; Wyatt et al., "Long-term morbidity associated with delayed treatment;" Haas, G.L. et al., "Delay to first antipsychotic medication in schizophrenia;" Carbone, S., Harrigan, S., McGorry, P.D., Curry, C., and Elkins, K., "Duration of untreated psychosis and 12-month outcome in first-episode psychosis: The impact of treatment approach," *Acta Psychiatrica Scandinavica*, 100: 96–104, 1999; Larsen, T.K., Friis, S., Haarh, U. et al., "Early detection and intervention in first-episode schizophrenia: A critical review," *Acta Psychiatrica Scandinavica*, 103: 323–34, 2001; Drake, R.J., Haley, C.J., Akhtar, S. and Lewis, S.W., "Causes and consequences of duration of untreated psychosis in schizophrenia," *British Journal of Psychiatry*, 177 (suppl.): S11–515, 2000; Browne, S., Clarke, M., Gervin, M. et al., "Determinants of quality of life at first presentation for schizophrenia," *British Journal of Psychiatry*, 176: 173–6, 2000.

68 Linszen, D., Lenior, M., de Haan, L. and Dingemans, P., "Early intervention, untreated psychosis and the course of early schizophrenia," *British Journal of Psychiatry*, 172: 84–9, 1998; Craig, T.J., Bromet, E.J., Fennig, S. et al., "Is there an association between duration of untreated psychosis and 24-month clinical outcome in a first-admission series?" *American Journal of Psychiatry*, 157: 60–6, 2000; Ho, B.-C., Andreasen, N.C., Flaum, M. et al., "Untreated initial psychosis: Its relation to quality of life and symptom remission in first-episode schizophrenia," *American Journal of Psychiatry*, 157: 808–15; de Haan, L., van der Gaag, M. and Wolthaus, J., "Duration of untreated psychosis and the long-term course of schizophrenia," *European Psychiatry*, 15: 264–7, 2000; Barnes, T.R.E., Hutton, S.B., Chapman, M.J. et al., "West London first-episode study of schizophrenia: Clinical correlates of duration of untreated psychosis," *British Journal of Psychiatry*, 177: 207–11, 2000; Warner, R., "Response to McGorry and Edwards," *Schizophrenia Bulletin*, 28: 181–5, 2002.

69 Mosher, L.R., "The Soteria Project: The first generation American alternatives to psychiatric hospitalization," in Warner, *Alternatives to Hospital for Acute Psychiatric Treatment*, pp. 111–29; Lehtinen, V., Aaltonen, J., Koffert, T. et al., "Two-year outcome in first-episode psychosis treated according to an integrated model. Is immediate neuroleptisation needed?", *European Psychiatry*, 15: 312–20, 2000; Ciompi, "Catamnestic long-term study on the course of life and aging of schizophrenics; Bola, J.R. and Mosher, L.R., "Treating psychosis without drugs: Soteria two-year outcomes," in *World Psychiatric Association International Congress*, Madrid, Spain, 2001.

70 Scheper-Hughes, N. and Lovell, A.M., *Psychiatry Inside Out: Selected Writings of Franco Basaglia*, New York: Columbia University Press, 1987, p. xvii.

71 Donelly, M., *The Politics of Mental Health in Italy*, London: Routledge, 1992.

72 Ibid., p. 67.

73 Reda, S., "Attitudes towards community mental health care of residents in north London," *Psychiatric Bulletin*, 19: 731–3, 1995.

74 Wolff, G., "Attitudes of the media and the public," in J. Leff (ed.), *Care in the Community: Illusion or Reality?* New York: Wiley, pp. 144–63, 1997.

75 Ibid.

76 Penn, D.L., Guynan, K., Daily, T. et al., "Dispelling the stigma of schizophrenia: What sort of information is best?" *Schizophrenia Bulletin*, 20: 567–78, 1994.

77 Frean, A., "EastEnders praised for breaking taboo on schizophrenia," in *The Times*, London, May 10, 1997.
78 Wahl, O.F., *Media Madness: Public Images of Mental Illness*, New Brunswick, New Jersey: Rutgers University Press, 1995.
79 Ibid., p. 145.
80 Ibid.
81 Personal communication, Otto Wahl.
82 Rogers, E.M., *Diffusion of Innovations*, New York: Free Press, 1995.
83 Ibid.
84 Ibid.; Rogers, E.M., "The field of health communication today: An up-to-date report," *Journal of Health Communication*, 1: 15–23, 1996.
85 Rogers, *Diffusion of Innovations*.
86 Paykel, E.S., Hart, D. and Priest, R.G., "Changes in public attitudes to depression during the Defeat Depression Campaign," *British Journal of Psychiatry*, 173: 519–22, 1998.
87 Ibid.
88 Sartorius, N., "Fighting schizophrenia and its stigma: A new World Psychiatric Association educational programme," *British Journal of Psychiatry*, 170: 297, 1997.
89 Schulze, B., Richter-Werling, M., Matschinger, H. and Angermeyer, M.C., "Crazy? So what!? Effects of a school project on students' attitudes towards people with schizophrenia," unpublished manuscript, Department of Psychiatry, University of Leipzig, Germany.
90 Meise, U., Sulzenbacher, H., Kemmler, G. and De Col, Ch., "A school programme against stigmatization of schizophrenia in Austria," unpublished manuscript, Department of Psychiatry, University Clinics, Innsbruck, Austria.
91 For more information on the Boulder anti-stigma campaign check the mental health center web page, www.mhcbc.org

Bibliography

STUDIES OF THE OUTCOME OF SCHIZOPHRENIA IN TABLE 3.1

Ackner, B. and Oldham, A.J., "Insulin treatment of schizophrenia: A three-year follow-up of a controlled study," *Lancet*, i: 504–6, 1962.

Astrup, C., Fossum, A. and Holmboe, R., *"Prognosis in Functional Psychoses,"* Springfield, Illinois: Charles C. Thomas, 1963.

Astrup, C. and Noreik, K., *Functional Psychoses: Diagnostic and Prognostic Models*, Springfield, Illinois: Charles C. Thomas, 1966.

Beck, M.N., "Twenty-five and thirty-five year follow up of first admissions to mental hospitals," *Canadian Psychiatric Association Journal*, 13: 219–29, 1968.

Benazzi, F., "DSM-III-R schizophreniform disorder with good prognostic features: A six-year follow-up," *Canadian Journal of Psychiatry*, 43: 180–2, 1998.

Biehl, H., Maurer, K., Schubart, B. et al., "Prediction of outcome and utilization of medical services in a prospective study of first onset schizophrenics: Results of a prospective 5-year follow-up study," *European Archives of Psychiatry and Neurological Sciences*, 236: 139–47, 1986.

Bland, R.C. and Orn, H., "Fourteen-year outcome in early schizophrenia," *Acta Psychiatrica Scandinavica*, 58: 327–38, 1978.

Bland, R.C., Parker, J.H. and Orn, H., "Prognosis in schizophrenia," *Archives of General Psychiatry*, 35: 72–7, 1978.

Bleuler, E., *Dementia Praecox, or the Group of Schizophrenias*, New York: International Universities Press, 1950.

Bleuler, M., *The Schizophrenic Disorders: Long-term Patient and Family Studies*, New Haven: Yale University Press, 1978.

Bond, E.D., "Results in 251 cases five years after admission to a hospital for mental diseases," *Archives of Neurology and Psychiatry*, 6: 429–39, 1921.

Bond, E.D. and Braceland, F.J., "Prognosis in mental disease," *American Journal of Psychiatry*, 94: 263–74, 1937.

Braatöy, T., "The prognosis in schizophrenia, with some remarks regarding diagnosis and therapy," *Acta Psychiatrica et Neurologica Scandinavica*, 11: 63–102, 1936.

Breier, A., Scheiber, J., Dyer, J. and Pickar, D., "National Institute of Mental Health longitudinal study of chronic schizophrenia: Prognosis and predictors of outcome," *Archives of General Psychiatry*, 48: 239–46, 1991.

Briner, O., "Zentralblatt für die gesamte Neurologie und Psychiatrie," 162: 582, cited in E. Guttman, W. Mayer-Gross and E. Slater, "Short-distance prognosis of schizophrenia," *Journal of Neurological Psychiatry*, 2: 25–34, 1939.

Brown, G.W., Bone, M., Dalison, B. and Wing, J.K., *Schizophrenia and Social Care*, London: Oxford University Press, 1966.

Carter, A.B., "The prognostic factors of adolescent psychosis," *Journal of Mental Science*, 88: 31–81, 1942.

Cheney, C.O. and Drewry, P.H., "Results of non-specific treatment in dementia praecox," *American Journal of Psychiatry*, 95: 203–17, 1938.

Cole, N.J., Brewer, D.L. and Branch, C.H.H., "Socioeconomic adjustment of a sample of schizophrenic patients," *American Journal of Psychiatry*, 95: 203–17, 1963.

Coryell, W. and Tsuang, M.T., "Outcome after 40 years in DSM III schizopheniform disorder," *Archives of General Psychiatry*, 43: 324–8, 1986.

Cottman, S.B. and Mezey, S.B., "Community care and the prognosis of schizophrenia," *Acta Psychiatrica Scandinavica*, 53: 95–104, 1976.

Eitinger, L., Laane, C.L. and Langfeldt, G., "The prognostic value of the clinical picture and the therapeutic value of physical treatment in schizophrenia and the schizophreniform states," *Acta Psychiatrica et Neurologica Scandinavica*, 33: 33–53, 1958.

Engelhardt, D.M., Rosen, B., Feldman, J. et al., "A 15-year follow-up of 646 schizophrenic outpatients," *Schizophrenia Bulletin*, 8: 493–503, 1982.

Errera, P.A., "Sixteen-year follow-up of schizophrenic patients seen in an outpatient clinic," *Archives of Neurology and Psychiatry*, 78: 84–8, 1957.

Evensen, H., *Dementia Praecox*, Oslo: Kristiania, 1904.

Freyhan, F.A., "Course and outcome of schizophrenia," *American Journal of Psychiatry*, 112: 161–7, 1955.

Fromenty, L., "Les remissions dans la schizophrénie statistique sur leur fréquence et leur durée avant l'insulinthérapie," *Encephale*, 1: 275–86, 1937.

Fröshaug, H. and Ytrehus, A., "The problems of prognosis in schizophrenia," *Acta Psychiatrica Scandinavica*, supplement 169: 176–87, 1963.

Gerloff, W., "Über Verlauf und Prognose der Schizophrenie," *Archiv für Psychiatrie und Nervenkrankheiten*, 106: 585–98, 1936.

Guttman, E., Mayer-Gross, W. and Slater, E., "Short-distance prognosis of schizophrenia," *Journal of Neurological Psychiatry*, 2: 25–34, 1939.

Hall, J.C., Smith, K. and Shimkunas, A., "Employment problems of schizophrenic patients," *American Journal of Psychiatry*, 123: 536–40, 1966.

Harris, A., Linker, I., Norris, V. and Shepherd, M., "Schizophrenia: A prognostic and social study," *British Journal of Social and Preventive Medicine*, 10: 107–14, 1956.

Harrow, M., Grinker, R.R., Silverstein, M.L. and Holzman, P., "Is modern-day schizophrenia outcome still negative?" *American Journal of Psychiatry*, 135: 1156–62, 1978.

Hastings, D.W., "Follow-up results in psychiatric illness," *American Journal of Psychiatry*, 114: 1057–65, 1958.

Helgason, L., "Twenty years' follow-up of first psychiatric presentation for schizophrenia: What could have been prevented?" *Acta Psychiatrica Scandinavica*, 81: 231–5, 1990.

Henisz, J., "A follow-up study of schizophrenic patients," *Comprehensive Psychiatry*, 7: 524 8, 1966.

Hoenig, J. and Hamilton, M.W., "Schizophrenia in an extramural service," *Comprehensive Psychiatry*, 7: 81–9, 1966.

Holmboe, R. and Astrup, C., "A follow-up study of 255 patients with acute schizophrenia and schizophreniform psychoses," *Acta Psychiatrica et Neurologica Scandinavica*, supplement 125, 1957.

Holmboe, R., Noreik, K. and Astrup, C., "Follow-up of functional psychoses at two Norwegian mental hospitals," *Acta Psychiatrica Scandinavica*, 44: 298–310, 1968.

Horowitz, W.A. and Kleiman, C., "Survey of cases of dementia praecox discharged from the Psychiatric Institute and Hospital," *Psychiatric Quarterly*, 10: 72–85, 1936.

Huber, G., Gross, G. and Schuttler, R., "A long-term follow-up study of schizophrenia: Psychiatric course of illness and prognosis," *Acta Psychiatrica Scandinavica*, 52: 49–57, 1975.

Hunt, R.C., Feldman, H. and Fiero, R.P., "Spontaneous remission in dementia praecox," *Psychiatric Quarterly*, 12: 414–25, 1938.

Jablensky, A., Sartorius, N., Ernberg, G. et al., "Schizophrenia: manifestations, incidence and course in different cultures. A World Health Organization ten-country study," *Psychological Medicine*, monograph supplement 20, 1991.

Johanson, E., "A study of schizophrenia in the male: A psychiatric and social study based on 138 cases with follow-up," *Acta Psychiatrica et Neurologica Scandinavica*, supplement 125, 1958.

Johnstone, E.C., Frith, D.C., Gold, A. and Stevens, M., "The outcome of severe acute schizophrenia illness after one year," *British Journal of Psychiatry*, 134: 28–33, 1979.

Johnstone, E.C., Frith, C.D., Lang, F.H. and Owens, D.G.C. "Determinants of the extremes of outcome in schizophrenia," *British Journal of Psychiatry*, 167: 604–9, 1995.

Johnstone, E.C., Frith, C.D., Leary, J. and Owens, D.G.C., "IX. Concluding remarks," *British Journal of Psychiatry*, 159 (suppl.13): 43–6, 1991.

Jönnson, H. and Nyman, A.K. "Predicting long-term-outcome in schizophrenia," *Acta Psychiatrica Scandinavica*, 83: 342–6, 1991.

Jönnson, S.A.T and Jönnson, H., "Outcome in untreated schizophrenia: A search for symptoms and traits with prognostic meaning in patients admitted to a mental hospital in the preneuroleptic era," *Acta Psychiatrica Scandinavica*, 85: 313–20, 1992.

Kelly, D.H.W. and Sargant, W., "Present treatment of schizophrenia," *British Medical Journal*, 1: 147–50, 1965.

Kraepelin, E., *Dementia Praecox and Paraphrenia*, Edinburgh: Livingstone, 1919.

Kurihara, T., Kato, M., Reverger, R. and Yagi, G. "Outcome in schizophrenia in a non-industrialized country: Comparative study between Bali and Tokyo," *Acta Psychiatrica Scandinavica*, 101: 148–52, 2000.

Langfeldt, G., "The prognosis in schizophrenia and factors influencing the course of the disease," *Acta Psychiatrica et Neurologica Scandinavica*, supplement 13, 1939.

Lay, B., Blanz, B., Hartmann, M. and Schmidt, M.H., "The psychosocial outcome of adolescent-onset schizophrenia: A 12-year followup, *Schizophrenia Bulletin*, 26: 801–16, 2000.

Leary, J., Johnstone, E.C. and Owens, D.G.C. "II. Social outcome," *British Journal of Psychiatry*, 159 (suppl.13): 13–20, 1991.

Leiberman, D.M., Hoenig, J. and Auerbach, I., "The effect of insulin coma and E.C.T. on the 3 year prognosis of schizophrenia," *Journal of Neurology, Neurosurgery and Psychiatry*, 20: 108–13, 1957.

Lemke, R., "Untersuchungen über die soziale Prognose der Schizophrenie unter besonders Beruchsicktigung des encephalographischen Befundes," *Archive für Psychiatrie und Nervenkrankheiten*, 104: 89–136, 1935.

Levenstien, S., Klein, D.F. and Pollack, M., "Follow-up study of formerly hospitalized voluntary psychiatric patients: The first two years," *American Journal of Psychiatry*, 122: 1102–9, 1966.

Leyberg, J.T., "A follow-up study on some schizophrenic patients," *British Journal of Psychiatry*, 111: 617–24, 1965.

Lynge, I. and Jacobsen, J., "Schizophrenia in Greenland: A follow-up study," *Acta Psychiatrica Scandinavica*, 91: 414–22, 1995.

Malamud, W. and Render, I.N., "Course and prognosis in schizophrenia," *American Journal of Psychiatry*, 95: 1039–57, 1939.

Mandelbrote, B.M. and Folkard, S., "Some factors related to outcome and social adjustment in schizophrenia," *Acta Psychiatrica Scandinavica*, 37: 223–35, 1961.

Marengo, J., Harrow, M., Sands, J. and Galloway, C., "European versus U.S. data on the course of schizophrenia," *American Journal of Psychiatry*, 148: 606–11, 1991.

Marneros, A., Deister, A. and Rohde, A., "Comparison of long-term outcome of schizophrenic, affective and schizoaffective disorders," *British Journal of Psychiatry*, 161 (suppl. 18): 44–51, 1992.

Mason, P., Harrison, G., Glazebrook, C. et al., "The course of schizophrenia over 13 years: A report from the International Study on Schizophrenia (ISoS) coordinated by the World Health Organization," *British Journal of Psychiatry*, 169: 580–6, 1996.

Masterson, J.F., "Prognosis in adolescent disorders: Schizophrenia," *Journal of Nervous and Mental Disease*, 124: 219–32, 1956.

Mayer-Gross, W., "Die schizophrenie," in O. Bumke (ed.), *Handbuch der Geisteskrankheiten*, vol. 9, Berlin: Springer, 1932, p. 534.

Möller, H.-J., von Zerssen, D., Werner-Eilert, K. and Wüschner-Stockheim, M., "Outcome in schizophrenic and similar paranoid psychoses," *Schizophrenia Bulletin*, 8: 99–108, 1982.

Müller, V., "Katamnestische Erhebungen über den Spontanverlauf der Schizophrenie," *Monatsschrift für Psychiatrie und Neurologie*, 122: 257–76, 1951.

Munk-Jørgensen, P. and Mortensen, P.B., "Social outcome in schizophrenia: A 13-year follow-up," *Social Psychiatry and Psychiatric Epidemiology*, 27: 129–34, 1992.

Murdoch, J.H., "Crime in schizophrenic reaction types," *Journal of Mental Science*, 79: 286–97, 1933.

Niskanen, P. and Achté, K.A., "Prognosis in schizophrenia: A comparative follow-up study of first admissions for schizophrenic and paranoid psychoses in Helsinki in 1950, 1960 and 1965," *Psychiatria Fennica Year Book 1971*, 1971, pp. 117–26.

Norton, A., "Mental hospital ins and outs: A survey of patients admitted to a mental hospital in the past 30 years," *British Medical Journal*, 1: 528–36, 1961.

Otto-Martiensen, J., *Zeitschrift für Psychiatrie*, 77: 295 et seq., 1921, cited in R. Lemke "Untersuchungen über die soziale Prognose der Schizophrenie unter besonders Beruchsichtigung des encephalographischen Befundes," *Archives für Psychiatrie und Nervenkrankheiten*, 104: 89–136, 1935.

Prudo, R. and Blum, H.M., "Five-year outcome and prognosis in schizophrenia: A report from the London field research centre of the International Pilot Study of Schizophrenia," *British Journal of Psychiatry*, 150: 345–54, 1987.

Rennie, T.A.C., "Follow-up study of 500 patients with schizophrenia admitted to the hospital from 1913–1923," *Archives of Neurology and Psychiatry*, 42: 877–91, 1939.

Romano, J. and Ebaugh, F.G., "Prognosis in schizophrenia," *American Journal of Psychiatry*, 95: 583–96, 1938.

Rosanoff, A.J., "A statistical study of prognosis in insanity," *Journal of the American Medical Association*, 62: 3–6, 1914.

Rupp, C. and Fletcher, E.K., "A five to ten year follow-up study of 641 schizophrenic cases," *American Journal of Psychiatry*, 96: 877–88, 1940.

Salokangas, R.K.R., "Prognostic implications of the sex of schizophrenic patients," *British Journal of Psychiatry*, 142: 145–51, 1983.

Salokangas, R.K.R. and Stengård, E., "Gender and short-term outcome in schizophrenia," *Schizophrenia Research*, 3: 333–45, 1990.

Scottish Schizophrenia Research Group, "The Scottish first episode schizophrenia study: VIII. Five-year follow-up: Clinical and psychosocial findings," *British Journal of Psychiatry*, 161: 496–500, 1992.

Shepherd, M., Watt, D., Falloon, I. and Smeeton, N., "The natural history of schizophrenia: A five-year follow-up study of outcome and prediction in a representative sample of schizophrenics," *Psychological Medicine*, monograph supplement 15: 1–46, 1989.

Stalker, H., "The prognosis in schizophrenia," *Journal of Mental Science*, 85: 1224–40, 1939.

Stearns, A.W., "The prognosis in dementia praecox," *Boston Medical and Surgical Journal*, 167: 158–60, 1912.

Stephens, J.H., "Long-term course and prognosis in schizophrenia," *Seminars in Psychiatry*, 2: 464–85, 1970.

Stone, M.H., "Exploratory psychotherapy in schizophrenia-spectrum patients: A reevaluation in the light of long-term follow-up of schizophrenic and borderline patients," *Bulletin of the Menninger Clinic*, 50: 287–306, 1986.

Strecker, E.A. and Willey, G.F., "Prognosis in schizophrenia," *Journal of Mental Science*, 73: 9–39, 1927.

Tsuang, M.T., Woolson, R.F. and Fleming, J.A., "Long-term outcome of major psychoses: I. Schizophrenia and affective disorders compared with psychiatrically symptom-free surgical conditions," *Archives of General Psychiatry*, 36: 1295–301, 1979.

Vaillant, G.E. and Funkenstein, D.H., "Long-term follow-up (10–15 years) of schizophrenic patients with Funkenstein (adrenalin-mecholyl) tests," in P.H. Hoch and J. Zubin (eds), *Psychopathology of Schizophrenia*, New York: Grune & Stratton, 1966.

Vaillant, G.E., Semrad, E.V. and Ewalt, J.R., "Current therapeutic results in schizophrenia," *New England Journal of Medicine*, 271: 280–3, 1964.

Vázquez-Barquero, J.L., Cuesta, M.J., Castanedo, S.H. et al., "Cantabria first-episode schizophrenia study: Three-year follow-up," *British Journal of Psychiatry*, 174: 141–9, 1999.

Wiersma, D., Wanderling, J., Dragomirecka, E. et al., "Social disability in schizophrenia: Its development and prediction over 15 years in incidence cohorts in six European centers," *Psychological Medicine*, 30: 1155–67, 2000.

Wieselgren, I.-M. and Lindström, L.H., "A prospective 1–5 year outcome study in first-admitted and readmitted schizophrenic patients; relationship to heredity, premorbid adjustment, duration of disease and education level at index admission and neuroleptic treatment," *Acta Psychiatrica Scandinavica*, 93: 9–19, 1996.

Wirt, R.D. and Simon, W., *Differential Treatment and Prognosis in Schizophrenia*, Springfield, Illinois: Charles C. Thomas, 1959.

Wootton, L.H., Armstrong, R.W. and Lilly, D., "An investigation into the after-histories of discharged mental patients," *Journal of Mental Science*, 81: 168–72, 1935.

World Health Organization, *Schizophrenia: An International Follow-Up Study*, Chichester, UK: John Wiley, 1979.

Author index

Subject index